Questioning Credible Commitment

Financial capitalism emerged in a recognisably modern form in late seventeenth- and eighteenth-century Great Britain. Following the seminal work of Douglass C. North and Barry R. Weingast (1989), many scholars have concluded that the 'credible commitment' that was provided by parliamentary backing of government as a result of the Glorious Revolution of 1688/89 provided the key institutional underpinning on which modern public finances depend. In this book, a specially commissioned group of historians and economists examine and challenge the North and Weingast thesis to show that multiple commitment mechanisms were necessary to convince public creditors that sovereign debt constituted a relatively accessible, safe, and liquid investment vehicle. *Questioning Credible Commitment* provides academics and practitioners with a broader understanding of the origins of financial capitalism, and, with its focus on theoretical and policy frameworks, shows the significance of the debate to current macroeconomic policy making.

D'MARIS COFFMAN is the Mary Bateson Research Fellow at Newnham College, Director of the Centre for Financial History, and an Affiliated Lecturer in the History Faculty, University of Cambridge.

ADRIAN LEONARD is a Bateman Scholar at Trinity Hall and an Affiliated Researcher at the Centre for Financial History at Newnham College, University of Cambridge.

LARRY NEAL is Emeritus Professor of Economics at the University of Illinois at Urbana-Champaign, Research Associate of the National Bureau of Economic Research, and Visiting Professor at the London School of Economics.

Macroeconomic Policy Making

Series editors

Professor JAGJIT S. CHADHA *University of Kent, Canterbury*

Professor SEAN HOLLY *University of Cambridge*

The 2007–2010 financial crisis has asked some very hard questions of modern macroeconomics. The consensus that grew up during 'the Great Moderation' has proved to be an incomplete explanation for how to conduct monetary policy in the face of financial shocks. This series brings together leading macroeconomic researchers and central bank economists to analyse the tools and methods necessary to meet the challenges of the post-financial crisis world.

Published titles:

Chadha and Holly *Interest Rates, Prices and Liquidity: Lessons from the Financial Crisis*

Forthcoming titles:

Chadha, Durré, Joyce & Sarno *Developments in Macro-Finance Yield Curve Modelling*

Questioning Credible Commitment

Perspectives on the Rise of Financial Capitalism

Edited by

D'Maris Coffman, Adrian Leonard, and Larry Neal

CAMBRIDGE
UNIVERSITY PRESS

CAMBRIDGE
UNIVERSITY PRESS

University Printing House, Cambridge CB2 8BS, United Kingdom

Published in the United States of America by Cambridge University Press, New York

Cambridge University Press is part of the University of Cambridge.

It furthers the University's mission by disseminating knowledge in the pursuit of education, learning and research at the highest international levels of excellence.

www.cambridge.org
Information on this title: www.cambridge.org/9781107039018

© Cambridge University Press 2013

First published 2013

Printed in the United Kingdom by Clays, St Ives plc

A catalogue record for this publication is available from the British Library

Library of Congress Cataloguing in Publication data
Questioning credible commitment : perspectives on the rise of financial capitalism / edited by D'Maris Coffman, Adrian Leonard, and Larry Neal.
pages   cm. – (Macroeconomic policy making)
Includes bibliographical references and index.
ISBN 978-1-107-03901-8 (hardback : alk. paper)
1. Finance, Public – Europe – History.   2. Capital – Europe – History.
3. Credit – Europe – History.   4. Europe – Economic policy.   I. Coffman, D'Maris, 1973–
HJ1000.Q47   2013
336.4109′03 – dc23   2013026464

ISBN 978-1-107-03901-8 Hardback

Contents

Figures

Tables

Contributors

ANN M. CARLOS is Professor of Economics and Professor of History (courtesy) at the University of Colorado Boulder. She earned a Ph.D. in economics from the University of Western Ontario, Canada. Her current research has two foci: the impact of the commercial fur trade on native peoples in western Canada in the eighteenth century and the microfoundations of London's capital market in the late seventeenth and early eighteenth centuries. She has also examined the development of the joint-stock trading company. She is currently working on the operation of bankruptcy in Early Modern England. She is a coauthor (with Frank Lewis) of *Commerce by a Frozen Sea: Native Americans and the European Fur Trade* and numerous articles in economic, financial, and business history.

D'MARIS COFFMAN is the Mary Bateson Research Fellow at Newnham College, Cambridge, the Director of the Centre for Financial History, and an Affiliated Lecturer, History Faculty. She works on the relationship between public finance and private capital markets in eighteenth- and nineteenth-century Europe. Most of her recent publications arise from her doctoral thesis on the advent of excise taxation during the English Civil Wars and Interregnum. With Dr Anne Murphy of the University of Hertfordshire, Dr Coffman comanages the *European State Finance Database*. She sits on the Council of the Economic History Society. Dr Coffman received her M.A. and Ph.D. in history from the University of Pennsylvania and her B.Sc. in economics from the Wharton School.

ERIN K. FLETCHER is a Visiting Assistant Professor of Economics at Gettysburg College. She holds a doctoral degree from the University of Colorado at Boulder and conducts research on gender, families, finance, and economic history.

REGINA GRAFE is Associate Professor of History and the Director of Latin American and Caribbean Studies at Northwestern University

(Chicago). She has published three monographs on Spanish and European economic history, the most recent of which, *Distant Tyranny: Markets, Power and Backwardness in Spain, 1650–1800* (Princeton University Press, 2012), offers a radical revision of the coevolution of nation-state formation and market integration in Early Modern Spain. She is also the author of a number of articles on the economic history of the Hispanic world, as well as on commercial and maritime institutions published in journals such as the *Economic History Review*, the *Journal of Interdisciplinary History*, and the *Hispanic American Historical Review*.

RON HARRIS is a Dean and Professor of Law and Legal History at the Faculty of Law, Tel-Aviv University. He earned a Ph.D. in history from Columbia University. Harris works on the intersection of legal history and economic history. His main research fields are the history of the corporation and of other forms of business organisation, the history of bankruptcy and consumer credit, and Israeli legal history. He is the author of *Industrializing English Law: Entrepreneurship and Business Organization, 1720–1844*, the editor of two other books, and the author or coauthor of numerous articles in economics, business, history, and law journals.

ALEJANDRA IRIGOIN is an economic historian of Early Modern Latin America and a lecturer in the Department of Economic History at the London School of Economics. Her articles on the fiscal, monetary, and economic history of colonial Latin America and the political economy of the Spanish Empire have been published in the *Economic History Review*, the *Hispanic American Historical Review*, the *Journals of Global and World History*, the *Journal of Latin American Studies*, and *Historia Mexicana*. Jointly with Regina Grafe, she is preparing a manuscript on the Spanish Empire for Cambridge University Press.

MICHAEL KWASS, Associate Professor of History at Johns Hopkins University, studies the political and economic history of Early Modern Europe. Recipient of the David Pinkney Prize for *Privilege and the Politics of Taxation in Eighteenth-Century France: Liberté, Égalité, Fiscalité* (Cambridge University Press, 2000), he has published numerous articles on consumer culture in the age of the Enlightenment. He is currently completing a book entitled *Louis Mandrin: Globalization, Smuggling, and Rebellion in Eighteenth-Century France*, which examines heretofore hidden connections between world trade, the illicit economy, and popular politics in pre-revolutionary France. His is also at work on *Consumer Revolution, 1650–1800*, which explores the social, cultural, and political implications of Western consumption before the Industrial Revolution.

ADRIAN LEONARD is an Affiliated Researcher at the Centre for Financial History at Newnham College, University of Cambridge. His research focuses on the development and role of marine insurance, from its medieval origins to the early nineteenth century, in the advent of financial capitalism. Publications include 'Underwriting British Trade to India and China, 1780–1835' (*Historical Journal*, December 2012) and 'Reinsurance Issues in the Baltic Countries' (OECD, 2004). Prior to returning to academia in 2007, he spent ten years as a commercial writer, editor, and communications consultant, including appointments as editor of the *Financial Times World Insurance Report* and news editor of *Lloyd's List Insurance Day*.

JAMES MACDONALD is an independent scholar who specializes in the history of public finance. He is the author of *A Free Nation Deep in Debt: The Financial Roots of Democracy* (Princeton University Press, 2006). He was educated at Cambridge University and subsequently worked in the public debt markets on Wall Street before concentrating on financial history.

LARRY NEAL is Emeritus Professor of Economics at the University of Illinois at Urbana-Champaign, Research Associate of the National Bureau of Economic Research, and Visiting Professor at the London School of Economics. He specialises in financial history and European economies. Professor Neal is author of *The Rise of Financial Capitalism: International Capital Markets in the Age of Reason* (Cambridge University Press, 1990) and *'I Am Not Master of Events': The Speculations of John Law and Lord Londonderry in the Mississippi and South Sea Bubbles* (Yale University Press, 2012), as well as *The Economics of Europe and the European Union* (2008) and *The Origin and Development of Financial Institutions and Markets* (coedited with Jeremy Atack, 2009). Professor Neal is Past President of the Economic History Association.

LUCIANO PEZZOLO is Associate Professor of Early Modern History in the Department of Humanities of the Ca' Foscari University of Venice. He has published extensively on the economic history of Venice and the military and financial history of late medieval and Early Modern Italy. He is currently finishing a book on war and finance in Italy, 1350–1700.

JULIA RUDOLPH is Associate Professor of History at North Carolina State University. Her publications include *Revolution by Degrees: James*

Tyrrell and Whig Political Thought in the Late Seventeenth Century (Palgrave Macmillan, 2002), various articles on gender, crime, and the history of the book in Early Modern England, and, as editor, *History and Nation* (Bucknell University Press, 2006). Her latest book, *Common Law and Enlightenment in England 1689–1750* (forthcoming, Boydell & Brewer), is a history of common law that explores the origins of a jurisprudence of precedent and the intersections between legal ideas, practices, and publications and other eighteenth-century enlightened trends in philosophy, science, historiography, commerce, and print.

NATHAN SUSSMAN is the Alexander Brody Chair in Economic History at the Hebrew University of Jerusalem and the Director of the Research Department at the Bank of Israel. He earned his Ph.D. in economic history from UC Berkeley. His research focuses on financial history and medieval monetary and economic history. He is the author of *Emerging Markets and Financial Globalisation* with Yafeh and Mauro and the author and coauthor of numerous articles in economic and financial history.

KIRSTEN WANDSCHNEIDER is Associate Professor of Economics at Occidental College in Los Angeles. She holds an M.S. in finance and a Ph.D. in economics from the University of Illinois at Urbana. Her research focuses on historical financial markets and financial institutions in Europe, most recently the development of mortgage markets in Prussia. Her work has been published in academic journals such as the *Journal of Economic History* and *Cliometrica*.

YISHAY YAFEH is Associate Professor at the School of Business Administration of the Hebrew University and a Research Fellow of the London-based CEPR and the Brussels-based ECGI. He holds a Ph.D. in economics from Harvard University and has taught at Oxford and Montreal. His research interests are financial systems and financial intermediation, the economies of East Asia, and economic and financial history. Dr Yafeh has served as advisor to the Bank of Israel, the Israel Securities Authority, and the International Monetary Fund. His research has been published, among others, in the *Journal of Finance*, the *Quarterly Journal of Economics*, the *Journal of Economic Literature*, and the *Journal of Business*. He coauthored, together with Paolo Mauro and Nathan Sussman, the book *Emerging Markets and Financial Globalization* (Oxford University Press, 2006).

Preface

As the Series Editors of *Modern Macroeconomic Policy Making*, we were eager to include a volume in the series that brought us some insights from a serious study of economic history. This is partly because, even though the ongoing financial crisis has promulgated so much disagreement and noise, it seems the one point on which all are agreed is that we should study more economic history. We were delighted, therefore, to able to build on the original contribution of North and Weingast, which had suggested that the Glorious Revolution of 1688/89 had provided a political and fiscal settlement so profound that it had laid an important foundation for both the subsequent Financial and Industrial Revolutions. The question of institutional capability dovetails neatly into a crucial development in modern macroeconomic theory, the so-called 'Barro–Gordon–Kydland–Prescott paradigm' that thrust the problem of time inconsistency permanently onto the policy making agenda. This analysis led to wide-ranging assessment of the importance of commitment technologies that could tie the hands of future policy makers and so promote the credibility and optimality of current plans. Thus, macroeconomic policy began to emphasise the importance of bringing forward-looking expectations into line with policy makers' objectives, and therefore the credibility of policy itself became a crucial element in the design of policy frameworks. It also turned out that a study of economic history allowed us to locate many examples in which the question of policy makers' credible commitment was central.

In this volume, which follows a successful conference at Newnham College, Cambridge, in 2010, we are pleased to see several key events in English and European economic history re-examined. Thus, this volume brings together a number of contributions from economic historians who question the conventional wisdom and offer a much more nuanced approach to understanding events both before and after 1688. This volume has been expertly edited by D'Maris Coffman, Adrian Leonard, and Larry Neal and has benefitted greatly from the detailed comments of two external, and sadly anonymous, referees in whose debt we, as nonspecialists, remain.

JAGJIT S. CHADHA AND SEAN HOLLY

Acknowledgements

This volume has been three years in the making. In the first instance, the project was inspired by the success of a conference: 'Questioning Credible Commitment: Re-thinking the Glorious Revolution and the Rise of Financial Capitalism', held at the Centre for Financial History at Newnham College, University of Cambridge, 20–23 March 2010. Dr Coffman co-organised the conference with Dr Anne Murphy of the University of Hertfordshire. The editors would especially like to thank Dr Murphy, and also to thank the conference's sponsors and participants, including Professor Ron Harris, Professor Julia Rudolph, Mr James Macdonald, Professor Ann Carlos, Professor Luciano Pezzolo, Professor Michael Kwass, and Professor Nathan Sussman, whose contributions have formed the basis for the chapters that they and their colleagues have contributed to this volume.

This four-day conference was made possible by generous grants from the Newnham College Senior Members' Research Fund (SMRF), the Cambridge Endowment for Research in Finance (CERF), and the Centre for Financial History (CFH). As this was the inaugural plenary conference for the Centre for Financial History, the editors would also like to thank Winton Capital Management for their indirect support of the event.

The editors would like also to thank the series editors, Professor Jagjit S. Chadha of the University of Kent and Professor Sean Holly of the University of Cambridge, along with two anonymous reviewers. Thanks too to Dr Coşkun Tunçer of the London School of Economics for his timely research assistance.

1   Introduction

D'Maris Coffman and Larry Neal

'Credible commitment' has become one of the most widely used phrases in the literature of both economics and political science. A search of *EconLit*, an electronic bibliography of economics articles, brings up 1,932 hits for the phrase in texts published between 1976 and 2012. Of these, 1,894 occur after the publication of North and Weingast's classic 1989 article 'Constitutions and Commitment: The Evolution of Institutions Governing Public Choice in Seventeenth-Century England'. Clearly the attraction of the phrase derives largely from the appealing story they tell: institutional change arising from England's 1688/89 Glorious Revolution created, for the first time, a 'credible commitment' that the government would not default on its debt in the future. 'Whig historians', from Henry Hallam and James Mackintosh forward, had also pointed to the importance of the Glorious Revolution for the increasing military success of the English mercantile state after 1688, in contrast with its inconsistent performance in the three Anglo-Dutch Wars from 1652 to 1674. The ability of William III and Marlborough to challenge the forces of Louis XIV from 1689 to 1713 presaged a century of rising economic and political power. North and Weingast, however, put their emphasis on the economic consequences of the political changes that occurred in 1688. They argued that the contrast between the lacklustre performance of the English economy before 1688 and the increasing strength of its overseas trade afterwards resulted directly from the change in political institutions.

Their narrative fits well with the implications of economic models of control systems being developed in the late 1980s. These found that credible commitment mechanisms had to be in place to keep political authorities from making time-inconsistent policy decisions. Beginning with Lucas's critique of macroeconomic models based on existing patterns of economic behaviour by the private sector (1976), economists realised that private agents would have an incentive to change their behaviour in response to changes in economic policy. For example, a persistent increase in inflation rates generated by permissive monetary policy would not lead to a permanent decrease in unemployment. The

Lucas critique was followed by Kydland and Prescott's demonstration (1977) that initially optimal plans would turn out to be suboptimal even if planners changed policies in response to new behaviour by private agents. The resulting 'time inconsistency' of public policy would, for instance, lead private decision-makers to respond by restricting investment in light of the resulting uncertainty. Economic growth would be permanently lowered. The result of the persistent disruptions to the international and domestic economies after the oil shocks of the 1970s and the rise of globalisation after 1971, and again after 1990, has led macroeconomists to develop ever more sophisticated models to help policy-makers devise appropriate responses to exogenous shocks. A major effort has been the search for micro foundations of macroeconomic models that would establish incentive-compatible contracts between, for example, central banks and the financial sector, or governments and debt holders.

In this context Persson and Tabellini, policy-oriented economists deeply involved in the formation of a new international economic order, beginning with the founding of the European Central Bank in 1998, found the North and Weingast story very appealing. They remark that 'delegating much of the power over fiscal-policy decisions to the Parliament . . . relaxed the previous incentive constraints and increased the government's credibility for repayment' (Persson and Tabellini 1994, 1: 21). More recently, Daron Acemoglu (an economist) and James Robinson (a political scientist) state boldly that 'The Glorious Revolution was the foundation for creating a pluralistic society, and it built on and accelerated a process of political centralization. It created the world's first set of inclusive political institutions' (Acemoglu and Robinson 2012, 102).

The thrust of analysis of the failures of economic policymaking, repeatedly evident since the end of the 'golden age of economic growth' in the early 1970s, has been for both economists and political scientists to explore the interactions of economics and politics. Lacking experimental evidence from laboratories, theorists seeking validation of their arguments must turn to the material generated by political and economic historians. Too often, however, the evidence useful for economists has to be teased out from the pages and pages of contextual descriptions that are so characteristic of the history profession. The North and Weingast article did exactly that for both economists and political scientists. From the massive collection of details presented in Dickson's classic work on the financial revolution in England (1967), North and Weingast extracted the pertinent details that illustrate the importance of institutions for determining economic outcomes. It was Dickson's demonstration that the rise of the capital market for British government debt followed the accession of William and Mary in 1689 that North and Weingast took as 'the single most important piece of evidence' that the necessary condition of securing contracts across time and space, and therefore enabling impersonal exchange, had been fulfilled. That breakthrough, they argue, followed (albeit gradually and with setbacks) from Britain's continued economic and military success, and led to victory in the wars against France, and eventually to the Industrial Revolution.

Among historians, however, the 'credible commitment' thesis has been subjected to both criticisms and elaborations. The critics picked away at the historical evidence North and Weingast used to support their argument that the constitutional break in 1688 was definitive for England. North and Weingast acknowledged then, and in all subsequent writings by each of them, that constitutional change is subject to historical contingency, which means it is not sufficient for establishing credible commitment mechanisms, and is potentially reversible. North (2005), for example, emphasises the complexity of the interplay of beliefs, institutions, implicit incentives, and political systems for enforcing the formal and informal rules that make it so difficult to displace dysfunctional institutions with more effective alternatives. He argues that the ultimate test of new institutions is their adaptive efficiency in responding to new economic challenges. Weingast (2005) takes up the question of why the constitutional commitment made in 1689 was self-enforcing. He argues that the prior disposal of James II as monarch made it clear, from then on, that Parliament could depose the king, the ultimate sanction to ensure that future monarchs would keep their commitments to maintain the new constitution. At the end of that essay, moreover, he concludes that 'Both crises and ongoing constitutional adjustments seem central to the creation of self-enforcing constitutions that are stable for multiple generations' (Weingast 2005, 106).

Both North and Weingast had to clarify and sharpen their original argument about the sources and results of England's constitutional commitment in light of earlier challenges by economic historians. O'Brien and Hunt (1997) argue that the evolution of British public finance began much earlier, at least during the English Civil War, and some improvements were made during the Stuart Restoration. Epstein (2000) notes that interest rates on British government debt remained well above those already achieved in the Netherlands and various Italian city-states well into the eighteenth century. Sussman and Yafeh (2006) take up the interest-rate argument to show that market interest rates remained high on most British government debt for several decades after 1688. They refer to Quinn (2001), who showed that private interest rates remained high due to wartime demands for government finance during the reign of William III. Quinn, however, does note that the huge increase in the size of government debt provided a useful reserve asset for private bankers, whose business increased as well. The enormous quantity of government debt issued after 1688, which continued to increase in each war thereafter, remains the most impressive evidence in support of the original North and Weingast thesis, a point made repeatedly by Weingast in later work (Weingast 1997; Weingast 2005).

Examining the importance of constitutional provisions in general, Clark (1996) argues that property rights were already well protected in English law. He found no changes in yields on land mortgages in response to increases in Parliament's authority. DeLong and Schleifer (1993) had earlier demonstrated that European cities with absolutist institutions grew more slowly in population than cities within nonabsolutist regimes between 1000 and 1800. Acemoglu, Johnson, and Robinson (2005) demonstrate that constraints on executives helped cities to grow larger on the Atlantic seaboard. Stasavage (2007) shows that European cities governed by merchant elites found it easier to borrow, and at lower interest rates, especially if the cities had constitutional constraints on their rulers. He finds less support, however, for the argument that constitutional checks by themselves increased the credibility of debt commitments for either city-states or territorial states. Stasavage (2011) finds that merchant elites in control of cities whose geography allowed them to remain compact and defensible were the most successful in achieving long-term credible commitments for their sovereign debts. Acemoglu and Robinson (2012) emphasise the importance of historical contingency for institutional change in general. They also make the point that, to adapt effectively to changing economic circumstances, constitutions must provide newcomers with access to power.

Most recently Cox (2012) argued that the Glorious Revolution was indeed a 'constitutional watershed', but for more precise reasons than simply controlling the king's access to long-term finance. For him, private property rights were not at issue in England under either Tudor or Stuart rule, so Clark's evidence on the stability of private returns, especially for land throughout the sixteenth to eighteenth centuries, is simply irrelevant to the constitutional question. Rather, the real issue for the Stuarts was how to assert absolutist rule in place of representative assemblies, as the Bourbon monarchs had achieved in France. To accomplish this goal, Stuart rulers had variously tried to rule without convening Parliament, to sidestep Parliament by expanding use of royal prerogatives, or simply to buy parliamentary support. He then shows that the post-1688 Parliament took meaningful steps to counter each possibility. It insisted on regular elections (initially every three years), limited revenue sources to fixed and ever-shorter terms for specific purposes, and, most effectively, controlled the appointments of the king's ministers responsible for collecting and dispensing the revenue. In this way, he emphasises a point, made earlier by Getzler (1996): in light of the irrationality of traditional English property law, which limited the possibility of more efficient use of property by re-allocation through market processes, an effective legislative power was needed to direct resources towards more profitable endeavours. 'In other words, the costs of irrational private law were balanced by the benefits of a legitimate and effective system of public taxation. A stronger governmental participation in the definition and control of private property rights at the microeconomic level might have undermined the legitimacy and success of the larger fiscal system' (Getzler 1996, 650). Several of the contributions in this volume highlight the growing importance of excise taxes as the basis for funding government debt, while land taxes remained stagnant and irregular, as did customs revenues after 1688 (Chandaman 1975; Braddick 1996).

Clearly it is the details of history that matter for determining the success of any institutional change, and examination of those details is the particular province of historians. Looking at the process of creating credible commitments between monarch and Parliament, and then between Parliament and the British public, scholars contributing to this volume find multiple instances of historical contingency creating watershed moments, as well as multiple mechanisms for creating commitments. A much more nuanced and complicated narrative emerges, which suggests not that North and Weingast were wrong in 1989, but that their story was incomplete.

Much of the attraction of their narrative was the apparent simplicity of the government's role in the economy at the time, unencumbered as it was by the expenditure demands of modern welfare states. Economic policy-makers today have to confront the multiple demands of an enfranchised public who desire full employment and access to health care and education, as well as public order and prosperity. In contrast, Britain's central government authorities in the seventeenth and eighteenth centuries confronted a much narrower, but equally pressing challenge: to maintain the British Isles free from foreign domination, whether military, dynastic, or religious. The international context was the increasing scale and expense of the warfare necessary to maintain both the authority of central governments and the territorial integrity of the emerging nation-states of continental Europe, in a period when the military revolution, which began in the fourteenth century, led to continued advances in technology, logistics, and finance.

Not all European powers followed the same paths. Some evolved solutions that North and Weingast label 'absolutist', whereas others developed a 'constitutional' model. North and Weingast's formulation of this dichotomy is consistent with, and to some degree an inspiration for, the subsequent use of the terms by historical sociologists, who approach absolutism by employing it as part of a set of typologies that delineate the possible solutions to the problem of rule for the composite monarchies of Early Modern Europe (Gorski 2003, 3–15). These typologies are useful because they suggest a range of possibilities, but they say nothing about what happened in practice.

As with most late-twentieth-century debates, Marxist and non-Marxist variants were advanced. In *Coercion, Capital, and European States, 990–1990*, Tilly sees three divergent paths of political development: the 'capital-intensive' city-states of Northern Italy, Switzerland, and southern Scandinavia; the 'coercion-intensive' hinterlands of Russia, Poland, Hungary, and northern Scandinavia; and the 'centrally-ruled' national states of France, England, and eventually Prussia (Tilly 1990, 7–20). In his account, Tilly is heavily indebted to Wallerstein's neo-Marxist world-systems theory, which recasts class relations as exchange relations within a capitalist world system (Tilly 1990, 61). Unfortunately the Marxist version does not help historians to distinguish between elements within each set. As Abrams points out, 'Marxist theory needs the state as an abstract-formal object in order to explain the integration of class societies', and thus takes the state as a relatively unproblematic locus for the exercise of power (Abrams 1988, 70). The only way to get a different outcome in the Marxist account is through a different alignment of class or (now) exchange interest. Thus, for Marxists, absolutism (or constitutionalism) is not, strictly speaking, a modality of the exercise of power because, given a specific set of material realities and social relations, Marxist theory admits no competitive solutions. Variations in the forms of absolutism and styles of absolutist rule are of only passing interest. What made 'absolutism' absolutist was the nature of the monopoly on coercive power that it purportedly encouraged.

Downing (1992) and Parker (1996) see the military revolution as the impetus for political change. Downing claims that 'military-bureaucratic absolutism' emerged in Prussia and France because the ruling regimes there could mobilise vast domestic resources to finance their respective participation in the Thirty Years War. Downing then contrasts these regimes with those that he believes saw liberalism evolve from medieval constitutionalism. Ertman's account in *Birth of Leviathan: Building States and Regimes in Medieval and Early Modern Europe* (1997) is more sophisticated, offering a two-dimensional typology with two variables: organisation of local government at the time of state formation and timing of 'sustained geo-military competition'. From this, Ertman adduces four variants: patrimonial absolutism (France, Spain), bureaucratic absolutism (Prussia), bureaucratic constitutionalism (Britain), and patrimonial constitutionalism (Hungary, Poland). In this account absolutism versus constitutionalism denotes state structure, whereas bureaucratic versus patrimonial denotes regime structure. He explains the 'absolutist' outcome, usually in the 'core' states, in terms of a fledging *Ständestaat* divided among itself, unable to resist the ambitions of 'imperial' princes. In order to sidestep charges of overly schematic conclusions, Ertman introduces an element of contingency. Owing to the strength of her parliaments, Britain might have become patrimonial and absolutist under the Stuarts, but instead evolved a state bureaucracy under William. The chief advantage of Ertman's account is that it de-links bureaucratisation from absolutism, thereby making it possible to distinguish between France, Prussia, and Britain.

Ertman did not have the last word. Gorski's bold new synthesis, in *The Disciplinary Revolution* (2003), combines Michel Foucault, Max Weber, Norbert Elias, and Gerhard Ostreich to develop a 'comprehensive theory' of social discipline, one that includes self-, corrective, communal, and judicial discipline. His aim is not to explain absolutism, but rather to describe the Early Modern nonabsolutist state par excellence, the Dutch Republic. For him, the 'Reformation unleashed a profound and far-reaching process of disciplinary revolution – that greatly enhanced the power of the Early Modern states, and the effects of this revolution were deepest and most profound in the Calvinist parts of Europe'. Nevertheless his model can be applied to absolutist regimes as well, for he redefines 'state capacity' as 'a function, not only of administrative rationalisation, but of the strength of social infrastructure, and the rationality of sociopolitical ethics'. His model holds equally well in his analysis of the nonabsolutist Dutch and absolutist Prussian cases. This leads him to a revised state theory, under which states are 'not only administrative, policing, and military organisations, but also pedagogical, corrective and ideological' (Gorski 2003, 32, 38, 165). They operate as frequently through cooptation as through coercion; state power is not always dependent on state structure (but also on human resources, organisational fidelities, and infrastructure). State formation is as often a bottom-up as a top-down process. Early modern rulers, whether absolutist or constitutional, 'had multiple and potentially conflicting interests – ideal and material, geopolitical and eudaemonistic, personal and dynastic, long-run and short-run, and so on – and their efforts to prioritise and reconcile them were invariably influenced by individual *habitus* and collective valuations' (Gorski 2003, 168).

How well did these theoretical formulations of historical sociologists correspond to reality? England avoided most seventeenth-century wars, in part due to its defeat of the Spanish Armada in 1588, so its contribution to the military revolution really began at the conclusion of the Thirty Years War (1618–48). The Treaty of Westphalia (1648) forced a permanent retrenchment of the Holy Roman Empire, as the German states were divided along religious lines. Further, the Habsburg dynasty yielded the northern provinces of the Low Countries to a republic, which, along with the confederation of the mountain cantons of Switzerland, was recognised by the traditional sovereign powers of Europe as an equal power when they implemented the terms of the Treaty of Westphalia. For the Dutch Republic the treaty marked the successful end of an Eighty Years War for independence from Spain, and a new phase of political governance that focused on maintaining the prosperity of the Dutch mercantile elite under the political guidance of the long-established merchant guilds in control of the major port cities (Lesger 2006). For France, however, the Westphalia agreement merely meant that Cardinal Mazarin could now focus on continued war with Habsburg Spain, which ended with the Peace of the Pyrenees in 1669. The signing of that treaty completed the outlines of the borders of modern France, as well as the ascendancy of Louis XIV over the aristocratic revolt of the Fronde led by the Prince de Condé, which had threatened control over state revenues by parliament similar to that in the English and Dutch examples. By 1651, however, the revolt was subdued, and France could focus on the war with Spain.

The Peace of Westphalia mattered little for England, a country in the final throes of a civil war which climaxed the following year with the regicide of Charles I. The military victory of the New Model Army led by Oliver Cromwell and financed on a continuous basis by monthly levies of the land tax in 1650 was followed by the Navigation Act of 1651, which restricted coastal trade and fisheries to English and Welsh vessels. Presumably intended to thwart foreign incursions in support of Charles II, who had fled to Scotland, the Navigation Act provoked a short-lived and decisive naval war with the Dutch, who had been taken by surprise. The upshots were a flourishing English merchant marine, which was bolstered by 1,000 vessels captured from the Dutch, and regular amendments, over the next two centuries, of the Navigation Acts, which were finally expunged from British law in 1849.

So lay the future of European mercantilism in the play of Great Power politics among Spain, France, Britain, and the Dutch Republic over the

period from 1648 to 1815. Each state consolidated its political position domestically, while exploring the possibilities for expanding trade
and treasure from abroad. The early examples of treasure streaming into
Spanish Seville on the annual fleets from Vera Cruz and Cartagena,
and of trade profits from pepper sold at persistently high prices by the
Portuguese state monopoly, excited the imitative efforts of all three fol-
lower countries. Already the Dutch and English East India companies
were proving successful in undercutting the existing spice and silk trades,
which had been dominated in earlier periods first by Italians and later
by Portuguese merchants. Under Jean-Baptiste Colbert the French East
India Company attempted to mimic Anglo-Dutch success, with state
support and control. The overall context of the economic policies of all
three mercantile powers was the endeavour first to define, and then to
maintain, the geographical limits of the emerging nation-state. This was
the historical setting within which a series of natural experiments were
conducted by the three powers to determine, essentially, how to wage and
win large-scale wars. In the process major innovations in war finance were
necessary, while coming up against the limits of what modern macroeconomists call the 'trilemma of open economies'. Economics students
today learn, along with newly appointed finance ministers, that no country can long sustain all three desirable economic policies of independent
monetary policy, fixed exchange rates, and open capital markets.

France, as the largest kingdom in Europe after 1648, naturally
attempted to expand its trade overseas while protecting its domestic
industries from competition by Italian and Dutch city-states. While
attempting at times to import capital, especially under the guidance of
John Law during the Regency period of 1715, and then to keep fixed
exchange rates with the rest of Europe after 1726, the absolutist regime
of France was persistent in pursuing independent monetary policies. By
the end of the Thirty Years War the Dutch realised that they needed to
encourage foreign capital, but could not hope to maintain independent
monetary policies among their several fiscally separate provinces, so the
Dutch Republic's focus was always on maintaining fixed exchange rates,
basically to sustain its commodity trade with the rest of Europe. Britain
variously flirted with independent monetary policies within Scotland,
Ireland, or northern England, and occasionally was forced into floating
exchange rates as a result, but always persisted in maintaining access to
foreign capital.

From this broader historical perspective, then, the ultimate success
of Britain in learning how both to finance and to wage war effectively
– starting with its attempts in the seventeenth century and culminating
with its success by 1815 – is a natural experiment already run. Within

it, economists and political scientists may find evidence to test their assumptions about the nature of the essential determinants for creating credible commitment mechanisms. The historical context in which the British state focused on building a fiscal–military regime to compete with the other European mercantile powers, but paid scant attention to public education, health, or employment and retirement security, moreover, makes this natural experiment neater for analytical purposes. Just as accounts of the Industrial Revolution have furnished models of industrialisation and prescriptions for developmental economists (Rostow 1960; Gerschenkron 1962), North and Weingast's thesis has furnished similar inspiration to those who aspire to pair financial capitalism with economic growth (Levine 2001; Graff 2003). Consequently, the thesis has proven influential in an extraordinary range of disciplines, from financial and economic history to sociology, development studies, and legal and political theory, and in modern public policy circles. It is possible to see in their historical model support for the Washington Consensus.

The essays collected in this volume grew out of a conference entitled 'Questioning Credible Commitment: Re-thinking the Glorious Revolution and the Rise of Financial Capitalism', held at the Centre for Financial History at Newnham College of the University of Cambridge in March 2010. They by no means represent the first attempts by historians to critique the North and Weingast formulation on empirical grounds. Yet, as editors, we feel they represent fairly the principal lines of approach, with one caveat. If fiscal institutions were neither based on the Dutch model nor formed as a result of regime change in 1688, similar claims may be made for monetary institutions, which were noticeably absent from North and Weingast's discussion, despite their centrality to debates about time-inconsistent policy making (Persson and Tabellini 1994). Mayhew argues in a recent edited collection (Munro 2012) that the Williamite Recoinage came not as a result of predation by Stuart monarchs after the Restoration, but rather from the Crown's insistence on maintaining a 'high value silver coinage of unchanging worth, despite major shifts in the international value of precious metals'. Over the course of the seventeenth and eighteenth centuries, resistance to adjusting the mint price of silver to align it with the market price was so entrenched that clipping became commonplace. Quinn's now-classic study of the operation of the bills–bullion arbitrage market demonstrates vividly the opportunities and costs associated with this policy (Quinn 1996). Subsequently, Isaac Newton's fixed peg of one gold guinea to twenty-one silver shillings in 1717 had the not-unsurprising consequence that bimetallism soon became a dead letter, and a de facto gold standard emerged over the eighteenth century (Redish 1990). Whether these developments had anything to do with constitutional change is debatable, but if so, it would seem more reasonable to interpret the relative probity of British monetary institutions not to Parliament, but to a reassertion of the Crown's prerogative powers vis-à-vis the institution of the Royal Mint to ensure an adequate supply of bullion to meet the costs of keeping armies in the field.

Acemoglu and Robinson's tendency to collapse North and Weingast's argument into an assertion of the seminal role of the Revolution of 1688/89 in securing property rights has been bolstered by Niall Ferguson's Reith Lectures for the BBC, but both overlook earlier caveats (Elster 1995) and a wholesale rebuttal of the argument by Hoppit (2011), who argues convincingly that parliamentary supremacy did not have the consequence of better securing the property of Englishmen, let alone of Scots. In fact, as he demonstrates, under more aggressive and more frequent parliamentary rule, 'property was often heavily taxed, frequently expropriated, and exceptionally, eradicated through redefinition'.

By the same token, despite occasional reassertions of the old canard (Carruthers 1996; Pincus 2009) about the significance of the Whig Supremacy, recent research has effectively debunked crude assumptions about the respective appetites of 'Whig merchants' and 'Tory landowners' for government finance (Stasavage 2007; Murphy 2013). The best recent scholarship on merchants and their communities (Hancock 1995; Grassby 2001; Gauci 2001, 2007; Bowen 2006; Zahedieh 2010) argues persuasively that their networks were not organised chiefly along political lines. Moreover, as Neal demonstrated twenty years ago (Neal 1990), English capital markets were genuinely international in character from the beginning of the eighteenth century onwards (Neal 2000). Unsurprisingly, there was genuine cross-party consensus about the need to preserve the public credit. Rehabilitation of the Tory Robert Harley's skilful management of the 1710–11 public finance crisis suggests that it might have been as much a turning point in terms of reassuring public creditors as North and Weingast supposed that 1688 should have been (Murphy 2013).

Murphy emphasises the steep learning curve that Parliament faced in managing the issuance of long-term debt. In her view it took nearly thirty years for the average public creditor to see Parliament as protecting investors' interests. As North and Weingast themselves acknowledge, there were moments in which the path dependency they identify might have been dislodged. Wells and Wills (2000) find one such possibility amidst the Jacobite threat. Sussman and Yafeh (2006) lend empirical support to the 'primacy of the political' in their study of long-term interest rates, which did not begin to fall until the middle of the eighteenth century.

How far polemical print literature provided a 'voice' to the ordinary creditor remains debatable, but the advent of *Early English Books Online* and *Eighteenth Century Collections Online* has produced a turn towards studies of the vast print literature of the early eighteenth century (McGrath and Fauske 2008; Moore 2010; Reinert 2011; Wennerlind 2011; Murphy 2013). In a different vein, Harris (2004) argues that truly effective creditor action and the required tools for effective oversight of the public finances were not available until the nineteenth century. More provocatively, Macdonald (2006) argues that it was the British public debt that secured English liberties, rather than the other way around.

Yet despite the available critiques, many elements of the North and Weingast presentation retain the stature of 'stylised fact'. Truly effective criticism eventually must yield an alternative formulation. The essays collected in this volume try to help those fascinated by the complexities of institutional design by examining in depth precisely the historical details that preceded and followed the regime change of 1688 in England, but with the explicit objective of identifying the underlying mechanisms for the establishment of credible commitments by the government, whether it was the Crown, Parliament, or 'the king in Parliament'.

What emerges from this exploration is a sense that a multiplicity of mechanisms contributed to 'credible commitment'. There were multiple institutional roots of legitimacy, and there is little reason to give the constitutional framework a privileged position among them. At the same time, significant legal developments were not limited to presumptive protections of individual property rights or to developments solely at the King's Bench. Demands for transparency and probity of the public accounts had a distinctly English provenance, and owed their genesis to the vicissitudes of public finance during the English Civil Wars and Interregnum. That these demands were reasserted after 1688 points less to the presumptive strengths than it does to the weaknesses of the constitutional settlement and to public wariness of the legitimacy and permanence of the post-Revolution regime. The secondary market, far more than the primary one, provided the key vehicle for democratisation of the public debt, allowing access by women, religious minorities, and relatively small investors.

The ability to 'exit' a trade by selling financial assets in a secondary market represents the most effective form of creditor action conceivable (other sorts are contemplated today only after secondary markets fail), as long as the investor has an adequate basis for confidence that there will be a buyer. In the eighteenth century, as today, liquidity is key. The strength of any primary market for financial assets depends on the existence, smooth operation, and depth of secondary markets. The existence of secondary markets not only provided the catalyst for the reduction of interest rates, but also meant that it was possible to increase the volume of debt issues markedly. This finding should have significant policy implications amidst the worst sovereign debt crisis in eighty years, especially given the disapprobation heaped upon financial intermediaries during the subprime lending crisis.

The first seven substantive chapters of this volume, taken together, offer both an elaboration of, and an alternative to, the classic account offered by North and Weingast. The three chapters that follow offer comparative views of the Italian states, the Spanish Empire, and the French monarchy. The final chapter in the volume uses a national comparative framework to advance an empirical argument for the primacy of politics in acknowledging the importance of perceptions of political risk to investors' appetites for sovereign bonds. The interdisciplinary nature of this volume, coupled with the wide variety of themes and institutions explored, makes it impossible and imprudent to replace one stylised fact with another. Nonetheless the editors hope that, by exposing the multiplicity of commitment mechanisms necessary to achieve 'credible commitment', coupled with the role of political contingency in that process, this volume will provide rich material for economists and economic historians alike to rethink their assumptions about the genesis and origins of financial capitalism in Early Modern Europe.

Chapter 2 begins these explorations by presenting a twofold shift in the application of the 'credible commitment' concept as laid down by North and Weingast. Harris examines the concept in the context of charter-granting, rather than that of the national debt and the government bond market, and applies the concept to the pre-Civil War period, rather than the post-Glorious Revolution period. This is particularly important because the *quo warranto* challenges to town and corporate charters in the 1680s contributed to North and Weingast's notions of a predatory Stuart monarch. Harris finds instead that during the period from 1558 to 1640, 'credible commitment' mechanisms did evolve for the protection of corporate charters. Charter-granting was not solely the province of the crown prerogative; Parliament and the common-law courts played a role. Harris concludes with the finding that constitutional changes over this period conferred an advantage to England vis-à-vis continental rivals in conveying such commitments with credibility.

In Chapter 3, Adrian Leonard continues in a similar vein by arguing that the theoretical framework offered by North and Weingast does not necessarily characterise the actual nature of relations among the Crown, Parliament, and the financial and business communities, either before or after the Glorious Revolution. Adrian Leonard argues that a series of related initiatives by these actors, taken between the last quarter of the sixteenth century and the first of the eighteenth (a period which straddles the putative establishment of the institutions of 'credible commitment'), illustrate a progressively diminishing commitment on the part of Crown and Parliament to the protection of merchants' private wealth and of the trade which generated customs duties. This was the case despite the importance of customs revenue to the servicing of government borrowing during the rise of the fiscal-military state. Through the application of the lessons of New Institutional Economics, Adrian Leonard concludes that London's marine insurance market developed in support of the advance of trade, despite the largely harmful effects of state intervention or inaction post-1688.

Coffman argues in Chapter 4 that many of the conditions taken to be *sine qua non* of 'credible commitment' in the English case, specifically parliamentary supremacy, transparency in public accounting, accountability via direct creditor action, robust secondary markets, and a stated commitment to maintaining the 'public faith', were, in fact, in place during the Civil Wars and Interregnum under the Long Parliament and Commonwealth regimes (1643–53), but they did not, in themselves, produce credible commitment mechanisms for generating support for a long-term public debt. The author finds that these are 'necessary but not sufficient' conditions, and suggests instead that perceptions of the stability of the regime are the key ingredient. Coffman also suggests that the constitutional fissures of the Civil Wars and Interregnum provided the context for a conceptual shift, whereby the abstract concept of the 'state' evolved in opposition to the 'public'. After 1688 the Crown and Parliament became servants of that state: the Crown oversaw the increasingly bureaucratised and efficient revenue establishment, while Parliament voted sufficient revenues to service the public debt. Although the Civil Wars and Interregnum provided a dress rehearsal, it would take nearly three generations for the public to find credible representations that successive regimes would not default on the previous regime's debts.

In Chapter 5, Rudolph argues that the impeachment of Macclesfield in 1725 was a turning point in resolving jurisdictional controversies between law and equity in commercial disputes in Britain. The trial and subsequent conviction were offered as a gesture to appease public anger. He served as a scapegoat, sacrificed in an effort to restore public confidence in economic policies. Most importantly, however, on a jurisdictional and jurisprudential level, Macclesfield's impeachment stood as an indication that in England, common-law tradition and stability were the keys to continued financial innovation and successful economic growth. Such a conclusion about the flexibility and importance of the common law in furnishing commitment mechanisms is consistent with the findings of Harris, Adrian Leonard, and Coffman for the earlier period. Yet unlike the North and Weingast account, this argument does not turn specifically on private property rights.

If credit standing is measured by interest rates, it is clear that England did not suddenly become a good credit risk just because of the 1688/89 Revolution. In Chapter 6, Macdonald argues that it took until 1717 for the English public debt to attain 'investment-grade' status. Macdonald shows that a key point in this process was the election of 1710, when a party strongly opposed to the new form of debt-based public finance won a sweeping majority. However, the new Tory-backed government not only avoided default in spite of the gravity of the financial crisis that it inherited, but also managed the public finances in a manner that was arguably sounder than that of its Whig predecessor. The fiscal responsibility shown under the parliamentary system by the natural opponents of debt-based finance was critical for demonstrating a 'credible commitment' to public solvency. In that sense, Macdonald provides elaboration and embellishment of the dynamic described by Coffman in Chapter 5.

Carlos, Fletcher, Neal, and Wandschneider argue in Chapter 7 that the expense of the War of the Spanish Succession (1702–13) left each of the great powers of Europe (Austria, Britain, France, the Dutch Republic, and Spain) with unprecedented burdens of government debt. The overlapping Great Northern War (1700–1721) between Sweden and Russia also encumbered those two European powers with pressing financial obligations. The competitive experiments in dealing with the amassed debt that followed over the next decade left Britain alone among the contesting military powers of Europe holding the key to success in war finance: the development of a robust secondary market. Only Britain managed to convince a large and diverse number of individuals to hold onto their claims against the government. This was due to British institutions that allowed individuals to trade their claims with each other, rather than redeeming them directly from the government.

In Chapter 8, Pezzolo reminds us that the cities of northern and central Italy in the late Middle Ages have furnished generations of financial historians with insight into the genesis of public finance. The early establishment of deficit financing through short- and long-term borrowing has attracted interest among those seeking the origins of financial capitalism. A line of continuity – more or less ephemeral – has been drawn from Italian communes to eighteenth-century England, which is regarded as the birthplace of modern state debt. His chapter examines the means that some governments exploited to raise resources to wage war. Renaissance and Baroque Italy offer an excellent field to verify the model linking institutions to financial efficiency. Republics, monarchies, and principalities actually presented different financial and economic structures and performances. A long-term approach permits one both to highlight major changes in financial development, and to control for relationships – if any – with political structures.

In contrast, Irigoin and Grafe, in Chapter 9, agree that that the ability of rulers to commit credibly to protecting subjects' or citizens' property rights distinguished fast-growing European countries from the laggards, but, although the North and Weingast model laid the foundation for the belief that state predation was the most important political threat to economic growth in Early Modern Europe, the authors argue that coordination and integration of fragmented political units were also important. Following recent work by Besley and Persson (2009), they emphasise the complementarity of state fiscal capacity and legal capacity, which is especially present in the phase of European nation-state building. They thus shift attention toward a larger issue that bedevilled Early Modern European states: how to maintain effective legal and fiscal control over larger geographical units, including overseas empires and contiguous territories within Europe. Predation was not the typical strategy, certainly not in the Spanish case.

In Chapter 10, Kwass begins with the observation that the financial revolution that catapulted Britain to great-power status in the eighteenth century never took root in old-regime France. According to the 'credible commitment' thesis, France lacked the two institutions responsible for the spectacular rise in British public credit: a national parliament and a central bank. The only representative assembly in France that could have conceivably seized control over taxation and credibly serviced the public debt, the Estates General, lay dormant between 1614 and 1789, a casualty of Bourbon absolutism. The one great experiment with a French national bank, John Law's tentacular *Banque Royale*, went bust in 1720, casting a pall over French finances for decades to come. This chapter uses case studies of the salt and tobacco monopolies to examine the workings of court capitalism in France closely, and concludes that conflicts over whether consumption taxes might credibly service the public debt persisted until a political settlement was reached during the Third Republic in the nineteenth century.

In the final chapter, Sussman and Yafeh revisit their earlier work that focused on Britain following the Glorious Revolution, and extend the time-series data on the cost of Britain's debt to 1850. During that period both the cost and the total volume of British government debt increased substantially. Whereas the neoclassical position attributes higher borrowing rates to the effect of temporary military spending on crowding-out of private consumption, the results presented by the authors demonstrate that the rising cost of debt mainly reflects a direct increase in the risk premium due to the uncertainty associated with the outcome of war. The analysis includes a novel variable – the size of the British navy – which provides a direct measure of the effect of war-induced risk on government borrowing costs. These findings confirm that risk associated with war was the primary driver of variation in the cost of Britain's government debt, even when the country was already rich, industrialised, and institutionally developed. The rest of the chapter presents, in a unified framework, results from different data sets and time periods presented in the authors' previous work and considers the Early Modern period and the beginning of the modern era in a national comparative framework.

Taken together, these ten essays illustrate how far modern scholarship has advanced the debate inaugurated by North and Weingast over twenty years ago. They amount less to a trenchant critique than to an elaboration and embellishment of the multiple commitment mechanisms necessary to convince public creditors that sovereign debt constituted a relatively accessible, safe, and liquid investment vehicle. This volume's additions and amendments to the 'credible commitment' thesis will doubtlessly not be the final word on the subject, but the editors expect that they will furnish academics and practitioners alike with a broader understanding of the origins of financial capitalism, and perhaps even some useful operating guidelines.

References

Abrams, Philip 1988. 'Notes on the Difficulty of Studying the State', *Journal of Historical Sociology*, 1(1) (March), 58–89.
Acemoglu, Daron and Robinson, James 2012. *Why Nations Fail: The Origins of Power, Prosperity, and Poverty*. New York: Crown Publishers.
Acemoglu, Daron; Johnson, Simon; and Robinson, James 2005. 'The Rise of Europe: Atlantic Trade, Institutional Change and Economic Growth', *American Economic Review*, 95(3), 546–79.
Besley, T. and Persson, T. 2009. 'The Origins of State Capacity: Property Rights, Taxation, and Politicism', *American Economic Review* 99, 1218–44.
Bowen, Huw 2006. *Business of Empire: The East India Company and Imperial Britain, 1756–1833*. Cambridge: Cambridge University Press.
Braddick, Michael 1996. *The Nerves of State: Taxation and the Financing of the English State, 1558–1714*. Manchester: University of Manchester Press.
Carruthers, Bruce 1996. *City of Capital: Politics and Markets in the English Financial Revolution*. Princeton: Princeton University Press.
Chandaman, C. D. 1975. *The English Public Revenue, 1660–1688*. Oxford: Clarendon Press.

Clark, Gregory 1996. 'The Political Foundations of Modern Economic Growth: England, 1540–1800', *Journal of Interdisciplinary History*, 26(4), 563–88.

Cox, Gary W. 2012. 'Was the Glorious Revolution a Constitutional Watershed?' *Journal of Economic History*, 72(3) (September), 567–600.

DeLong, J. Bradford and Schleifer, Andrei 1993. 'Princes and Merchants: European City Growth before the Industrial Revolution', *Journal of Law and Economics*, 36, 671–702.

Dickson, P. G. M. 1967. *The Financial Revolution in England, A Study in the Development of Public Credit, 1688–1756*. New York: Macmillan.

Downing, George 1992. *The Military Revolution and Political Change*. Princeton: Princeton University Press.

Elster, Jon 1995. 'Forces and Mechanisms in the Constitution-Making Process', *Duke Law Journal*, 45, 364–96.

Epstein, S. R. 2000. *Freedom and Growth, Markets and States in Europe, 1300–1750*, London: Routledge.

Ertman, Thomas 1997. *Birth of Leviathan: Building States and Regimes in Medieval and Early Modern Europe*. New York: Cambridge University Press.

Gauci, Perry 2001. *Politics of Trade: The Overseas Merchant in State and Society, 1660–1720*. New York: Oxford University Press.

Gauci, Perry 2007. *Emporium of the World: The Merchants of London, 1660–1800*. London: Hambledon Continuum.

Gerschenkron, Alexander 1962. *Economic Backwardness in Historical Perspective*. Cambridge, MA: Harvard University Press.

Getzler, Joshua 1996. 'Theories of Property and Economic Development', *Journal of Interdisciplinary History*, 26, 639–69.

Gorski, Philip 2003. *The Disciplinary Revolution: Calvinism and the Rise of the State in Early Modern Europe*. Chicago: Chicago University Press.

Graff, Michael 2003. 'Financial Development and Economic Growth in Corporatist and Liberal Market Economies', *Emerging Markets Finance and Trade*, 39, 47–69.

Grassby, Richard 2001. *Kinship and Capitalism: Marriage, Family, and Business in the English Speaking World, 1580–1720*, Cambridge: Cambridge University Press.

Hancock, D. 1995. *Citizens of the World: London Merchants and the Integration of the British Atlantic Community*. Cambridge: Cambridge University Press.

Harris, Ron 2004. 'Government and the Economy, 1688–1850', in Roderick Floud and Paul Johnson (eds.), *The Cambridge Economic History of Britain since 1700, Volume I, 1700–1850*. Cambridge: Cambridge University Press.

Hoppit, Julian 2011. 'Compulsion, Compensation, and Property Rights in Britain, 1688–1833', *Past and Present*, (210), 93–128.

Kydland, Finn E. and Prescott, Edward C. 1977, 'Rules Rather than Discretion: The Inconsistency of Optimal Plans', *Journal of Political Economy*, 85, 473–91.

Lesger, Cle 2006. *The Rise of the Amsterdam Market and Information Exchange: Merchants, Commercial Expansion and Change in the Spatial Economy of the Low Countries, c. 1550–1630*. Burlington, VT: Ashgate Publishing Company.

Levine, Ross 2001. *Financial Structure and Economic Growth: A Cross-Country Comparison of Banks, Markets, and Development* (with Asli Demirgüç-Kunt). Cambridge, MA: MIT Press.

Lucas, Robert 1976. 'Econometric Policy Evaluation: A Critique', in *Carnegie-Rochester Conference Series on Public Policy*, 1, 19–46.

Macdonald, James 2006. *A Free Nation Deep in Debt: The Financial Roots of Democracy*. Princeton: Princeton University Press.

Mauro, Paolo; Sussman, Nathan; and Yafeh, Yishay 2006. *Globalization and Emerging Markets in the Nineteenth Century: Sovereign Debt and Institutions in the Golden Era of Globalization*. Oxford: Oxford University Press.

McGrath, Charles Ivar and Fauske, Chris 2008. *Money, Power, and Print: Interdisciplinary Studies of the Financial Revolution in the British Isles*. Newark: University of Delaware Press.

Moore, Sean 2010. *Swift, the Book, and the Irish Financial Revolution: Satire and Sovereignty in Colonial Ireland*. Baltimore: Johns Hopkins University Press.

Munro, John H. A. (ed.) 2012. *Money in the Pre-industrial World: Bullion, Debasements and Coin Substitutes*. London: Pickering & Chatto.

Murphy, Anne L. 2013. 'Demanding "Credible Commitment": Public Reactions to the Failures of the Early Financial Revolution', *Economic History Review*, 66, 178–97.

Neal, Larry 1990. *The Rise of Financial Capitalism: International Capital Movements in the Age of Reason*. Cambridge and New York: Cambridge University Press.

Neal, Larry 2000. 'How It All Began: The Monetary and Financial Architecture of Europe from 1648 to 1815', *Financial History Review*, 7(2) (October), 117–40.

North, Douglass C., 2005. *Understanding the Process of Economic Change*. Princeton: Princeton University Press.

North, Douglass C. and Weingast, Barry 1989. 'Constitutions and Commitment: The Evolution of Institutions Governing Public Choice in Seventeenth-Century England', *Journal of Economic History*, 43(4), 803–32.

O'Brien, Patrick K. and Hunt, Philip 1997. 'The Emergence and Consolidation of the Excises in the English Fiscal System before the Glorious Revolution', *British Tax Review*, 1997, 35–58.

Parker, Geoffrey 1996. *The Military Revolution: Military Innovation and the Rise of the West, 1500–1800*, 2nd edn. Cambridge: Cambridge University Press.

Persson, Torsten and Guido Tabellini 1994. *Monetary and Fiscal Policy*. 2 vols. Cambridge, MA: MIT Press.

Pincus, Steve 2009, *1688: The First Modern Revolution*. New Haven, CT: Yale University Press.

Quinn, Stephen 1996. 'Gold, Silver, and the Glorious Revolution: Arbitrage between Bills of Exchange and Bullion', *Economic History Review*, 49, 473–90.

Quinn, Stephen 2001. 'The Glorious Revolution's Effect on English Private Finance: A Microhistory, 1680–1705', *Journal of Economic History*, 61(3) (September), 593–615.

Redish, Angela 1990. 'The Evolution of the Gold Standard in England', *Journal of Economic History*, 50(4) (December), 789–805.

Reinert, Sophus A. 2011. *Translating Empire: Emulation and the Origins of Political Economy*. Cambridge, MA: Harvard University Press, 2011.

Rostow, W. W. 1960. *The Stages of Economic Growth: A Non-Communist Manifesto*. Cambridge: Cambridge University Press.

Stasavage, David 2007. 'Cities, Constitutions, and Sovereign Borrowing in Europe, 1274–1785', *International Organization*, 61 (Summer), 489–525.

Stasavage, David 2011. *States of Credit: Size, Power, and the Development of European Polities*, Princeton, NJ: Princeton University Press.

Sussman, Nathan and Yafeh, Yishay 2006. 'Institutional Reforms, Financial Development and Sovereign Debt: Britain 1690–1790', *Journal of Economic History*, 66(4) (Dec), 906–35.

Tilly, Charles 1990. *Coercion, Capital and European States: 990–1990*. Cambridge, MA: Blackwell.

Weingast, Barry R. 1997. 'The Political Foundations of Limited Government: Parliament and Sovereign Debt in 17th- and 18th-Century England', in John N. Drobak and John V. C. Nye (eds.), *The Frontiers of the New Institutional Economics*. San Diego: Academic Press.

Weingast, Barry R. 2005. 'The Constitutional Dilemma of Economic Liberty', *Journal of Economic Perspectives*, 19, 89–108.

Wells, John and Wills, Douglas 2000. 'Revolution, Restoration, and Debt Repudiation: The Jacobite Threat to England's Institutions and Economic Growth', *Journal of Economic History*, 60(2) (June), 418–41.

Wennerlind, Carl 2011. *Casualties of Credit: The English Financial Revolution, 1620–1720*. Cambridge, MA: Harvard University Press.

Zahedieh, Nuala 2010. *The Capital and the Colonies: London and the Atlantic Economy, 1660–1700*. Cambridge: Cambridge University Press.

2   Could the crown credibly commit to respect its charters? England, 1558–1640

Ron Harris[1]

This chapter offers a twofold shift in the application of the 'credible commitment' concept laid down by North and Weingast (1989). It examines the concept in the context of charter-granting, rather than in that of the national debt and the government bond market, and applies the concept to the pre-Civil War period, rather than the post-Glorious Revolution period.

Standard analytical frameworks

Since the 1950s, the classic economic theorisation of charters has been within the frameworks of regulation, public choice, and rent-seeking. Under these frameworks entrepreneurs are conceived as buyers. The crown or the state, or their agents, are perceived as sellers. The charter is the regulatory good being sold (Buchanan 1968; Stigler 1971, 3–21). Buyers are willing to pay for charters as part of their rent-seeking activity (Krueger 1974, 291–303). They particularly aim at the monopoly provided by the charter, which allows entrepreneurs to add a monopolistic rent to the free-market price of goods imported into England. The payment that entrepreneurs are willing to make to the crown for a charter depends on the expected value of monopoly rents over the lifetime of the charter. The better a group of merchants can organise to lobby the crown for the regulatory product it wishes to buy, the more likely it is to win in competition against other bidding groups. The smaller and more coherent the group, and the more it is based on pre-existing organisational infrastructure and the like, the more likely it is to be better organised and better able to solve free-rider problems (Olson 1971; Olson 1982; Miller 1989, 83–132; Macey and Miller 1991, 347–98).

[1] I would like to thank the organisers of the 'Questioning Credible Commitment' conference, D'Maris Coffman and Anne Murphy, and its participants for their helpful comments; Richard Helmholz, Guy Lurie, and Neil Nathanel for invaluable suggestions; and Rachel Klagsbrun for her research assistance.

Another way of conceptualising a charter is as an agreement between the crown and a group of merchants, analogous to a loan contract between the sovereign and lenders and future creditors. The charter details the exchange. The crown provides monopoly, incorporation, and enforcement of the monopoly against interlopers, possibly naval support, and political backing. The group of merchants provides money in various ways, including upfront cash and future custom and tax payments, promotion of the crown's foreign policy, and ships for the navy in times of war. In both conceptualisations – as a piece of regulation or as an agreement – the chartering system is viewed as a cornerstone of mercantilism (Ekelund and Tollison 1981).

The puzzle

Although this analytical framework provides some valuable insights, it does not deal with the 'credible commitment' problem. This is understandable, in that the framework was developed before North and Weingast published their now-classic article. However, if one considers the issue through the 'credible commitment' perspective, this lack is clearly detrimental. After all, the same problem that North and Weingast identified with respect to the crown's commitment to repay debts also applies to its commitment to respect charters. The crown, as long as it is an absolute sovereign, can do whatever it wishes. It cannot restrain itself in the present from doing things in the future. Therefore, the traditional analytical framework is revealed to be somewhat limited. From the perspective of charters as regulation, the crown can revoke a charter at will, issue a new, competing charter, or refuse to enforce privileges granted in a charter. From the perspective of charters as agreements, there is no third-party enforcer of the agreement. One of the parties to the contract is the intended, but unidirectional, enforcer.

Initially chartering was not the exclusive prerogative of the crown. Corporations were created by church authorities; they were recognised as created by prescription or common law. By the sixteenth century, the crown had assumed exclusivity over incorporation. An explicit, *ex ante*, and direct authorisation by the monarch became the only mode of incorporation (Blackstone 1756, 460–63; Kyd 1793–4, 39–41). In contemporary constitutional terms incorporation was considered an essential component of the monarch's exclusive and voluntary prerogative to create and grant dignities, jurisdictions, liberties, exemptions, and, in this case, franchises (monopolies and corporations) (Maitland 1908; Hale 1976). This authorisation was normally given in the form of charters or letters patent. The sovereign could exercise his prerogative to revoke or abolish such franchises at will. The law of corporations was classified by contemporaries as part of the Law of the King, the core of the English constitution. In practice, the authority to grant charters, and implicitly also to revoke them, was less contested than many other crown actions during late Tudor and even early Stuart reigns. For example, the raising of income by the crown, independent of Parliament, in the form of levies and impositions such as ship money, tonnage and poundage, and forced loans was much more controversial, because it contradicted the emerging constitutional principle of parliamentary approval of taxation.

This is a classic 'credible commitment' problem. The crown, as a sovereign that exercises prerogative authority, could backtrack and revoke commitments. Thus, the crown could not credibly commit not to revoke. Further, it could do much to breach its obligations even before reaching the stage of outright annulment of a charter: nonenforcement of the monopoly, granting charters to direct or indirect competitors, extorting additional payments, imposing new taxation, and expropriating capital/accumulated wealth. As a result, the buyers of the regulatory charter (or the counterparty to the charter as an agreement) would not have viewed the crown's commitments as credible, and should have been willing to pay less, or should have been unwilling to pay at all. The charters would thus lose their value, and the market for charters would be doomed to collapse altogether.

This did not happen. The period 1550–1630 was a heyday for corporate charters, most of them monopolistic. Most of England's overseas trade was incorporated, as a partial list (with dates of first incorporation) illustrates: Merchant Adventurers, 1505; Russia, 1553; Spanish, 1577; Eastland, 1579; Turkey, 1581; Venice, 1583; Levant, 1592; French, 1611; East India, 1600. Discovery, enslavement, extraction, and plundering voyages were chartered: the Morocco Company, 1585; Senegal River Adventurers, 1588; North West Passage Company, 1612; Gynney and Bynney Company, 1618; Guiana Company, 1609; Guinea Company, 1631. North American colonies and plantations were also chartered: Virginia, 1606; Plymouth Company, 1606; Newfoundland Company, 1610; Bermuda, 1615; New England, 1620; Nova Scotia, 1621; Massachusetts Bay, 1629; Providence Island Company, 1630 (Scott 1951; Cawston and Keane 1968; Tomlins 2001, 315–72). There must have been some 'credible commitment' devices in operation that kept the market for charters viable.

This chapter will proceed as follows. It begins with a survey of five distinct commitment devices that could potentially assist sovereigns to restrain themselves and credibly commit to upholding their promises and grants. It then examines which of these devices applied in England of 1558–1640. In the following section, it provides four case studies to examine which of these devices actually came into operation in late Tudor and early Stuart England and how the devices interacted with each other. Finally, it offers a preliminary comparative perspective to evaluate whether England was in any way unique in terms of the availability of commitment devices and of the economic performance that could be derived from the availability of a credible chartering system.

Availability of commitment devices

The literature presents a range of commitment devices, not all of which were originally suggested by their framers as commitment devices. The availability of each, in the context of charter-granting, varied over the period. Repeated transactions can sustain credibility through a bilateral reputation mechanism, but often the intensity of the transaction is not sufficiently high, or the payoffs at the endgame are detrimentally too high, to maintain credibility. Greif shows that multilateral, coalition-based reputation mechanisms can function when bilateral reputation does not work (Greif 1989, 857–82; Greif 2006). Olson suggests that the clustering of interest groups around a regulatory arrangement that benefits them, and active lobbying in its favour funded by profits extracted thanks to that regulation, may prevent the government from amending the regulation in a manner that hampers these interest groups (Olson 1971; Olson 1982). North and Weingast note that, among other things, appropriate institutional design, in their case the establishment of the independent Bank of England, can create self-imposed constraints on the sovereign's ability to backtrack from commitments (North and Weingast 1989, 821; Weingast 1997, 213–46; North, Wallis, and Weingast 2009). Landes and Posner suggest that an independent judiciary can serve as the third-party enforcer of agreements between the sovereign – in this case the executive branch or legislature – and its subjects (Landes and Posner 1975, 875–901). The most obvious commitment device in modern liberal states is an entrenched constitution. A prime example is the United States constitution, which requires for amendment a two-thirds supermajority in both houses of Congress and a three-quarters supermajority among the states. The 'Taking Clause' is an example of a 'credible commitment' not to expropriate private property. The 'Contract Clause' was understood to prohibit exactly what is of interest here, the dilution of privileges granted to incorporators in charters, which were equated to contracts between the state and its subjects (*Trustees of Dartmouth College* v. *Woodward*, 17 US [4 Wheat.] 518, 1819; *Charles River Bridge* v. *Warren Bridge*, 36 US 420, 1837). North and Weingast assert that more than one commitment device was used in their case, but for analytical purposes devices of different sorts are examined below one by one, to determine which of them could have possibly functioned to reinforce the crown's credibility and sustain the market for charters.

Reputation

The most elementary way to achieve a reputation was through repeat transactions. The more the crown granted charters and respected their terms, the higher its repute and credibility. Repeat transactions functioned along two dimensions. The first is the diachronic history of the chartering of a single enterprise. The longer the crown kept its promise to respect a charter, the better was its reputation. At first sight, it seems that a charter or monopoly set up for a reasonable term of years, and prolonged from time to time, serves reputation accumulation better than a perpetual charter or monopoly, although this insight requires analysis beyond the scope of the present chapter. The second dimension is spatial, the multiplicity of concurring grants. The more future charters are valued in accordance with the commitment of the crown to pending charters, the more reluctant the crown will be to revoke or not respect charters. In other words, the negative externality of the revocation of the commitment to the receivers of a given charter on the value of other charters increases the incentive of the crown to respect its commitments and maintain its general reputation. In the case of England, the sheer passage of time after the beginning of the use of charters in the middle of the sixteenth century and into the seventeenth century facilitated the accumulation of reputation. The expansion of the use of charters from long-distance trade to shorter-distance trade and to domestic manufacturing and retail also supported the function of reputation as a commitment device.

Entrepreneurs could also act strategically by threatening not to fulfil their obligations. They could invest less than promised. They could fail to perform the kinds of activities that supported the crown's diplomatic and naval policies. They could defect and cooperate with other European states, say the Spanish, Portuguese, or Dutch, or with local rulers in Asia, such as the Mughals or the Ming Dynasty, or simply remain overseas, leaving their wealth thousands of miles from the closest royal official. This is a reminder that the 'credible commitment' problem is two-sided. Admittedly, as the weaker and not sovereign party, the receivers of the charter could find it easier to commit credibly. Credible threats by the incorporators to tit-for-tat could support a reputation mechanism. The grant of the charter was only the first stage in the repeated interactions that built a reputation for both parties. The merchants would aim, as far as possible, to increase their reliance and investments in keeping with the crown's ongoing respect for the charters' terms, and vice versa. The frequent renewal of a charter was another interaction in which positive reputation could accumulate, although as shown in the following in the case of the East India Company, this prediction was not always fulfilled. Corporations or the crown could end up damaging their reputation because of external pressures.

Institutional devices

Institutional devices could be employed by both parties to the charter, the receivers and the grantors. The basic institutional response of receivers to the 'credible commitment' problem was in the way the business was organised. The level of vulnerability of business corporations to revocation can be assessed through an examination that intermingles somewhat with the discussion of reputation, one which distinguishes between different types of business activities performed through charters, and analyses them one by one. (Nonbusiness charters, such as municipal charters, will not be considered, nor will those which were granted only after activities began. These were prone to expropriation irrespective of the charter, and their incorporators did not have to decide whether to pursue the activity based on the credibility of the crown.)

One-shot ventures, such as privateering and exploration charters, were, in a sense, less vulnerable. All the incorporators needed was for the crown to allow them to depart England, and, at the end of their voyage, if successful, to allow them to keep their agreed-on share of the fortune. In another sense, if the adventurers were not likely to be repeat players, say Francis Drake or John Hawkins, the crown had no incentive to establish a reputation with them (though it could have incentive to establish a general reputation by respecting its commitment). The next level up is composed of companies that provided infrastructure to their members, but did not conduct the transaction in their corporate capacity and account. This category includes regulated corporations, an incarnation of the merchant guilds. The regulated corporation did not pool the resources of its members, and thus had only limited capital, which was invested in a few physical assets, such as warehouses and residential dwellings overseas, and a meeting hall in England. Thus, its exposure to expropriation by the crown was limited. Individual merchants remained at risk of expropriation of the goods they traded and of the money they received, but this problem is common to all business activities and accumulations of wealth, and not unique to charters.

The next, and last, level up is joint-stock companies. In them resources were pooled in order to meet higher investment thresholds and to spread greater risks, since the capital of such companies was mostly invested in ships, goods, forts, factories, port facilities, etc. When calling up external equity investors and when taking investment decisions with respect to the level of activity and investment in the construction of facilities, such companies relied on the charter and its monopoly, state support, and incorporation components. Thus these companies were more vulnerable to revocation of charter commitments. However, some mitigating factors existed regarding that vulnerability. A significant proportion of the property in danger of expropriation was located overseas in destination markets, where the crown could find it harder, though not impossible, to touch. Revocation or dilution of the monopoly (by lapse of enforcement or by issuing competing charters) was only partially detrimental if not accompanied by withdrawal of the license to trade overseas and expropriation of property, because after the chartered company had established its leading position in the overseas market and *en route* to that market, newcomers or interlopers might face entry barriers that they could not overcome even with some support from the crown. This is a good example of the influence of 'credible commitment': although the joint-stock company was the more vulnerable form of organisation, over time it nevertheless became the more ubiquitous one, thanks to the ability of such companies to enter distant markets, cross entry barriers, invest in infrastructure, and establish leading market positions. All of these were made possible through the formation of more 'credible commitment' by the crown.

On the grantor's side, within the state an institutional division of labour was developed regarding chartering, enforcement of charters, and revocation. No new independent entity, such as the Bank of England, which played a pivotal role in North and Weingast's thesis, was formed in the context of chartering, but a division of labour between the three pre-existing branches of government did evolve. The crown was still undoubtedly the central player. It granted charters, negotiated with the entrepreneurs, and on the side of the state was the prime benefactor of the chartering system. The common-law courts supervised the use of charters and criticised the grant of bad monopolies by the crown. Although Parliament was not yet an incorporator and grantor of monopolies through the legislative process (a role it assumed later in the seventeenth century), it was a forum in which agitation against monopolies granted by the crown could be expressed. Parliament objected to the crown's bypassing of parliamentary approval of taxation by selling charters (as well as by other methods). Eventually, in the 1624 Statute of Monopolies (discussed later in this chapter), Parliament restricted the prerogative of the crown to grant monopolies. The division of powers between the crown, the courts, and Parliament weakened the former's ability to grant charters, but also made those charters that were granted more consensual and less easily revocable.

Independent judiciary and the common law

North and Weingast highlight the importance of separation of powers, but stress the role of an independent representative parliament as a branch separate from the executive branch associated with the crown, and only in passing mention the judiciary. A 1975 article by Landes and Posner complements this. It was the first to integrate the judiciary into the theory of regulation. They argue that the judiciary, unlike the legislature, was independent of interest-group politics, and thus could provide a long-term enforcement mechanism for regulatory contracts made between the legislature and a given interest group. Judicial enforcement thus raised the value of the regulatory commodity (Landes and Posner 1975; Klerman and Mahoney 2005, 1–17). A slight tilt of their argument can view the creation of an independent judiciary as a commitment device. Even if not fully independent, the common-law courts in late Tudor and early Stuart times could constrain the crown's power to revoke charters through a number of channels.

The writs of *quo warranto* and *scire facias* are two companion prerogative writs (Holdsworth 1922, 382–407; Baker 1990, 166–7; Harris 2000, 16–19). The writ of *quo warranto* is a legal proceeding during which an individual's or corporation's right to a privilege or franchise is challenged. Those who pretended to act like a corporation, in the case of a charter of incorporation, had to show *quo warranto* (literally, 'by what authority or warrant'), that is, by which valid charter they claimed the corporate privileges they exercised. The writ of *scire facias*, literally 'to know the causes', was used if the charter had been obtained by fraud or misrepresentation, or if the crown had granted a charter by mistake, or under a misapprehension as to the construction of the effect of the charter, or if the corporation had done something prohibited or not authorised by its charter. *Quo warranto* challenged the validity of charters, whereas *scire facias* annulled them. Initially, in the thirteenth century, both were used by the king to strengthen his authority at the expense of mostly municipal corporations (Sutherland 1963). By the sixteenth century the effect of these two writs had changed somewhat. They constrained the monarch by requiring legal proceedings, typically in the Court of King's

Bench, for the annulment of business corporations' charters. Annulment before expiration was thus legalised. This forced the King's Counsel to go to court, make legal arguments, and present evidence (Patterson 2005, 879–906) in a court that was quite independent, and generally not very favourable to the early Stuarts. By the Restoration the writs were again used to strengthen royal authority by revoking charters granted during the Commonwealth (George 1940, 47–56; Dunn 1963, 488–512; Levin 1969; Haffenden 1985a, 298–311; Haffenden 1985b, 452–66).

A related legal tool is visitation of corporations. Visitation was originally meant to allow bishops and other senior church officials to supervise ecclesiastical corporations, but this tool changed over time. After the Reformation it lost its original function, and came to be used by the king to assert authority (Pound 1936, 369–95). Technically, the tool could be used through the prerogative writs of *mandamus* or *quo warranto* or through equity. This type of intervention was also a manifestation of the growing legalisation of the relationship between the crown and the chartered corporations. The doctrine of *ultra vires* (literally, 'beyond the powers') was also used sporadically to challenge the activities of corporations in a manner that rendered the corporate environment increasingly legalistic (Smith 1946–47, 28–33). The case of Sutton's Hospital (1610) deals with several aspects of the formation and governance of corporations, most of which are not directly relevant here (Sutton's Hospital, 10 Co. Rep. 23a 1612). However, it is a good demonstration of the growing role of law and of litigation in governing corporate affairs. It was a particularly long and high-profile report by contemporary standards. This is one more indication of the growing rule of law with respect to the granting of charters by the crown.

Constitution

For a constitution to convey 'credible commitment', it must be entrenched. The presence or lack of entrenchment is a fundamental feature of constitutions. An entrenched constitution cannot be altered in any way by a legislature or the crown as part of their normal business of passing ordinary laws and decrees, but can only be amended by a different and more onerous procedure. In the England of the late Tudors and early Stuarts the entrenchment of the constitution was contested. According to some scholars, three contemporary constitutional theories can be identified: royalist, parliamentarian, and common law (Goldsworthy 1999).

According to royalist theories, God conferred governmental powers on the king alone. He was God's vicar, and as such, had not only authority to rule, but also the divine qualities needed for doing so. He could not be constrained in any way by Parliament or the courts. His prerogative with respect to granting and revoking charters and attaching privileges to them was not constrained in any way. As the dominant theory of the day, the royalist theory implied the inability of the crown to commit credibly to the value of the charters it granted.

According to parliamentarian theories, God originally conferred the highest powers of government on the community as a whole. The community delegated the powers to the king subject to certain conditions. One of them was that Parliament would make laws and impose taxes (Elton 1989, 151–74, 223–302). Another was that the king would use his powers subject to statute and common law. The community was represented (though not through elections) by Parliament, and only Parliament could act on its behalf. The question of to what extent the king could raise income from nonparliamentary sources was the cause of grave contention between Parliament and the early Stuarts (Maitland 1908, 258–60; Kenyon 1986, 24–32; Hart 2003, 89). Parliament in that period meant King, Lords, and Commons in conjunction. The king's chartering powers were constrained by statutes of Parliament, notably the 1624 *Statute of Monopolies* (Maitland 1908, 260–61).

Common-law theories held that the common law embodied the wisdom of the community, as expressed in immemorial customs. The common law was manifest in institutions, rules, and statutes that evolved over the years and could not be abolished by the king. These theories, whose main protagonist at the time was Edward Coke, held that the judges were committed to the principles of the common law and not to the dictates of the king who appointed them (Kenyon 1986, 90–94; Maitland 1908, 261–75). The question of whether the common law constrained Parliament's legislative authority was not clearly answered by these theories. Some later observers interpreted Coke's holding in Bonham's Case (*Thomas Bonham* v. *College of Physicians*, 8 Co. Rep. 114a; 77 Eng. Rep. 646, CP 1610) as asserting that parliamentary statutes which violated fundamental law were void. Others said that he did not go so far.

Common-law theories are relevant to chartering on three counts. First, prerogative writs could not be exploited at will by the crown to annul charters. Second, some of the privileges granted by the charters, notably monopolies that are detrimental to the public interest, were against the law (discussed below the case of *Darcy* v. *Allen*). Third, and related, the judiciary was independent and could not be dismissed by the crown for enforcing the law against the crown's interests (Hart 2003, 56–74).

As parliamentarian and common-law theories of the English constitution – theories that adhered to a mixed constitution, to some Englishmen's rights, and to constraints by conventions and historical traditions – became more popular, so did the ability to commit credibly to chartered corporations.

Interest groups

One of the insights gained from North and Weingast's contribution is that once a commitment is made by the sovereign, under certain institutional configurations interest groups will be formed to prevent the sovereign from revoking that commitment. In the case of the national debt, North and Weingast identify state creditors – holders of government bonds – as organised around Parliament in such a way as to ensure that Parliament did not backtrack from collecting taxes for debt repayment. Carruthers takes this idea one step forward. The three 'monied companies' of the late seventeenth and early eighteenth centuries, the Bank of England, East India Company, and South Sea Company, served as the focal point for interest groups to ensure that the state would honour its commitment to repay its loans. The charters of these companies were one of the commitment devices. Once chartered, the companies served not only as institutional intermediaries, but also as interest group organisers and as party politics players within the Whig and Tory parties in Parliament (Carruthers 1996, 137–59; Alborn 1998; Harris 2000, 53–9; Harris 2009, 145).

The same interest group analysis can be applied to the late Tudor and early Stuart periods. The rising commercial classes gradually aligned with the major political players of the time, the crown and Parliament. Brenner identifies three socio-economic-political groups of merchants. The first, in the middle of the sixteenth century, comprised the members of the Merchant Adventurers, who forged a strong political alliance with Henry VIII and Elizabeth. The second, by the late sixteenth century, was the Russia–Levant–East India group of merchants, which gradually replaced the Merchant Adventurers in terms of business success and political power. Elizabeth was more dependent on their willingness to be taxed and to lend her money. The leading Levant and East India merchants and directors were the elite of the City of London; they were made magistrates and members of Parliament. Brenner describes the workings of interest groups in the first decades of the Stuart reign:

Above all the Levant-East India merchants shared with all of the other company merchants of London a profound dependence on the Crown-sanctioned commercial corporations that provided the foundation for their protected trades. This dependence united the generality of company merchants in defence of privilege and, all else being equal, in support of the royal government, which was of course the guarantor of their protected status. (Brenner 2003, 83)

The third interest group Brenner identifies is members of colonial companies, membership of which was distinct in that it included both merchants and landed gentry. The merchants who joined the colonial companies trading to North America and the Caribbean mostly came from the City margins, were less wealthy, and lacked political connections in that period, but in a pioneering, large-scale quantitative study of the background of company members, Rabb finds that the gentry joined these companies, comprising some twenty per cent of their members. This is in contrast to the East Asia merchant companies, in which the gentry were not present in any significant numbers (Rabb 1967). The gentry created a solid political basis for the colonial companies in Parliament. Brenner claims that the city merchant elite – the leading shareholders and directors of the East Asia corporations – supported the crown all the way, until the early 1640s. He claims that by the 1630s colonial merchants sided with Parliament (Ashton 1979; Brenner 2003, 199–315). This is in line with Rabb's finding of significant gentry membership. These members were on Parliament's side.

In a recent quantitative study of the Long Parliament, Jha concludes that 'three of four shareholder MPs supported the expansion of parliamentary control in the Civil War, compared to around half of non-shareholders'. Furthermore, 'share ownership is associated with a twenty percentage point rise in the probability of support for Parliament, an effect that is strongly significant and remarkably unchanged with the addition of rich controls for wealth, religion, and geographical features' (Jha 2010, 14–15). It is not necessary here to decide upon the accuracy either of Brenner's position that East Asia merchants supported the crown in order to protect their charters, or of Jha's that company shareholders switched to Parliament because they felt threatened by the crown's ability to revoke their charters and expropriate their wealth. Important for the purposes of the current chapter is that interest-group politics mattered for the credibility of the crown when chartering was on the table. Interest group coalitions could, under some political circumstances, though definitely not radical circumstances such as the Civil War, add another layer, in addition to the reputational, institutional, judicial, and constitutional layers, to the credibility of crown commitments.

Five types of commitment devices have been identified, and their availability in the period 1558–1640 examined. Their functioning in actual historical contexts, and in conjunction with each other, is studied below through four historical case studies. The cases are not representative of the period as a whole, though each was important in the view of contemporaries. They were selected because each of them exemplifies a different interplay of devices and different facets of the chartering phenomenon.

The Spanish Company

The final round of negotiations that predated the chartering of the Spanish Company lasted three years, during which various groups of merchants lobbied for and against the company. The Privy Council held several hearings, and the eventual charter embodied a compromise between veteran Spanish merchants and newcomers. The charter, dated 8 July 1577, granted jurisdiction over the entire Iberian coastline. The Company was granted all the usual powers of a corporate body, including that of punishing interlopers (Croft 1973a, 7–29). Within eighteen months of its foundation, the Company was at odds with the Merchant Adventurers, the outports, and the government itself.

Of the various port towns affected by the Spanish Company's charter, Bristol, Chester, and Exeter present the most interesting cases, because their merchants had been involved in Spanish trade before, based on royal privileges. The legal configuration of the challenges they posed was quite similar. They continued trading with Spain, claiming that the new charter did not undermine their right to trade granted under earlier privileges obtained from the crown. On the authority of its charters, the Spanish Company arrested some of them for interloping on its monopoly zone. The traders turned to the Court of King's Bench, based on a *habeas corpus* writ, claiming that they were arrested without proper authority.

In the case of Bristol, in which a previous local chartered company did not exist in September of 1577, the Privy Council ordered the Lord Chief Justice of England and the Lord Chief Justice of the Common Pleas not to grant writs of *habeas corpus* to those arrested by the company for violation of its regulations (Ponko 1968, 1–63). Moreover, in 1578, the Council wrote to the mayor of Bristol, ordering him to take action against 'one Philippe Langley' who, contrary to the ordinances of the Spanish Company, continued retail trade with Spain. If the mayor could not persuade Langley to listen to reason, he was to bond him to appear before the Council.

Chester's merchants traded with Spain based on a charter granted by Queen Mary in 1554 and confirmed by Elizabeth in 1559. Upon incorporation, the Spanish Company suggested that the Chester Merchant Adventurers merge with it, to form the Chester branch of the Spanish

Company, but the lesser retailers of Chester refused, insisting that they had the right to trade independently with Spain. In November 1581 the Privy Council intervened in the Chester affair, ordering the Lord Chief Justice and the Master of the Rolls to hear the conflicting arguments put forward by the company and by some of the merchants of Chester and Liverpool. The law lords concluded that the Spanish Company had acted beyond its powers in attempting to prevent the retailers from trading. The Privy Council thereupon permitted the merchant retailers to continue their commerce (Unwin 1927, 35–64). Several more rounds followed. Finally, when the cessation of commerce following the Armada and the outbreak of war with Spain rendered the conflict pointless, legal action ended in July 1589 (Croft 1973b).

Immediately upon his coronation in 1603, James improved relations with Spain, and thus opened new opportunities to the few remaining traders to the peninsula. They wished to rely on the 1577 charter, and to reassert their monopoly over the re-established trade. They again faced opposition from the outports and from London retailers. This vested-interest opposition aligned with growing anti-monopoly sentiments in Parliament, which was suspicious of James' diplomatic, theological, fiscal, and constitutional intentions (Rabb 1964, 646–70; Ashton 1967, 40–55). An assault on the revival of the long-defunct monopoly of the Spanish Company would have had far more chance of success, so some MPs believed, than would campaigns mounted against much wealthier, politically powerful, and legally sound corporations such as the Merchant Adventurers and the Muscovy Company.

The first bill against the reuse of the old charter for enforcing the trade monopoly, drafted and passed in the Commons in 1604, was blocked in the House of Lords. The next stage was the legal scrutiny of the company's old privileges and of the charter of 1577. Defects were found by lawyers in the drafting of the charter and in its application, notably the fact that a President had not been elected for eighteen years. A new charter was drafted in 1605 to overcome these legal defects. A bill was reintroduced in 1606 to prohibit the monopolisation of trade with Spain (and France). This time the bill passed the Lords as well as the Commons. The Spanish Company was to be open to all merchants with a legitimate interest in the Spanish trade, as a corporation whose purpose was to promote trade, and not as a monopoly. However, the compromise satisfied neither the outports nor Parliament, and attempts at renegotiation were unsuccessful. A Commons committee was formed to consider the legality of the charter and, if needed, to draft a bill to counter it. Coke provided his legal opinion. The Spanish Company directors suggested several compromises, but they were rejected, and the bill for free trade into Spain, Portugal, and France went through the Commons with little opposition. Following some reservations, it passed the Lords, and was enacted in 1606, abolishing the Spanish Company (Croft 1975,17–27).

The case of the Spanish Company thus involved two rounds, the first in 1577–88, the second in 1603–6. The first round demonstrates the role of a multiplicity of institutions, the crown represented by the Privy Council, the judiciary, and the municipalities. It also demonstrates the turning of vested-interest conflicts into legal conflicts adjudicated in courts. The second round also demonstrates the interplay between institutions, this time Parliament and the crown, and a struggle between interest groups. Here, too, part of the controversy was turned into a legal controversy over the validity of the charter. The case of the Spanish Company demonstrates the vulnerability of charters granted for short-distance trade that could be engaged in by outport merchants and London retailers, as well as involvement of the City merchant elite in interest-group politics. However, it also suggests that chartering gradually became a more legalistic and adjudicated matter. This case and the following ones demonstrate the beginning of a nascent rule of law in the area of crown chartering.

Darcy v. Allen

This case deals with the grant of monopoly privileges by the crown to an individual, Edward Darcy, but its legal applicability covers the grant of monopolies to corporations as well. In 1588 Queen Elizabeth granted a twenty-one-year monopoly (originally granted in 1576) to Ralph Bowes for the manufacture, import, and sale of playing cards. In 1598 the letters patent were reissued for twelve years and assigned to Darcy, a groom in the royal court. In 1600 he appealed to the Privy Council to enforce his privilege against infringers. In 1601 the Council sent a letter, presumably at Darcy's request, to the Lord Chief Justice of the Common Pleas asking the Court not to review the validity of the playing cards monopoly, as its grant was part of the royal prerogative (Mossoff 2001, 1266–7).

Thomas Allen, a London haberdasher, was making and selling playing cards in 1601. Darcy brought an action for infringement against Allen in King's Bench. In his defence Allen initially argued that the monopoly contradicted privileges granted from time immemorial to his company, a London Livery Company chartered in 1448. His attorneys then made a more principled argument. The monopoly grant was defective because it contradicted Acts of Parliament as well as the common law. Coke, Attorney General at the time, argued for the validity of the monopoly, but in 1603 the King's Bench ruled unanimously that the monopoly grant was void, marking an additional step in the gradual development of a refined and detailed law which governed monopolies for inventions (Corre 1996, 1261–1327; Bracha 2005, 31–6). The court held that though the Queen had the prerogative to grant privileges and charters, they should be granted only to promote the common weal. Before the grant of the playing-cards monopoly to Darcy, traders had produced cards, and people could buy them at reasonable prices. Darcy used the patent for his own profit at the expense of others. The Queen was cleared; she had been deceived by Darcy into granting him the monopoly. Though Coke's report of the case suggests that the Court ruled against monopolies as such, two other reports of the case limit the ruling to the specific circumstances mentioned above, while in fact approving monopolies that would fit the traditional guidelines (11 Co. Rep. 84b, 77 Eng. Rep. 1260, 1603; Moore 671, 72 Eng. Rep. 830, 1603; Noy 173, 74 Eng. Rep. 1131, 1603).

Darcy v. Allen demonstrates the institutional rivalry between the judiciary and the crown. This rivalry was translated into constitutional rivalry with respect to the scope of the prerogative of the King and the role of common law in England's constitution. This case can be interpreted as providing a venue for challenging and annulling grants made by the crown. As such, it could be seen as weakening the ability of the crown to commit credibly, but a more compelling interpretation is that the case better clarifies the range of the crown's prerogative in granting monopolies. Grants within this range became more secure and credible following Darcy, even as the scope of Royal charters was restricted. The issues raised in Darcy were dealt with extensively in the next case to be considered.

The statute of monopolies

The grant of monopolies was high on the agenda following the accession of James I to the English throne in 1603. The Commons frequently attacked the grant of specific monopolies, and of monopolies in general, by Elizabeth and James. As shown in the preceding, the issue was litigated in the courts. The King made several declarations regarding his attitude toward monopolies and his policy in granting them, notably in 1603 and 1610. In 1621 a bill to limit the grant of monopolies by the monarch passed the Commons, but was rejected by the Lords. On the first day of the 1624 session of Parliament, Coke again moved the 1621 bill forward. This time a conference was held between the Lords and Commons, in which leaders of both houses, including the Archbishop of Canterbury and other Privy Councillors, Coke, and the Attorney-General, devoted time to sorting out the disagreements and carefully drafting the general prohibition and the exceptions to it. Petitions from vested interests, including livery and municipal corporations, as well as individuals and MPs holding various charters and letters patent, were accounted for. The list of exceptions to the rule grew as the 1624 session progressed. Eventually everybody involved, from Coke to Prince Charles, was satisfied with the draft. The bill passed the Lords and received royal assent in late May 1624.

Although some historians view the *Statute of Monopolies* as the origin of modern patent or antitrust law, or as a blow inflicted by Parliament on the king's prerogative and his fiscal and economic policy, more recent studies suggest that the *Statute* in fact reflected contemporary understanding of the state of the common law and the constitution. The *Statute of Monopolies* was not imposed on the king against his will, but rather was the product of a consensus arrived at after prolonged negotiations between all the interested political players of the time (Kyle 1998, 203–23; Bracha 2005, 43–51; Dent 2009, 415–53).

Indeed, the first section of the statute states, 'be it enacted that all monopolies and all commissions, grants, licenses, charters and letters patent . . . granted to any person . . . body politic or corporate for the sole buying, selling, making anything within this realm . . . are altogether contrary to the laws of this realm, and so are and shall be utterly void'. A long list of exceptions, carefully added by the Commons and Lords at the request of vested interests and public-good seekers, follows. The more general exceptions include monopolies enacted by Parliament, those approved by the common-law courts, privileges granted to 'true and first inventors' of new manufactures, and privileges granted to corporations. Also included is a long list of particular exceptions of individuals and economic activities. The process of enactment, as well as the final outcome, supports the revisionist conclusion. The *Statute* reflected a relative consensus. Charters granted to corporations following its enactment in 1624 were within the consensus even if endowed with monopoly, were unlikely to be declared illegal by common-law judges or Parliament, and were less likely to be revoked on the whim of the king.

The case of the *Statute of Monopolies* is in many respects a continuation of *Darcy v. Allen*. It deals with similar issues, though in a different institutional configuration. This time, the crown was in conflict with Parliament, rather than with the judiciary. At the forefront were constitutional issues such as the extent of the crown's prerogative, the division of power between the executive and the legislative branches, and the entrenchment of constitutional arrangements. Vested interests influenced and shaped the final outcome.

East India Company

The first charter of the East India Company, granted by Queen Elizabeth on 31 December 1600, contains numerous contractual features. The crown provided incorporation, with attached privileges of purchasing land, pleading in court, and having a common seal. In addition, it granted a trade monopoly for fifteen years over the territory extending east from the Cape of Good Hope to the Straits of Magellan. The Company was empowered to make bylaws and to impose penalties on interlopers. In return, it had to make regular voyages to India using six ships of specified size and crew. It also committed to deliver these ships to the navy in times of war. The crown committed to preventing other English subjects from visiting the East Indies, and implicitly committed not to grant competing charters. The Company committed to paying customs and duties, subject to specified exemptions for the first few years. It was agreed that interloping ships and their goods would be forfeited, and their value split equally between the Company and the crown. The crown permitted the Company to export bullion, as long as equal quantities were imported (the first voyage was exempt from this requirement). Admirals, sheriffs, and other state officials were required to aid the Company on land and sea as needed. To this detailed and seemingly balanced contract, in the form of a charter, were added several background complementary rules, notably the subjection of the Company and its trade to duty and taxation.

The charter envisioned its own prolongation. It indicated that 'if at the end of the said term of fifteen years it shall seem . . . convenient unto the said Governor and Company . . . and if that also it shall appear unto us, our heirs and successors, that the continuance thereof shall not be prejudicial or hurtful to this realm . . . but profitable for us . . . and for our realm, with such conditions as are herein mentioned, or with some alteration or qualification . . . grant . . . new letters patents . . . in due form of law' (Shaw 1887). The charter also envisioned its own termination, and that of the monopoly. It stated that if the grant 'shall not be profitable' to the crown or to the realm, then 'after two years warning' given to the Company, the charter could be terminated.

In 1609 James I issued a second charter for the confirmation and extension of its Elizabethan predecessor. It stressed that the company 'for ever be' a corporate body. The first charter did not expressly declare the perpetuity of the corporation. More importantly, the second charter granted the East India Company the trade monopoly over the same huge territory 'for ever'. Nevertheless, it provided the crown with an exit clause quite similar to the one in the 1600 charter, but fixed 'three years warning'. It is true that such prolongation and exit clauses do not establish a fully 'credible commitment' not to revoke the charter unilaterally and without advance warning, but their careful drafting at least suggests that attention was paid to this issue when the charter *cum* contract was negotiated and drafted (Shaw 1887).

The 1609 charter was not formally revoked in the period under review; it was finally replaced by a 1661 charter granted by Charles II (Shaw 1887). Its longevity is somewhat indicative of the credibility of the crown, but as mentioned previously, formal revocation was only one way open to the crown to dishonour its commitments. Nonenforcement was another option; the grant of charters to competitors was another. Charles I eroded his father's 1609 commitment in both ways. In 1630 he licensed English privateers to prey on local ships between the Red Sea and India. In 1635 he licensed William Courteen, an eminent London merchant, to organise a syndicate to trade with all areas of the East not previously exploited by the East India Company. In 1637, after receiving a £10,000 interest in the venture as a bribe, Charles granted Courteen's syndicate a full charter. In the years 1637–9 an initiative to colonise Madagascar, led by landed aristocrats, received the King's support. This was a threat to the East India Company, which used the island as a supply station *en route* to the East (Brenner 2003, 168–73).

These acts may seem a unilateral revocation of commitment by the crown, but in fact the King's use of his sovereign power to erode the charter was in retaliation for the East India Company's dodging of the agreement in 1627–9. The Company had refused the King's request for a loan, and to invest in fortifications and war with the Dutch in accordance with the King's policy. It had not raised sufficient capital to allow operations on the expected scale, and petitioned Parliament, accusing the King of having failed to provide military support against Dutch aggression (Scott 1951, 110–17; Chaudhuri 1965, 56–73). This can be interpreted as strategic behaviour by both parties to the agreement, with each act aimed at forcing the other to comply with their own interpretation of their opposites' obligations. Eventually, in 1639, the king withdrew his support from the competing ventures, and the parties reached yet another truce. A partial explanation for this is that Eastern trade, unlike short-distance trade such as the trade with Spain, involved a high investment threshold and institutional governance and finance structures which individual interlopers, or even newly entering syndicates, were unable to meet. Further, outsiders who wished to invest in eastern trade, and share in its profits, could do so by purchasing shares in primary or secondary markets. Such an entry option did not exist in closed, regulated corporations such as the Spanish Company. The interest groups that pressed the king to revoke his commitment to joint-stock long-distance trading corporations were weaker than those that pressed him to withdraw commitments to the small group of merchants that enjoyed other charters.

The long history of the charters of the East India Company seems like a success story in terms of 'credible commitment'. For forty years, Elizabeth I, James I, and Charles I respected the basic terms of the charter. In truth, challenges and crises occurred, but the charter held. It did so because the reputation mechanism was gaining momentum. It held because the charter was granted in a zone of consensus. Parliament, the judiciary, and the crown all viewed it as constitutional. The vested interests that pressed the crown not to respect it were not formidable, first, because of the natural entry barriers involved in oceanic Eastern trade, and second, because, as a result of the joint-stock nature of the corporation, outsiders could buy a share in the potential profits on the open market, which further broadened the base of the group that had vested interests in the venture.

Comparison with the Continent

In France, grants of privileges to corporations, municipalities, and the like were for the life of the granting king (Collins 2009, 8). When discussing the grant of privileges to print books in France, Armstrong states that 'the grant of privilege from royal chancery was [an] exercise of royal prerogative, and in principle a personal favour. It was thus uncertain whether a privilege granted by one king was valid under his successor' (Armstrong 2002, 26–7). She brings several examples of people who obtained grants for printing a book, and following the death of the reigning king sought legal advice. On the basis of advice received, they then petitioned for a new letters patent from the new king. In Portugal, privileges granted to foreigners, particularly foreign merchants, to reside in Lisbon, to trade with Portugal, and later also to participate in its eastern trade were viewed as personal grants of the king. Privileges granted by João II were either renewed by Manuel I upon his accession in 1495, or expired. The same applied to privileges granted by Manuel with the accession of João III in 1521 (do Amaral and Valentina 1965).

Thus, on the Continent the king was limited in his ability to commit credibly to his charters by his inability to commit credibly not to die during the term of the granted privilege. The formal legal continuation of commitment across rulers was an important precondition for the possibility to convey 'credible commitment' in England. Indeed, the successor to the throne could reconfirm and renew the charter, and some of them did so, but he had no formal commitment to do so. His reputational damage could not be prohibitive, as he did not breach his own commitment. Furthermore, the identity of the successor and his future policy could not be predicted *ex ante*, at the time of granting and pricing the charter. What can explain the Continental difference? Kantorowicz provides a compelling explanation for England's peculiarity.

It was in connection with the case of the Duchy of Lancaster, argued in court in 1561, that the Tudor judges produced their most striking formulation concerning the king's 'two Bodies'. Since those formulations eventually passed into juristic textbooks and dictionaries such as those of Crompton, Kitchin, Cowell, and perhaps also of other authors around 1600; and since they were quoted by authorities such as Coke, Bacon, and later also countless others . . . The originality of the Tudor lawyers should be sought chiefly in the fact that they replaced the commonly used notion of Dignitas by the notion of 'Body politic', and thereby were led to certain elaborations and conclusions which the civilians and canonists had not deemed it necessary to indulge in. (Kantorowicz 1957, 405–6)

The different path of constitutional jurisprudence taken by Tudor lawyers and judges allowed the English crown to grant charters and privileges through its eternal corporate body, rather than through the earthly body of the living monarch. These charters could include the grant of monopoly for a long term or even eternally, as was the case with the grant of James I to the East India Company in 1609.

While France, Portugal, and Spain were at a constitutional and institutional disadvantage compared to England when wishing to convey 'credible commitment', the Dutch Republic encountered a somewhat different disadvantage. It was not an absolute monarchy in which kings had the prerogative to grant and revoke charters at will. Merchant families played a dominant role in Dutch municipal, provincial, and federal politics (Adams 2005). In England mercantile interest groups challenged the crown when the latter wished to revoke commitments. In the Dutch Republic the mercantile interest groups were on the side that conveyed commitments: the state. There were no balancing powers. The example of the charter of the Dutch East India Company is instructive. The Company was chartered on 20 March 1602 by the States-General, the federal assembly of the Dutch Republic. It was established for twenty-one years. The state granted the Company a trade monopoly over the entire area between the Cape of Good Hope and the Straits of Magellan

(Gepken-Jager 2005, 29, 41). The first accounting was set to take place after ten years. Investors were allowed to withdraw their capital and undistributed profits from the company at that stage, but not before. The Company's structure reflected its formation through the merger of six predecessor companies. It had six city-based chambers in charge of raising capital and fitting ships.

Each chamber had two classes of shareholders, active and passive: *bewindhebbers* and *participanten*. The former had the status of governors, and took an active role in managing the chamber. The latter had no voting rights and did not take part in decision-making. The demand of the passive investors to participate in management and receive information about the state of trade and the accounts was avoided throughout the first joint stock. In 1612 the state assisted the active shareholders in delaying, and eventually refusing, the demand of passive investors that they distribute the original capital investment and accrued profits to those wishing to withdraw. That is, the active shareholders used their positions as both merchants and city magistrates to exercise political influence on the provincial and federal governments, and unilaterally to lock in the external investors by way of the charter. They could, and did, lock in the passive investors again, after the end of the ten-year period, by using their political clout to amend the terms of the original charter and extend the duration of the joint stock (Harris 2009).

Thus, the commonality between the charter-granting state and the vested interest of the merchants made the state's commitment to support the Dutch East India Company a 'credible commitment' vis-à-vis the outer world, but the commitment to the passive investors to respect the terms of the 1602 charter and allow withdrawal of the investment in 1612 was not credible. Interest group devices could not function because the passive investors lacked organisation and political power. Reputation did not function because the active shareholders, the big merchants, viewed the game as an endgame. They believed that by the end of the twenty-one-year period, when eastern trade was well established, the Company would be sufficiently stable and profitable to regain its reputation, or to manage without the passive investors. Although the Dutch had some similarities to the English in constitutional and institutional respects, they differed from them in others, such as the form of the interest group and the function of reputation.

The differences identified and discussed above amount to an anecdotal comparison, not a comprehensive exploration of the differences between England and the Continent. A future systematic comparison is definitely due, but at least a preliminary agenda is set here for the issues that require explanation.

Conclusion

The evolution of 'credible commitment' devices in England in the period 1558 to 1640 is impressive. The crown, even if not formally, ceased to have an exclusive and voluntary prerogative to grant charters. Parliament and the judiciary became important institutions in the charter-granting business. New constitutional ideas constrained the crown's prerogative. These ideas were shrewdly mixed with old narratives and memories, and became entrenched. The crown had to take into account the vested interests both of the charter grantees and of their competitors, because these interest groups had access to Parliament and the courts of law, and had the options of refraining from doing business or of seeking alternatives overseas. All of these amounted to a gradual shift from an absolute monarchy to a nascent rule-of-law monarchy.

The developments discussed in this chapter do not amount to the formation by the English crown of an absolute ability to convey a foolproof 'credible commitment' to respect its charters. Indeed, in some cases the crown's overall ability to grant charters actually weakened. With respect to some of the activities for which the crown wished to grant charters and monopolies, the outcome was an inability to grant or commit to them, because Parliament or the judiciary could override the crown's decision. With respect to other grants, uncertainty as to the validity of the charters grew. At the end of the period, when England deteriorated into full-blown civil war, the king obviously could not uphold his commitments, and thereafter the Commonwealth had to decide which to preserve. However, the test of commitment devices is not whether they hold through a revolution, but rather whether they hold during the normal life of a regime. Furthermore, the commitment to repay sovereign debts, created in the aftermath of the Glorious Revolution, was also not foolproof. Debasement of the coinage, inflation, and the South Sea debt conversion scheme were among the strategies employed by the state to bypass this commitment, despite the Bill of Rights and the establishment of the Bank of England. After all, even modern liberal democracies are not fully committed and fully credible. They often have to pay a reputational and political price for this, but so did Elizabeth, James, and Charles when revoking their charters.

The argument made here is relative, and not absolute, on several levels. It is not absolute because it presents neither a counterfactual nor a historical English state which offered fully credible commitments, or was altogether predatory, against which to compare the late Tudor and early Stuart state. There is no benchmark to which the level of chartering activity in the period 1558–1640 could be compared in order to infer from this level the credibility of the English state. The crown was relatively better able in this period to convey 'credible commitment' with respect to charters than to loans, because the use of charters had a longer history which, over the generations, facilitated the development of legal and institutional constraints. The crown was able to convey greater 'credible commitment' than in the past because of the general constitutional developments of the period, which strengthened the status of Parliament and the common law. The English crown could convey commitments that were more credible than those of other European countries because of its judicially developed constitutional doctrines and the balance of powers between merchants and the state. The 'credible commitment' framework provides an interesting explanation for the widespread use of charters and corporations in late Tudor and early Stuart England.

References

Adams, Julia 2005. *The Familial State: Ruling Families and Merchant Capitalism in Early Modern Europe*, Wilder House Series in Politics, History, and Culture. Ithaca: Cornell University Press.

Alborn, Timothy L. 1998. *Conceiving Companies: Joint-Stock Politics in Victorian England*. London: Routledge.

Armstrong, Elizabeth 2002. *Before Copyright: The French Book-Privilege System, 1498–1526*. Cambridge: Cambridge University Press.

Ashton, Robert 1967. 'The Parliamentary Agitation for Free Trade in the Opening Years of the Reign of James I', *Past and Present*, 38.

Ashton, Robert 1979. *The City and the Court: 1603–1643*. Cambridge: Cambridge University Press.

Baker, John H. 1990. *An Introduction to English Legal History*, 3rd edn. London: Butterworths.

Blackstone, William 1756. *Commentaries on the Laws of England*, 1st edn, 4 vols. Oxford: Clarendon Press, vol. I.

Bracha, Oren 2005. *Owning Ideas, A History of Anglo-American Intellectual Property*. S.J.D. Dissertation, Harvard Law School.

Brenner, Robert 2003. *Merchants and Revolution: Commercial Change, Political Conflict, and London's Overseas Traders, 1550–1653*. London: Verso.

Buchanan, James M. 1968. *The Demand and Supply of Public Goods*. Chicago: Rand McNally.

Carr, Cecil Thomas (ed.) 1913. *Select Charters of Trading Companies, A.D. 1530–1707*, Selden Society Publications, 28. London: Selden Society.

Carruthers, Bruce G. 1996. *City of Capital: Politics and Markets in the English Financial Revolution*. Princeton, NJ: Princeton University Press.

Cawston, George and Keane, A. H. 1968. *Early Chartered Companies: A.D. 1296–1858*. New York: Burt Franklin.

Chaudhuri, Kirti N. 1965. *The English East India Company: The Study of an Early Joint-Stock Company 1600–1640 (Rise of International Business)*, Reprints of Economic Classics Series. New York: A. M. Kelley.

Collins, James B. 2009. *The State in Early Modern France*, 2nd edn. Cambridge: Cambridge University Press.

Corre, Jacob I. 1996. 'The Argument, Decision, and Reports of Darcy v. Allen', *Emory Law Journal*, 45, 1261–1327.

Croft, Pauline (ed.) 1973a. 'Introduction: The First Spanish Company, 1530–85', in *The Spanish Company*, London Record Society 9, available at www.british-history.ac.uk/report.aspx?compid=63964. Date accessed: 14 June 2012.

Croft, Pauline (ed.) 1973b. 'Introduction: The Revival of the Company, 1604–6', in *The Spanish Company*, London Record Society 9, available at www.british-history.ac.uk/report.aspx?compid=63965. Date accessed: 14 June 2012.

Croft, Pauline 1975. 'Free Trade and the House of Commons, 1605–6', *Economic History Review*, 28, 17–27.

Dent, Chris 2009. 'Generally Inconvenient: The 1624 Statute of Monopolies as a Political Compromise', *Melbourne University Law Review*, 33, 415–53.

do Amaral, Cotta and Valentina, Maria 1965. *Privilégios de mercadores estrangeiros no reinaldo de D. João III*. Lisbon: Instituto de Alta Cultura, Centro de Edtudos Históricos.

Dunn, Richard S. 1963. 'The Downfall of the Bermuda Company: A Restoration Farce', *William and Mary Quarterly*, 20, 488–512.

Ekelund, Robert B., Jr. and Tollison, Robert D. 1981. *Mercantilism as a Rent-Seeking Society: Economic Regulation in Historical Perspective*. College Station: Texas A & M University Press.

Elton, Geoffrey R. 1989. *The Parliament of England 1559–1581*. Cambridge: Cambridge University Press.

George, Robert H. 1940. 'The Charters Granted to English Parliamentary Corporations in 1688', *English Historical Review*, 47–56.

Gepken-Jager, Ella 2005. 'The Dutch East India Company (VOC)', in Ella Gepken-Jager, Gerard Van Solinge, and Levinus Timmerman (eds.), *VOC 1602–2002: 400 Years of Company Law*, Law of Business and Finance, vol. VI. Deventer, Netherlands: Kluwer Legal Publishers.

Goldsworthy, Jeffrey 1999. *The Sovereignty of Parliament: History and Philosophy*. Oxford: Clarendon Press

Greif, Avner 1989. 'Reputation and Coalitions in Medieval Trade: Evidence on the Maghribi Traders', *Journal of Economic History*, 49, 857–82.

Greif, Avner 2006, *Institutions and the Path to the Modern Economy: Lessons from Medieval Trade*. Cambridge: Cambridge University Press.

Haffenden, Philip S. 1985a. 'The Crown and Colonial Charters, 1675–1688, Part I', *William and Mary Quarterly*, 15, 298–311.

Haffenden, Philip S. 1985b. 'The Crown and Colonial Charters, 1675–1688, Part II', *William and Mary Quarterly*, 15, 452–66.

Hale, Matthew 1976. 'The Prerogatives of the King', Selden Society Publications, vol. XCII. London: Selden Society.

Harris, Ron 2000. *Industrializing English Law: Entrepreneurship and Business Organization – 1720–1844*. Cambridge: Cambridge University Press.

Harris, Ron 2009. 'Law, Finance and the First Corporations', in James J. Heckman, Robert L. Nelson, and Lee Cabatingan (eds.), *Global Perspectives on the Rule of Law*. London: Routledge.

Hart, James S. 2003. *The Rule of Law, 1603–1660: Crowns, Courts and Judges.* Harlow, UK: Pearson/Longman.

Holdsworth, William S. 1922. 'English Corporation Law in the 16th and 17th Centuries', *Yale Law Journal*, 31, 382–407.

Jha, Saumitra 2010. 'Financial Innovations and Political Development: Evidence from Revolutionary England', Research Paper 2005, Stanford University Graduate School of Business, available at http://ssrn.com/abstract=934943. Date accessed: September 28, 2011.

Kantorowicz, Ernst H. 1957. *The King's Two Bodies.* Princeton, NJ: Princeton University Press.

Kenyon, J. P. 1986. *The Stuart Constitution*, 2nd edn. Cambridge: Cambridge University Press, pp. 24–32, 90–94.

Klerman, Daniel and Mahoney, Paul 2005. 'The Value of Judicial Independence: Evidence from Eighteenth Century England', *American Law and Economics Review*, 7, 1–17.

Krueger, Anne O. 1974. 'The Political Economy of the Rent-Seeking Society', *American Economic Review*, 64, 291–303.

Kyd, Stewart 1793–4. *A Treatise on the Law of Corporations*, 2 vols. London, vol. I.

Kyle, Chris R. 1998. 'But a New Button to an Old Coat: The Enactment of the Statute of Monopolies, 21 James I cap.3', *Journal of Legal History*, 19, 203–223.

Landes, William M. and Posner, Richard A. 1975. 'The Independent Judiciary in an Interest-Group Perspective', *Journal of Law and Economics*, 18, 875–901.

Levin, Jennifer 1969. *The Charter Controversy in the City of London, 1660–1688, and Its Consequences.* London: University of London.

Macey, Jonathan R. and Miller, Geoffrey P. 1991. 'Origin of the Blue Sky Laws', *Texas Law Review*, 70, 347–98.

Maitland, Frederic W. 1908. *The Constitutional History of England: A Course of Lectures Delivered*, 1st edn. Cambridge: Cambridge University Press.

Miller, Geoffrey P. 1989. 'Public Choice at the Dawn of the Special Interest State: The Story of Butter and Margarine', *California Law Review*, 77, 83–132.

Mossoff, Adam 2001. 'Rethinking the Development of Patents: An Intellectual History, 1550–1800', *Hastings Law Journal*, 52, 1255–67.

North, Douglas C. and Weingast, Barry R. 1989. 'Constitutions and Commitment: The Evolution of Institutional Governing Public Choice in Seventeenth-Century England', *Journal of Economic History*, 49, 803–32.

North, Douglass C., Wallis, John J., and Weingast, Barry R. 2009. *Violence and Social Orders: A Conceptual Framework for Interpreting Recorded Human History.* Cambridge: Cambridge University Press.

Olson, Mancur 1971. *The Logic of Collective Action: Public Goods and the Theory of Groups*, 2nd edn. Cambridge, MA: Harvard University Press.

Olson, Mancur 1982. *The Rise and Decline Of Nations: Economic Growth, Stagflation, and Social Rigidities*, New Haven, CT: Yale University Press.

Patterson, Catherine 2005. 'Quo warranto and Borough Corporations in Early Stuart England: Royal Prerogative and Local Privileges in the Central Courts', *English Historical Review*, 120, 879–906.

Ponko, Vincent, Jr. 1968. 'The Privy Council and the Spirit of Elizabethan Economic Management, 1558–1603', *Transactions of the American Philosophical Society*, 58, 1–63.

Pound, Roscoe 1936. 'Visitatorial Jurisdiction over Corporations in Equity', *Harvard Law Review*, 49, 369–95.

Rabb, Theodore K. 1964. 'Sir Edwin Sandys and the Parliament of 1604', *American Historical Review*, 69, 646–70.

Rabb, Theodore K. 1967. *Enterprise and Empire: Merchant and Gentry Investment in the Expansion of England, 1575–1630*. Cambridge, MA: Harvard University Press.

Scott, William R. 1951. *The Constitution and Finance of English, Scottish and Irish Joint-Stock Companies to 1720*. New York: Peter Smith, vol. II.

Shaw, John 1887. *Charters Relating to the East India Company from 1600 to 1761*. Madras: Madras Government Press.

Smith, Airlie 1946–7. 'Ultra vires: A Problem of Sovereignty', *Res Judicata*, 3, 28–33.

Stigler, George J. 1971. 'The Theory of Economic Regulation', *Bell Journal of Economics and Management Science*, 2, 3–21.

Sutherland, Donald W. 1963. *Quo warranto Proceedings during the Reign of Edward I, 1278–1294*. Oxford: Clarendon Press.

Tomlins, Christopher 2001. 'The Legal Cartography of Colonization, the Legal Polyphony of Settlement, English Intrusions on the American Mainland in the Seventeenth Century', *Law and Social Inquiry*, 26, 315–72.

Unwin, George 1927. 'The Merchant Adventurers' Company in the Reign of Elizabeth', *Economic History Review*, 1, 35–64.

Weingast, Barry R. 1997. 'The Political Foundations of Limited Government: Parliament and Sovereign Debt in 17th- and 18th-Century England', in John N. Drobak and John V. C. Nye (eds.), *The Frontiers of the New Institutional Economics*. San Diego: Academic Press.

3 Contingent commitment: The development of English marine insurance in the context of New Institutional Economics, 1577–1720

Adrian Leonard[1]

North and Weingast's 'credible commitment' thesis is among the leading applications of the theoretical branch of historical analysis known as New Institutional Economics (NIE). It has proved durable and, despite challenges, enduring. Through the conception of an institutional development – the supremacy of Parliament over the sovereign following the Glorious Revolution – the authors argue that England was able to raise unprecedented levels of state finance from a lending constituency increasingly less worried about arbitrary sovereign default. By implication, this classical NIE development led to British international success, Empire, the Industrial Revolution, and arguably to the modern world.

This chapter does not set out to question the institutional theory behind North and Weingast's discussion of Parliament's elevation following 1688, nor does it attempt to challenge the acknowledged whiggishness of the 'path dependency' which proponents of NIE so often claim (North believes it was 'sequentially more complex organization that eventually led to the rise of the western world') (North 1991, 105). Instead, it shows that the grand theory presented in 'Constitutions and Commitment' does not always reflect the actual conduct of affairs between the monarch, Parliament, and the financial community, both before and after the Glorious Revolution. A series of related initiatives by these actors illustrates the crown's progressively diminishing commitment to the protection both of merchants' private wealth and of the trade which underpinned crown customs revenues, despite the importance of these income streams to the servicing of government borrowing during the rise of the fiscal–military state. These initiatives, examined in this chapter, were taken between the last quarter of the sixteenth century and the first of the eighteenth,

[1] I am grateful to my coeditors, D'Maris Coffman and Larry Neal, and to Martin Daunton for their invaluable feedback on earlier drafts of this chapter, and to David Ibbetson for his insights.

a period bisected by the establishment of the institutions of 'credible commitment'. They relate to an institution constituting one of the 'evolving organisations that accompanied economic expansion' which North and Weingast acknowledge as important, but admit in their seminal article to 'slight' (North and Weingast 1989, 805). Through the framework of NIE theory, it shows how London's marine insurance market developed in support of the advance of trade, despite negative state intervention or inaction post-1688. Historical contingencies matter for the way that economic institutions evolve, and in the case of marine insurance in London, a strong monarch (Elizabeth I) turned out to be more supportive than a weak one (George I).

Marine insurance is plainly an important example of the institutions which NIE theorists argue 'had to be created to mitigate the many kinds of contractual problems associated with long-distance trade' (Greif, Milgrom, and Weingast 1994, 746). Early modern ocean-going commerce was an essentially precarious, unpredictable system. Huge distances greatly distorted the fundamentals of supply, demand, and pricing by depriving merchants of current information. Oceans and privateers sometimes denied traders their goods; princes and pirates sometimes seized their liberty. The loss of a season's invested capital could spell ruin for an individual merchant. Such risks and uncertainties produced an economic rationality, and hence a series of economic behaviours, broadly different from those of modern economics (Musgrave 1981, 10–19). Insurance in London was adapted and widely adopted to mitigate some of these uncertainties.

Greif argues that 'the nature of the institutions that govern . . . exchange relations affect trade's magnitude and direction', in combination with endowments, technology, and preferences (Greif 1992, 128). According to North, economic institutions are crucial to the reduction of transaction costs, which themselves are 'a critical determinant of economic performance'. Institutions 'define the choice set and therefore determine transaction and production costs and hence the profitability and feasibility of engaging in economic activity'. Among the transaction costs impacted by institutions are enforcement costs, which in international trade include the costs related to 'protection of goods and services *en route*' and of 'contract . . . enforcement in alien parts of the world'. Because 'there was continuous interplay between the state's fiscal needs and its credibility in its relationships with merchants', political institutions also play a key role (North 1991, 97–107).

Since the publication of 'Constitutions and Commitment' in 1989, North and other NIE theorists have often discussed 'credible commitment', which can 'evolve to enable agreements to be reached when the payoffs are in the future and on completely different issues':

Self-enforcement is important in such exchange, and in repeat dealings a reputation is a valuable asset. But as an economic exchange, the costs of measurement and enforcement, discovering who is cheating whom, when free-riding will occur, and who should bear the cost of punishing defectors make self-enforcement ineffective in many situations. Hence political institutions constitute *ex ante* agreements about cooperation among politicians. They reduce uncertainty by creating a stable structure of exchange. (North 1990, 50)

Further, 'the shackling of arbitrary behavior of rulers and the development of impersonal rules that successfully bound both the state and voluntary organisations were a key part of this whole process' (North 1991, 107). In earlier work, North identified productivity growth in ocean shipping of between half and one per cent per annum during the period 1600 to 1750 as one of the key contributions to seventeenth-century English economic growth, which occurred despite a generally rising population. He attributed at least a portion of this success to premium-based marine insurance (North and Thomas 1973, 137). However, the institutional growth, development, and operation of this important market have been analysed only sporadically within the framework of NIE, without definitive conclusions (two such works are discussed below).

Marine insurers, disputes, and NIE

The London marine insurance market, concentrated first in Lombard Street, later in the Royal Exchange, and still later in Lloyd's Coffee-house, has been active since at least the middle of the fifteenth century. Following long-established practice developed by Italian merchants a century or more before, multiple men of wealth would each underwrite relatively small proportions of the total value of an individual risk insured under a single marine insurance policy. For example, in 1555 each of twenty-two men and partnerships assumed a share of an insurance policy granted to cover the trade goods of Antwerp merchant Anthony de Salizar, 'from any porte of the Iles of Ind[ia] of Calict unto Lixborne [Lisbon] in the ship called Sancta Cruz' (TNA HCA/24/29 fol. 45). Within the market, individual underwriters acted as 'leaders'. These specialists (for example, in Levant or East Indies sailings) would set the prices, terms, and conditions to be granted under relevant policies, often in cooperation with brokers, who were already well established (Stow 1720, 242–3). Other underwriters would 'follow' to provide the contingent capital necessary to support the total values insured.

The community of underwriters was small. Over forty-seven months from 1664, Charles Marescoe purchased 108 policies underwritten by just thirty-one discrete individuals, ten of whom accounted for almost 84% of the total value of the policies (Roseveare 1987, 582–8). The total number of underwriters active in the market appears to have grown over time, as trade expanded. Between 1709 and 1717, Ralph Radcliffe purchased policies underwritten by eighty-six different underwriters, although in 1716, from whence eighteen Radcliffe policies survive, only forty-four individuals underwrote a share of his risks (HALSC DE/R/B293/1–47). Selection of favourites may have limited the number of underwriters involved in these examples, and higher wartime rates encouraged dabblers to assume more risk. No comprehensive enumeration exists for the sixteenth and seventeenth century, but in 1720 Attorney General Nicholas Lechmere reported that 'there are about one hundred Persons of very Good Repute, who Insure Ships and merchandizes at Sea' (The Commons 1720, 44).

This extremely cooperative market was also highly integrated horizontally. Many underwriters, perhaps most, were also active merchants. For example, alongside John Barnard,[2] who was primarily a wine merchant, Marescoe and Jacob David, merchants trading between London, Baltic, French, and Spanish ports after the Restoration, were both buyers of insurance and underwriters of other people's cargoes and vessels (Roseveare 1987, 582–8). This pattern continued: in 1818 the India merchant Stewart Majoribanks underwrote £50 on Sarah Wilde's share of the vessel *Frances* returning from Quebec, and in 1824 he purchased numerous policies at Lloyd's for goods he was shipping to China.[3] Such horizontal integration appears to have been significant, so the small community of regular traders must have been aware of the profits to be made in the business, as well as the potential for large losses.

Price differentiation was sometimes made by buyers (or their brokers) between the credit quality (expressed as reputation) of the individuals underwriting risk (intermediaries preferred to use 'good men', a phrase which occurs often in merchant correspondence). Some paid more for the perceived better security of the chartered companies (The Commons 1824, 59), and evidence from underwriters' risk books suggests that some buyers paid fractionally more (e.g., BL Add. MSS 34672–83). It was common for brokers outside England to accept risk from foreign

---

[2] Barnard later became an MP for London, and was heavily involved in parliamentary legislation concerning the stockjobbing of sovereign debt.

[3] Sanderson, Brothers (insurance brokers), Insurance policy 27.11.1818, in the possession of the author; Clagett & Pratt: 'Risk Book 1824', *Lloyd's of London*.

merchants, and then reinsure those risks at a lower price in London, as Barnard's testimony to a parliamentary committee shows: 'Foreigners have allowed their correspondents here a *Premium* to Insure the Insurers, which . . . has been occasioned by Foreigners not knowing the Insurers here, and that they can afford to give it, by reason of the Lowness of the *Premiums*' (The Commons 1720, 44). To expand the risk pool, and thus diversify their risk portfolios, underwriters appear frequently to have insured merchants plying different trades. Marescoe, for example, frequently insured voyages to and from Virginia, Barbados, and India – destinations to which his Baltic trade did not extend (Roseveare 1987, 586). Awareness of the importance of ensuring a geographical spread of risk was the norm (The Commons 1824, 67).

The Early Modern London marine insurance market was thus unlike the U.S. health insurance market of the twentieth century, which Akerlof uses to illustrate his 'lemons principle'. In Akerlof's model both buyer and seller practise adverse selection: insurance buyers over the age of sixty-five purchase expensive insurance only if their health is poor, whereas insurers themselves tend to insure through employment plans, guaranteeing a minimum level of health (that sufficient for employment) among the population they cover (Akerlof 1970, 492–4). In contrast, marine insurers and their clientele operated in a smaller and therefore potentially better-informed market. Although it is clear that many merchants bought cover only when their vessels were to sail into the most seasonally inhospitable seas, or during wartime, this information was obviously known to underwriters, and prices were adjusted accordingly. Rates charged by the Lloyd's underwriter William Braund to insure cargos for America in 1759 and 1764 clearly illustrate wartime adjustments. In 1759, during the Atlantic naval conflicts of the Seven Years War, Braund charged ten discrete rates, including seven different rates in the month of March alone, for the voyage from London to a named American port (with no significant correlation between the specific port and the rate). The mean rate is 7.1%; the standard deviation 5.1%. In sharp contrast, Braund charged only three rates in peaceful 1764 (2.5%, 3%, and 4%), for a mean of 3.2%, and a standard deviation of 0.76%. From March 1764 his rate for the voyage did not vary from 2.5% (ECRO, D/DRu B7). Nor was information overload a problem. In the years 1715 to 1717, only ninety-five sailings from London departed for the Mediterranean (Davis 1962, 256). It cannot have been difficult for underwriters to keep track of these voyages and vessels, nor of their fortunes, nor of the merchants who had cargo aboard. Such information would limit opportunities for knowledge shortfalls to lead to adverse selection among regular traders. Thus, within the small community of regular marine insurance buyers and sellers in London, information was as complete as perhaps is possible. In the words of North, 'Under these conditions, it simply pays to live up to agreements' (North 1990, 33).

Information asymmetry is the focus of an argument by Kingston which employs NIE theory to argue that private insurers' superior information gave them a significant advantage over corporate rivals in the post-1720 environment (Kingston 2007). An information advantage may have existed, but Kingston acknowledges in a footnote that at least one of the companies had equal access to the same information networks as private underwriters. Brokers who worked with both the companies and the private insurers were another source of knowledge equalisation. Kingston does not acknowledge the existence of information asymmetries among Lloyd's underwriters, although they surely existed. Lloyd's, as a market of individuals, was fiercely competitive internally. Further, even if an information deficit did disadvantage the companies, other relevant factors were at least equally important, including the fundamental desirability of employing multiple underwriting bodies to spread large risks as widely as possible, and the companies' self-imposed limitations on the types of risks and maximum values they would underwrite. Of £148,100 insured on the Indiaman *Scaleby Castle* in 1799, one of the companies wrote only £10,000, the other nothing, despite the vessel owners' desire for even greater coverage than was achieved. Private underwriters did the rest (The Commons 1824, 21).

The companies' greatest disadvantage, however, was pricing. They regularly set rates higher than private underwriters for the same risks. The Royal Exchange Assurance charged twenty per cent more than every other underwriter involved in the *Scaleby Castle* policy (The Commons 1824, 21). Unlike at Lloyd's, both companies regularly charged more to insure vessels considered inferior (Eden 1806, 31), which implies not reduced access to information, but a greater willingness to employ that which they possessed. Such underwriting and pricing policies reflect primarily the companies' more limited appetite for marine risk, rather than negative exogenous disadvantages. According to Supple, 'the two chartered corporations approached the expanding demand for [marine] insurance with such caution as to retain only a very small proportion', approximately four per cent between them (Supple 1970, 53). A more comprehensive analysis of the competing institutional dynamics of Lloyd's and the companies can be found in Oliver Westall's article 'Invisible, visible, and direct hands' (Westall 1997).

The contractual mechanism of the insurance instrument is almost identical to policies familiar to modern commercial insurance buyers. It provides, in exchange for an advance fee (the premium), contingent capital to be delivered in case of the actual whole or partial loss of a vessel or cargo during transport. In effect, the insurers provide the insured merchant with sufficient capital to withstand the loss of his vessel or trade goods – but only if such a loss actually occurs. 'Parliament represented wealth holders', North and Weingast state (1989, 804). However, some parliamentary initiatives after 1688 weakened or damaged commitment mechanisms designed to support the wealth-holders who comprised the insurance trading community. Further, some of its post-Revolution actions served to weaken the market as a whole, endangering state revenues. In contrast, much earlier acts of the Privy Council, the executive committee of less-restrained monarchs which was responsible for royal proclamations related to economic regulation, sometimes moved to introduce or strengthen commitment mechanisms through directives related to the governance of the London marine insurance market. In all cases, the leading motive for action was to support ocean-going trade by cooperatively managing exogenous challenges to the system, which since at least the late thirteenth century, when Edward I imposed the *maltote*, a wool export tax, had been an important source of royal finance (Mann 1986, 427). The income stream had always been (in principle, if not practice) dedicated to the support of the navy, the primary instrument of English and British trade and imperial expansion since the seventeenth century.

Buyers and underwriters in London conducted their business under the tenets of the Law Merchant. Milgrom, North, and Weingast describe the institution comprising the Law Merchant, along with the systems of judges used to enforce it, as having the fivefold effect of successfully encouraging merchants to behave honestly, of imposing sanctions on violators, of securing information about the behaviour of others, and of compelling merchants both to provide evidence against cheaters and to pay any judgements assessed against them (Milgrom, North, and Weingast 1990, 1). Recourse to the Law Merchant and to merchant judges drawn from the community and familiar with the code was very often agreed in the language of insurance policies. A contemporary English translation of the earliest policy in the archives of the High Court of the Admiralty – written originally in Italian, although issued in London – states that 'it is to be understood this preasente writinge hathe as muche forse as the beste made or dicted byll of surance w'ch is used to be made in this lombarde streete of London' (TNA HCA 24/27/199). A document with the character of a modern 'expert opinion', intended to inform Admiralty adjudicators, accompanies another policy under suit. It likens the practice of marine insurance – and thus the Law Merchant which governs enforcement – to that of Antwerp, stating 'That the use and custome of makynge bylls of assurance in the place comonly called Lumbard Strete of London and likewyse in the Burse of Antwerpe, is and tyme oute of mynde hathe byn emonge m'chants usinge and frequentinge the sayde severall places and assuraunces' (TNA HCA 24/35 fol. 46).

Clauses mentioning Lombard Street, and later the Royal Exchange, appear in almost all of the policies preserved in sixteenth-century Admiralty records, and in almost all formal British and even American policies issued until the eighteenth century and beyond. A printed policy prepared in the 'Insurance Office kept in King Street, Boston [Massachusetts], by Samuel Philips Savage' in 1762 declares the policy to have '*as much Force and Effect as the Surest Writing or Policy of Assurance heretofore made in* Lombard-Street, *or in the* Royal Exchange, *or elsewhere in* LONDON' (LMA CLC/B/063/MS32992/002). The legal historian Holdsworth suggests that such clauses 'probably had the result of producing a uniformity in the legal effect' of all of the policies in which they appear. The clause provided all parties to an insurance contract, and any courts which may be called to adjudicate disputes between those parties, with a known – if uncodified – body of customary practice to govern proceedings (Holdsworth 1917, 98). More recently, Jones argues that, with the clause, 'the merchant attempted to bolster up his position by incorporating [into his policy] the entire body of the Law Merchant, in so far as it was worked out in relation to marine insurance' (Jones 1970, 55).

As was the Italian practice, the usual and initial method of dispute resolution among merchant-insurers in London was arbitration within the merchant community. This norm is shown by the policy of 1555 cited above, which states that the underwriters, 'yf godes will be that the said shippe shall not well procede we promys to remyt yt to honist m'chaunts and not to go to the lawe' (TNA HCA 24/29 f. 45). Although the arbitration clause was not present in all policies, it was common. Another policy, underwritten March 1564, requires the parties in case of dispute 'to stande to the judgement of m'chaunts indifferently chosen w^thoute goying to any other lawe' (TNA HCA 24/35 f. 283). A piece of Elizabethan legislation (Anno 43 Elizabethæ, cap. 12, *An Act Conc'ninge matters of Assurances, amongste Merchantes*, on which much more below) attests to a long history of arbitration within the insurance community. It declares that 'Assurers have used to stande so justlie and p'ciselie upon their credites, as feweor no Controv'sies have risen thereupon, and if any have growen, the same have from tyme to tyme bene ended and ordered by certaine grave and discreete Merchantes, appointed by the Lorde Mayor of the Citie of London, as Men by reason of their experience fittest to understande, and speedilie to decide those Causes'. The policy underwritten in Boston and cited above states '*in Case of any Dispute arising hereupon, the Matter in Controversy shall be submitted to, and decided by Referees, chosen by each Party, agreeable to Rules and Customs in* LONDON' (LMA CLC/B/063/MS32992/002).

Milgrom, North, and Weingast show that extrajudicial systems of dispute resolution operating under the Law Merchant can be effective mechanisms for ensuring the honest behaviour of trading partners, even in the absence of a centralised authority with wide jurisdiction to enforce contracts. They accomplish this by enhancing the reputation system of enforcement. Further, they do so in a cost-efficient way (Milgrom, North, and Weingast 1990, 1–23). 'The commercial sector is completely capable of establishing and enforcing its own laws', Benson argues, stating that commercial law was made largely by the merchant community, despite governments' efforts to assume the role of commercial law-making. Merchant institutions became ever more effective in a Smithian 'spontaneous order' of evolution, such that commerce and commercial law have developed 'coterminously without the aid of, and often despite the interference of, the coercive power of nation states', because the evolving mechanism of merchant law developed before and alongside it (Benson 1989, 647).

Benson's view did not always play out in reality, however, and thus marine insurance contracts did sometimes reach formal courts. Intentional fraud certainly occurred, but such cases were the exception, despite their celebrity. Extant contemporaneous records of individual marine insurance relationships which did not involve a dispute are rare, but a great deal of evidence survives for those cases which were argued in the public courts. Barbour's claim of 1928, that the insurance system was 'open to considerable frauds and abuses' (Barbour 1929, 572), is often misinterpreted as meaning that criminality was the norm. Clearly, the utility of the insurance market would be diminished to the point of uselessness if no one, a few, or even only a majority of the players chose to abide by the rules. Common sense says that under such circumstances the institution would not have lasted very long.

That said, the sixteenth-century policies cited have survived only because they were subject to suit in the High Court of the Admiralty. In addition, the Privy Council fairly regularly entertained insurance disputes, hearing at least sixteen cases between 1573 and 1587 (Dasent 1894; Dasent 1895; Dasent 1901). Greif argues that it was institutions supporting bilateral and multilateral enforcement mechanisms that allowed rulers to commit to providing an environment in which foreign merchants could trade securely in the knowledge that the ruler would uphold their property rights (Greif 1992, 129). Such rights can logically be extended to include a right to enforcement of third-party contracts, including contracts of marine insurance made with English underwriters. Much of the discussion below centres on efforts to establish such multilateral mechanisms in England in the sixteenth and seventeenth centuries, in order to allow the trade of foreign merchants in London, who were present in significant numbers, to proceed and expand in a period when adherence to the established Law Merchant was no longer nearly universal, and when the expansion of trade left recourse to merchant arbitration insufficient in the eyes of some participants.

Nine of the cases which drew the attention of the Privy Council between 1573 and 1587 involved disputes brought by foreign merchants, often through the intervention of an ambassador. By longstanding convention, alien traders fell under the special protection of local monarchs. In England their disputes were heard before the Chancellor, before the Privy Council, or by a special commission (Prichard and Yale 1993, lxxx). The third approach was typically favoured by the Privy Council when it was faced with insurance matters. It usually first referred matters to arbitration by London's Lord Mayor and aldermen, or to a panel appointed by the Lord Mayor, and heard cases in Council only when arbitration failed. Even then, Councillors typically sought, as a guide to settlement, direction from local merchants as to the prevailing custom under the Law Merchant. In July 1574 their Lordships heard a complaint from the Spanish merchant Peter Mertines against his London insurers, 'certein merchaunts', about an insurance policy issued for a ship sailing from Southampton to Bilbao. In the first instance the Privy Council instructed the Judge of the Admiralty 'to committe the cause to certein indifferent persons to whom it might be heard and determined acording to right and equitie' (Dasent 1895, 262). The case dragging on, in February the Council called the parties before them, and appointed arbitrators from amongst the merchant elite. Should the arbitration fail, they were to abide by the binding judgment of Alderman Hayward, a former Lord Mayor.

The records of insurance transactions which survive in court records and elsewhere from this early period in the development of London's insurance market reveal not only aspects of that development, but also the nature of London's trade at the time and the preponderance of exchange within Europe. Records of only three of the seventeen cases heard by the Privy Council reveal the voyage; all relate to trade with France or Spain. All of the policies of the merchant-stranger Bartholomew Corsini, underwritten in London in the 1580s, insure European trade. Seven of the eight voyages insured under policies issued to 1630 and retained in the records of the High Court of the Admiralty also insure European ventures; one covers a voyage to New Spain and home. Recently, Ebert has applied NIE theory to marine insurance to argue that Atlantic trade drove institutional change in the marine insurance sector 'to 1630' which involved increased state involvement in enforcement (Ebert 2011). However, evidence such as these early London policies does not support his assertion. Ebert employs Greif's distinction between collectivists and individualists to frame his argument, as this chapter does below. However, neither NIE theory nor the balance of extant documents – from London and elsewhere – supports his thesis about the driving role of the Atlantic. Ebert shows that changes in insurance institutions occurred concurrently with the rise of Atlantic trade, but provides no evidence that they were linked. In fact, the great majority of the extant evidence of the drivers of the institutional changes he outlines relates to European, Mediterranean, or East Indies trade. The case discussed above brought in London in 1555 by a Portuguese merchant is a typical example. The absolute growth of trade in the period Ebert examines was the key driver of new imbalances which demanded institutional change in marine insurance markets, not Atlantic trade exclusively, or even particularly.

NIE proffers both simple and advanced explanations for the increase in formally adjudicated marine insurance disputes, and for the subsequent development of new, state-backed enforcement institutions to resolve them. North argues that 'institutional evolution entailed not only voluntary organisations that expanded trade and made exchange more productive, but also the development of the state to take over protection and enforcement of property rights as impersonal exchange made contract enforcement increasingly costly for voluntary organisations which lacked effective coercive power' (North 1991, 109). Greif employs a distinction, borrowed from the social sciences, between societies which can be classified as 'collectivist' and those which are 'individualist'. He compares eleventh-century Maghribi traders and Genoese merchants of the twelfth and thirteenth centuries to illustrate the institutional impact of this division. His example has been roundly criticised by Edwards and Ogilvie, who 'find no evidence that the Maghribi traders had more "collectivist" cultural beliefs than their European counterparts' (Edwards and Ogilvie 2012, 423), and robustly defended (Greif 2012, 444 ff.). Goldberg has also identified shortcomings (2012, 149–50). Nonetheless the classification – with modifications – provides a useful analytical framework for the development of marine insurance institutions. In brief summary, in socially segregated 'collectivist' communities, individuals' economic interactions take place mainly with other members of their religious, ethnic, or familial groups. The enforcement of commercial agreements occurs through informal institutions. In contrast, in 'individualist' societies with an integrated social structure, trade is carried out by and among people from different groups. Enforcement is achieved through institutions such as courts, usually with the backing and authority of the monarch or the state (Greif 1992).

Greif focuses his exploration of the collectivist/individualist division on principal–agent relationships in international trade. However, the distinction is telling in the context of London's growing insurance market of the sixteenth to eighteenth centuries. Informal arbitration under the Law Merchant provided a satisfactory dispute resolution system while the insuring merchant community was 'collectivist' in character, comprising a relatively small number of individuals who acted as both underwriters and insureds, who did so repeatedly (thus making reputation a critical asset to protect, as NIE dictates), and who used the marine insurance system to obtain the contingent capital necessary to operate with a margin of comfort sufficient to ensure that an unforeseen loss of a vessel or cargo would not mean ruin. Notably, however, it was a shared culture of entrepreneurialism, rather than creed, blood, or kinship, which tied the community together. This is a broader definition of collectivists than Greif employs, but one which its inventors in the social sciences would be comfortable with (see, for example, Triandis, McCusker, and Hui 1990). These collectivist institutions proved inadequate when outsiders – 'individualists' who either did not wish to play by the rules of the game, or worse, who wished to commit outright fraud against the merchant-insurers – began regularly, as trade expanded, to take up London's insurance offer.

The model holds when extended to further planks supporting Greif's argument (Greif 1997, 71–6). Collectivists are likely to be horizontally integrated; the mere description 'merchant-insurer' indicates this to have been the case. Collectivists can be forced to forego 'improper behaviour' through collective economic punishment; the London insurance community would exclude those who did not follow the rules, such as on 12 January 1779, when the subscribers to 'New Lloyd's Coffee House' agreed a standard form of contract, and 'That We will not Underwrite to any Person or Persons who may hereafter tender any Policy *otherwise Printed*' (GHL CLC/B/148/A/001). Information sharing is key to enforcement in collectivist societies, which reduce transaction costs by making investments in the distribution of information within their trading communities. Lloyd's once again fits this pattern, for example through the publication of *Lloyd's List*, a news sheet with current shipping intelligence, at least as early as July 1692 (McCusker 1995, 53). The *List* was widely circulated, and provided a collective monitoring service for passive investors in insurance and trade, as well as for underwriters (including Lloyd's competitors; free riding was not seen as a problem, because extending the customer base to expand the risk pool was more important). Later *Lloyd's Register* provided subscribers with current details of vessels active in the world's merchant fleet. In addition, the market established a shared network of correspondents in ports around the world to deliver timely news of shipping movements and other events (Wright and Fayle 1928, 353).

Greif further argues that 'the Genoese [in their transit to an individualist society] ceased to use the ancient custom of entering contracts by a handshake, and instead developed an extensive legal system for the registration and enforcement of contracts'. While Italian insurance policies were typically notarised, in order to give them legal force in the Roman law tradition, in London no such notarial seal was applied, and thus 'there could be no remedy at law' (Jones 1970, 55) (although, as shown, legal solutions were sometimes adopted). Finally, Greif states that contract enforcement in individualist societies is achieved mainly through specialised organisations such as courts, whereas collectivists prefer informal means of enforcement. As a result, the 'customary' law that had governed the behaviour of Genoese merchants and insurers – the Law Merchant – ultimately was codified, and permanent courts were established. As shall be shown below, the entrance of individualists into the London marine insurance market required that just such steps be taken.

Acts of the Privy Council

As London became an increasingly important centre of international trade, the number of merchants, both local and foreign, purchasing insurance in the city multiplied. A concurrent increase in insurance-related disputes was widely recognised. The Act of 1601 mentioned above makes specific reference to this phenomenon, stating 'of late yeeres that divers p'sons have withdrawen themselves from that arbitrarie course, and have soughte to drawe the parties assured to seeke their money of everie severall Assurer, by Suites comenced in her Majesties Courtes, to their greate charges and delayes'. The occasional failure of arbitration was weighing even on the Privy Council, which in February 1573/4 wrote to the Lord Mayor to complain that an unresolved dispute between the merchant William Soninge and several of his insurers 'tendeth to the derogacion of so auncient a custome as assuraunce amongst merchauntes is, and breadeth grete discredit to the parties' (Dasent 1895, 196). Over the next several years the Council attempted to resolve the problem of insurance disputes with a three-pronged programme. It was to formalise, through the existing City governing institutions at the Guild Hall, the resolution of marine insurance disputes under the Law Merchant; to codify that law to create a more concrete set of regulations than the nebulous 'custom of Lombard Street'; and finally to establish an information system which could help to counteract the involvement of newcomers who were unwilling to play by the rules (Ibbetson 2008, 295). Through this programme (almost certainly perceived by its formulators as three separate actions, rather than a cohesive plan), the Privy Council was to create a new institution of enforcement which was intended to answer the arrival of individualists into a collectivist market.

In February 1575/6 the Privy Council responded decisively to a 'suit of the principal merchants of England' which complained that 'for want of good registration of assurances . . . merchants have been greatly abused by evil-disposed persons who have assured one thing in sundry places, so that the ancient custom of merchants in Lombarde Streete, and now the Royal Exchange, has fallen out of esteem, though hitherto regarded as the foundation of all assurances made throughout Christendom' (TNA C 66/1131, 17). Unscrupulous merchants and sea captains were attempting to maximise their returns from short-term plays in the insurance market by overinsuring, then making multiple fraudulent claims. Richard Candeler, a mercer and agent of Thomas Gresham, was granted monopoly rights over the 'making and registering of all assurances, policies and the like upon ships and goods going out of or into the realm made in the Royal Exchange or any other place in the city of London'. His patent stated that 'assurances not made with Candeler . . . shall be void'. However, his action did not constitute plain rent-seeking, nor was his post a simple sinecure. He was involved in a protracted negotiation with Walshingham over the level of fees he could charge (Raynes 1964, 42–50), and he performed the responsibilities of his office himself. His own signature appears on nine extant insurance policies issued in 1580–83 (LMA CLC/B/062/MS22281, CLC/B/062/MS22282).

Thus was erected the 'Office of Assurance'. It was located in a ground-floor shop on the Royal Exchange, and was the only one accessible from the interior quadrangle of the building (Glaisyer 2006, 29). The new institution met with opposition from London's sizeable community of established insurance brokers and notaries, who complained they were 'like utterly to be undone . . . upon a Patent obtained by Candler, that none but he, or his Deputies, should make and register Policies and Instruments of Assurance. Which Time out of mind were done by Notaries Public, and by the sworn Brokers of the City' (Stow 1720, 242–3). Nor were merchants unanimously supportive of the Office, which had no power to compel merchants to use its services. In July 1576 the Privy Council wrote to the Lord Mayor complaining that 'certain evill disposed persons do refuse to bring their assuraunces to be registred' (Dasent 1894, 177). Individual motivations for nonregistration obviously cannot be determined, but the desire for commercial secrecy in the time-sensitive arena of Early Modern trade (Price 1991, 296) is a more likely explanation for widespread avoidance than intent to defraud. Registration threw policies open to public scrutiny, which could reveal to competitors sensitive details about the timing and nature of merchants' voyages and cargoes.

It is likewise impossible to know what share of marine insurance policies underwritten in London were prepared and/or registered by Candeler and his successors in the Office, although it follows that policies which were not registered were more likely to be made among the collectivist group of merchant-insurers, comprising men known to underwriters or to an established broker. However, regardless of its rate of penetration, it is clear that the institution was a feature of the London insurance market for over a century, surviving Civil War, Commonwealth, and Restoration, if not Revolution. In 1640 the Court of Committees of the East India Company noted the payment of £25 to 'Mr Pryor, of the Assurance-house' for writing up a policy covering pepper re-exported to Italy (Foster 1909, 40); George Prior and William Couper had taken over the operation of the office from Candeler in 1610, after it was subcontracted to them by the new patent holders for the substantial annual fee of £400 (Raynes 1964, 56). Charles Molloy in 1676 distinguished between '*Publick*' and '*Private*' insurances, the former 'made and entered in a certain Office of Court... on the *Royal Exchange*' (Molloy 1744, 282). Over the next twenty-three years the patent appears to have lapsed, although the institution of optional policy registration had become entrenched practice, and the Office of Assurances privatised. The 1699 edition of Edward Hatton's *Comes Commercii* explains that 'Insurances for Merchants are either made in publick or in private. Publick insurances are such as are Registered in a Publick Office, as Mr. *Tucker's*, Mr. *Bevis's*, &c. on the East Side of the *Royal Exchange, London*' (Hatton 1699, 289). Although the solution was not universal, the Privy Council, through a new institutional source of information sharing, had begun to overcome one of the problems caused by the entry of individualists into the expanding London insurance market.

The second institutional development ordered by the Privy Council was the codification of insurance regulation, as it was understood according to the Law Merchant. In doing so, the Councillors set out not to change the customary rules of the game, but instead to give them regulatory teeth by definitively recording the ancient practices of Lombard Street. In 1574 their Lordships wrote to the Lord Mayor, requesting that he 'by conference with suche as be moste skilfull in [insurance] causes, should certifie my Lordes what lawes, orders, and customes are used in those matters of assuraunce, to thend they may be put in use acordinglie'. Clearly the third-party enforcement required in individualist societies cannot be conducted adequately without consistent rules of the game. By June 1575 the Orders must not have been transmitted, because the Privy Council again wrote to the Lord Mayor 'to certifie their Lordships what had been done for the setting downe of some orders for matters of assuraunce which their Lordships required to be donne long agoe'. Following the election of a new Lord Mayor, a further letter was despatched, and a sharper, fourth missive in July 1576 (Dasent 1894, 163; Dasent 1895, 321, 397).

The *Booke of Orders of Assurances within the Royall Exchange, c.* 1577, set out standard marine insurance practice under the Law Merchant (BL ADD MS 48023 fols. 246–73). The code was never adopted by statute – that would take another 330 years, until the 1906 passage of *An Act to codify the Law relating to Marine Insurance* – although Kepler's scepticism that the rules 'were ever used by merchants' is odd, because by definition they comprised the merchants' established practice (Kepler 1975, 47). Based on a contemporaneous petition by an aspiring monopolist intermediary (usurped by Candeler, no doubt with Gresham's backing and patronage), Kepler describes the late sixteenth-century marine insurance market as 'unorganised'. However, it does not appear to have been disorganised. The original petitioner had probably exaggerated market dysfunction to further his cause. In contrast, Wright and Fayle found 'nothing to show that [the] system had proved inadequate to the requirements of commerce' (Wright and Fayle 1928, 35). As shown above, the 1601 Act declared that 'few or no controversies' over marine insurance had occurred, and those that did were typically 'ended and ordered' by panels of merchant arbitrators.

On several occasions the Privy Council had called for the formation of such arbitration panels on an *ad hoc* basis to handle specific disputes. In its third action to address the challenges of the changing institution of marine insurance in London, their Lordships instructed the Lord Mayor to formalise the arrangements for arbitration of insurance disputes. The arrangements are set out in the records of the Court of Aldermen. In January 1576/7 the Court voted to 'ellecte nomynate and chuse, for the desidinge and endinge of the causes [of assurance, seven men] . . . as indifferent p'sons to order, judge, and determyne all suche casues touching assurance made or hereafter to be made, w'thin the Royall Exchange, or the cittie of London'. The named men were to be 'comynge two dayes in the weeke, that ye to be mundays and Thursdays, sitt in the office howse of assurance in the Royall Exchange'. Candeler – now styled Registrar of Assurances – or his designate was to act as recorder, incorporating new decisions into the *Book of Orders* to form an evolving, and thus flexible, body of insurance law (LMA COL/AD/01/022 [MR X109/037], Letter Book Y, fos. 126–7).

Shortly afterwards, the Admiralty Judge Dr David Lewis was appointed by the Privy Council to sit as an additional commissioner, bringing an outsider into the group, but it remained collectivist in character. This did not suit everyone. The Privy Council complained to the Lord Mayor in 1593 that 'Marchant strangers, having occasion to deale in matters of assurance, remaine discontented that no strangers are admitted to joyne with suche Englishe Comissioners as you appoint in theis casues'. The Councillors attempted to resolve the problem with a letter to the Court of Aldermen, whereby their Lordships 'doe order that you add yearlie unto the rest [of the Commissioners] alreadie established or in liewe of some of them, three strangers of forrein nations, being marchantes knowne to be of worthe, judgement and integritie' (Dasent 1901, 313).

With this third set of actions the Privy Council, in the name of the monarch, had made a valiant attempt to resolve the issues raised by the changing societal nature of the London marine insurance market. It had established a system of information exchange, a set of rules of enforcement, and a permanent tribunal to deal with the upset caused in the collectivist market by the arrival of individualist players, some foreign and therefore unfamiliar with the custom of Lombard Street, some genuinely unfamiliar with the rules of the game, and some simply unscrupulous. In so doing, the Queen's policy-makers had taken steps to keep flowing the contingent capital which allowed trade to proceed and grow, and thus to keep moving the stream of customs revenue available to the crown for the repayment of debt. In practice, this resulted in strengthened commitment mechanisms intended equitably to protect wealth.

The insurance act

The effort was not entirely successful. In March 1601 several merchants petitioned the Privy Council to act to improve it (Ibbetson 2008, 305). Shortly afterwards a further attempt – this time parliamentary – was made to rationalise conflicting cultures of marine insurance practice, through the 1601 *Act Conc'ninge matters of Assurances, amongste Merchantes*, which was written and championed by Privy Councillor Francis Bacon. It established a 'Court of Assurances' built on the foundation of the Guild Hall's commissioners of arbitration. The new panel was to comprise the Judge of the Admiralty, the Recorder of London, two doctors each of civil and common law, and eight merchants – or any five of them. These men had authority to effect enforcement through imprisonment. The provisions of the Act were strengthened under the restored monarch, when *An Additional Act concerning matters of Assurance used amongst Merchants* (Anno 14 Caroline, cap. 23) was passed in 1662, amending slightly the composition of the panels of commissioners. Some insight into the popularity and functioning of the Court can be gleaned from a letter of the Canaries merchant John Paige. In March 1652 he met with underwriters about a claim related to the vessel *Susan*. 'I was fain to put them to suit in the Insurance Court before could bring them to any reason', he wrote to an agent. In a later dispute, Paige predicted victory because 'there's several precedents of the very same nature upon record in the Insurance Court' (Steckley 1984, 64, 97–8).

Despite the changes under Charles II, this institution of royal enforcement continued to suffer shortcomings, largely because competing courts progressively eroded its jurisdiction. In the 1658 case *Came v. Moye* (KB 1658, 2 Siderfin 121, 82 E.R. 1290), an insured had sued his insurer in the specialist court, where his claim had been dismissed. At the Court of King's Bench, the insurer-defendant's barrister, Sir Thomas Twisden (later a judge of the regicides), agreed to jurisdiction, because the Admiralty had overlapping jurisdiction in many matters over which the common-law courts also held sway, but declared it was not correct for one to overrule the judgement of another. He argued further that the plaintiff had made his choice of venue and, in the common interest, there was no need to hear the case again, and, finally, that the statute which established the Court of Assurances specifically allowed for appeal to the Chancery Court, not King's Bench. However, Lord Chief Justice John Glynne found that the Court of Assurances, as a Court of Equity, held jurisdiction *in personam* (where action is against an individual), rather than *in rem* (where action relates to property), and that Equity Court decisions *in personam* did not remove the remedy of common law, and thus, that the case could lie before him.[4] The decision was a clear victory of the common law over the courts of equity.

Some thirty-five years later, in *Delbye v. Proudfoot & Others* (1692, 1 Shower KB 396, 89 ER 662), the reporter, Bartholomew Shower, as defending attorney, argued successfully that 'the court of commissioners of policies of insurance only extends to suits by the insured against the underwriters' and that 'any other construction would make a clashing

---

[4] I am grateful to Neil Jones of Magdalene College, Cambridge, for his translation of *Came v. Moye*.

of jurisdictions'. The insurers had wished to sue their clients for having acted fraudulently. Shower argued that this voided the policy, and therefore removed the case from a court established to make rulings under insurance policies. 'It was never intended further than the relief of the insured against the insurers, and being such a law, was not to be extended further than the words', he argued, claiming that the intention of the policy was to limit litigation by providing a venue in which the insured could sue all underwriters at once under a policy, rather than pursuing each individually. Indeed, the wording of the Act, cited above, provides support for this argument, although pursuing only a single suit seems to have been normal practice amongst the collectivist community of merchant insurers (The Commons 1720, 43–4).

Legal erosion of the Court of Assurances was not its sole shortcoming. Merchants and insurers typically continued to avoid formal courts where possible, preferring *en camera* arbitration, which preserved their trade secrets, and was probably cheaper (Price 1991, 296). Barnard's 1720 testimony stated that 'in Disputes about Losses or Averages the Insurers are generally desirous to have them adjusted by Arbitration, it being in their Interest to do so, and that the Insurers very often pay unreasonable Demands, rather than suffer themselves to be sued' (The Commons 1720, 44). Better yet, parties would often opt simply for negotiation. In a third dispute, Paige brought underwriters around to settlement having 'given the insurers upon the *Swan* a dinner at tavern, where I found them inclining to reason' (Steckley 1984, 86). The Court of Assurances survived the Glorious Revolution, as *Delbye* v. *Proudfoot & Others* proves, but it falls from the record after this date. Although short-lived from a long-term perspective, the Court was hardly the abject failure sometimes portrayed (Grassby 1995, 217). The parliamentary effort to reconcile collectivist and individualist cultures in the London marine insurance market diluted the collectivist community's traditional method of dispute resolution, but represents a clear pre-revolutionary attempt by the monarch's representatives, with Parliament, to strengthen the efficacy, and thus the credibility, of commitment mechanisms which, through marine insurance underwriting, protected trade capital and customs revenue.

The merchant insurers bill

About the same time that the Court of Assurances was vanishing – and as London's insurance market was thriving, having now taken up residence, at least in part, at Edward Lloyd's Coffee-house – a great calamity, one of the storms of war, met the nation, her merchants, and her merchant-insurers. In 1693 the Anglo-Dutch Smyrna convoy to the Levant was attacked by the French fleet. About 400 merchantmen were overwhelmed by privateers and men-of-war. Perhaps ninety-two merchant vessels, valued with their cargoes at over £1,000,000, were captured or destroyed (Palmer 2005, 78–9). Members of the Levant Company alone lost £600,000 in ships and cargo (Holmes 1993, 197). The Smyrna catastrophe hit the nascent Lloyd's insurance market very hard. At least thirty-three private underwriters were driven into bankruptcy (The Commons 1720, 43). A parliamentary rescue plan, introduced to the Commons in December 1693, called for binding settlements between the stricken underwriters and their policy holders, to prevent the former from falling into bankruptcy. London merchants owed 'very great sums' by the insurers petitioned to be heard on the issue, and a committee of MPs was struck to consider the Bill. It included Levant merchants Sir Samuel Barnardiston and Sir Thomas Vernon; Robert Waller and Thomas Blofield, the mayors of York and Norwich, respectively; the tobacco merchant Jeffrey Jeffreys; George England, a merchant of Great Yarmouth; both of the Bristol MPs appointed by their guild of Merchant Adventurers; brewing magnate and joint-stock investor John Perry; plantation owner Samuel Swift; and 'all the Members of the House who are Merchants'. Through this selection, Parliament was following the long-established practice of the collectivist merchant community by calling on insiders (albeit an unrepresentative group of them) to help to settle the details of the question, although like the range of commissioners appointed by the 1601 Act, it also included externals with different interests.

The legislation they framed, called the *Bill to enable divers Merchants-Insurers, that have sustained great Losses by the present War with France, the better to satisfy their several Creditors*, would have made partial payment agreements between each distressed underwriter and two-thirds of his creditors binding upon the remaining third, whether the latter group liked it or not (The Lords 1900, 358–60). It would have created a new, statutory commitment mechanism. Under the proposed system, a single creditor would not be able to drive a debtor into bankruptcy, with the attendant attachments and costs that such actions inevitably brought to bear on all creditors, the debtor, and the state. Instead, debtors' assets would be swiftly and efficiently distributed *pro rata* among creditors. (Provisions for such distributions are possible today under English law through a process called a 'scheme of arrangement', which is widely used by distressed insurers. However, 'schemes' were not introduced into law until the passage of the *Companies Act 1985*.)

The 1693 Bill attracted significant debate. In January, five additional members were appointed to the committee, and an undated broadsheet pamphlet, called *REASONS Humbly offered for the Passing of a BILL to enable divers Merchants that have been great Sufferers by the present War with France, the better to satisfy their Creditors*, was published in support (BL GRC 816.m.12 [16]). It argued that the provision would benefit insureds, as the few underwriters who had failed would bring down agreements with solvent insurers; that the 'Practice and Custom of Assurance in the Kingdom is both Antient and Creditable', and would be damaged in the absence of a statutory arrangement; and that the Bill, which would require registration of affected policies, would be the only way for insurers to 'accommodate their affairs with their respective Creditors, which are very Numerous, many of them unknown; because the Assurances are made in Trust for divers Persons in remote Parts of the Kingdom, and Places beyond the Seas'. Each point highlights a continuing tension between collectivist and individualist practice in the London marine insurance market. The tract goes on to highlight an important collectivist underpinning of the institution. Posing the question 'Why may there not be some Design of Fraud, by the Persons desiring this BILL?' its anonymous authors went on to answer, 'There [*sic*] Reputations are so generally known, they humbly presume, there is no ground for such Objection, having been known Merchants and Traders beyond the Seas for many Years past, and have paid great Sums of Money for Customs, and always honestly and truly discharged their several Debts, as well in England as elsewhere'. The broadsheet also argued that it was only a small group of insurers that was unable to reach settlement.

In February the name of merchant-insurer Daniel Foe (later Defoe) was inserted into the Bill, and shortly afterwards it passed the Commons. No record of the debate in the House of Lords survives, but the *Journal* records that the peers rejected the bill upon its second reading in March. Narcissus Luttrell, with characteristic terseness, recorded only that 'The Lords have flung out the bill for merchants ensurers' (Luttrell 2011, 281). This legislation was caught in one of the gravest political issues of the day. The Smyrna disaster was widely blamed (to use the language of the *Bill*) on 'miscarriages of the sea affairs'. These in turn were the product of what the Commons described as the 'notorious and treacherous mismanagement' of the navy (Rodger 2004, 153–4). The destruction of the Levant fleet led to the collapse of government credit in the City, as Godolphin warned the king in July (Horwitz 1977, 116). Further, the Bill was brought to the Lords at almost exactly the same moment that the new land tax, which fell most heavily on Country Tories, was beginning to bite (Holmes 1993, 289, 336). The resentment against City financiers by aristocratic landholders (later satirised by Tory propagandist Joseph Trapp's 1711 pamphlet *The Character and Principles of the Present Set of Whigs*) was emerging with strength, and probably helped to scuttle the legislation. Thus, a political battle between nascent parliamentary constituencies was probably more important to this post-1688 parliament than strengthening creditors' confidence in their counterparties' ability to pay. In contrast to the acts of the monarch's Privy Council more than a century earlier, Parliament failed to authorise a costless initiative which would have allowed debts to be met partially, 'according to right and equity', and strengthened the state's commitment to the important income stream arising from international trade.

The Bubble Act

The financial events of 1720, including the passage of the *Bubble Act* (6 George 1, cap. 18), which restricted the formation and operation of joint-stock companies, are well known. Less familiar is the impact of the Act on the London marine insurance market, but it must count as a significant state intervention into underwriters' business.

After a protracted lobbying campaign and significant debate, Parliament permitted 'two several and distinct corporations' to underwrite marine insurance, and prohibited all other corporations, societies, and partnerships from conducting the business anywhere in Britain or her colonies. Substantial capital was raised through subscriptions for the Royal Exchange Assurance and the London Assurance, companies projected respectively by two gentlemanly capitalists, the Lords Onslow and Chetwynd. They joined with leading merchants to back the two corporate marine insurers which, they argued, would support trade, and thus benefit the nation.

The insurance-company projects attracted much debate in the City, in pamphlets, and in Westminster. Allegations of bribery of the Attorney General, Nicholas Lechmere, were widespread, but were dismissed after examination by the House of Commons (The Commons 1720, 5, 13). For his part, Lechmere argued that there was no argument in law against a corporate insurer, and that such a foundation 'may be of great advantage to trade', but he stated that there was no need for two such companies, and no need for a joint stock as large as had been subscribed (if not paid), in excess of £1 million (The Commons 1720, 48, 57). Merchant opinion about the proposals was divided. A petition opposed to Onslow's request for a charter was signed by the prominent Levant merchant Ralph Radcliffe and thirteen of the underwriters of policies issued to him between 1709 and 1717. However, a later petition arguing in favour of

Chetwynd's rival scheme was also signed by Radcliffe, and by twelve of the merchant-insurers who underwrote his insurances (although just two of the latter men were included in the first group of signatories) (HALSC, DE/R/B23/1–47). Outport merchants were also engaged. Bristolians, led by their Lord Mayor, petitioned against Onslow's project, although later they too shifted to favour an incorporation (The Commons 1720, 24–53). Wright and Fayle argue that collaboration between Onslow and Chetwynd was 'plain fact', but the evidence of Radcliffe's underwriters shows that the competing proposals divided the insurance community. After much clamouring, the issue was solved with twin gifts to the King of £300,000 each, to be skimmed from the subscriptions and applied to Civil List debts (Wright and Fayle 1921, 49, 58–9). On top of this, each company promised to subscribe £156,000 to a government loan. Although in the years ahead they were to play a continued role in the financing of state debt, the immediate impact of these commitments on the new joint-stock companies was financial strife and shareholder revolt (Supple 1970, 35). The incident is reminiscent of the rent-seeking arrangements surrounding Edward I's *maltote*.

The architect of the £600,000 plan was Robert Walpole. Under it, not only would the leading pair of proposed marine insurance companies be granted charters (a third, called 'Shales Insurance' and projected by Philip Helbut, 'fell to the ground') (Eden 1806, 13), but they were also granted an official duopoly. Meanwhile Walpole doubled his personal £2,550 investment in the shares in just two weeks (Plumb 1956, 285–92). Although the Commons, amidst the bubble-fuelled environment of outrage at stock-jobbing, had stated its intention to 'restrain the extravagant and unwarrantable practice of raising money by voluntary subscription', which it did soon after with the *Bubble Act*, it was, in stark contrast, 'delighted at the prospect of paying for government without the need to raise taxes or borrow money', and 'quickly agreed' to Walpole's proposal. The King too was 'favourably inclined' to the proposals to grant royal sanction to the two insurers. Charters and a duopoly were duly granted. The large subscriptions decried by the Attorney General were approved (Supple 1970, 26–32). The wealth of subscribers had been diverted directly to the sovereign. Only a detail prevented the duopoly from destroying the London marine insurance market: individuals underwriting against their personal capital were allowed to stay in the business. (Underwriting at Lloyd's continued exclusively on this basis until the 1990s.) A few partnerships were affected, but they had only to switch to individual underwriting. However, corporate underwriting remained monopolised until 1824, and the successful and well-functioning market was interfered with and restrained.

Outcomes

During the early years of the period covered by this chapter, London's marine insurance market was relatively small and primarily insular, but with links to international traders who played by similar rules to those prevailing in London. The institution's characteristics map very well onto the model of 'collectivist' societies described by Greif, despite the absence of defining racial, confessional, or familial ties. It was the shared culture of capitalist commerce which tied these men together; London's collectivist merchant community crossed the boundaries of faith and kinship, comprising French, German, Italian, Dutch, and Jewish traders (Gauci 2001, 39). In this way, the community of London underwriters adheres better to sociologists' conceptions of individualism and collectivism than to the typically narrower adoption of the framework under NIE. In the eighteenth century, as London became a much more important centre for oceanic trade, and its marine insurance market the international leader, it began to serve a much wider community, including an expanded home market, which included the entry of many more 'individualists' into the institution. This was accompanied by an increasing tendency for players, especially buyers of insurance, to lack vertical integration with insurance provision. Over this period, in line with Greif's model, the enforcement and information provision components of transaction cost control had to be modified, requiring increasing involvement of state actors in the operation of the institution.

The state's response does not track well with North and Weingast's 'credible commitment' thesis. The four incidents described illustrate a journey away from commitment, one which gathered pace as the Glorious Revolution of 1688/89 receded into history. The pre-revolutionary monarch behaved in a way which was neither rent-seeking nor confiscatory, and instead responded constructively to the challenges faced by merchant-insurers, in the 1570s through the Privy Council, and in 1601 through Parliament. Yet post-1688 the crown and Parliament in combination refused to endorse a plan to sustain the solvency of the community when it was needed in 1693, and returned, in 1720, to naked rent-seeking behaviour. In the case of marine insurance the trajectory of commitment went in the direction opposite to that proposed by North and Weingast. As Britain's fiscal–military state developed, the security of merchant shipping, fundamental to the sustained flow of customs revenue which underpinned an important share of state debt repayment, was an important backstop to 'credible commitment', yet the actions of the King in Parliament did not exhibit credibility to those who ventured their capital in support of that security.

In the first example, the Queen, through the Privy Council, worked closely with merchants on a project of institution-building. The monopoly granted to Candeler, and supported by City champion Gresham, was feared by some and eschewed by others, but was useful to the overall security of trade. At the bidding of merchants, the Office of Assurances should have helped to reduce intentional fraud by interloping individualists through improved transparency of information, while setting down the traditional rules governing the game for newcomers to follow. The establishment of a permanent panel of Commissioners of Arbitration merely formalised an existing merchant institution. In the second example, Parliament and the Privy Council took further steps to build a new legal institution, again on the foundation of longstanding merchant practice, and again in response to merchant petitions. The opening line of the Act makes clear its underlying purpose: 'to advance and increase the generall weatlthe of the Realme, her Majesties Customes, and the strengthe of Shippinge'. It allowed loopholes, however, which favoured collectivist merchants' interests: policies not registered at Candeler's office were not within the Court's jurisdiction, and registration was not made mandatory through binding regulation. A cooperative compromise had been reached which allowed merchant practice to prevail where merchant-insurers were trading risk amongst themselves.

In the third example, following catastrophe, a new commitment mechanism was agreed between merchants and the Commons, but blocked by the Lords, a majority of whom, it can be assumed, found point-scoring in royal politics and the protection of their own wealth and status more important that reinforcing commitment mechanisms. The result was the bankruptcy of perhaps a quarter of London's merchant-insurers, which cannot have helped anyone. The final example, the granting of Royal charters and a restrictive monopoly to a pair of marine insurance companies in exchange for a very large grant to the King, exemplifies the opposite of 'credible commitment'. With the enthusiastic support of Parliament, and against the advice of state officials, it was a clear throwback to the pre-Revolutionary model of state finance: the grant of exclusive Royal Charters in exchange for cash and loans. The move deprived the many hundreds of investors in the new joint-stock insurers of a large percentage of their capital, in exchange for duopolistic trading rights which blocked further development of the market through corporate foundations. In this case, three decades after the institutions of 'credible commitment' had been established, its major actor – the King in Parliament – did not hesitate to accept investors' funds from their agents. The chain of commitment did not yet extend to these investors.

Key to archive references

BL: British Library
ECRO: Essex Country Records Office
GHL: Guildhall Library
HALSC: Hertfordshire Archives and Local Studies
             Centre
LMA: London Metropolitan Archives
TNA C: National Archives, Chancery
TNA HCA: National Archives, High Court of Admiralty

References

Akerlof, George A. 1970. 'The Market for Lemons: Quality, Uncertainty, and the Market Mechanism', *Quarterly Journal of Economics*, 84(3), 488–500.

Barbour, Violet 1929. 'Marine Risks and Insurance in the Seventeenth Century', *Journal of Economic & Business History*, 1, 561–96.

Benson, Bruce L. 1989. 'The Spontaneous Evolution of Commercial Law', *Southern Economic Journal*, 55(3), 644–61.

Commons, The 1720. *The Special Report from the Committee Appointed to Inquire into, and Examine the Several Subscriptions for Fisheries, Insurances, Annuities for Lives, and All Other Projects Carried on by Subscription . . .* London: House of Commons, printed by Tonson, J., Goodwin, T., Lintot, B., and Taylor, W.

Commons, The 1824. *Report from the Select Committee on Marine Insurance (Sess. 1810), 18 April, 1810.* London: House of Commons.

Dasent, John R. 1894. *Acts of the Privy Council of England, New Series, vol. IX, 1575–77.* London: H.M.SO.

Dasent, John R. 1895. *Acts of the Privy Council of England, New Series, vol. VIII: 1571–75.* London: H.M.SO.

Dasent, John R. 1901. *Acts of the Privy Council of England, New Series, vol. XXIV: 1592–93.* London: H.M.SO.

Davis, R. 1962. *The Rise of the English Shipping Industry in the Seventeenth and Eighteenth Centuries.* Newton Abbot: David & Charles.

Ebert, Christopher 2011. 'Early Modern Atlantic Trade and the Development of Maritime Insurance to 1630', *Past & Present*, 213, 87–213.

Eden, Sir Frederick 1806. *On the Policy and Expediency of Granting Insurance Charters.* London.

Edwards, Jeremy and Ogilvie, Sheilagh 2012. 'Contract Enforcement, Institutions, and Social Capital: The Maghribi Traders Reappraised', *Economic History Review*, 65(2), 421–44.

Foster, William (ed.) 1909. *Court Minutes of the East India Company, 1640–1643.* Oxford: Clarendon Press.

Gauci, Parry 2001. *The Politics of Trade: The Overseas Merchant in State and Society, 1660–1720.* Oxford: Oxford University Press.

Glaisyer, Natasha 2006. *The Culture of Commerce in England, 1660–1720.* Woodbridge: Royal Historical Society & Boydell Press.

Goldberg, Jessica 2012. *Trade and Institutions in the Medieval Mediterranean: The Genzia Merchants and Their Business World.* Cambridge: Cambridge University Press.

Grassby, Richard 1995. *The Business Community of Seventeenth-Century England.* Cambridge: Cambridge University Press.

Greif, Avner 1992. 'Institutions and International Trade: Lessons from the Commercial Revolution', *American Economic Review*, 82(2), 128–33.

Greif, Avner 1997. 'On the Interrelations and Economic Implications of Economic, Social, Political, and Normative Factors: Reflections from Two Late Medieval Societies', in John Drobak and John Nye (eds.), *The Frontiers of the New Institutional Economics.* London: Academic Press.

Greif, Avner 2012. 'The Maghribi Traders: A Reappraisal?' *Economic History Review*, 65(2), 445–69.

Greif, Avner; Milgrom, Paul; and Weingast, Barry R. 1994. 'Coordination, Commitment, and Enforcement: The Case of the Merchant Guild', *Journal of Political Economy*, 102(4), 745–76.

Hatton, Edward 1699. *Comes Commercii, or the Trader's Companion*, 1st edn. London: printed by 'J.H. for Chas. Coningsby' and three others.

Holdsworth, W. S. 1917. 'The Early History of the Contract of Insurance', *Columbia Law Review*, 17(2), 85–113.

Holmes, Geoffrey 1993. *The Making of a Great Power: Late Stuart and Early Georgian Britain, 1660–1722.* London: Longman.

Horwitz, Henry 1977. *Parliament, Policy and Politics in the Reign of William III.* Manchester: Manchester University Press.

Ibbetson, D. 2008. 'Law and Custom: Insurance in Sixteenth-Century England', *Journal of Legal History*, 29(3), 291–307.

Jones, W. J. 1970. 'Elizabethan Marine Insurance: The Judicial Undergrowth', *Business History*, 2, 53–66.

Kepler, J. S. 1975. 'The Operating Potential of the London Insurance Market in the 1570s', *Business History*, 17, 44–55.

Kingston, Christopher 2007. 'Marine Insurance in Britain and America, 1720–1844: A Comparative Institutional Analysis', *Journal of Economic History*, 67(2), 379–409.

Lords, The 1900. *Manuscripts of the House of Lords*, vol. **I** (New Series), 1693–1695. London: H.M.S.O.

Luttrell, Narcissus 2011. *A Brief Historical Relation of State Affairs from September 1678 to April 1714*, vol. **3**. Cambridge: Cambridge University Press (reprint of Oxford University Press edition, 1857).

Mann, M. 1986. *The Sources of Social Power, Vol. I: A History of Power from the Beginning to A.D. 1760.* Cambridge: Cambridge University Press.

McCusker, John J. 1995. *European Bills of Entry and Marine Lists: Early Commercial Publications and the Origins of the Business Press.* Cambridge, MA: Harvard University Press.

Milgrom, P. R.; North, D. C.; and Weingast, B. R. 1990. 'The Role of Institutions in the Revival of Trade: The Law Merchant, Private Judges, and the Champagne Fairs', *Economics and Politics*, 2(1), 1–23.

Molloy, C. 1744. *De jure maritimo et navali: or, A Treatise of Affairs Maritime, and of Commerce*, 8th edn. London: J. Walthoe (printer) (first published 1676).

Musgrave, P. (1981). 'The Economics of Uncertainty: The Structural Revolution in the Spice Trade, 1480–1640', in P. L. Cottrell and D. H. Aldcroft (eds.), *Shipping, Trade, and Commerce: Essays in Memory of Ralph Davis*. Leicester: Leicester University Press.

North, Douglass 1990. *Institutions, Institutional Change and Economic Performance*. Cambridge: Cambridge University Press.

North, Douglass 1991. 'Institutions', *Journal of Economic Perspectives*, 5(1), 97–112.

North, Douglass and Thomas, R. P. 1973. *Rise of the Western World: A New Economic History*. Cambridge: University Press.

North, Douglass and Weingast, B. 1989. 'Constitutions and Commitment: The Evolution of Institutions Governing Public Choice in Seventeenth-Century England'. *Journal of Economic History*, 49(4), 803–32.

Palmer, M. 2005. *Command at Sea*. Cambridge, MA: Harvard University Press.

Plumb, J. H. 1956. *Sir Robert Walpole: The Making of a Statesman*. London: Crescent Press.

Price, J. 1991. 'Transaction Costs: A Note on Merchant Credit and the Organisation of Private Trade', in Tracy, J. (ed.), *The Political Economy of Merchant Empires*. Cambridge: Cambridge University Press.

Prichard, M. J. and Yale, D. E. C. (eds.) 1993. *Hale and Fleetwood on Admiralty Jurisdiction*. London: Selden Society.

Raynes, H. E. 1964. *A History of British Insurance, 2nd edn*. London: Pitman & Sons.

Rodger, N. A. M. 2004. *The Command of the Ocean: A Naval History of Britain, 1649–1815*. London: Penguin.

Roseveare, Henry (ed.) 1987. *Markets and Merchants of the Late Seventeenth Century: The Marescoe–David Letters, 1668–1680*. Oxford: Oxford University Press.

Steckley, G. F. (ed.) 1984. *The Letters of John Paige, London Merchant, 1648–1658*. London: London Record Society.

Stow, John 1720. *A Survey of the Cities of London and Westminster (Strype's Edition)*. London: printed for A. Churchill and nine others (first published 1598).

Supple, Barry 1970. *The Royal Exchange Assurance: A History of British Insurance 1720–1970*. Cambridge: Cambridge University Press.

Trapp, J. 1711. *The Character and Principles of the Present Set of Whigs*. London.

Triandis, H. C.; McCusker, C.; and Hui, C. H. 1990. 'Multimethod Probes of Individualism and Collectivism', *Journal of Personality and Social Psychology*, 59(5), 1006–20.

Westall, Oliver 1997. 'Invisible, Visible, and "Direct" Hands: An Institutional Interpretation of Organisational Structure and Change in British General Insurance', *Business History*, 39(4), 44–66.

Wright, C. and Fayle, C. E. 1928. *A History of Lloyd's*. London: Macmillan & Co.

4   Credibility, transparency, accountability, and the public credit under the Long Parliament and Commonwealth, 1643–1653

D'Maris Coffman[1]

In the two decades since the publication of North and Weingast's 'Constitutions and Commitment' article, scholarship has moved away from their central claim about the importance of parliamentary supremacy over a predatory monarch for the protection of property rights (North and Weingast 1989). Instead, modern commentators have built on the original framework to advance additional conditions which they present as the *sine qua non* of 'credible commitment' in the British case, specifically parliamentary supremacy over public finance, transparency in public accounting, accountability via direct creditor action, and robust secondary markets in the decades following the Revolution of 1688/89 (Stasavage 2003; Murphy 2013). Are these conditions sufficient unto themselves, or are other considerations equally or more important? Natural experiments are rare in the historical profession, but the Civil Wars and Interregnum provide an opportunity to test this new consensus.

All of these elements (parliamentary control over the public finances, transparency in public accounts, accountability via creditor action, and surprisingly deep secondary markets), as well as a stated commitment to maintaining the 'publike faith' and the use of common-law procedure to adjudicate disputes between taxpayers and the regime, were in place under the Long Parliament and Commonwealth regimes. Yet they did not, in themselves, produce 'credible commitment' mechanisms for generating support for a long-term public debt. Rather, these appear to be necessary but not sufficient conditions. If anything, there is strong evidence that the most important ingredient in the durability of commitment mechanisms is also the most elusive and contingent: the perception of the stability and permanence of a given regime, whether it be representative and deliberative or monarchical and autocratic.

---

[1] I would like to express my appreciation to my coeditors, Adrian Leonard and Larry Neal, for their invaluable assistance and careful reading of earlier drafts and to two anonymous referees for their helpful suggestions.

This chapter argues that North and Weingast were essentially correct, in their original article, to focus attention on constitutional structure. However, by failing to engage meaningfully with the mid-seventeenth-century experience of constitutional fracture, they did not apprehend that during the decades preceding the Revolution of 1688/89 contemporaries had begun to abstract a notion of 'the state', which was sovereign, permanent, and continuous. The first half of this essay takes up that mid-century experience; the second contextualises the evolving contemporary discourses about the public credit within longer narratives of state formation. After 1688, Parliament and the crown's servants jointly had the responsibility to ensure that the state did not default on its debts. As other chapters in this volume argue, it took decades for the public to find this re-configuration to be a credible one. Rather than a game played between predatory monarchs and self-interested parliaments, Britain's fiscal–military state depended equally upon a disciplined and efficient revenue establishment and upon the willingness of Parliament to vote fiscal impositions that were adequate to service debts. The conceptual distinctions maintained by North and Weingast, which sharply demarcate 'executive', 'legislative', and 'judicial' powers, mattered less than the sense in which Parliament and the crown were both servants of the state after the Revolution. Insofar as the eighteenth-century fiscal–military state was dismantled in the decades of peace that followed the Napoleonic Wars, it would be a mistake to accept the judgments of nineteenth-century Whig historians and their intellectual heirs about the nature of the Revolution Settlement. Rather, it is necessary to look to the mid-seventeenth century for the origins of these developments.

O'Brien and Hunt (1999) have also argued forcefully that the institutions required for the good governance of public finance pre-dated the Glorious Revolution. In doing so, they built on the work of Roseveare (1969), Chandaman (1975), and Roseveare (1991), both of whom located the origins of 'Treasury Control' (which is to say the primacy of the Treasury as the department responsible both for supervising the revenue and for controlling expenditure) in the Restoration period. In the two decades before the Glorious Revolution, the Treasury establishment grew out of the clerks of the lower Exchequer, which had been re-established by Cromwell in 1654. The Long Parliament abolished both the upper Exchequer court and the office of the lower Exchequer during the Civil Wars. The Lord Treasurer presided over the lower Exchequer, but the institution that came to be known as 'the Treasury' ironically grew most rapidly in the periods in which the office of Lord Treasurer was held by Treasury Commissions that shared power amongst themselves (1667–73, 1679–83) and encouraged bureaucratisation in turn.

Pride of place in the Treasury's growing arsenal belonged to the excise establishment, but equally important was their increasingly successful assertion of control over departmental expenditure (Chandaman 1975, 251).

How far specific developments belonged to the Restoration as such, and how far they were an outgrowth of the preceding republican period, remains open to debate. In a recent account, Murphy (2013) takes up the traditional view, which credits Sir George Downing with the key innovation, the introduction of numbered tallies in 1667, upon his return from the Netherlands (Roseveare 1969; 1991; Scott 2003). Yet close examination of the parliamentary funds in place under the Long Parliament and Commonwealth regimes reveals that even then they were administered according to the same principle later championed by Downing. Moreover, inspection of Treasury minute books from the 1660s suggests that the first Restoration Lord Treasurer, the Earl of Southampton, was actually responsible for the retention of the 'best practice' of the Interregnum experience (Coffman 2008; 2010).

Despite the preconditions of 'credible commitment', Parliament's disposal of capital assets in the late 1640s and early 1650s, in the form of lands seized by the regime that generated revenue in the form of rents, represented the loss of the most immediate mechanism for rescheduling short-term debts into debts of longer duration. Insofar as these land sales rewarded the regime's allies (in a manner reminiscent of the disposal of monastic lands under Henry VIII), their sale was as much a political manoeuvre as a financial one. Furthermore, Oliver Cromwell's aversion to financial intermediation frustrated the development of permanent secondary markets for government debt in the 1650s (Ashley 1962; Coffman 2010). It is clear, however, that British fiscal institutions were by no means a product of the Revolution of 1688/89 (Brewer 1990). Very little support remains for the old canard about 'England's Apprenticeship' to Dutch masters in the wake of William's ascension to the throne (Wilson 1984; 't Hart 1991).

North and Weingast associate legal protection of creditors and taxpayers, a commitment to servicing debt, and the idea of 'public credit' with the Revolution of 1688/89. In so doing, they neglect the mid-century origins of the Financial Revolution. In part this neglect is a function of their apparent desire to sidestep debates about the origins of the fiscal state by ascribing a 'fiscal revolution' to 1688, when, in fact, most of the fiscal innovations were a product of the earlier period (Coffman 2008). Modern use of the term 'fiscal–military state' dates from Brewer's *Sinews of Power* (1990). More recently, Braddick (2000) distinguished four dimensions of the Early Modern state in seventeenth-century England:

the patriarchal, the confessional, the dynastic, and the fiscal–military. The authors agree that the seventeenth-century British state was a 'small state' compared to France, Spain, or even the Austrian Empire at the time, let alone by modern standards (Brewer 1990; Braddick 2000). The Poor Law was administered at the parish level, educational and medical institutions funded largely through charity, and the legal system, save insofar as the crown paid salaries to the upper judiciary, was successful in passing the cost of administration onto voluntary officialdom, and the costs of prosecution onto the plaintiff (Braddick 2002).

Although the other dimensions remained part of the constitution, by the mid-eighteenth century the British state can be best characterised as a fiscal–military state if judged by how it spent its revenues. Unlike the seventeenth-century state, which struggled with the practicalities of enforcing religious conformity at home, the eighteenth-century British 'fiscal–military' state was geared for making war, and the overwhelming majority of crown expenditure, post-Revolution, was directed overseas. The consequences are difficult to over-emphasise. Whereas the Long Parliament and Commonwealth had been forced to raise funds from the populace to fight a civil war, and then to quell a disquieted kingdom, William III used Britain as a tax province from which to pursue an aggressive foreign policy. This implies, as in the North and Weingast model, what they formulate as a significant difference in the 'sovereign's time preference or discount rate'. Civil wars are, by their nature, moments which make tremendous fiscal demands on sovereign states, where, indeed, 'the survival of the sovereign and the regime was placed at risk' (North and Weingast 1989, 807). In other words, one might expect the Parliamentary and Commonwealth regimes to show a willingness to engage in hyperbolic discounting, for instance, by debasing the coinage as Henry VIII had done. They did not do so. Instead, both the Long and Rump Parliaments recognised that their very survival depended on maintaining the 'publike faith' (which equates to the modern maxim that 'those who live outside the law have to be honest'). Whatever the dubious constitutional stature of the 'abdication' of James II in 1688, the Whigs and Tories of the Revolution Settlement enjoyed comparatively stronger constitutional and legal positions than their fathers and grandfathers, from whose example they nevertheless stood to profit (Scott 2000).

Yet for all of the significance of mid-seventeenth-century experiments in public finance for the shape of the post-Revolution settlement, the fiscal and financial innovations of the 1640s and 1650s cannot be divorced from their immediate contexts. Whether or not Parliament enjoyed more legitimacy, in the eyes of the majority of Englishmen, than William III did in the wake of the Revolution, the Long Parliament in the 1640s struggled to establish its authority amidst the splintering of the constitution that the English civil wars precipitated. The Long Parliament's fiscal exactions were arguably both extra-legal and extra-constitutional. They required different legitimising rhetoric than burdens imposed by the crown. Parliament emphasised 'necessity' and, as such, the temporary nature of the revenue ordinances, and used them to collateralise monies borrowed. Yet it would be a mistake to reduce these developments to the discursive logics of extra-constitutional rule. In the 1640s and 1650s the conditions of parliamentary supremacy over public finance, transparency in public accounting, accountability via creditor action, and robust secondary markets now associated with 'credible commitment' grew out of the weakness of the regime and its need to win the public trust, not out of any putative relative strength of Parliament vis-à-vis the king, let alone the superiority of, or public enthusiasm for, limited government or participatory political culture.

On an institutional level, excise taxation (and with it the growing excise establishment) was the primary fiscal innovation to survive regime change in 1660 (O'Brien 1988; Braddick 1996; O'Brien and Hunt 1999; Coffman 2010). Yet this was far from a foregone conclusion. There were powerful forces working against the permanent settlement of the excise. Domestic commodity taxation appeared to violate the Tudor conception of the kingdom as the 'manor of England', in which the landed voted impositions on themselves to supply their king. For those who wanted to restore a pre-Civil War financial regime that can best be termed 'fiscal feudalism', excise taxation was anathema (Hurstfield 1955). When it did not bear the taint of Dutch republicanism, the excise smacked of continental absolutism. Proponents thought it the 'most insensible imposition', but as disaffected royalists, radicals, and independents alike pointed out, the taxation of domestic commodities fell heaviest on the poor. Many Englishmen thought that the poor should not pay taxes at all. In the mercantile community, approval of the excise was far from universal. Special interests argued that specific excises hurt trade, destroyed fledgling industries, and rewarded professional tax collectors at the expense of more productive members of society. Yet excise taxation was established as a permanent part of the ordinary revenue and the primary source of extraordinary revenues after the Restoration (Chandaman 1975). Excise taxation then provided the engine of Schumpeter's transformation from a demesne to a tax state, the catalyst for a shift in ideological justifications of parliamentary taxation, and ultimately the rhetoric of legitimisation for the public credit (Schumpeter 1954; Braddick 1994; Coffman 2008).

This argument rests on three related findings. The first is that excise taxation proved far more successful than anticipated, both in its capacity to raise needed funds, and in the speed with which the parliamentary regime was able to create a durable and disciplined revenue establishment. Second, the relative regularity and transparency of collection, the high degree of centralisation, and the new methods of auditing and control permitted the development of new short-term debt instruments, which could be secured by the ordinances and priced by the market. The market pricing of short-term debt broadened and deepened credit markets and provided an important intermediate step towards the development of long-term debt instruments after 1690. Third, the excises had no legal precedent (or dubious ones at best) and thus required a new rhetoric of legitimacy. By voting to retain the excise in exchange for the permanent abolition of the Court of Wards (one of the prerogative courts identified by North and Weingast as essentially extractive), the Cavalier Parliaments maintained a legal fiction based on medieval doctrines of supply. In effect, the excise offered a solution, acceptable both to adherents of an older model of fiscal feudalism, and to those who pressed for reform (Coffman 2008).

Implementing all three operations – excise taxes, short-term debt backed by specific revenues, and development of legal justifications – by the Long Parliament's practice of 'administration by legislation', coupled with aggressive oversight by the Commonwealth Committee for Regulating the Excise, created a body of procedures and precedents that the Restoration Treasury preserved and adapted in its attempts to settle the revenue (Coffman 2010). The development of the British excise establishment shows a high degree of path dependence. This was largely because the excise ordinances had proved such an effective way to raise funds from 'neutrals' and even 'malignants' during the Civil Wars, as well as a remarkably useful and flexible tool for securing the public debt (Coffman 2008; Coffman 2010).

The close connection between excise revenue and government debt service (Figure 4.1) observable over the course of the eighteenth century arose from the Long Parliament and Commonwealth regimes' practice of assigning specific revenues to service particular debts (Brewer 1990; Coffman 2008). Unfortunately current scholarship follows North and Weingast (1989, 821) in ascribing the practice of assigning revenue ordinances to service particular debt instruments exclusively to the post-Revolutionary period (Murphy 2013). The practice actually began during the 1640s under the Long Parliament, and was fundamental to the manner in which public debt instruments were issued. Creditors both

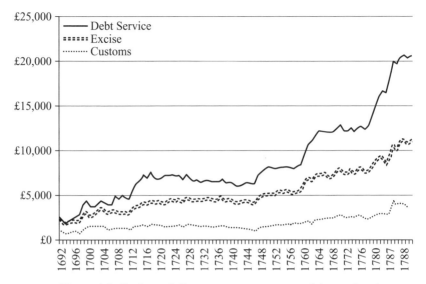

Figure 4.1. Excise and Customs revenues versus debt service charges, 1690–1790, £000. *Source*: Mitchell 1988, 575–80.

large and small understood the regime's debts to be secured by revenue ordinances, and would refuse to lend unless they understood the collateral to be sufficiently unencumbered and judged the security to be 'good' (Coffman 2008).

The Parliamentary regime, as will be shown, took very seriously indeed the need to maintain the 'publike faith'. It is no exaggeration to say that the propensity for creditor action that Murphy ascribes to the post-Revolution period can also be perceived in the Interregnum.

Parliamentary supremacy? 'Administration by legislation'

Parliamentary supremacy during the Civil Wars and Interregnum was the product of constitutional crisis. The Westminster Parliament functioned without a formal Treasury or even an Exchequer to administer the revenue. This produced 'administration by legislation'. To give but one example, the Long and Rump Parliaments issued over sixty ordinances for the establishment and regulation of some aspect of the Excise, including its use as collateral for public debt (Coffman 2013b). The Long Parliament was responsible for more than half of these. From 1643 to 1649 it further passed dozens of resolutions and parliamentary orders specifying disbursements, demanding advances from the commissioners (in the form of loans), or pledging the excise as collateral for loans made by third parties. Cumbersome as this system was, there was no clear alternative (Coffman 2013b). Once Charles I and his supporters had retreated to Oxford after the king's defeat at Turnham Green, Parliament confiscated coin and other treasure remaining in the Court of Wards, the Exchequer, the Duchy Courts, and the First-fruits Office (Ashley 1962, 39). Most of the officials and their under-clerks had joined the royalist side. Without the king, these prerogative courts ceased to function. Over time, Parliament arrived at the expedient of conducting routine financial operations by standing committee as authorised by Commons.

These committees represented complex institutional arrangements with different standings in law. Most of the revenue committees were simply an alternative to the aforementioned royal courts. They issued *warrants* for payments of the Parliamentary regime's debts, which were numbered and had to be paid sequentially. They were struck off of, and then assigned to, one of ten parliamentary funds which received monies anticipated by the various ordinances. Both committees and Commons as a whole could also contract short-term bankers' *loans* (usually with a maturity of twenty-four months), which would be secured by the actual revenue ordinances, and issue 'publike-faith' *bills*, which were unsecured by a specific ordinance but backed by the 'public faith' (Coffman 2008). The ordinances appointed commissioners, who were not parliamentarians themselves but often their relatives or close associates (Wheeler 1999). They often had to make *advances* to the regime. Although these advances were not legally secured by the ordinances, the receivers were well positioned to reimburse themselves once the revenues materialised. As a general rule, advances by customs and excise commissioners were repaid in six months at a rate of eight per cent per annum. Parliament's ability to repay these loans often depended upon the willingness of other creditors to advance additional monies, on the same terms, to meet current expenses. A minority of taxpayers were also allowed to make *compositions* (negotiated settlements in advance, in lieu of assessed duties) to the commissioners. Compositions represented a negotiated discount on the duty rate, rather than a direct levy, but also offered commissioners lump-sum payments with which to reimburse themselves (Coffman 2010).

Many of the committees were national in scope and staffed by Parliamentarians; others were local, manned by the hated 'local committeeman'. Distinctions could also be made between 'standing' committees of Parliament and 'ad hoc' committees, especially regional committees that handled military governance. Their constitutional stature was also elusive: some were extensions of existing institutions, whereas others appeared de novo. The *Committee for the King's Revenue* at Wiche House (renamed the *Committee for the Public Revenue* after the regicide) dates from the negotiations of 1626. In November of 1642 Parliament added the *Committee for the Advance of Money* at Haberdashers' Hall, followed closely by the *Committee for Compounding* (with delinquents) at Goldsmith's Hall, and the *Committee for Sequestrations*. Not surprisingly, the latter committees were essentially penal in function, insofar as they imposed forced loans on the generality of the Commonwealth and confiscated the lands and personal property of those deemed insufficiently loyal to the regime (Scroggs 1907). In that respect, the conduct of these penal committees bore similarities with the prerogative Star Chamber they replaced, a fact not lost on the regime's opponents.

Excise matters were handled by the revenue committee, which made recommendations to Commons as a whole, until June 1645, when a separate *Committee for Improving and Regulating the Excise* was established. Parliament's system of disbursing monies by 'warrant' on the 'public-faith' proved cumbersome. A *Committee for Taking Accounts of the Kingdom*, established in 1644, enjoyed very little success in auditing this system. In June 1649 the Council of State appointed a committee to consider reforms, but no action was taken until Cromwell dissolved the Rump in late 1653. This system of parliamentary finance meant that pronouncements about routine administrative matters, including instructions for officers, judicial procedures to combat frauds, accounting rules and regulations governing comptrollers, as well as numerous clarifications, had to be issued by parliamentary ordinance (Scroggs 1907; Ashley 1934; Coffman 2010).

Because Parliament understood its task, before the regicide, to include saving the king from evil counsel, these ordinances were careful to emphasise the 'defence of the King, Parliament, and Kingdom, both by Sea Land, as for and towards the payment of the Debts of the Commonwealth, for which the Publike Faith is, or shall be ingaged'. This set-piece language also stressed the 'great necessity of providing present supply for the preservation of this Kingdom, our Religion, Laws and Liberties from utter ruine and destruction', and promised constantly that the exactions would be temporary (Coffman 2013b). One consequence of 'administration by legislation' was that the term-structure of the debt was limited by the original ordinance. Parliament had to renew the ordinances annually, biennially, or occasionally triennially to avoid defaulting on its debts.

A robust money market grew up around this system. Revenue commissioners collected the duties from taxpayers, who could only pay in coin or specie (but not in the regime's paper – its publike faith bills, military debentures, or warrants). In principle, the commissioners then turned those monies over to the parliamentary fund. More often than not, the commissioners had already made advances to the fund sufficient to cover the monies received. Alternatively, if they held additional

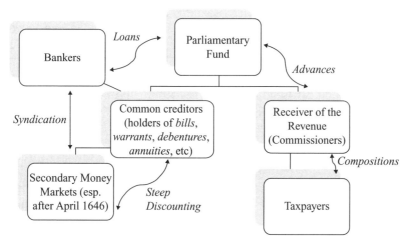

Figure 4.2. The money market.

monies, they might be ordered to have their clerks pay the regime's creditors directly. After April 1646, when these debts became assignable, goldsmith-bankers began to syndicate their loans and to buy up, at a discount, debts held by common creditors.

This system, complete with 'numbered' warrants and other varieties of both secured and unsecured debt, looks remarkably like the payment system that many historians imagine the Revolutionary Settlement in 1690 to have inaugurated (Roberts 1977). Although long-term debt instruments (callable life annuities) made up a small proportion of the total, they did exist, and were used occasionally to reschedule debts. Two vignettes illustrate both the circumstances in which they might be offered to very different classes of creditors and the standing of these instruments under the law.

The Widow Abercromie, Susan Denton, was the maiden aunt of a royalist gentry family whose seat, Hillesden House, had been overrun in skirmishes along Buckinghamshire's border with Oxfordshire. Sir Alexander Denton, the baronet, had died in a parliamentary prison, and his son and heir, John, was killed while fighting royalist troops to regain Abingdon (Purkiss 2006, 303–4). After a whirlwind courtship, Susan Denton married Captain Jeremiah Abercromie, a Scots-Irish Covenanter and leader of the troop of dragoons whom Cromwell had dispatched from Newport to destroy her home (Calton 1994, 298; Purkiss 2006, 303; Brown 2007, 50). They were married in June 1644. Despite her family and friends' disapproval, Abercromie was a man of means, who even had substantial land in Ireland (Williams-Hay Verney 1892, 200). The Captain was also one of a handful of officers whom the House of Lords wanted to reinstate after the Self-Denying Ordinance. Although both a moderate and a Presbyterian, this Ulster officer also maintained close ties to Cromwell (Temple 1986). Whatever their misgivings, the Denton family accepted Abercromie after the wedding, but less than a year later he was killed by a scouting party from the nearby Royalist garrison at Boarstall. The Dentons dutifully buried Jeremiah in the churchyard at Hillesden.

Susan Abercromie (née Denton) lobbied to recover the £512.3s.2d which her husband had advanced the Parliamentary cause. By January 1647 she obtained a certificate from the Committee for Accounts for that sum, which she presented the following May in a petition to Parliament (CJ V, 174, 14 May 1647). The Commons ordered that the 'sum of three hundred pounds be paid unto Suzanna Abercromie, widow of the said Jeremiah, in her assigned in full satisfaction of all demands whatsoever, demandable upon said Captain Abercromie's entertainment in the service of the Parliament'. As was the practice for payments to widows and maimed soldiers, 'the sum of 300*l* [is to] be charged upon the Receipts of the Grand Excise in course together with interest for the same from the date hereof after the rate of eight per cent per annum payable every six months'. The Commons appointed John Goodwin to draft an ordinance for that purpose. In spite of their support of Captain Abercromie in 1645 the Lords would take another seven months to issue the annuity to his widow (LJ, IX: 580, 17 Dec. 1647, 602, 20 Dec. 1647). After entering the order they sent a copy to the *Committee for Improving and Regulating the Excise* (TNA CUST 109/14, f. 14b). Thirteen years later, Mrs Abercromie was listed in the Declared Accounts of the Excise Commissioners under the section marked 'annuities', as she was still receiving twice-annual interest payments of £12 (TNA E 351/1299, Declared Accounts, Excise Commissioners, 1659, 9; TNA E 351/1300, Declared Accounts, Excise Commissioners, 1660, 7). Despite the 'haircut' she accepted on the principal, Mrs Abercromie did rather well compared to other holders of common army pay warrants, who were unlikely to recover more than a couple of shillings in the pound.

What one widow had negotiated for herself on a small scale, 'smarter money' obtained on a larger one. In March 1648 the Commons settled, for £9,625 secured on the excise, a debt of £19,250 owed to a foursome led by Richard Turner (TNA CUST 109/14, f. 15a). In September 1642 Turner, a prominent member of the Common Council, along with citizen and Draper of London Maurice Gethin, Merchant Tailor and alderman of the City Tempest Milner, and goldsmith banker and nephew of the Lord Mayor Richard Wollaston, had, together with Turner's father, lent £27,927.15s.4d to Parliament for provisions to be sent to Ireland. In October 1643 this sum, as well as another £14,854.3s.4d (for a total of £40,051.18s.8d), had been secured by a parliamentary ordinance for the sequestration and sale of delinquent estates (CJ VI: 278–279, 27 Oct. 1643). Four sophisticated members of London's financial community thought it prudent to accept as settlement a life annuity worth less than half what they were owed. As with the Widow Abercromie, these men were in receipt of their annuity payments at the Restoration and into the 1660s. The alternative was to go to the back of the queue. In another instance, the Commons confirmed a debt at face value (for £2000) to Sir Charles Coote for his Irish campaigns, but ordered the excise commissioners to pay his warrant only 'after other assignments already charged shall be first satisfied' (TNA CUST 109/14, fo. 15b).

To summarise, the Long Parliament and Commonwealth employed a surprising array of debt instruments. Because of the extra-constitutionality and dubious legality of domestic commodity taxation and the necessity of satisfying creditors, most of these were short-term debt instruments, subject to repayment of the principal or capitalisation of the interest after a period of twenty-four months. Long-term debt instruments existed, but represented an insignificant portion of the total. Why did these annuities never number more than a few dozen, given their attractiveness to both parties and given their adoption after 1688? The answer points to additional modifications of the North and Weingast model.

Transparency, accountability, and the 'publike faith'

Parliamentary revenue committees were held accountable in two senses in the 1640s. First was through formal mechanisms of audit and oversight embedded in the redundant committee structure described above. Equally, however, Parliament was accountable to the public, and, as such, operated with a remarkable degree of transparency about public accounts. Moreover, in the absence of a legal system which permitted the sale of privileges that served to exempt individual subjects or citizens from taxation, as in Early Modern France, a regime that respects its creditors only to mistreat its taxpayers is apt to discover that they are the same people. The Long Parliament and Commonwealth regimes understood this, particularly with respect to their dealings with the London Common Council, and so handled complaints about the behaviour of revenue officials and committeemen alongside concerns about the creditworthiness of the regime, since the authorities regarded them as inextricably linked.

Those loyal to the regime were also eager to offer advice or their services as financial intermediaries. As early as August 1644, the Scriveners advertised a meeting of 'divers persons of quality' to advise Parliament on how 'just Debts may be secured, upon honourable and advantageous propositions, to the Parliament' (*It Is Thought Fit . . .* 1644). In the same advertisement, they encouraged 'all persons who have any Debts owing to them, by such who are with the King, do summe up a total thereof, without nominating either Debitor or Creditor' and send them to the Scriveners for inspection. The spectre of coordinated creditor action meant the regime had to tread carefully.

It is difficult to comprehend the workings of the committees without inspecting their minute books. The revenue committees often had dozens of members, but only a core group would sit regularly. In the case of the *Committee for Regulating the Excise*, the ten most active members handled over forty per cent of the 483 decisions in the period from November 1649 to May 1652 (Coffman 2013b). During the busiest periods it met daily; in the slower months, at least twice a week. The committee could, at any time, be called to account to a supervisory committee or to the Commons as whole. More often than not, the Commons simply required the committee to command the excise commissioners to submit their accounts for inspection or, in particularly contentious cases, to publish them in answer to popular printed polemics.

Given the deprivations of the Civil War and the fact that a significant portion of the population remained hostile, or at least neutral, towards the regime, it should come as no surprise that the voluminous output of hand presses complained bitterly about the hardships presented by all forms of parliamentary taxation. What made the complaints dangerous was not their scale (even the Smithfield Riot against the excise on flesh in 1647, which was the only large-scale disturbance, was limited to property damage and theft), but rather the difficulty in deciding if the disaffection stemmed from the fiscal exactions or from more generalised disapproval of the regime (Braddick 1991; Coffman 2008). Judging by the *Thomason Tracts* and related surviving material on *Early English Books Online*, there were hundreds of such attacks before the imposition of the *Treason Act* of May 1649, which made it a capital crime to argue that the 'government is tyrannical, usurped or unlawful' (McElligott 2007). Afterwards, specific complaints continued to appear, but they did not draw specific inferences about how such abuses reflected on the legitimacy of the regime. One pamphlet from a hand press written two days after the Smithfield Riot against the excise on flesh illustrates contemporary awareness of the unprecedented scale of war finance. The author reserved most of his disapprobation for the assessments, which were a direct tax, but presented an estimated total of £17,512,400 that he thought Parliament had extracted from the kingdom in four years. It was not lost on him that this exceeded the crown's annual revenues of £1,100,000 by a factor of more than four (*London's Account* ... 1647, 11).

In late June another pamphlet attacked the committees of the Associate Counties (Essex, Suffolk, Norfolk, Kent, Sussex, Surrey, Middlesex, and Hertfordshire) for arbitrary and illegal proceedings, but this time advanced the claim that heavy taxation had caused the author's sympathies to shift to the Royalist cause (*An Account* ... 1647a). If direct taxation could cause defections from the Parliamentary cause, then indirect taxation was the safer strategy. Royalist writers, emboldened by both the inability of the regime to censor criticism of the committees and the unwillingness of the army to intervene, took their polemic a step further. The conflicting loyalties of local elites could easily aggravate charges of hypocrisy, as was made plain by both the subtitle and the text of Samuel Sheppard's comedy *The Committeeman Curried* (1647). The play, which was almost certainly never performed (but was meant to mimic those performed in coffeehouses), also served as a protest against the continuing closure of the theatres (Wright 1934; Wiseman 1998). It was so popular that Sheppard published a follow-up in October. The gist of the plot involves the perfidy of the Committee-man called Suck-dry, who, with the assistance of an excise officer Common-curse and their clerks Sneake and Shallow-braines, plunders loyal citizens. His appetites unsated, he next compromises their wives.

Sexual libels, which owed their origins to classical republican rhetoric, were an especially favoured strategy (Rudolph 2000; McElligott 2004); likening the regime's fiscal appetites to sexual ones was not limited to the Royalist camp. The Leveller Richard Overton's anonymous pamphlet *Westminister Fayre, Newly Proclaimed* (1647) introduced 'the close committee-man that loves a W[hore]' (Wolfe 1958). In this tract the Devil was no worse than an excise-man or a sequestrator. After detailing the abuses, Overton told the targets of the vitriol that their 'wares were not worth a fart, for all your cogging', and promised them that the King and Army 'will cast you from your sphere, for dire aspects, that you have caused there'.

While it may be tempting to see these as marginal discourses, the authorities took such print polemics about the behaviour of the committees seriously, and were more than prepared to dignify them with thorough and thoughtful replies. As the relations between the Presbyterians and the Army degenerated over the summer, this became even more urgent. In a dramatic move, Giles Grene, MP for Weymouth and the man who brokered the repeal of the excises on flesh after the Smithfield Riot, published his twenty-three-page *Declaration in Vindication of the Honour of the Parliament* on 1 September 1647. On the title page he acknowledged his membership in the House of Commons. Grene produced for his readers a detailed account of Parliament's fiscal regime, including the contributions of the Customs, the Excise on Flesh and Salt, and receipts from prize goods. He took pains to collect the complaints of the regime's critics, and to answer them in turn. In his discussion of commodity taxation, for instance, he justified the distinction between 'necessaries' and 'superfluities', and defended the care and caution taken by the Customs Commissioners in developing the book of rates (Grene 1647, 12). Two days later, Henry Parker, the Observerator, published a systematic defence of excise taxation under the pseudonym Philo-Dicæus, entitled *The standard of equality, in subsidiary taxes and payments: or, a just and strong preserver of publick liberty* (Parker 1647), which answered systematically all manner of complaints, theoretical and practical, about the excise (Coffman 2008). In a similar vein, the petitions of the various companies of soap-makers, Parliament's reply, and the investigations of the *Committee for Regulating the Excise*, including detailed public accounts, were published under the Commonwealth in 1650 (Coffman 2013a).

Despite the tone of much of the Royalist polemic, which attacked the ruthlessness with which the regime confiscated the assets of its opponents, the revenue committees dealt assiduously with those taxpayers they judged to be loyal to the regime. The Committee for Regulating the Excise, for instance, followed common-law procedure in its dealings with the public, routinely allowed redemption of property seized for nonpayment of duty upon satisfaction of the fines (despite legislation permitting the state to sell the goods), granted habeas corpus to those who might be able to pay their debts if released from prison, and even took security, such as brewers' tools, as surety while nevertheless allowing the brewer to keep them for use in his trade (Coffman 2013b). The committee dealt far more mercilessly with the alleged misconduct of revenue officers, and constantly enjoined their excise commissioners to act 'for best advantage to the state', and to emphasise to their subordinates their 'publique service'.

The atmosphere of freedom of the press described by Murphy (2013) after the lapse of the Licensing Acts in the wake of the revolution might apply equally to the Interregnum. Although some of this material reflected widespread grievances, many of the pamphlets could be best characterised as projecting, punting, special pleading, or even careful management of print culture by the Parliamentary regime. For instance, Thomas Fauntleroy's pamphlet, *Lux in Teneberis. Or a Clavis to the Treasury in Broad-street* (1654) was a printed version of a scribal copy presented to the 'Treasury' (by which the author meant the London Office of the excise treasurer) in November 1653. In this tract Fauntleroy alleged abuses and oversights by the Commonwealth's excise sub-commissioners and recommended a tightening of accounting procedures. The incident gives every appearance of having been part of a successful patronage bid (as Fauntleroy became Clerk of the Pells from 1656 to 1658 after the re-establishment of the Exchequer), despite the fact that most of his claims do not withstand close scrutiny (Coffman 2013a). Instead, in this case, it was convenient to the Cromwellian regime to see them published.

It was, in fact, the Long Parliament's commitment to the 'publike faith' that made it difficult to reschedule the debt at a crucial moment in 1647. In January, a parliamentary report concluded that total remaining unpaid charges on the Grand Ordinance of the Excise stood at £398,211, exclusive of interest (Wheeler 1999, 153; Coffman 2008, 132). Another £400,000 for the payment of the Scots army had been charged on the Grand Excise, but secured by the pending sale of Episcopal lands (Habakkuk 1962, 70–88; Gentles 1980, 573–96). The London Common Council had refused to lend unless they obtained security of the principal on the sale of the Episcopal lands, and security for the interest on the receipts of the excise. Moreover, the excise ordinances would serve as secondary collateral for the principal if the sale of the Episcopal lands proved insufficient. This offer was credible enough to raise the initial £200,000 needed as a down payment to the Scots within the first eight days. The strategy of 'doubling' (often confused with the scheme for dual security) evolved in response to the success of the House of Commons in brokering the deal.

In an effort to clear the remaining debts on the excise, the Commons proposed to capitalise them (by securing the original principal and any interest owed on the Episcopal lands plus allowing another eight per cent in interest) in exchange for the lender agreeing to make an additional loan of the same amount of principal on the same terms of eight per cent (Gentles 1980, 574; Coffman 2008, 133). Under such a scheme, had Mrs Abercrombie been able to lend the regime another £512.3s.2d in January 1647, she would have received a new public faith bill (paying eight per cent per annum) for £1024.6s.4d secured on the excise, which she might have used to bid for land. Instead, she accepted a life annuity with a face of £300 paying the same interest. Inasmuch as Mrs Abercrombie lived at least another twenty years, and the principal reverted to her heirs upon her death, the net present value of her annuity was remarkably close to the original debt. Contemporaries were aware of this: two manuals appeared in 1647 which taught readers how to value annuities

(Johnson 1646; Webster 1647). Insofar as the Episcopal lands themselves earned rents, there would have been a steady revenue stream with which to service debt. Yet amidst the standoff between the Independents and the Presbyterians, there was no attempt to do so, despite calls from those like Sir Thomas Fairfax to use the rents from the Episcopal lands to pay the army (Coffman 2008, 133).

Instead, the effect of the 'doubling' was to release an additional £400,000 in short-term government paper into the London capital markets. According to one scholar, the majority of those holding public faith bills opted wisely to exercise their statutory right to bid for the land using the bills rather than to wait for the sale (Gentles 1980, 575). In principle, when the sales were complete, the cashiers would 'retire' any outstanding bills. As another scholar explained, this system created an incentive to redeem the bills for the land, because each land sale decreased the value of the remaining collateral (Habakkuk 1962, 72–3). As a consequence, a secondary market in government paper developed to discount the bills as the land sales progressed. Speculators bought up the remaining bills in order to redeem them for land (Gentles 1980, 594). Unsurprisingly, sixty-seven members of Parliament ended up with over a quarter of the lands. This scheme reduced government debt by £660,000 within the first two weeks (of which £400,000 represented retirement of the paper issued for the payment to the Scots and the balance debts charged on the excise). The auditors reported that only £17,502 of the total was actually received in cash, which was not even enough to cover the costs of actually administering the sales, which included surveying and valuation (Gentles 1980, 576). That was to take years. Meanwhile, the short-term success of this scheme proved its undoing.

While the land sales occurred, the excise commissioners were to service the eight per cent interest on these debts. The Commons tried to float another loan of £200,000 to disband the army, but the London Common Council refused, realising that the Episcopal lands (which were being liquidated via the adjudication of the bids made in January) were no longer good security for the debt. Their refusal hastened the end of the Presbyterian faction, and paved the way for the army's seizure of power (Coffman 2008, 135). Meanwhile, the excise (though cleared of some £250,000 in charges) was saddled with debt service on the £660,000 (which was owed until settlement occurred) in addition to charges still outstanding. The result was predictable. According to the Declared Accounts for 29 September 1647 to 29 September 1650, the commissioners paid £193,017 in interest on secured debt. This represented 22.4% of the £860,671 in declared revenue. Meanwhile, another

Table 4.1. *The realised value of land sales*

Property	Value	£ from Doubling	£ from Sales
Episcopal	£676,387	£320,000	£17,501
Capitular	£1,170,000	£455,621	£22,951
Royal	£1,434,000		£84,763
Fee-farm rents	£816,834	£288,031	£239,206
Royalist	£1,224,916	£604,934	£15,048

Source: Habakkuk 1962, 87.

£524,192 went to the army. Despite popular opposition, there was little choice but to renew the excise revenue ordinances yet again.

Even without the political crisis of 1647 and the resultant blow to receipts, it was doubtful that the regime could have disciplined itself to paying down the debt during the Second Civil War. As the Council of State's figures reveal, by October of 1649 'the whole charge therefore upon the receipts of the excise, besides the said 484,000 *l.* [which served as secondary collateral for loans originally rescheduled on the sale of the Episcopal lands], was £1,505,497.3s.7d½' (CSPD 1648–50, 358), almost five times the value of the previous year's excise receipts. The disposal of the Episcopal lands left the public finances in an even worse position, but knowledge of that did not deter the practice. As has been well documented, the sale of other seized lands fared little better (see Table 4.1).

The disposal of seized lands was less a financial decision than a political one. Much as the sale of monastic lands during the Henrician Reformation had generated support for ecclesiastical reform amongst the gentry, the Commonwealth land sales shored up support for the regime amongst those who might otherwise view it as illegitimate. The public faith bills, by virtue of the doubling and their higher denominations, traded at a premium in the market next to other types of government paper. Their price after discounting was commonly sixty to eighty per cent of face value, whereas military debentures and routine army pay warrants, which could be used to buy the crown lands, circulated for as little as twenty per cent of face. The losers were ordinary soldiers, whereas the winners were usually their officers, who bought the warrants, and then purchased lands in turn. The disposal of the Commonwealth regime's capital assets represented a transfer of wealth from the official losers (the bishops, the crown, and their Royalist allies) to the official winners of the Civil Wars, but the administration of the sales, although transparent, was far from equitable. It should come as no surprise, then, that there was little appetite for a proposal in 1652 to abolish all taxes and duties, and instead use the proceeds of the sale of the 'houses, lands, goods whatsoever, belonging to the nobility of Scotland, who have any ways aided or assisted their pretended King against England' (*A New Way. . . ;* 1652, 8). By the same token, plans to retire the public debt with the sale of Irish lands after the Revolution also failed to find traction. Instead, as Dickson and Macdonald have documented, life annuities became the Williamite regime's debt instrument of choice (Dickson 1967; Macdonald 2006).

To summarise, the Long Parliament and Commonwealth regimes operated under expectations of transparency and accountability, and maintained a stated commitment to maintaining the 'publike faith'. There were robust secondary markets with speculators as liquidity providers, and a vibrant print culture with unrelenting creditor action, but there was no Financial Revolution to follow the Fiscal Revolution of the 1640s and 1650s (Coffman 2008). Instead of rescheduling the public debt, the Long Parliament and Commonwealth regimes oversaw the liquidation of capital assets that could have easily generated revenues sufficient to service a long-term public debt. The Civil Wars and Interregnum generated the necessary pre-conditions for 'credible commitment', but fears of the impermanence and illegitimacy of the regime dogged efforts at financial restructuring. As Mauro *et al.* (2006) have shown for the later period, perception of political risk is the key determinant of investors' appetites for debt securities (see also Sussman and Yafeh, this volume).

Constitutional monarchies and bureaucratic states: model specifications

If convincing, these findings pose fundamental challenges to the account given by North and Weingast, whereas the Interregnum experience suggests something of the nature of the misspecification of their model. The problem lies in the tendency within their account to conflate regime structure and state structure, taking them as a single variable. Their framework also depends upon the ability to distinguish amongst executive, legislative, and judicial powers, which are taken to rest respectively with the sovereign and the prerogative courts, the houses of Parliament, and the common-law courts. For North and Weingast the game can be played most effectively when each side can anticipate *ex ante* what punishments *ex post* can and should be imposed upon those who violate the established set of rules (North and Weingast 1989, 808). The 'state' in their account is synonymous with the sovereign and the institutions and resources commanded by it.

For North and Weingast the sweet spot is the one which allows each type of institution to keep the others in check in the constitutional equivalent of rock–paper–scissors. As North and Weingast make clear, 'although parliamentary supremacy meant that Parliament dictated the form of the new political institutions, it did not assume the sole position of power within the government, as it did after the Civil War or in the nineteenth century' (1989, 816–17). Yet this 'separation of powers', so admired by Montesquieu in *The Spirit of the Laws* (1748), and so thoroughly enshrined in American jurisprudence today, is anachronistic by seventeenth- and early eighteenth-century standards. Understanding why is essential to identifying what is particular and even peculiar about the eighteenth-century British 'fiscal–military state'. It is not just, as North and Weingast argue, the constitutional arrangement between king and Parliament that undergoes another fundamental transformation in the early nineteenth century. The fiscal–military state itself did not survive the decades of peace that followed in the wake of the Napoleonic wars. Its gradual dismantling was accelerated by changes to the franchise in 1832; moreover, the emergence of laissez-faire doctrines that made both limited state interference in the economy, and little to no regulation of economic life, into normative ideals altered the nature of the game identified by North and Weingast. The result was not a predatory Parliament, but rather a Parliament that protected its own interests by shrinking the liberal state wherever possible.

The extent to which nineteenth-century Parliaments succeeded can be illustrated by an examination of total and per capita debt for the eighteenth and nineteenth centuries (see Figure 4.3). In 1815 both reached their 1690–1913 zenith, in nominal terms, and both declined thereafter. By the same token, and in keeping with North and Weingast's analysis of the 1690s and 1700s (1989, 823), this correlated with only moderate price inflation. From 1700 to 1815 the price level increased 2.5 to 3.5 times (depending upon whether RPI or CPI figures are used in the estimation), but it then remained stable, despite some volatility, until the outbreak of the First World War (Mitchell 1988).

Capturing the peculiarities of the eighteenth-century fiscal–military state requires a portrait of the constitutional framework more nuanced than that furnished by North and Weingast. To provide an alternative conceptualisation, it is necessary to unravel the use of the term 'state' in the late seventeenth century, which, in turn, is inextricably wrapped up in discourses about sovereignty, and in the historiography of that elusive phenomenon called 'absolutism'. North and Weingast understood the term very differently than historians did when they employed 'absolutism' as a term of art. For North and Weingast, 'absolutist monarchs' were

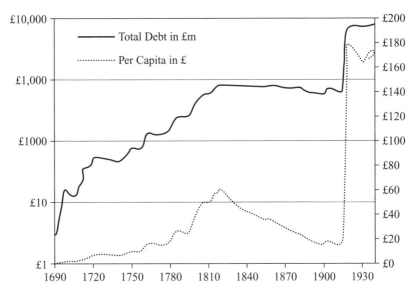

Figure 4.3. The public debt of Britain, 1690–1939 (nominal). *Source:* Mitchell 1988, 578–83.

free to disregard the law, to ignore constitutive assemblies, and to abuse the liberties of their subjects. This is a functionalist definition in which 'absolutists' are constrained in their view only by the practical limits of coercive power and the rational limits of predation. Yet that usage is both anachronistic and terminologically inaccurate and as such obscures the realities of Early Modern statecraft and state formation.

Contrary to what many students of the seventeenth century might suppose, 'absolutism' (as distinguished from 'absolute power' or even 'absolutist monarch') first entered the language of politics during the decade after the French Revolution. French writers wanted to characterise the political system of the *ancien régime*, and then subsequently to understand what was restored in 1815 (Burns 1990, 20–21). Naturally they looked to Jacques-Bénigne Bossuet's *Politics Derived from Holy Scripture* (1709), which had been written to instruct the dauphin, and its central claims that the king's power was absolute, paternal, sacred, and limited by reason as by 'fundamental law'.

Such a definition not only represented a particular strain of thought, but also was the product of a century of debate. Jean Bodin's theory of sovereignty, as articulated in *The Six Books of the Commonwealth* (1583), had contributed notions of 'absolute power' because, in Bodin's view, true sovereignty is absolute, perpetual, and indivisible, and involves, above all else, the power of rightful command. Bodin instructed his readers: 'the best expedient for preserving the state is never to grant a prerogative of sovereignty to any subject, much less a stranger, for it is a stepping stone to sovereignty'. In Bodin's analysis Polybian mixed monarchy (such as that of the English) could not be sovereign; the 'king-in-parliament' had delegated his prerogative sovereignty away. More importantly, Calvinist resistance theory (including that favoured by English Parliamentarians in the Civil Wars sixty years later) was a recipe for anarchy. Bodin thus made pains to distinguish legitimate royal monarchs from despots and tyrants, a distinction that turns on the ruler's power over his subject's private property. He stated unequivocally that the sovereign power of the prince would not ordinarily encroach upon the power of the *paterfamilias* in his own household, for what he was describing is a 'commonwealth, with sovereign power, of several households and of that which they have in common' (Bodin 1992). This much, at least, was consistent with how seventeenth-century Englishmen understood their own body politic, which North and Weingast identify as the expectation that a Tudor or early Stuart monarch 'live on his own' under ordinary circumstances. The conceptual 'manor of England' conferred legitimacy upon the raising of extraordinary revenues to fight wars to protect the kingdom or the true religion.

Sir Robert Filmer took up this analogy between the patriarchal authority of the *paterfamilias* and the fatherly power of kings in *Patriarcha* (1680) and *The Free-Holders Grand Inquest* (1648). Although Filmer's *Patriarcha* was not seen in print before 1680, it circulated in scribal form during the Interregnum. Coupled with Filmer's own thoughts on *The Anarchy of a Limited or Mixed Monarchy* (1648) and *The Necessity of the Absolute Rule of Kings* (1648), the emergence of absolute kingly power was seen as the apex of paternal power. The king was the father above other fathers, and Filmer believed that a sovereign could, theoretically, 'limit or assume the authority of inferior fathers for the public benefit of the commonwealth' (Filmer 1991, 228). As one modern scholar argues, proponents of divine-right theory of kingship, based in scripture on the maxim that 'God gives not Kings the style of Gods in vain, for on his throne his sceptre do they sway', could obtain added legitimacy in divinely ordained paternal authority (Burns 1990, 31). This is why Whig resistance theorists went to the trouble of refuting Filmer in the 1680s (Rudolph 2002) and why Whig historians of the nineteenth century imagined that their forefathers had triumphed over 'absolutism' in 1688.

A focus on how nineteenth-century Frenchmen read Bossuet and how seventeenth-century Englishmen read Bodin can obscure the confessional context for the advent of theories of absolute monarchy. Any such discussion must begin with Skinner's *Foundations of Modern Political Thought*. First published in 1978, his account has dominated the field for the past thirty-five years. His lasting influence owes as much to his revolutionary methodology, a strict contextualist approach which situates a text in its linguistic and ideological context via the explication of 'minor', noncanonical texts, as it does to his explicit claims. Although his narrative account is contestable, it offers a good beginning. Skinner explicitly tied 'absolutism' to the Lutheran Reformation. First, Luther denied the church's right to claim temporal authority in Christian society; second, he gave that worldly jurisdiction to princes, and made resistance to them resistance to the will of God. Religious conformity, in both Catholic and Protestant countries, became bound up in questions of political obedience. Toleration was possible only insofar as Catholics and Calvinists abjured any resistance theory that claimed the right to depose heretical kings. In the religious conflicts that followed, theorists such as Bodin became 'unyielding defenders of absolutism, demanding the outlawing of all theories of resistance and the acceptance of a strong monarchy as the only means of restoring political unity and peace' (Skinner 2000, II: 284).

Much like the Western Marxists who saw 'absolutism' as a stage between 'feudalism' and 'capitalism', Skinner's aim was not to take monarchical absolutism on its own terms, but to understand it as a transitional discourse – one that evolved into the modern concept of 'state'. His analysis of Bodin, Suarez, and even Bossuet served as a prelude to his reading of Thomas Hobbes, who offered an altogether different account of absolute sovereignty in his *Leviathan* (1651), one that created an artificial person in the 'state' and was not dependent upon the idea of monarchy. Although Hobbes saw the sovereign as bound by the laws of nature and the laws of God, he had no patience for schemes to limit sovereign power via paternal authority and fundamental law, or to shroud it in divine-right kingship. As Skinner concluded, 'the idea that the supreme authority within a body politic should be identified as the authority of the state was originally the outcome of a particular theory of politics, a theory [that of Hobbes] at once absolutist and secular-minded in its ideological allegiances' (Skinner 1989, 122). In Britain, as Skinner noticed, the Long Parliament adopted this usage in the decade before Hobbes elaborated it.

During the Civil Wars and Interregnum, Parliament used the abstraction of 'the state' to refer to the exercise of powers which, under other circumstances, were the preserve of the sovereign. The result was that contemporaries distinguished the 'state' from the 'publike' and saw the duty of Parliament to maintain the 'publike faith' and the 'publike credit'. Although references to the 'state' by the Crown, its servants, and

Parliament did not entirely disappear after the Stuart Restoration (and had currency especially within the growing Treasury establishment), the usage receded only to be reasserted after 1688. In Skinner's account, the period from 1648 to 1789 was one during which this idea spread to continental Europe and fanned the radical Enlightenment. Around 1750,

The immediate outcome of this conceptual revolution was to set up a series of reverberations in the wider political vocabularies of the western European states. Once 'state' came to be accepted as the master noun of the political argument, a number of other concepts and assumptions bearing on the analysis of sovereignty had to reorganized or in some cases be given up. (Skinner 1989, 123)

This account differs dramatically from that proposed by North and Weingast. In the new model, 'public finance' becomes possible when a century-long contest between crown and Parliament over the supply of the revenue gets reformulated into terms of a state which raises tax revenues to service the public debt, thereby maintaining the public faith and ensuring the public credit. The Civil Wars and Interregnum provide a dress rehearsal for this conceptual shift. The mid-century experiment in England failed because persistent and widespread fears of both regime change and renewed civil strife limited the state's capacity to borrow from the public, and made it necessary to dispose of capital assets to buy support for the regime. By preserving the institution of the monarchy in 1689, Parliament sidestepped the problems encountered in the 1640s and 1650s about where to locate executive power after deposing a king. In that respect North and Weingast are correct that parliamentary supremacy did not mean parliamentary rule (1989, 816, 818). Yet in reality, by allowing a foreign prince to use England and Wales as a tax province, the English Parliament settled the constitution. That bargain, in turn, served to aggrandise the British fiscal–military state in proportion to William's revenue requirements, a process that continued more or less unabated until 1815.

The British state, in a historical and ideological sense, evolved out of the need to develop a political language that abstracted sovereign power so that it was not dependent on a particular type of rule. Once established as a discursive category, the state was taken to be transcendental. In a practical sense, the bureaucratic state developed independence from the crown, and from Parliament, as successive rulers became dependent upon taxation and public borrowing to finance the increasing scale and scope of warfare. All of this adds up to a much different specification of the 'evolution of the constitutional arrangements in seventeenth-century England' both before and after the Glorious Revolution (North and Weingast 1989, 803), and points to a different genesis of 'credible commitment'.

It is not sufficient to categorise the relationship between post-Revolutionary 'institutions' and 'government' as that of 'limited monarchy' or 'parliamentary supremacy'. Crown and Parliament were integral parts of an increasingly permanent British state. What public creditors needed was evidence of both the state's *willingness* and its *ability* to pay. The evidence that was missing in the summer of 1647 was *ex ante* expectations of domestic peace, political stability, and the continuity of the state amidst potential changes in either the person of the sovereign or the faction in control of government. As Macdonald (2006) has shown, however, a great irony underpins this story. Had the London Common Council and the army been content to receive callable life annuities collateralised by the rents for seized lands, rather than funded through their sale, in exchange for monies advanced and remuneration owed, they would have been in a position to coerce the regime to honour commitments which had the force of common law. In this respect the Widow Abercromie's investment in the Parliamentary regime, and the subsequent commitment of the Restoration regime to her, was a harbinger of things to come.

Key to references

CJ:	Journal of the House of Commons
CSPD:	Calendar of State Papers Domestic
LJ:	Journal of the House of Lords
TNA CUST:	National Archives, Customs and Excise Series
TNA E:	National Archives, Exchequer

References

A New Way, to Pay Old Debts . . . 1652. London.

An Account of the Arbitrary, Exactions, Taxations, Impositions . . . 1647. London.

Ashley, Maurice 1962. *Financial and Commercial Policy under the Cromwellian Protectorate*, 2nd edn. London: Frank Cass & Co. Ltd.

Bodin, Jean 1992. *On Sovereignty*. Cambridge Texts in the History of Political Thought. Edited and translated from the French by Julian Franklin. Cambridge University Press.

Braddick, Michael J. 1991. 'Popular Politics and Public Policy: the Excise Riot at Smithfield in February 1647 and Its Aftermath', *Historical Journal*, 24, 597–626.

Braddick, Michael J. 1994. *Parliamentary Taxation in Seventeenth-Century England: Local Administration and Response*. Woodbridge: Boydell Press.

Braddick, Michael J. 1996. *The Nerves of State: Taxation and the Financing of the English State, 1558–1714*. Manchester University Press.

Braddick, Michael J. 2000. *State Formation in Early Modern England*. Cambridge University Press.

Brewer, John 1990. *Sinews of Power: War, Money and the English State, 1688–1783*. Harvard University Press.

Brown, John 2007. *John Bunyan: His Life, Times and Works*. London: Kessinger Publishing.

Burns, J. H. 1990. 'The Idea of Absolutism', in John Miller (ed.), *Absolutism in Seventeenth-Century Europe*. New York: St Martin's Press.

Calton, Charles 1994. *Going to the Wars: The Experience of the British Civil Wars, 1638–1651*. London: Routledge.

Chandaman, C.D. 1975. *The English Public Revenue 1660–1688*. Oxford: Clarendon Press.

Coffman, D'Maris 2008. *The Fiscal Revolution of the Interregnum: Excise Taxation in the British Isles, 1643–1663*. Ph.D. Thesis, University of Pennsylvania.

Coffman, D'Maris 2010. 'The Earl of Southampton and the Lessons of Interregnum Public Finance', in David Smith and Jason McElligott (eds.), *Royalists and Royalism during the Interregnum*. Manchester University Press.

Coffman, D'Maris 2013a. *Excise Taxation and the Origins of the Public Debt*. Basingstoke: Palgrave Macmillan.

Coffman, D'Maris 2013b. 'Towards a New Jerusalem: The Committee for Regulating the Excise, 1649–1653'. *English Historical Review*, 128: 535.

Dickson, Peter G. M. 1967. *The Financial Revolution in England: A Study in the Development of Public Credit, 1688–1765*. New York: St. Martin's Press.

Fauntleroy, Thomas 1654. *Lux in Teneberis. Or a Clavis to the Treasury in Broad-Street*. London.

Filmer, Sir Robert 1991. *Patriarcha and Other Writings*. Edited and translated by J. P. Somerville. Cambridge University Press.

Gentles, Ian. 1980. 'The Sales of Bishops' Lands in the English Revolution, 1646–1660', *English Historical Review*, 95, 573–96.

Grene, Giles 1647. *Declaration in Vindication of the Honour of the Parliament*. London.

Habakkuk, H. J. 1962. 'Public Finance and the Sale of Confiscated Property during the Interregnum', *Economic History Review*, 15, 70–88.

Hurstfield, Joel 1955. 'The Profits of Fiscal Feudalism, 1541–1602', *Economic History Review*, 8, 53–61.

It Is Thought Fit by Divers Persons of Quality . . . 1644. London.

Johnson, John 1646. *Johnsons Arithmetick . . .* London.

London's Account: or, A Calculation of the Arbitrary and Tyrannical Exactions, Taxations, Impositions, Excises, Contributions, etc. 1647. London.

Macdonald, James 2006. *A Free Nation Deep in Debt: The Financial Roots of Democracy*. New York: Farrar, Straus and Giroux.

Mauro, Paolo; Sussman, Nathan; and Yafeh, Yishay 2006. *Emerging Markets and Financial Globalization: Sovereign Bond Spreads in 1870–1913 and Today*. Oxford University Press.

McElligott, Jason 2004. 'The Politics of Sexual Libel: Royalist Propaganda in the 1640s', *Huntingdon Library Quarterly*, 67, 75–99.

McElligott, Jason 2007. *Royalism, Print and Censorship in Revolutionary England*. London: The Boydell Press.

Mitchell, Brian R. (ed.) 1988. *British Historical Statistics*. Cambridge University Press.

Murphy, Anne L. 2013. 'Demanding 'Credible Commitment': Public Reactions to the Failures of the Early Financial Revolution', *Economic History Review*, 66, 178–97.

North, Douglass C. and Weingast, Barry 1989. 'Constitutions and Commitment: The Evolution of Institutions Governing Public Choice in Seventeenth-Century England', *Journal of Economic History*, 43, 803–32.

O'Brien, Patrick K. 1988. 'The Political Economy of British Taxation, 1660–1815', *Economic History Review*, 50, 1–32.

O'Brien, Patrick K. and Hunt, Philip A. 1999. 'Excises and the Rise of a Fiscal State in England' in Mark Ormrod, Margaret Bonney, and Richard Bonney (eds.), *Crises, Revolutions and Self-Sustained Growth: Essays in European Fiscal History*. Stamford: Shaun Tyas.

Parker, Henry (pseud. Philo-Dicæus) 1647. *The Standard of Equality, in Subsidiary Taxes and Payments: or, A Just and Strong Preserver of Publick Liberty*. London.

Purkiss, Diane 2006. *The English Civil War: Papists, Gentlewomen, Soldiers, and Witchfinders in the Birth of Modern Britain*. London: Basic Books.

Roberts, Clayton 1977. 'The Constitutional Significance of the Financial Settlement of 1690', *Historical Journal*, 20, 59–76.

Roseveare, Henry 1969. *The Treasury: The Evolution of a British Institution*. London: Allen Lane.

Roseveare, Henry 1991. *The Financial Revolution, 1660–1760*. London: Longman.

Rudolph, Julia 2000. 'Rape and Resistance: Women and Consent in Seventeenth-Century English Legal and Political Thought', *Journal of British Studies*, 39, 157–84.

Rudolph, Julia 2002. *Revolution by Degrees: James Tyrrell and Whig Political Thought in the Late Seventeenth Century*. New York: Palgrave Macmillan.

Schumpeter, Joseph A. 1954. 'The Crisis of the Tax State', *International Economic Papers*, 4, 5–38.

Scott, Jonathan 2000. *England's Troubles: Seventeenth-Century English Political Instability in European Context*. Cambridge University Press.

Scott, Jonathan 2003. '"Good Night Amsterdam". Sir George Downing and Anglo-Dutch Statebuilding', *English Historical Review*, 118, 334–57.

Scroggs, William O. 1907. 'English Finances under the Long Parliament', *Quarterly Journal of Economics*, 21, 463–87.

Sheppard, Samuel 1647. *The Committee-Man Curried. A Comedy...* London.

Sheppard, Samuel 1647. *The Second Part of The Committee-Man Curried. By the First Author, S.S.* London.

Skinner, Quentin 1989. 'The State', in Terence Ball, James Farr, and Russell B. Hanson (eds.). *Political Innovation and Conceptual Change*. Cambridge University Press.

Skinner, Quentin 2000. *Foundations of Modern Political Thought*, vol. 2. Cambridge University Press.

Stasavage, David 2003. *Public Debt and the Birth of the Democratic State: France and Great Britain, 1688–1789*. Cambridge University Press.

Storr, Christopher (ed.) 2009. *The Fiscal-Military State in Eighteenth-Century Europe. Essays in Honour of P.G.M. Dickson*. Farnham: Ashgate.

Temple, Robert K. G. 1986. 'The Original Officer List of the New Model Army', *Historical Research*, 59, 50–77.

't Hart, M.C. 1991. '"The Devil or the Dutch": Holland's Impact on the Financial Revolution England, 1643–1694', *Parliaments, Estates and Representation*, 11, 39–52.

Webster, William 1647. *Websters Tables, for Interest Direct and to Rebate . . .* London.

Westminster Fayre, Newly Proclaimed 1647. London.

Wheeler, James Scott 1999. *The Making of a World Power: War and the Military Revolution in Seventeenth Century England*. Stroud: Sutton Publishing.

Williams-Hay Verney, Margaret Maria 1892. *Memoirs of the Verney Family*, vol. 2. London: Longmans.

Wilson, Charles H. 1964. *England's Apprenticeship, 1603–1763*. London: Longman.

Wiseman, Susan 1998. *Drama and Politics in the English Civil War*. Cambridge University Press.

Wolfe, Don M. 1958. 'Unsigned Pamphlets of Richard Overton, 1641–1649', *Huntington Library Quarterly*, 21, 167–201.

Wright, Louis 1934. 'The Reading of Plays during the Puritan Revolution', *Huntington Library Bulletin*, 6, 73–108.

5   Jurisdictional controversy and the credibility of common law

Julia Rudolph[1]

On Thursday, 27 May 1725, Lord Chancellor Thomas Parker, Earl of Macclesfield, was impeached from office. His removal was the culmination of a trial that had occupied the House of Lords for most of the month. The Lords sat for thirteen full days, presided over by their speaker, Peter King, to consider twenty-one articles of impeachment brought before them by the managers of the House of Commons (*Journal of the House of Lords* 1725, 1–10). Prominent among the accusations against the disgraced Lord Chancellor were charges of extortion, abuse of trust, encouragement of risky investment with court funds by his subordinates, and orchestration of a cover-up when such investment led to embezzlement, culminating in a program of perjury and deceit. The Lords' verdict against Macclesfield was extensive and unanimous. He was found guilty of 'taking of several of the Masters in *Chancery* very great and exorbitant Sums of Money, for their Admission into their respective Offices' (Salmon 1737, 874). Moreover, it was found that Macclesfield not only frequently sold the office of Chancery master, but also allowed unfit men – men who could not afford the price of office – to pay for their places out of suitors' assets held by their predecessors in office. It was the revelation that some of these masters had speculated with suitors' monies in the hopes of making up the difference in their suitors' accounts (as well as enriching themselves) that led to the initial investigations. When these masters' accounts suffered losses because of failed investments, caused especially by the bursting of the South Sea Bubble, Lord Chancellor Macclesfield tried to conceal the problem. He sought to make up the missing monies out of other masters' funds as a way to

[1] This essay is drawn, with some modification, from a chapter in my book, *Common Law and Enlightenment in England, 1689–1750* (Boydell & Brewer, 2013). I'd like to extend special thanks here to one of my series editors, Stephen Taylor, for his willingness to share with me some manuscript materials relating to the Macclesfield impeachment. Thanks, too, to the organisers and participants involved in the 'Questioning "Credible Commitment" Conference' for their stimulating questions and comments.

prevent an enquiry (Howell 1812, 778–79, 1070, 1074–80; Holdsworth 1938, 206; Heward 1983, 46–48).

The enquiry was launched, and the trial ensued. The wider controversy of 1725–7 revolved around varying interpretations of commercial and financial change. In the course of debate a sharp contrast was drawn between the flexibility of Chancery law, where equity fostered the development of new credit practices, and the stability and certainty of common law. In light of crisis and scandal common law came to be especially valued, because it was seen to promote the kind of security of property rights necessary for lasting economic prosperity and positive commercial growth.

Scandal might have been avoided, and the Chancery masters' scheme might have worked, if their investment of suitors' fees and assets had been successful. But the underlying fraud that fuelled the sale of office was exposed when more suitors sought to reclaim their monies than could be accommodated by the existing assets in the masters' accounts (Heward 1983, 50). Indeed, calculations regarding deficiencies in the accounts, and payments directed to make up the funds, continued after the trial (CUL Cholmondeley [Houghton] MS 65 29 fol. 3). The general economic and political crisis caused by losses suffered in the South Sea Bubble is clearly an important context for this particular crisis in Chancery. In the aftermath of the market crash there were calls for vengeance against corrupt ministers, duplicitous company directors, and other well-placed men who had profited from speculating in the market before the bubble burst. Macclesfield was not accused of illicit speculation himself. He had purchased South Sea stocks in the third subscription of June 1720 at the peak of the bubble, and authorised the sale of his stock in August 1723 when prices had already fallen, so it is not clear that he aimed to 'ride the bubble' (Carswell 1960, 161; FLP Carson Collection Letters, Form for the Sale or Transfer of Stock DS 27 Aug. 1723). However, he became an emblem of such greed, gambling, and deceit. Since he had already resigned from the chancellorship in early January 1724/5, impeachment was seized upon as a way for opponents to embarrass Whig ministers. It was also a way for those ministers to restore public confidence, and, by offering up a scapegoat, to preserve their own power.

Macclesfield's impeachment demonstrates the impact of a major political event that was plainly intended to reassure a public anxious about the financial probity and fiscal responsibility of their governors. Part of an effort to rebuild trust in public institutions and financial markets after the South Sea crisis, Macclesfield's fall helped to persuade investors that it was again safe to participate in the stock market, and even to commit capital to the state. One significant reason that the impeachment could have this effect was that it was tied to a broader process of law reform and institutional change. After this scandal the Bank of England took on an enhanced role in its relationship with Chancery: whenever masters deposited suitors' monies and securities at the Bank of England, the records of these transactions were to be held at the Bank, as well as at the Chancery Report Office. Most importantly, all interest on these securities was also deposited at the Bank, and recorded in the masters' books there. Subsequent legislation established a new financial–judicial office, the Accountant-General of the Court of Chancery, in whose name all cash and securities were to be held. This put even greater distance between the masters and their suitors' funds (Heward 1983, 52–3; Carlos and Neal 2006, 503). All of these innovations were tied to an insistence upon procedural regularity and effective administration. These changes signalled legal adaptability in the face of commercial change, and in response to new financial instruments and institutions in early eighteenth-century England. Such responsibility and adaptability fostered public trust.

The crisis in Chancery equally indicates the influence of jurisdictional controversy in eighteenth-century England. Macclesfield's trial was one among many disputes regarding the proper relationship between common law and equity, and it stimulated jurisprudential debate about what kind of law provided stronger protections and surer justice. In the course of debate those essential ideas about the benefits of common-law tradition and stability were articulated. Special emphasis was placed on the law's effectiveness in protecting the security of property rights, and this too helped to engender public trust.

These kinds of debates about the balance of authority between common law and equity had long been a familiar feature of English legal and political discourse. Jurisdictional controversies had emerged as early as the fifteenth century, not long after the Chancellor had begun to exercise judicial power in his court. The Chancellor was tasked with administering justice according to reason and conscience; he acted on principles of natural law with the end of fulfilling the just intentions of common law. In Chancery, equity offered new kinds of remedies where the rigidity of common law – with its closed system of Latin writs and formalised pleading in Law French – meant either that new problems could not be dealt with at common law, or that the common law would produce an unjust result. Chancery's jurisdiction had expanded, and a body of equitable doctrine had developed, between the sixteenth and the eighteenth century. At the same time, however, common-law courts such as King's Bench and Common Pleas competed with Chancery for business, and conflicts arose over just how far the authority exercised by an equitable judge such as the Chancellor should extend (Horwitz 1998, 40; Horwitz 1999, 168–9; Baker 2002, 100–111). Such conflicts and expansion actually strengthened both jurisdictions.

One area of conflict was trust doctrine. In the creation of a trust agreement, ownership of property was transferred at common law to the trustee. However, because that ownership was meant to be exercised for the good of the beneficiary of the trust, English law slowly came to recognise that the beneficiary had an equitable estate in, or beneficial ownership of, the trust. Although common law could only recognise the fact of property transfer and trustee ownership, the trustee's obligations and the beneficiary's ownership came to be protected by the law of equity in Chancery (Baker 2002, 250–57). Yet serious questions arose concerning this enforcement of trustee obligation. If a trustee was recognised as lawful owner, could the reason and conscience of a single chancellor override, and potentially erode, the legality and stability of a common law of property? These kinds of conflicts stimulated jurisprudential reflection on the nature of law and of justice, and helped to provide credibility to the common law not only as a vehicle for protecting property rights, but also as a critical component of responsible economic development.

One important reason that these jurisdictional and jurisprudential disputes persisted in eighteenth-century England was that new problems arose for the courts to address as a result of broad and rapid economic change. Such change was, of course, related to longer-term economic trends: the expansion of long-distance trade, the growth of international and domestic markets, and the employment of financial instruments such as bills of exchange, mortgages, and annuities. These had been evolving since the sixteenth century (Neal 1990; Muldrew 1998), but the late seventeenth and early eighteenth saw the beginning of a period of a dramatically increased rate of growth in public finance. After 1689 the creation of a national debt, of the Bank of England, and of means of state funding through new kinds of long- and short-term loans presented new challenges for the common law. These changes had serious implications for the courts' role in maintaining established protections for the security of property (North and Weingast 1989; Rogers 1995; Banner 1998; Harris 2004, 208–11, 225–30). This was also the beginning of a period of advances in private finance, a period in which there was greater popular awareness of, and greater diffusion of popular participation in, financial practices (Hoppit 1990, 305–22; Neal 1990, 10; Harris 2000, 53–9; Glaisyer 2006; Murphy 2009). The expansion of both the stock market and private investment was significant in stimulating the growth of new kinds of financial instruments, for example, and of new kinds of contractual expectations. These too had a real impact on the way in which English law negotiated the experience of change. As new issues came before the courts, and new remedies developed in common law and equity, jurisdictional conflicts sometimes emerged.

Early eighteenth-century judges and lawyers grappled with the consequences of these new market practices. In the process many of them made arguments on behalf of common-law stability and the authority of tradition, but now their conception of common law justice developed in new ways, in conjunction with contemporary ideological debate about commercial and financial innovation. These economic and jurisprudential debates were part of broader enlightened philosophical trends, affected by contemporary investigation into the moral-philosophical implications of economic change. In Macclesfield's impeachment trial, for example, several participants, including the Earl himself, were deeply engaged with arguments about human appetites, sentiment, and sensibility which stood at the centre of enlightened moral-philosophical debate (Quarrie 2004, 8–9, 11–16; Quarrie 2006, 8–13; Hanham 2009). Some, such as Speaker Peter King – who was also Chief Justice of the Common Pleas at this time – and Master of the Rolls Joseph Jekyll were notably active in the eighteenth-century movement for moral reform (Foss 1864, 32, 130–31, 157; Clark 1988, 75–7; Hayton 1990, 55, 61, 66, 72, 81; White 2003, 40). In Jekyll's and others' legal arguments against Macclesfield the concerns of the campaigns for moral reform became intertwined with arguments about financial innovation concerning, for example, the dangerous volatility of markets or the ephemeral nature of credit and trust.

There was also a specifically gendered aspect of these discussions, because concerns about women's engagement in commercial society as consumers, investors, and property-owners were another significant focus of contemporary debate. Anger was directed at the Lord Chancellor for his failure to protect female suitors' interests: those women who came to Chancery for protection where common law failed them, critics complained, were left violated and exposed. Macclesfield's guilt was here construed as a failure of male honour, and his corruption was described as a kind of venality equal to the violation of women's bodies. Finally, this gendered perception of corruption helped to foster an ongoing scepticism about legal doctrine regarding the equitable law of trusts, which contributed to the reaffirmation of the authority, stability, and justice of common law.

The critique of Macclesfield, then, was a critique of equity, and of Chancery's authority over these new commercial and financial trends. In the course of the trial the benefits of common-law tradition came to be aligned with morality and the public good. Such jurisprudential developments, understood in these cultural and philosophical terms, help to explain changes in legal doctrine and practice in this period. Further, attention to these jurisprudential developments helps us to gain a fuller appreciation of the complex ways in which English common law contributed to economic growth. The credibility of common law – even more than 'parliamentary supremacy', 'political liberties', or other elements of North and Weingast's conception of 'credible commitment' – was an essential factor in Britain's political and economic success.

The endorsement of common-law justice was notable from the start of Macclesfield's trial. Prosecutors defined their central charge, extortion, or the sale of office, as 'an Offence at the Common Law, and punishable by Fine and Imprisonment' (Salmon 1737, 880). Evidence of this common-law offense was first shown to be rooted in general custom and prescriptive example: accepted practice indicated that it was illegal to appoint 'subordinate Officers for Gift or Brocage' and, more broadly, illegal to accept gifts or payment for performing other official functions. 'The ancient Law of *England*', the Commons' managers insisted, 'was that none having any Office concerning the Administration of Justice, should take any Fee or reward of any Subject for the doing of his Office, to the End he might be free, and at Liberty to do Justice' (Salmon 1737, 879). Second, charters and statutes of former kings – the two most important examples being *12 Richard II c. 2* (1388) and *5&6 Edward VI c.16* (1552) – were adduced as confirmation of this custom, providing an 'additional Constraint or Obligation upon the superior Officer, by an oath not to commit the Offence' (Salmon 1737, 880). A good deal of legal debate revolved around the interpretation of these statutes, even though the prosecution maintained that Macclesfield's actions constituted a violation of common law whether or not he took the oath 'against buying and selling of offices' that was prescribed in such legislation (Salmon 1737, 880; Howell 1812, 1107–8).

One important point at issue here was the proper status of Chancery personnel, because the definition of Chancery masterships as judicial rather than ministerial offices was at the heart of the charge of corruption. The blurring between ministerial and judicial office had long been a feature of English governance, and it was further complicated by the identification between office and property. Tradition held that an office such as a mastership, or the chancellorship, was a species of property enjoyed by the officeholder (Peck 1990, 162–7). This was a tradition rooted in medieval law; however, it also raised questions about undue interest and venality, and was easily harnessed to polemical images of suspect French-style judicial practices.

Macclesfield's defence counsellors were aware of these traditions, and sought to exploit their useful ambiguities. For instance, the defence did define the Earl's right to nominate men to office as a species of property, and then strongly endorsed each man's 'natural right to dispose of his own estate or interest, his own friendship or favour, upon what consideration he pleases: it is his own and therefore he has a right to make any just and legal advantage of it' (Howell 1812, 1087–8). Such arguments were aimed to associate Macclesfield's actions with principles of natural justice and, even more, with the defence of property interests and stability, which was a key common-law theme. Macclesfield's adherence to custom and common law was further underscored by one of his advocates, the civilian lawyer Exton Sayer, in an explication of the relationship between custom and nature. Sayer reminded the Lords that the Chancellor was not accused of selling favourable verdicts, which was a clear violation of natural law, but simply of selling offices or places according to custom:

My Lords, the writers upon the law of nature have properly distinguished between selling justice, and offices concerning the administration of justice . . . With them the selling [of] justice is absolutely forbid, is absolutely corrupt and immoral. The selling [of] offices is [a] matter of mere policy, varied in different governments, prohibited in some, allowed in others. (Howell 1812, 1109)

Examples of such policies from different nations and different times were given to demonstrate the variability and historicity of custom (Howell 1812, 1088, 1364). The justice of Macclesfield's actions was a justice of common law, founded in prescription, reason, and legislation; the sale of masterships was prescriptive practice, illuminated by exemplary cases and consonant with natural justice.

Here, as elsewhere, Lord Chancellor Macclesfield's defence counsel argued from precedent and ancient usage, and denied that the sale of office was a violation of common law. Indeed, both Sayer and the principal counsellor for the defence, Serjeant Probyn, depicted the Lord Chancellor as unfairly singled out, because all Macclesfield had done was to follow the practice of 'the many great and learned persons who executed this high office before him' (Howell 1812, 1090, 1131). Probyn and Sayer then introduced testimony regarding the purchase of masterships under Macclesfield's immediate predecessors, Lord Chancellors Harcourt and Cowper. Indeed, Serjeant Probyn insisted that the practice of selling offices was sanctioned, in the language of the common law, by reference to 'time immemorial', explaining that 'The precedent is too ancient for us to discover when it was first made, and I humbly submit it to your lordships, that the immemorial, constant usage and practice of it in all ages since, will sufficiently establish the reasonableness and justice of the precedent' (Salmon 1737, 875, 879; Howell 1812, 1090; Holdsworth 1938, 206). Defence counsel John Strange asserted that any interpretation of relevant statutes regarding office-holding must also take into account this matter of ancient and constant usage, and Sayer added in his statement that witnesses could testify to that constant 'opinion and practice of the Earl's predecessors' (Howell 1812, 1108, 1133–4; Aylmer 1980). Such common opinion based on prescriptive practice, he explained, must be acknowledged as more authoritative than statute, and as constitutive of justice.

The Lord Chancellor was here depicted as an adherent of custom more than conscience. The conventional image of the Chancellor as guardian of natural law, concerned with universal justice that would 'fix' or 'fulfil' common law, was noticeably absent from both defence and prosecution claims about justice and right. For example, this emphasis on prescription and precedent also informed arguments meant to justify Macclesfield's failure to respond to contemporary crises in economy and law. Participants acknowledged that procedural reforms were long over-due in the court of Chancery. The business of the court had grown, they concluded, and the sums of money administered by Chancery masters had also increased, so that past practice was now insufficient for cur-rent circumstances. Yet defence counsel insisted that it would have been imprudent, if not impossible, for Macclesfield as a single Chancellor to effect such reforms because, in Serjeant Probyn's words, 'the ancient practice of every court is the law of that court; and it would be a dan-gerous experiment for any one presiding judge to vary it'. Probyn added the dictum that 'He that acts without a precedent, acts upon the peril of his own judgment' – another clear contrast to the usual image of the independent judgment of a Lord Chancellor (Howell 1812, 1093).

Although the usual image of the Chancellor as 'unfettered conscience' is largely absent from this trial, the prosecution did articulate conven-tional complaints against an 'arbitrary chancellor'. Here is another indi-cation that particular disputes about office and corruption in this trial were part of a wider engagement with jurisdictional controversy. In Mac-clesfield's trial the prosecution drew upon some notorious images and inflammatory arguments in order to reanimate an old association between a powerful Lord Chancellor and the dangers of arbitrary rule. For exam-ple, the twenty-first article of impeachment, charging that Macclesfield 'suspended' and 'dispensed' with law, clearly employed the language of Stuart tyranny (Howell 1812, 782). This language and these kinds of associations were also apparent in the prosecution's suggestion that the Lord Chancellor aimed at reviving the court of wards, and finally in the insinuations made about Macclesfield's suspected Jacobitism (and here, some did add, the sale of judicial offices must be seen as a French-absolutist practice too) (Wilson 1727, 57, 62; Howell 1812, 782–3).

Such arguments are an indication that this trial served as another venue for the contest over claims to 'Revolution Principles' between opposition and court Whigs. Framing this impeachment trial as an episode in the longer history of jurisdictional conflict between Chancery and the common-law courts, and between tyranny and the demands of 'National Justice', had a clear resonance and jurisprudential value (NLW Longueville 1187, fols. 7–8; Hoppit 2002, 159–60). In response to these tactics, Macclesfield highlighted his own part in the preservation of common law during the years he had spent at King's Bench as successor to the respected Chief Justice John Holt. Many were reminded, too, of his early successes in defending the liberty of the Whig printer John Tutchin, and in impeaching the Tory minister Henry Sacheverell, in those celebrated trials (Salmon 1737, 577; Howell 1812, 1086, 1322; Horsely 1973).

The fact that both defence and prosecution laid claim to Revolution Principles, to the traditions of the ancient constitution and the continuity of English liberties, is further proof that this trial was bound up with contemporary debate over that key result of 1688, the financial revolution. The pursuit of a modern, commercial, market-driven, and debt-ridden society was at the heart of domestic and foreign policy under Whig government in the early eighteenth century. In this new context commentators began to develop new arguments and ideas: they offered optimistic claims about the nature of human appetite and the role of human passion in social development, as well as more pessimistic critiques of the corrupting effects of prosperity. This was a moment when moral-philosophical debate intensified and multiplied, a time of sociological and republican discourse, when the ideas of men such as Fenelon, Mandeville, Shaftesbury, and Hutcheson circulated widely. Macclesfield's trial was influenced by a powerful contemporary discourse about luxury, avarice, and credit.

Attention to the work of Bernard Mandeville within these debates about luxury and public virtue is particularly important to the analysis of Macclesfield's impeachment, first because of the close association between the two men. The Lord Chancellor was a friend and patron of the physician–philosopher: Macclesfield owned at least one of Mandeville's books and likely read others; Mandeville was a frequent and witty companion at the Earl's dinner table; the two men enjoyed intimate conversation and correspondence (Mandeville 1924, xxvi–xxvii; Sotheby's 2006, 262, 344). Their relationship should be viewed as one among several indications of Macclesfield's engagement with contemporary philosophical discussion. Indeed, the Lord Chancellor was also a recognised patron of other intellectuals, including Edmond Halley, Isaac Newton, and William Jones, and even of 'freethinkers' such as John Toland and

Pierre Desmaizeaux (Quarrie 2006, 8–13; Hanham 2009). It thus came as no surprise to eighteenth-century observers that suspect philosophical commitments and controversial associations or friendships emerged as issues in the trial.

Bernard Mandeville is especially relevant to understanding the impeachment, second, because *The Fable of the Bees*, his notorious defence of vice as conducive to the public good, was published in its extended and most provocative version in 1723, shortly before Macclesfield's troubles began (Horne 1978, 33; Hont 2006, 387, 395). Mandeville's *Fable* was a statement made in defence of financial revolution. First published as *The Grumbling Hive* in 1705 to support Whig foreign policy, and to counter Tory–Jacobite attacks on 'the corrupt regime of debt and luxury', Mandeville's essay was republished and extended as *The Fable of the Bees* in 1714, and again in 1723 in the aftermath of the South Sea Bubble. It was Mandeville's elaboration on an 'already-established discourse on the volatile moral relations between public virtue and the demands of commerce' – a particularly heightened discourse in this period of recrimination against stockjobbers and speculators, and a discourse that was fundamental to the charges against Macclesfield (Pocock 1975, ch. 14; Sekora 1977; Goldsmith 1985; Goldsmith 1987, 238–51; Hundert 1994, 24; Hoppit 2002, 309–11; Mitchell 2003).

This discourse about virtue and commerce not only was conducted in these terms of English politics, between new and old Whigs and in the language of civic humanism, but also was a broadly European debate that notably engaged French and Scottish, as well English, thinkers. Clearly one important target for Mandeville was Archbishop Fenelon's *The Bees* (1689); Mandeville was also influenced by French Jansenist ideas about the operation of human appetites and passions (Horne 1978, 21–5, 31; Hundert 1994, 23–35; Hont 2006, 382–92). Yet by 1723 Mandeville was even more interested in challenging the ideology of the Earl of Shaftesbury; the latest edition of *The Fable of the Bees* included a pointed critique of Shaftesbury's philosophy of moral sense. In this essay, entitled 'A Search into the Nature of Society', Mandeville sought to demolish the philosopher's claims about natural sociability and necessary moral development aimed at the public good (Horne 1978, 32–50; Hundert 1994, 118–26; Cowan 1998; Hont 2006, 395, 399). Mandeville further tied the critique of Shaftesbury to an attack on the movement for moral reform by adding yet another text, the notorious 'Essay on Charity and Charity Schools', to this new edition of his *Fable*.

These same kinds of contemporary concerns with commercial development, and these same terminologies of moral sense and moral reform, were essential elements in the legal debate over Macclesfield's guilt.

Participants took the measure of the Lord Chancellor's animating passions, and made allusions to the ideas of Shaftesbury and Mandeville in courtroom argument over Macclesfield's motives. For example, prosecutors asserted that destructive passions overcame Macclesfield's rational interests and derailed his moral sense. These passions – the avaricious desire for wealth, an insatiable greed – clearly diminished the Chancellor's care for the public welfare, they argued, and ultimately undermined his professional actions (Howell 1812, 807–8, 1167, 1248, 1330, 1352). In his own courtroom speech Macclesfield insisted that the whole case against him rested upon false interpretation of his motives for acting. The prosecution focused on his alleged avarice and greed, yet that 'charge of [his] desire of gain' was misdirected, Macclesfield explained, because it entailed a fundamental misinterpretation of his feelings and intentions. In response to such misinterpretation the challenge for his defence was to demonstrate that 'amassing a great estate was never [Macclesfield's] view; and that rapacious and base ways of getting money are not consistent with [his] way of laying it out'. If the defence successfully confuted the charge of avaricious motives, Macclesfield concluded, then the 'sting of this impeachment is taken out': without this, though there should have been imprudence, indolence, too great confidence, perhaps credulity, irresolution, or any other defect or weakness, there has been nothing wicked (Salmon 1737, 879; Howell 1812, 1329). Macclesfield underscored the link between emotion, intentionality, and criminality, betraying the influence of philosophical discourse on legal concepts, when he explained that 'It is such a corrupt heart only can change actions that in themselves are innocent, and some of them perhaps commendable, into so many crimes' (Salmon 1737, 879; Howell 1812, 1328).

In signalling his conformity to moral sense and reason Macclesfield did not go so far as to claim that, when he took part in the customary practice of selling masters' offices, his actions were fundamentally aimed at securing the public good. However, he did suggest that his actions indicated some feeling and regard for public welfare, because he did not knowingly, or even carelessly, advance incompetent men to office. That kind of an act, which 'prejudiced the public', would clearly be immoral and criminal, he conceded. Any benefit accrued would simply be an aggravation of the crime. Macclesfield deliberately added, to these lords who were steeped in the traditions of patronage and place, that such an act would be criminal whether linked to monetary gain, or done 'for the sake of kindred, or friendship, or for recommendation', the other aggravating factors (Salmon 1737, 878; Howell 1812, 1274).

Finally, Macclesfield turned from this vocabulary of sentiment and sociability to an obviously Mandevillian argument about public benefits and private vices as justification for his actions. The Lord Chancellor maintained that he had fulfilled his duty by placing well-qualified men into office, and that he had simply benefitted, as his predecessors had done, by collecting monies for the appointment to Chancery masterships. 'If the public have all the benefit it can have, where is the immorality?' Macclesfield asked. 'Where is the crime, if I have an advantage too?' (Salmon 1737, 878; Howell 1812, 1274). Indeed, the individual pursuit of gain was, as Mandeville had shown in his *Fable*, the engine of common wealth, and the foundation of common good. Here Macclesfield's defence appealed to clearly controversial arguments about economic growth and financial opportunity. If one part of the Lord Chancellor's defence strategy was to lay claim to the values of common-law stability, another part was to embrace the arguments of unfettered capitalism.

Participants in this trial thus articulated familiar terms of debate over the relationship between commerce and social welfare, and regarding the place of the passions in human nature. References to the specific arguments of important authors, such as Mandeville or Shaftesbury, were also made in published commentaries on Macclesfield's case, and on other impeachments circulated by opponents and supporters soon after the Earl's conviction (*Enquiry* 1725; Gordon 1725; *Vindication* 1725; Wilson 1726). This enlightened moral-philosophical discourse was central to the expression of ideas about judging and about justice, and helped to determine both the outcome and the impact of Macclesfield's trial. A strong connection was forged between common law and positive moral values such as sociability and credibility. The justice of common law – the certainty of its principles and procedures – provided reassurance that stability could accompany economic growth, and the public good could be preserved.

For example, those who endorsed Macclesfield's impeachment focused clearly on the negative connotations of the Lord Chancellor's avarice. In depicting its dangers they turned to the language of status, honour, and masculinity, a discourse typical of a cultural ideology of politeness, taste, and civility, and, by the 1720s, strongly associated with the philosophical works of the Earl of Shaftesbury (Hundert 1994, 124). The construction of the problem of avarice within this 'polite' discourse appears in the trial records, and in associated texts, such as George Wilson's *Bribes no Perquisites, Or the Case of the Earl of Macclesfield, Being Impartial Observations Upon his Lordship's Tryal* (1726), and Thomas Gordon's *The Justice of Parliaments on Corrupt Ministers, in Impeachments and Bills of Attainder, Consider'd* (1725). One set of arguments advanced here defined Macclesfield's true guilt as valuing money above good breeding. Critics of the

Earl pointed to evidence of an ignoble reverence for money in Maccles-field's willingness to demean himself for as little as one hundred guineas, and in his propensity to advance 'mean men' – men of little fortune and less ability – to Chancery masterships (Salmon 1737, 875, 875b; Howell 1812, 898–9). The eleventh article of impeachment detailed the charge that Macclesfield 'did admit several persons to the said offices of Masters of the said Court of Chancery, who, at the time of such their admission, were of small substance and ability, very unfit to be trusted with the great sums of money and other effects of the suitors of the said Court, lodged in their hands by the orders of the said Court' (Howell 1812, 775). A false sense of value underlay the crime: rather than calculating an applicant's immediate worth and willingness to pay the Chancellor's fee, Macclesfield should have considered the potential master's entire wealth and social worth (Wilson 1727, 64–5).

From the perspective of the governing classes, including his fellow lords and ministers, Macclesfield had subverted their common interests and reputation when he admitted inferior men to masterships. These inferior men represented the sordid side of commercial development and pros-perity, 'for men of small fortunes', Commons manager Arthur Onslow reminded the Lords, 'as they have more temptations, so they run less hazard than others in preying upon money that is entrusted with them; and it is this, my lords, that encourages such men to give exorbitant rates for employments which afford them those opportunities' (Howell 1812, 899). Such men, focused solely on material gain and unaffected by the civilising and moralising effects of polite society, were the very oppo-nents of an urbane and sociable milieu. Civility and sociability thus were seen as the foundations of English governors' fiscal probity and financial responsibility – foundations that were being restored by Macclesfield's impeachment. Here Onslow extended another version of contemporary outrage as it was directed against the great impact of the burst bubble on 'high politics, high finance and high society' (Banner 1998, 65–72; Hop-pit 2002, 158; Murphy 2009). Had the Lord Chancellor been properly concerned with the social status of the masters, prosecutors explained, he would have been aware of their illicit motives, and he would have fore-seen their perilous behaviour. Macclesfield's endorsement of such men instead, and his own wholesale pursuit of luxury and pleasure, were con-strued as a total abandonment of gentlemanly and enlightened culture.

The impolite and dishonourable character of the Lord Chancellor's behaviour was also criticised by Thomas Gordon, but from a slightly different direction. It was Macclesfield's exploitation of his position and the inequity of his actions, Gordon explained, that were most offensive. At the very opening of *The Justice of Parliaments* Gordon emphasised the theme of dishonour, and called upon the authority of Sallust and Juvenal to make the case that elite men who performed criminal acts were, justly, more prone to publicity and censure than 'Men of an obscure Class' might be.

The Nature of their Crime alters, and takes a fresh Gloss, and Degrees of Heinousness, from the Character and Circumstances of the Persons by whom committed; and as the *Satyrist* justly remarks,

– Still more publick Scandal Vice extends,
As He is Great, and Noble, who offends.

We make Allowances to *poor* Rogues and *undignified* Delinquents, from Poverty and Necessities driving them to unwarrantable Shifts for a Subsistence; but we have not the same Room to excuse Criminals, who are paid largely and have ample Perquisites for doing Justice, yet cannot perswade themselves to act with Conscience and Integrity. (Gordon 1725, 1–2)

Gordon returns to this theme again and again, using the language of credit and debt to describe the dignity of nobility (Gordon 1725, 19–20, 22, 24, 27). Honour and reputation, which were critical for the amassing of wealth, should be indicative of trustworthy character, rather than a cover for fraud. In highlighting this comparison between the 'great and noble' and 'poor rogues and undignified delinquents', Gordon alluded to contemporary complaints that wealthy offenders were usually left alone, whereas the poor were subject to frequent fines and punishment. This was the thrust of Daniel Defoe's earlier critique of the Societies for the Reformation of Manners' campaign against prostitutes, bawds, and drunks. 'The punishing vices in the poor, which are daily practiced by the rich', Defoe explained, 'seems to me to be setting our constitution with the wrong men upward, and making men criminals because they want money' (Shoemaker 1991, 250). Gordon's defence of punishing the crimes of the Lord Chancellor included this kind of critique of the hypocrisy of the moral reformers. Even more, Gordon's opening attack was a critique of an offender like Walpole, who was left unscathed after 1720. Such inequitable outcomes and failure of legal restraints were even more troubling for Gordon than the passions that led men, wealthy or poor, to crime. Macclesfield's impeachment was regarded as a key element in the restoration, and reform, of law.

As Macclesfield's opponents advanced these kinds of arguments about honour and nobility, their depictions of Macclesfield's guilt articulated a number of gendered concerns that ultimately deepened the critique of equity. First, in characterising his actions as a kind of moral degeneracy, critics used sexual imagery long used by proponents of moral reform who depicted government ministers as 'pimps and panderers' and office-holders as 'common prostitutes' (Hayton 1990, 84–5). To Macclesfield belongs 'guilt without measure', Arthur Onslow insisted, for example, because the Earl 'brought a disgrace upon his country, by prostituting one of its highest courts of justice to his own avarice and corruption, to the rapine and corruption of his inferior officers, and to the undoing of those, who, by the constitution of the kingdom, have been forced into his power' (Howell 1812, 899–900, 1061, 1075). Most signally, those who were 'forced' and 'undone' by his 'prostitution' of justice were the large numbers of female suitors in Chancery. This kind of language brought the Chancellor's authority into dispute by calling upon the familiar association between arbitrary power and rape (Rudolph 2000). It further echoed the legal and physical attacks on prostitution, sodomy, and other 'lewd' and 'debauched' practices carried out by the Societies for the Reformation of Manners as they undertook prosecutions of brothels and bawdy houses in these years. The reference was deliberate: at this very moment in 1725 the prosecution of prostitutes and other 'lewd and disorderly persons' was a matter of legal controversy (Shoemaker 1991, ch. 9; Trumbach 1991; Hunt 1996, 112–13, 115; Hurl-Eamon 2004; Dabhoiwala 2007). The association of Macclesfield with prostitution would have aligned the case against him with the cause of the reformers in this set of other contemporary cases.

This species of argument against Macclesfield's 'prostitution of justice' was again specifically aligned with argument against Mandeville, because the physician–philosopher had very recently published an argument against the prosecution of brothels, and in favour of legalised prostitution, as part of his reevaluation of virtue and social good. Mandeville's *A Modest Defence of Publick Stews: Or, An Essay upon Whoring* first appeared in 1724 and was republished in 1725 with an 'Answer' appended in defence of the work of moral reform (Mandeville 1725). This 'Answer' to Mandeville advertised the progress made by the societies in combating 'the Prevalency of the most scandalous Vices, and', the author added, 'in many Instances, a visible Reformation has ensued' (Mandeville 1725, 61). When Macclesfield's crimes were viewed as another form of prostitution his impeachment could easily be identified with the good work of moral reform, and with the refutation of Mandeville's claims.

The example of prostitution as a money-making activity was, more generally, at the centre of the public discussion regarding the tendency for commercial activity to lead to corruption. 'For the reformers... and Mandeville himself', Rosenthal avers, 'prostitution became an emblematic vice of excessive desire that commercial society had to confront' (Burtt 1995; Rosenthal 2006, 57). Of course, prostitution was conventionally understood as a female money-making activity, and the connection made between Macclesfield's 'excessive desire' and prostitution, and the crackdown on prostitution itself, were also expressive of contemporary fears about female sexuality and female agency. These anxieties, and related ideas about women's proper roles as agents and objects of exchange within marriage, appear in other elements of the charges against Macclesfield. For example, prosecutors launched a powerful and sustained complaint against the Lord Chancellor's refusal to protect the property of female suitors in Chancery. Those women who rightly looked to him for protection and support of settlements, they said, were now left penniless and powerless. Counsel made the case for impeachment, in part, by providing evidence of women whose fortunes were lost in the Chancery masters' risky investment scheme (Wilson 1727, 22; Howell 1812, 778, 995–1001). Moreover, the masters' and chancellor's responsibility for their suitors' monies was defined as a trusteeship. This made it easier to advance the charge of betrayal of widows and orphans, which was another repeated discourse in the courtroom and in wider public discourse about the trial (NLW Longueville 1187, fols. 5–10; Wilson 1727, 14, 17, 20–21; Salmon 1737, 881, 887; Howell 1812, 784, 809, 811, 899, 1030, 1059, 1073, 1106, 1118, 1166–7, 1251, 1257, 1375). Indeed, trusteeship was seen as the essential factor that allowed corruption. And if trusts were prone to abuse even by those in Chancery who upheld them, it could be argued, then this kind of equitable remedy was inherently unstable and ultimately unjust. By contrast, recourse to common law, as it was associated with stability and honesty, could be envisioned as a way to restore justice.

The rage expressed against the Lord Chancellor's failure to protect female property must, finally, be seen as an expression of concern about women's involvement in speculation. This was a concern that was tied to specific anger about the burst South Sea Bubble, as well as wider anxiety about 'new money' and the financial revolution. When prosecutors and commentators relied upon sentimental images of female suitors as weak, dependent, and ruined they actually aligned the case for impeachment with contemporary hostility towards women's commercial activities. In this sense, the anger against the Lord Chancellor was not so much expressive of disquiet about the exploitation of powerless women. It was, rather, the manifestation of a fear that commercialisation was undermining conventional gender roles. Contemporaries articulated ambivalence about, and at times overt hostility towards, women's financial independence and engagement in commercial activities in a variety of ways. These concerns were often tied to contemporary discourses about luxury, nation, and class. Not surprisingly, the language of politeness, with its heightened attention to gendered definitions of civility, credit, and honour, was an important part of public debate, for example, over appropriate female trades (Phillips 2006, chs. 8–9). The outcry about the losses suffered by female suitors in Chancery was part of this broader ambivalence regarding women as property holders, and is another example of the relevance of gender concerns to contemporary arguments about financial innovation and commercial change. In the period of the South Sea Crisis, of course, the evils of commerce were underscored, and the dangers of gambling on the stock market were seen as equal for both men and women (Laurence 2006, 259–60), but the attack on Macclesfield's Chancery masters as investors was also part of a pointed critique of women in particular as investors.

All of these arguments formed part of a larger critique taking shape in which an unfettered and unmediated market culture, promoted by the Lord Chancellor, was characterised as the antithesis of refinement, sociability, judgement, and morality. Common law, in contrast, was valued as sociable, moral, and masculine, and it was associated, by both prosecution and defence, with public utility and the protection of property. Adhering to established procedures and allowing gradual, incremental change were not understood in opposition to enlightened reason and public utility, but rather were seen as the best ways to ensure justice. Moreover, this reaffirmation of common-law tradition and prescription was not understood as a rejection of financial and commercial change. It was seen rather as the best way to promote strong economic growth by preserving the stability, and ensuring the civility, of the post-Revolution economy, state, and society.

On a practical level, Macclesfield's impeachment resulted in some new regulations and reforms. The administration of Chancery funds was streamlined, and oversight was increased, in order to support new financial and judicial practices. The sale of Chancery masterships was finally discontinued, although clearly it was recognised that such practice had been a traditional perquisite of the office, because the pension of the succeeding Lord Chancellor, Peter King, was increased by £1,200 as compensation for lost revenue. This is another clue that, on a symbolic level, Macclesfield's impeachment operated as a gesture to appease public anger. He served as a scapegoat sacrificed in an effort to restore public confidence in economic policies. Most important, however, on a jurisdictional and jurisprudential level, Macclesfield's impeachment stood as an indication that in England, common-law tradition and stability were the keys to continued financial innovation and successful economic growth.

Key to archive references

CUL: Cambridge University Library
FLP: Free Library of Philadelphia
NLW: National Library of Wales

References

Aylmer, G. E. 1980. 'From Office-Holding to Civil Service: The Genesis of Modern Bureaucracy', *Transactions of the Royal Historical Society*, Fifth Series, 30, 91–108.

Baker, J. H. 2002. *An Introduction to English Legal History*. London: Butterworths.

Banner, Stuart 1998. *Anglo-American Securities Regulation: Cultural and Political Roots, 1690–1860*. Cambridge: Cambridge University Press.

Burtt, Shelley 1995. 'The Societies for the Reformation of Manners: Between John Locke and the Devil in Augustan England', in Roger D. Lund (ed.), *The Margins of Orthodoxy: Heterodox Writing and Cultural Response 1660–1750*. Cambridge/New York: Cambridge University Press.

Carlos, Ann M. and Neal, Larry 2006. 'The Micro-foundations of the Early London Capital Market: Bank of England Shareholders during and after the South Sea Bubble, 1720–25', *Economic History Review*, 59(3), 498–538.

Carswell, John 1960. *The South Sea Bubble*. Stanford, CA: Stanford University Press.

Clark, Peter 1988. 'The Mother Gin Controversy in the Early Eighteenth Century', *Transactions of the Royal Historical Society*, Fifth Series, 38, 63–84.

Cowan, Brian 1998. 'Reasonable Ecstasies: Shaftesbury and the Languages of Libertinism', *Journal of British Studies*, 37(2), 111–38.

Dabhoiwala, Faramerz 2007. 'Sex and the Societies for Moral Reform, 1688–1800', *Journal of British Studies*, 46(2), 290–319.

Dickson, P. G. M. 1967. *The Financial Revolution in England: A Study of the Development of Public Credit 1688–1756*. New York: St. Martin's Press.

An Enquiry into the Origin of Parliamentary Impeachments: With a History of the Most Remarkable 1725. London: Printed for J. Peele.

Foss, Edward 1864. *The Judges of England*, vols. VII–VIII. London: John Murray. Reprint New York: AMS Press, 1966.

Glaisyer, Natasha 2006. *The Culture of Commerce in England 1660–1720*. Woodbridge: Boydell & Brewer.

Goldsmith, M. M. 1985. *Private Vices, Public Benefits: Bernard Mandeville's Social and Political Thought*. Cambridge: Cambridge University Press.

Goldsmith, M. M. 1987. 'Liberty, Luxury and the Pursuit of Happiness', in Anthony Pagden (ed.), *The Languages of Political Theory in Early Modern Europe*. Cambridge: Cambridge University Press.

Gordon, Thomas 1725. *The Justice of Parliaments on Corrupt Ministers, in Impeachments and Bills of Attainder, Consider'd*. London: Sold by J. Roberts.

Hanham, A. A. 2009. 'Parker, Thomas, First Earl of Macclesfield (1667–1732)', in *Oxford Dictionary of National Biography*, Oxford University Press, online edn, available at www.oxforddnb.com/view/article/21341. Date accessed: 11 June 2012.

Harris, Ron 2000. *Industrializing English Law: Entrepreneurship and Business Organization 1720–1844*. Cambridge: Cambridge University Press.

Harris, Ron 2004. 'Government and the Economy 1688–1850', in Roderick Floud and Paul Johnson (eds.), *The Cambridge Economic History of Britain since 1700, Volume 1, 1700–1850*. Cambridge: Cambridge University Press.

Hayton, David W. 1990. 'Moral Reform and Country Politics in the Late Seventeenth-Century House of Commons', *Past & Present*, 128, 48–91.

Heward, Edmund 1983. 'The Early History of the Court Funds Office', *Journal of Legal History*, 4(1), 46–53.

Holdsworth, W. S. 1938. *A History of English Law*. London: Methuen & Co, vol. 12.

Hont, Istvan 2006. 'The Early Enlightenment Debate on Commerce and Luxury', in Mark Goldie and Robert Wolker (eds.), *The Cambridge History of Eighteenth-Century Political Thought*. Cambridge: Cambridge University Press.

Hoppit, Julian 1990. 'Attitudes to Credit in Britain 1680–1790', *Historical Journal*, 33(2), 305–22.

Hoppit, Julian 2002. 'The Myths of the South Sea Bubble', *Transactions of the Royal Historical Society*, Sixth Series, 12, 141–65.

Horne, Thomas A. 1978. *The Social Thought of Bernard Mandeville: Virtue and Commerce in Early Eighteenth-Century England*. London: Macmillan.

Horsley, Lee Sonsteng 1973. 'The Trial of John Tutchin, Author of the *Observator*', *Yearbook of English Studies*, 124–140.

Horwitz, Henry 1998. *A Guide to Chancery Equity Records and Proceedings 1600–1800*. London: PRO Publications.

Horwitz, Henry 1999. 'Chancery's "Younger Sister": The Court of Exchequer and its Equity Jurisdiction 1649–1841', *Historical Research*, 72(178), 160–82.

Howell, T. B. 1812. *A Complete Collection of State Trials and Proceedings for High Treason and Other Crimes and Misdemeanors*. London: Printed for T.C. Hansard, vol. 16.

Hundert, E. J. 1994. *The Enlightenment's Fable: Bernard Mandeville and the Discovery of Society*. Cambridge: Cambridge University Press.

Hunt, Margaret R. 1996. *The Middling Sort: Commerce, Gender, and the Family in England 1680–1780*. Berkeley: University of California Press.

Hurl-Eamon, Jennine 2004. 'Policing Male Heterosexuality: The Reformation of Manners Societies' Campaign Against the Brothels in Westminster, 1690–1720', *Journal of Social History*, 37(4), 1017–35.

Journal of the House of Lords, vols. 15, 22, British History Online, www.british-history.ac.uk/source.aspx?pubid=36, www.british-history.ac.uk/source.aspx?pubid=1223. Date accessed: 11 June 2012.

Laurence, Anne 2006. 'Women Investors, "That Nasty South Sea Affair" and the Rage to Speculate in Early Eighteenth-Century England', *Accounting Business and Financial History*, 16(2), 245–64.

Mandeville, Bernard 1724. *A Modest Defence of Publick Stews: Or, an Essay Upon Whoring, As it is Now Practis'd in these Kingdoms*. London: Printed by A. Bussy.

Mandeville, Bernard 1725. *A Modest Defence of Publick Stews: Or, an Essay Upon Whoring, As it is Now Practis'd in these Kingdoms. Answer'd*. London: Printed by A. Moore.

Mandeville, Bernard 1924. *The Fable of the Bees Or Private Vices, Publick Benefits*, with a commentary critical, historical, and explanatory by F. B. Kaye, 2 vols. Oxford: Clarendon Press; reprint Indianapolis: Liberty Fund, 1988.

Mitchell, Annie 2003. 'Character of an Independent Whig – "Cato" and Bernard Mandeville', *History of European Ideas*, 29(3), 291–311.

Muldrew, Craig 1998. *The Economy of Obligation: The Culture of Credit and Social Relations in Early Modern England*. New York: St. Martin's Press.

Murphy, Anne L. 2009. *The Origins of English Financial Markets: Investment and Speculation before the South Sea Bubble*. Cambridge: Cambridge University Press.

Neal, Larry 1990. *The Rise of Financial Capitalism: International Capital Markets in the Age of Reason*. Cambridge: Cambridge University Press.

North, Douglas C. and Weingast, Barry R. 1989. 'Constitutions and Commitment: The Evolution of Institutions Governing Public Choice in Seventeenth-Century England', *Journal of Economic History*, 49(4), 803–32.

Peck, Linda Levy 1990. *Court Patronage and Corruption in Early Stuart England*. Boston: Unwin Hyman.

Phillips, Nicola 2006. *Women in Business 1700–1850*. Woodbridge: Boydell Press.

Pocock, J. G. A 1975. *The Machiavellian Moment, Florentine Political Thought and the Atlantic Republican Tradition*. Princeton: Princeton University Press.

Quarrie, Paul 2004. 'Introduction', in Sotheby's *The Library of the Earls of Macclesfield Removed from Shirburn Castle, Part One: Natural History*. London: Sotheby's.

Quarrie, Paul 2006. 'Introduction', in Sotheby's *The Library of the Earls of Macclesfield Removed from Shirburn Castle, Part Eight: Theology, Philosophy, Law and Economics*. London: Sotheby's.

Quarrie, Paul 2006. 'The Scientific Library of the Earls of Macclesfield', *Notes and Records of the Royal Society*, 20, 5–24.

Rogers, James Steven 1995. *The Early History of the Law of Bills and Notes: A Study of the Origins of Anglo-American Commercial Law*. Cambridge: Cambridge University Press.

Rosenthal, Laura J. 2006. *Infamous Commerce: Prostitution in Eighteenth-Century British Literature and Culture*. Ithaca, NY: Cornell University Press.

Rudolph, Julia 2000. 'Rape and Resistance: Women and Consent in Seventeenth-Century English Legal and Political Thought', *Journal of British Studies*, 39(2), 157–84.

Salmon, Thomas (ed.) 1737. *A New Abridgment and Critical Review of the State Trials*, 2 vols. Dublin: Printed by and for R. Reilly.

Sekora, John 1977. *Luxury: The Concept in Western Thought, Eden to Smollett*. Baltimore: Johns Hopkins University Press.

Shoemaker, Robert 1991. *Prosecution and Punishment: Petty Crime and the Law in London and Rural Middlesex c. 1660–1720*. Cambridge: Cambridge University Press.

Sotheby's 2004–8. *The Library of the Earls of Macclesfield Removed from Shirburn Castle*, 12 vols. London: Sotheby's, vol. 8.

Trumbach, Randolph 1991. 'Sex, Gender and Sexual Identity in Modern Culture: Male Sodomy and Female Prostitution in Enlightenment London', *Journal of the History of Sexuality*, 2(2), 186–203.

A Vindication of the Lord Chancellor Bacon, From the Aspersion of Injustice Cast upon him by Mr. Wraynham 1725. London: Printed for J. Peele.

White, Jonathan 2003. '"The Slow but Sure Poyson": The Representation of Gin and Its Drinkers 1736–1751', *Journal of British Studies*, 42(1), 35–64.

Wilson, George 1726. *Bribes no Perquisites, Or the Case of the Earl of Macclesfield, Being Impartial Observations Upon his Lordship's Tryal*. London: Printed for A. More.

Wilson, George 1727. *The Trial of the Earl of Macclesfield, Faithfully Abridg'd. With Remarks Thereon*, 2nd edn. London: Printed for A. Moore.

6 The importance of not defaulting: The significance of the election of 1710

James Macdonald

When North and Weingast published their seminal paper in 1989, it is unlikely that they knew what a debate they would set off. They raised important issues, partly because the question of how to turn a poor credit rating into a good one, and so to reap the rewards of lower interest rates, remains highly topical. They are important also because the picture that North and Weingast painted of England after the 1688 revolution has been challenged. In particular, their central claim, that the establishment of parliamentary government and an independent central bank provided the credibility required to borrow cheaply, runs afoul of a significant obstacle. How was it that England's borrowing costs were so high not just in the 1690s, but for many years afterwards? If the English viewed their revolution as securing not just their liberties, but also their credit rating, they must have been sorely disappointed.

The thesis put forward by North and Weingast was essentially institutional. A reinforced parliament, an independent judiciary, and an independent central bank created multiple veto points that made a default less likely. Moreover, both Parliament and the Bank of England had specific interests in protecting private property rights: Parliament because it represented property holders the Bank because it was itself a public creditor.

Quite apart from the contrary evidence of interest rates, there are some theoretical questions about the sufficiency of the argument. Parliament may have represented property holders, but not all property holders owned government bonds, especially in a country such as England where the vast majority of all property was in the form of land. The interests of the 'landed' and the 'monied' classes were not identical, especially when the taxes required to support public debt fell on land. It is not clear, at least prima facie, why a parliament composed largely of landowners should always uphold the property rights of government bondholders. Indeed, there was a stream of pamphlets during this period reminding Parliament of its obligation to uphold the public credit, suggesting that public creditors did not feel entirely secure on this point (Murphy 2013).

Second, the Bank of England may have been an institutional bulwark for public creditors as a whole, but the history of France was evidence of the inadequacy of such bulwarks in the face of a government which found it convenient to default. The Farmers General and the Hôtel de Ville of Paris between them formed an institutional bulwark for public creditors that was arguably stronger than the Bank of England. The Bank may have acted as agent for the payment of a number of public debts, but it had no control of the taxes necessary to make such payments. In contrast, the Farmers General collected the bulk of French taxes, and then transferred the funds necessary for debt service to the Hôtel de Ville without the money even passing through the hands of the government. Who could ask for a better institutional bulwark? Finally, although an independent judiciary is undoubtedly to be preferred to a legal system that acts merely at the convenience of the state, one of the features of sovereign debt that makes 'credible commitment' so difficult to establish is the sovereign's de jure or de facto immunity to suit.

Clearly, there were other factors at play in the gradual fall of interest rates on the British public debt to levels that can be described as investment grade. To understand what they may have been, it is helpful to look at the non-institutional elements that go into a credit rating. These fall into two fundamental categories, relating first to ability to pay, and second to willingness to pay. In the first category lies the question of underlying economic capacity. To take an extreme example, a country such as Haiti, after suffering a devastating earthquake, may not be in a position to service its debts. The question of economic competence also falls into the category of ability to pay. A country may have sound enough economic fundamentals, but may mismanage its finances to such a degree that it is unable to pay its debts. An example of such mismanagement is Argentina in 2001. This issue of management turns out to occupy a central place in the history of the early English financial revolution.

The second element – willingness to pay – is clearly of particular importance in public debt, where the borrower is largely free from legal constraints. Creditors may be comforted by the presence of institutional barriers to default, as suggested by North and Weingast. However, they may require more solid reassurances. The most indisputable of these is the effective control of the levers of power by public creditors when they constitute the majority of the electorate. However, although this may have been true in mercantile republics such as those of Italy and the Netherlands, and was to become true of Britain by the end of the eighteenth century, it was not true of Britain at the beginning of the century. An alternative explanation has been put forward by David Stasavage, who has argued that although the public creditors were not a majority of the ruling class, they were able to keep a near monopoly over control of the reins of power for much of the eighteenth century through an alliance with a part of the aristocracy in the Whig party (Stasavage 2003; Stasavage 2007). However, in a parliamentary system of government, it is scarcely prudent for a public creditor to rely on the permanence of such arrangements. Such a creditor is likely to require the additional reassurance that the government will not default even if the non-creditors come to power. This is where the election of 1710 comes in. In that year, the Whig majority in Parliament was overturned when the Tories won a landslide victory, returning 329 members versus 169 Whigs and 14 others (Hayton 2002, 229–30).

The election of 1710 has been noted by many historians of the period as an interesting political moment because of the violence of the political debate, the completeness of the change of government, and the attempt of the City to influence events in Westminster (Hill 1971, Morgan 1921, Roberts 1982, Wennerlind 2011). This article seeks to look at it as a financial crisis as well as a political one, and in particular to analyse its financial outcome.

If the Whigs represented an apparently disparate coalition of merchants, religious nonconformists, and aristocrats, the Tories were also a coalition of interests centred around high-church landowners. The Tories denounced the Whigs not just because the latter accepted and even encouraged religious nonconformity, or because they insisted on continuing an expensive war against France even when favourable peace terms were available, but because the new, debt-based system of war finance was overturning the traditional power relations of the country. Their feelings were best expressed by Jonathan Swift in his 1711 pamphlet *The conduct of the allies and of the late ministry*. In Swift's view, the public debt was a political scam with insidious consequences.

In order to fasten wealthy people to the new government, they proposed those pernicious expedients of borrowing money by vast premiums, and at exorbitant interest: a practice as old as Eumenes, one of Alexander's captains, who setting up for himself after the death of his master, persuaded his principal officers to lend him great sums, after which they were forced to follow him for their own security... Let any man observe the equipages in this town; he shall find the greater number... to be a species of men quite different from any that were ever known before the Revolution, consisting either of generals and colonels, or of such whose whole fortunes lie in funds and stocks: so that power, which according to the old maxim, was used to follow land, is now gone over to money. (Swift 1711)

Given views such as these, and the background of a severe fiscal crisis, it was not unreasonable for a public creditor to fear that an incoming Tory government might default, for one of several reasons. The new government might simply repudiate some or all of the debt, or find excuses to reduce or write it down on grounds similar to those so frequently rehearsed in France. This certainly was the fear of some Whigs such as Benjamin Hoadly:

Many will ask...what is to become of those, who...have trusted to *Parliamentary Funds*, and supported the *Cause* of the *Nation* with their *Money*? The *Suspicions* of Men cannot be remedied; and when it is seen that there are those who care not what becomes of *Money-Credit* at this moment; who are forcing an inglorious *Peace* upon their own Nation; who think no measures are too precipitous to...place themselves in *Offices* of *Profit* and *Trust*; they cannot help suspecting that will not be over tender on the point of National *Justice*, and that the *lot* of those who have depended upon it, will be very hard at last. This suspicion is mightily increased by an *Ugly Discourse* now too frequent amongst those who are impatiently awaiting for a *Thorough Alteration* concerning a *Political Sponge* to wipe out the Debts of the *Nation*, and at one dash the very Memorial, if possible, of the demands of those who have been too forward to place confidence in *Parliamentary Security*. (Hoadly 1710)

This was not the only reason to fear a default. The government might find itself unable to borrow owing to a lack of confidence in the credit market, or it might fail to handle the financial crisis properly because of a lack of experience and competence. ('This is no time for a novice', a British Prime Minister would warn exactly three centuries later, in an attempt to scare voters away from electing another Tory government during another financial crisis.) The extent of investor concerns about the outcome of the election is shown by the twenty per cent fall in the price of Bank of England shares between the beginning of June and the end of October. Some 'Dons of the City and the Bank' tried to persuade the Queen to keep the existing government in order to avert a financial crisis, but without success (Hoppit 2000, 128).

Yet, in the event, creditors' fears proved unfounded. The new government did not deliberately repudiate or write down the debt. The central debate in the run-up to the election was whether the new government would be able to avoid default in the face of a creditors' strike. This was the background for Daniel Defoe's pamphlet *An essay upon loans*, written at the behest of Robert Harley, the leader of the new government (Downie 1979). Defoe's argument was that because no one would willingly hoard their money if there were decent lending opportunities around, the money of the Whig financiers would find its way into the hands of the government indirectly, even if they refused to lend it directly.

Perhaps you won't lend it to the government, well you will then lend it upon private security...and those you lend it to will lend it to the government...Will you run it into trade? Do so by all means. Some of those hands it will circulate through will lend it to the government...No party can be so foolish to think

they can stop the flow of money to the government... Keep up but the credit
of Parliament... [and] it is not in the power of any party of men to stop the
current of loans, any more than they can stop the tide at London Bridge. (Defoe
1710)

Defoe's argument was based firmly on the premise that the new government would attempt to 'keep up the credit of parliament.' The issue
of whether there would be default, therefore, hinged on whether the
government would prove capable of handling the financial crisis that
it inherited from the outgoing Whig administration. This crisis was far
from being purely political, based on lack of confidence in the new government. Rather, it was the product of an unsustainable build-up of
short-term debt over many years, exacerbated by an economic downturn
brought on by the failure of successive harvests. An idea of the level of
economic hardship at the time can be seen in the rise in the index of
consumer prices from 92 in 1708 to 135 in 1711 (Mitchell and Deane
1962).

The credit crisis had been brewing for years, but had been hidden
from sight by the government's failure to account for some £7 million of
past-due debts until 1711. At the time, short-term borrowing took three
forms. The cheapest for the government was Exchequer Bills, which
were issued in limited amounts and were underwritten by the Bank of
England. By 1710 there was £3 million outstanding at an interest rate
of 2d per day, equivalent to 3.04% per annum. Next in line were the
Exchequer Tallies, which were issued either in exchange for cash, or
more frequently in payment for goods or services. Tallies were secured
against tax receipts, and their date of repayment was imprecise. Their
interest varied from four to six per cent, depending on the reliability of
the underlying tax receipts. They were often repaid with Exchequer Bills,
which increasingly served as a form of money. In 1710 there was close to
£5 million Tallies outstanding. The weak link in the government's short-
term finances was the notes issued by the Army and Navy departments in
payment for supplies. During a war these started to swell uncontrollably
unless the government was able to raise sufficient money from long-term
loans to keep the military machine liquid. By 1710 there was in excess of
£6 million departmental notes outstanding, and most of the unaccounted
£7 million debts also took this form. Altogether, the government's short-
term debt came to over £21 million, compared to revenues available after
paying long-term debt interest of £4.2 million. The imbalance between
debts and revenues was even worse than during the financial crisis of
1697, which had led to the protesting of Bank of England notes for
nonpayment in Holland, and, but for the end of the war, might have
ended in default.

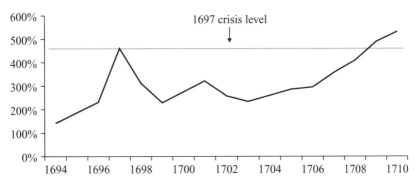

Figure 6.1. Short-term debt as a percentage of free revenues. *Source and notes:* Mitchell and Deane (1962), Dickson (1967), Jones (1988, 71). Free revenue is defined as total revenue less long-term debt interest. In 1711 the budget included over £7 million of previously unrecorded liabilities, some going back before 1702. These expenses have been allocated over the years 1700–1710 to give a more accurate picture of the growth of the short-term debt.

It was clear that the public finances could not be set on a sound basis until this debt overhang was reduced to manageable proportions. Because the total amount of floating debt was so far in excess of taxes, it was apparent that the only solution was a conversion of short-term into long-term debt. This was the method by which the crisis of 1697 had been resolved, and it is not surprising that it was adopted in 1711. In 1697 the excess debt had been exchanged for shares in the Bank of England, which had received perpetual annuities from the government in exchange for the short-term debts cancelled. In 1711 party politics precluded using the 'Whig' Bank of England, and a new, Tory-controlled trading company was established for the purpose. The flotation of the South Sea Company in September converted £9.2 million of the government's floating debt into perpetual annuities, and effectively brought the fiscal situation back under control.

The South Sea flotation was the flagship achievement of the new government. However, it is reasonable to ask whether it was not, in itself, an act of default. The question of exactly what constitutes a government default has sometimes been disputed, especially when it comes to restructurings. The advent of exchange-traded credit default swaps (CDS), however, has required the establishment of a standardised definition. This definition includes any restructurings that occurs under 'conditions of impaired credit', which would certainly include Britain in 1710–11. However, the definition also requires that the restructuring be

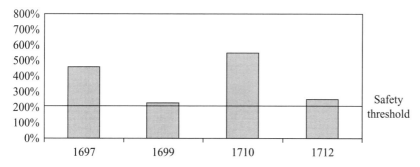

Figure 6.2. Short-term debts as a percentage of free revenues during and after fiscal crises. *Source:* Mitchell and Deane 1962, Dickson 1967.

mandatory on at least two-thirds of all creditors. By this standard, the South Sea flotation was not a default, because the creditors subscribed to the new issue voluntarily. However, under the most basic CDS definition of default – a missed payment – the debts exchanged for South Sea Company shares were certainly in default, because many had not been paid for years. In this case, it was not so much the 1711 restructuring that was an act of default, but rather the failure of earlier governments to service their short-term debts.

On the other hand, it is not clear that a modern definition of default is relevant to the early eighteenth century. Lenders then were more forgiving of delayed payments, of which there were many. What they would not accept was the repudiation or forced reduction of principal, interest, or arrears of interest. By this standard, the South Sea flotation was not a default, since principal and overdue interest were fully recognised, and the interest rate on the annuities given to the South Sea Company was at least as high as the interest, if any, on the short-term debts exchanged.

The restructuring of short-term debt was only one of the measures required to establish the country's credit on a firm footing. The underlying cause of the crises of 1697 and 1710 was the failure of successive governments to raise sufficient long-term debt. Just how far the country was from the funding practices which accompanied later wars is shown in Figure 6.3.

Without a major increase in long-term borrowing, the problem of excess short-term debt was bound to recur. This is where the Lottery loans issued by Harley come in. Their terms were described by Dickson as 'unrealistic generosity' (Dickson 1967, 74), and perhaps this has tended to colour the perceptions of later historians. It does, of course, fit neatly

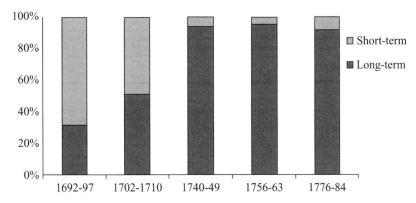

Figure 6.3. War borrowing patterns. *Sources*: Mitchell and Deane 1962, Dickson 1967.

with the Whig line that the Tories were a bunch of incompetent country squires who could not be trusted with the public finances.

In 1710 Britain's long-term debt consisted of an assortment of experiments conducted as the country felt (sometimes fumbled) its way towards a sustainable system of borrowing. The closest approximations to the form that became established later in the century were the perpetual annuities issued to the great chartered companies: the Bank of England, the East India Company, and, in 1711, the South Sea Company. These securities themselves were never traded, but the companies' shares provided a proxy vehicle for investing in the public debt. This was particularly true of the South Sea Company, which had almost no source of income other than its holdings of government debt. It was also true, to a lesser extent, of the Bank of England, whose income from banking was dwarfed by its income from government debt. The shares of the chartered companies were attractive to investors because they were easier to trade than government obligations (Sperling 1962, 4; Jones 1988, 285). Borrowing in this way also held advantages for the government by making any subsequent process of renegotiation easier (Quinn 2007). In 1710, perpetual annuities accounted for £8 million of the long-term debt. During the early years of the War of the Spanish Succession (1701–14), a similar amount had been raised in ninety-nine-year annuities at yields of between 6.64% and 6.23%, sold directly to investors. A fairly reliable secondary market existed for these annuities. A further £1.3 million of the debt took the form of life annuities, which by their nature were never traded.

Lottery loans were not an entirely novel idea when Harley took over the reins of government (Cohen 1953). The Million Adventure of 1694 had been among the very first attempts to raise long-term debt. In 1710, as the credit crisis started to take hold, Sidney Godolphin, the highly regarded Lord Treasurer, who the Whigs claimed was indispensable to national solvency, found that he could no longer raise money for ninety-nine years at relatively low yields, and had to resort to thirty-two-year annuities with a small lottery element that cost the government 8.3% per annum over their full life (Dickenson 1974). Harley maintained the thirty-two-year term and the lottery element for his new loans. However, instead of selling annuities, as had previously been the case, he incorporated changes in his new securities that effectively turned them into loans with a six per cent coupon sold at a twenty-three per cent discount to par. The resulting cost to the government was 8.55% per annum.

The question is: Was this unnecessarily expensive? The lottery loans were certainly designed to generate widespread appeal. In the first loan, issued in January 1711, 16.67% of the tickets had prizes, compared to only 2.5% in Godolphin's lottery annuities a year earlier (Ewen 1932, 134–9). The highest prize was 1,200 times the cost of a ticket. A second loan, the 'Classis' lottery issued in March 1711, contrived to make everyone a winner – albeit at the cost of reducing the scale of the largest prizes. All tickets were allocated into classes with basic prizes running from ten to thirty per cent. This generosity to the mass of ticket holders meant that the largest possible prize represented only 200 times the cost of a ticket. As a result, the subscription books were filled with ease – to the chagrin of the Whig financiers who had forecast their failure. They turned instead to accusations that the loans were unnecessarily generous, and thus were ruining the country.

Against such indictments there are two major counter-arguments. The first is the sheer scale of the loans, which inevitably increased the yield that had to be offered. Between 1704 and 1710, long-term borrowing had averaged £1.77 million per year (including £1.2 million raised from the East India Company in 1708, and £400,000 raised from the Bank of England in 1709, but excluding £1.6 million in short-term debts exchanged for long-term annuities by the Bank in 1709, because this was a refunding operation equivalent to the South Sea Company exchange in 1711, which has also been excluded). The average in 1711 to 1712 was £3.55 million. For the first time, Britain's war finance resembled its later reliance on long-term borrowing. During the War of the Austrian Succession (1740–48), the government's long-term borrowing averaged no more than £3.11 million per year. The scale of long-term borrowing in 1711 and 1712 was so great that it exceeded the budget deficit in both years, with the result that short-term debt was actually reduced. (The true 1711 budget figures are hard to determine because of previously unaccounted liabilities being included. In 1712 Robert Walpole attempted to justify the Whig government's record by arguing that most of the unaccounted debt came from either before or after their period of office. If his figures are accepted, the budget deficit attributable to 1711 falls from £10 million to £3.3 million – less than the £3.5 million raised in long-term loans. In 1712, the recorded deficit was £2.1 million, against long-term loans of £3.6 million.)

The second counter-argument relates to the structure of the loans. The term annuities issued by Godolphin had annual payments that covered both interest and principal, which made it difficult to know how much principal was outstanding at any moment. By the conventions of the period, they could not be redeemed before final maturity. However, because the lotteries took the form of interest-bearing loans, the amount of principal outstanding was always known; as a result, they could be repaid at face value. At the time of their issue this may have looked unlikely, because face value was thirty per cent higher than the amount received. However, if market interest rates fell below six per cent, it would become worth the government's while to redeem them or, more likely, to use the threat of redemption to encourage their holders to convert into lower-cost securities.

The inflexibility inherent in term annuities turned out to be a heavy price for the state to pay – one that was certainly not worth the modest 0.25% differential between the 8.3% interest cost of the thirty-two-year annuities and the 8.55% cost of the lottery loans. The extent of the financial advantage to the investor in irredeemable securities can be seen in Figure 6.4, which traces the market yield of the thirty-two-year annuities from early 1714 to their eventual disappearance in 1720.

Until late 1716, the thirty-two-year annuities followed the lottery loans in trading at progressively lower yields. By late 1716, interest rates had fallen to under six per cent, and by early 1717, the government could sell five per cent redeemable annuities at par. As the threshold of six per cent was reached, the lottery loans ceased to appreciate because of the possibility of prepayment. Similarly, the five per cent redeemable annuities never sold much above par, for the same reason. The thirty-two-year annuities appear to have sold at a modest discount to the lottery loans until the prospect of the latter's redemption loomed. At that point, the advantages of holding irredeemable securities struck home with investors, and they soared to a premium. Using the threat of repayment, it was relatively easy to persuade the holders of the lottery loans to exchange them for five per cent redeemable annuities in October 1717, but Walpole

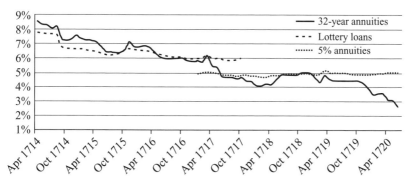

Figure 6.4. The advantage of being 'irredeemable': yield of the thirty-two-year annuities vs. redeemable securities. *Source and notes:* Yields calculated from John Freke, *The Prices of the Several Stocks, Annuities and Public Securities, &c., and the Course of the Exchange* (1714).

gave up the attempt to include the thirty-two-year and ninety-nine-year annuities in the conversion, because he was unwilling to offer the kind of premium that might have tempted their holders. It was only in the general folly of 1720 that the annuitants could be persuaded to part with their securities – and then only at valuations that implied yields of under three per cent at a time when the market for other long-term government securities was around 4.5%. In the case of the ninety-nine-year annuities, this represented a fifty per cent premium over their price at the beginning of the year, when they had traded more or less in line with other state debt.

Apart from putting the public finances on a firm ground for the first time since the start of the public debt in the 1690s, the lottery loans offered another advantage: they were remarkably inclusive. The tickets cost £10, which put them within range of a relatively wide public. In the general enthusiasm for this popular form of investing, there were proposals for lottery loans with tickets as low as £1. The number of public creditors in 1710 has been estimated at 10,000. The lottery loans attracted more than double this number (Dickson 1967, 271). Given that a wide dispersion of public debt in the population can only be positive for creating a 'credible commitment' to public solvency, this was a significant advance.

With these measures to restore the public solvency in mind, it is possible to review the history of interest rates in the period, in order to evaluate the impact of the political and financial factors that determined the cost of government borrowing.

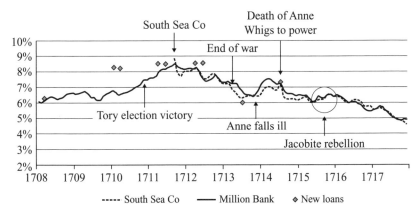

Figure 6.5. Dividend yields of the Million Bank and South Sea Company shares. *Source and notes*: Dividend yields of the Million Bank and South Sea Company shares. Prices from Castaing, *The Course of the Exchange* (1698). Yields smoothed to reflect market anticipation of the rise of Million Bank dividends from £5 to £6 in December 1713 and the reduction in South Sea Company dividends from £6 to £5 in September 1717.

Until 1711, the only security whose secondary market prices can be used as a reasonable proxy for government borrowing costs is the Million Bank.[1] After September 1711, the market yield on South Sea Company shares provides an alternative series, which turns out to coincide well with the yield on Million Bank shares.

Figure 6.5 reveals the influence of a number of factors, both political and financial, on yields. Politically, the change of government and the Tory landslide in the autumn of 1710 coincide with a significant rise in rates. However, the rise appears more as a gradual movement over a period of two years than as the short, sharp panic implied by the commentators at the time. Investor concerns over the threat of a possible repudiation or write-down of the debt following a Jacobite restoration in the months before Anne's death, and their resolution once the Hanoverian succession was assured, are also quite clear, as is the lesser effect of the Jacobite uprising in 1715 (Wells and Wills 2000). The impact of the end of hostilities in 1713 is very marked, with yields falling by almost two percentage points over a period of one year. Equally evident is the impact of the short-term debt crisis, with the reversal of the rise in yields coinciding perfectly with the flotation of the South Sea Company.

---

[1] A fund originally established in 1695 to invest in the Million Lottery annuities, and which subsequently invested in other government annuities.

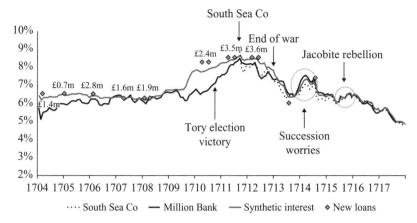

Figure 6.6. Yields against a synthetic interest rate series.

The final factor apparent in the chart is the effect of heavy issues of long-term debt, especially in 1711–12. However, there is a marked inconsistency between secondary market and new issues yields in 1710, which poses the question of how far the secondary market in Million Bank shares can be taken as a proxy for government borrowing costs. The likely explanation for the discrepancy is that when the government had to issue an unusually large amount of new debt, it was forced to pay rates higher than the market on seasoned loans. At the same time, because the Million Bank did not pay out its entire income as dividends, it was able to reinvest its surplus at market rates – a process that would gradually pull its yield towards the new, higher level at which new debt was issued. In 1713, the Million Bank was able to raise its dividend from £5 to £6 per share as a result of this process. A longer-term view of interest rates shows the same effect at the beginning of the war.

In 1704 the market yield on Million Bank shares was around 5.5%, yet the government had to pay 6.64% to raise new long-term debt for the war. By 1706, the yield on Million Bank shares had risen to reflect this new market reality, and for the following two years there was an almost perfect coincidence between primary and secondary market yields. There was then a fateful hiatus in the issue of long-term debt, with only £400,000 raised in 1709, against a deficit of $4 million. When Godolphin attempted to remedy this in 1710, he found that he had to pay a rate far above the secondary market. A synthetic interest rate series, weighted substantially towards new issue yields, can provide a plausible proxy for government borrowing costs over time. This gives a clearer idea of the impact of markedly higher levels of long-term debt issuance between 1710 and 1712.

The conclusion has to be that, although political factors played a role in the interest rate history of the period, they were outweighed by financial factors. Compare, for example, Sussman and Yafeh (this volume), who argue that wars and instability, rather than institutional reforms, are the prime determinants of interest rates. The largest rise and fall in rates which can be clearly attributed to political concerns occurred in the period between January and August 1714, when the succession crisis and its resolution drove rates up, and then down, by 80–100 basis points. The Jacobite rebellion of 1715 raised interest rates by less than fifty basis points. In contrast, the end of the war resulted in a fall in interest rates by 180–190 basis points. The effect of the election of 1710 on rates is hard to distinguish within the 250-basis-point rise in rates between 1708 and 1711 as a result of the growing short-term debt crisis. The rise in the yield of Million Bank shares in the six months leading up to the election amounted to 80 basis points, which is almost certainly an overgenerous estimate of the political element in this process, given that new issue yields had risen by 200 basis points before the political crisis got under way. In any case, whatever fears there may have been about a Tory government in 1710 had been fully dispelled by 1713, as can be seen in the fall of rates to levels that were not improved upon by the post-1714 Whig government until late 1716. As Roseveare put it, 'The myth of an omnipotent Whig monied interest had been exploded – and so too was the myth of rustic Tory innocence' (Roseveare 1991, 46).

It appears from this analysis that the most important element in the market's reaction throughout this period was the issue of the government's ability to service its debt – rather than concerns about its financial competence, or the risk that political change might bring in a government that questioned the legitimacy of the debt.

The ratio of floating debt to free revenues, when used as a proxy for the government's ability to run its finances on a sustainable basis, has the advantage of including not just short-term debts and revenues, but also long-term debt levels and interest rates. It therefore offers a relatively complete picture of the sustainability of the government's debt in a single number. With it, it is possible to look at a longer-term history of the early years of the financial revolution to see how this measure of fiscal sustainability correlates to interest rate movements. The fit turns out to be remarkably good, with a coincidence of peaks not only in 1710–11, but also in the crisis of 1697, in the relatively minor fluctuation of 1700–1701, and in the continued fall of both short-term debt and interest rates after 1716. It is also important to note that short-term debt levels remained dangerously high throughout the whole period from 1696 to 1717, as Figure 6.8 indicates.

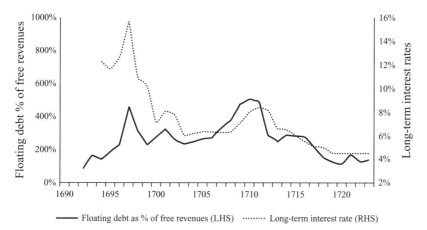

Figure 6.7. Floating debt as a percentage of free revenues vs. long-term interest rates. *Source and notes:* Annual average rates calculated as follows: 1694–1700, yield to maturity of the Million lottery annuities based on market prices in Houghton, *Collection for Improvement* (1692); after 1700, yield of Million Bank shares adjusted for new issue yields as outlined above.

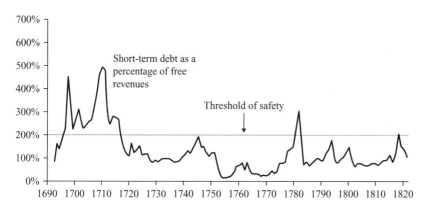

Figure 6.8. Short-term debt vs. free revenues. *Sources*: Mitchell and Deane 1962, Dickson 1967.

The levels of unfunded debt in the early years of the financial revolution were truly aberrant in a long-term perspective. After 1717, short-term debt only once rose above the danger level of 200 per cent of free revenues – towards the end of the War of American Independence. In contrast, before 1717 short-term debt was always above the danger level,

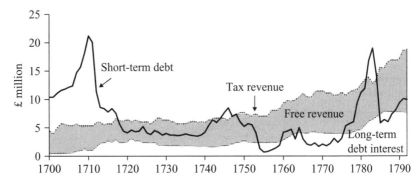

Figure 6.9. Short-term debt, tax revenues, and interest on the long-term debt. *Sources*: Mitchell and Deane 1962, Dickson 1967.

even when the immediate crises of 1697 and 1710–11 had been resolved. This in itself is sufficient to explain the stubbornly high interest rates that prevailed throughout the War of the Spanish Succession.

It is worth noting that, because of their volatility, changes in the level of short-term debt were more important than changing levels of taxes or interest payments in determining the movements of this ratio. Tax revenues were relatively static in the first half of the eighteenth century, starting to climb significantly only at the onset of the Seven Years War. The growth in long-term debt interest was a major contributory factor in the squeeze on free revenues in the early decades of the financial revolution, as is not surprising, given that debt started from almost nothing, interest rates were high, and interest costs were further increased by the exchange of short-term for long-term debt in 1697, 1709, and 1711. Thereafter interest costs stabilised, and started to grow only in the later decades of the century, but at a lower rate than taxes, except in times of war.

The reward for the sustainable funding practices that prevailed after 1717 was lower interest rates. The fall in interest rates was not the result of an easing debt burden in relation to GDP. By the outbreak of the French Revolution, British debt had risen from £40 million in 1710 to £245 million. This far outpaced the modest rate of economic growth over the period (around one per cent per annum), and there was no offsetting help from inflation, because price levels were unchanged in 1789. In contrast, the correlation between interest rates and the short-term debt ratio holds up remarkably well, at least until around 1797, as Figure 6.10 shows. After that date, other factors probably weighed at least as heavily on the bond market as floating debt. In particular, sterling

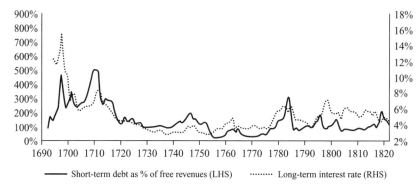

Figure 6.10. Short-term debt and long-term interest rates. *Sources*: As in previous charts, plus the average annual yields of three per cent annuities from Homer and Sylla 1991.

was no longer convertible into gold, raising the question of the real value of the currency in which debt would be repaid. Moreover, the total amount of debt outstanding was simply so great that its sustainability was questionable even if it was almost all long-term.

Interestingly, the greatest deviation in the correlation appears at the very beginning of the era of public debt. Until 1695 short-term debt was safely below the threshold of danger – if only because the practice of public borrowing was so new that large amounts of debt had not yet been built up. However, this did not make it possible for the government to borrow long-term at affordable rates. Ignoring the flotation of the Bank of England, where investors had substantial additional incentives over and above the income from the Bank's annuities (which were in any case scarcely cheap at eight per cent), the earliest successful long-term debt issues were the Million lottery of 1694, which cost 11.57%, and the life annuities of 1693–94, which also cost over ten per cent per year. The exact cost of the latter is difficult to estimate, but a clue is provided by the fact that in 1694 investors could get fourteen per cent on one life, twelve per cent on two lives, and ten per cent on three – obviously on the expectation that more lives would lead to a longer stream of payments. Thus, it cannot easily be argued that it was the government's failure to issue sufficient long-term debt that was the main cause of these high rates. It is likely that cause and effect worked the other way around. It was the near impossibility of raising affordable long-term debt that forced to government to rely on short-term borrowing.

The very low level of confidence in the security of the debt implied by these rates may have resulted from a number of factors: uncertainty over the durability of the Revolution; the untested nature of the new regime; the reluctance of Parliament to grant taxes in perpetuity; the poor credit record of almost all previous English regimes, including the Commonwealth; and the lack of experience of English investors with long-term debt instruments. In any case, the unwillingness of creditors to provide affordable long-term funds was an instance of self-fulfilling prophecy, because it ensured that the default that they feared would become a virtual certainty. The restoration of credit in 1697 without a write-down of debt meant that the regime had survived the crucial first test of its competence and good faith. It was rewarded by the largest fall in the yields of government securities in the history of British state debt. At the peak of the crisis in the spring of 1697, the Million Lottery annuities yielded almost eighteen per cent. By October 1700 this had fallen to little more than six per cent. The second greatest rally over a comparable period occurred between 1974 and 1977, when the yields of long-term government bonds fell from eighteen to eleven per cent.

During the War of the Spanish Succession the government was able to raise long-term debt at a cost that, although not cheap at over six per cent, was at least affordable. There seems little doubt that, had he insisted, Godolphin could have raised sufficient long-term debt to prevent the short-term debt crisis that erupted in 1710. That the market existed is proved by the ability of the Tories to raise very large sums during the following two years. Godolphin would probably have had to pay close to seven per cent to raise enough long-term debt to forestall the crisis, but had he done so, Harley would not have had to pay over 8.5% to restore public solvency in 1711–12.

After the successful resolution of the crisis of 1710–11, Britain gained a second reward from the markets for its demonstration of its commitment to financial solvency under adverse conditions. The restoration of credit was the more impressive precisely because it occurred under a government not representative of the interests of government creditors.

An interesting parallel with events in the early years of the English financial revolution is provided by the history of the early years of the United States. The refunding of unpaid revolutionary debts by Alexander Hamilton in 1790 displays a number of parallels with the refunding of unpaid British short-term debts in 1711. The interest rate was six per cent in both cases, and the process of conversion was voluntary. Nonetheless, creditors had to accept long-term securities that sold at a discount to par. The refunding restored the government's credit, and created a substantial body of long-term government creditors. The major difference, however, is that Hamilton was, in British terms, a Whig: a friend of

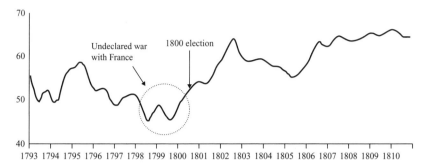

Figure 6.11. U.S. three per cent bond prices. *Source and notes:* Moving average of monthly prices on the New York stock exchange, compiled from the U.S. government bond trading database created by Robert E. Wright (2007).

mercantile interests, and a believer in central banks and financial markets. In order to consolidate the American financial revolution, the Hamiltonian system had to prove that it could withstand the transfer of power to its opponents. In 1800 the Jeffersonian Republicans, a party of the landed classes strongly opposed to Hamilton's 'British' system of finance (Ferguson 1983), swept to electoral victory. Yet, like the Tories in 1710, the Jeffersonian Republicans showed themselves to be far more responsible financially than suggested by the propaganda of their opponents. The Hamiltonian revolution was not overturned, and the debt was serviced punctually. The result was a strong rally in government bonds, illustrated in Figure 6.11.

The final question to be considered is why the Tories acted the way that they did, rather than as predicted by their opponents. One possible argument is that the government was not very 'Tory' after all. Harley was a former 'Country Whig' from a nonconformist background. His objective in 1710 was to establish a government open to all moderates, until the sweeping election result somewhat forced his hand. It is not clear what the outcome would have been if the government had been headed by some of the more extreme members of the party. However, Harley's position was in many ways typical of parliamentary systems, where the leadership is invariably more moderate than the rank and file. That this is so often the case is a reflection of the dictates of electoral politics. Parties need to appeal beyond their core voters if they are to get elected, and this need often results in leaders who are more centrist than their followers. Although the election campaign of 1710 was very heated, one of its strikingly modern features was the inherently centrist claim of both sides to be better able to run the country's finances.

Competition for power also goes to the heart of another reason for the success of the Tories in handling the nation's finances. One of the main complaints of the Whigs' opponents in 1710 was that they had monopolised the benefits of power. The ranks of the dyed-in-the-wool Country Tories were augmented by the presence of less deeply committed urban fellow travellers who were concerned mainly to overturn the Whig stranglehold on finance. A prime example is John Blunt, one of the main architects of the South Sea Company and of the lottery loans. His later justified disrepute as a result of the events of 1720 should not entirely overshadow his earlier achievements. This competition for the perks of handling government finances explains why the shares of the Bank of England declined by more than any others in the pre-election period – falling by twenty-one per cent compared to a fall of only nine per cent in Million Bank shares. This suggests that investors were more concerned about the possible erosion of the 'Whig' Bank's privileges than they were about a government default per se. In other words, the markets may have understood that the threat to government solvency from a Tory victory was never as real as Whig pre-election propaganda suggested.

All these moderating aspects of the competition for power are by-products of the principal virtue of electoral systems of government: their ability to co-opt opposition forces by giving them the prospect of coming to power. This makes it less likely that they will take actions that will undermine the political system. As an anonymous correspondent to the Tory mouthpiece *The Examiner* put it in August 1710, at the height of the heated campaign debate, 'Can any wise people think it possible . . . that any Parliament should be so unwise . . . as to destroy the credit of all Parliaments?' His rhetorical question was in answer to the rumour that the Dutch Estates General had intervened with the Queen to prevent a change of government and a general election. No people so wise as the Dutch, the declared 'country gentleman' wrote, can have made the mistake of confusing the credit of the nation with that of a single party, the Whigs (*The Examiner*, 24 August 1710).

Moreover, a turn in office, with all the responsibility it entails, gives opposition parties the chance to come to terms with reforms that are easy to attack from the safety of the opposition benches. The conclusion must be that if one is to seek a purely institutional element in the creation of 'credible commitment' in England after 1688, it is more likely to have come from the electoral system itself than from the establishment of multiple veto points.

References

Castaing, John 1698-. *The Course of the Exchange*. London.

Cohen, Jacob 1953. 'The Element of Lottery in British Government Bonds, 1694–1919', *Economica*, 20, 237–46.

Defoe, Daniel 1710. *An Essay upon Loans*. London.

Dickenson, W. C. 1974. *The Sword of Gold: Sidney Godolphin and War Finance, 1702–1710*. Avebury: Albion.

Dickson, P. G. M. 1967. *The Financial Revolution in England: A Study in the Development of Public Credit*. London: Macmillan Ltd.

Downie, J. A., 1979. *Robert Harley and the Press*. Cambridge: Cambridge University Press.

Ewen, C. L. 1932. *Lotteries and Sweepstakes*. London: Ayer.

The Examiner. London, 24 August 1710.

Ferguson, E. J. 1983. 'Political Economy, Public Liberty, and the Formation of the Constitution', *William and Mary Quarterly*, 40, 389–412.

Freke, John 1714-. *The Prices of the Several Stocks, Annuities, and Other Publick Securities, &c., with the Course of the Exchange*. London.

Hayton, D. 2002. *The House of Commons 1690–1815*. Cambridge: Cambridge University Press.

Hill, B. R. 1971. 'The Change of Government and the "Loss of the City" 1710–1711', *Economic History Review*, 224, 395–413.

Hoadly, B. 1710. *The Fears and Sentiments of All True Britains with Respect to National Credit, Interest and Religion*. London.

Homer, S. and Sylla, R. 1991. *A History of Interest Rates*. New Brunswick, NJ: Rutgers University Press.

Hoppit, J. 2000. *A Land of Liberty? England 1689–1727*. Oxford: Oxford University Press.

Houghton, J. 1692. *A Collection for Improvement of Husbandry and Trade*. London.

Jones, D. W. 1988. *War and Economy in the Age of William III and Marlborough*. Oxford: Oxford University Press.

Mitchell, B. R. and Deane, P. 1962. *Abstract of British Historical Statistics*. Cambridge: Cambridge University Press.

Morgan, W. T. 1921. 'The Ministerial Revolution of 1710 in England', *Political Science Quarterly*, 36(2) 184–210.

Murphy, A. L. 2013. 'Demanding "Credible Commitment": Public Reactions to the Failures of the Early Financial Revolution', *Economic History Review*, 66, 178–97.

North, D. C. and Weingast, B. 1989. 'Constitutions and Commitment: The Evolution of Institutions Concerning Public Choice in Seventeenth Century England', *Journal of Economic History* 43, 803–32.

Quinn, S. 2007. *Securitization of Sovereign Debt: Corporations as a Sovereign Debt Restructuring Mechanism in Britain, 1688–1750*. Fort Worth: Texan Christian University.

Roberts, C. 1982. 'The Fall of the Godolphin Ministry', *Journal of British Studies*, 22, 71–93.

Roseveare, H. 1991. *The Financial Revolution, 1660–1760*. London: Longman.

Stasavage, D. 2003. *Public Debt and the Birth of the Democratic State*, Cambridge: Cambridge University Press.

Stasavage, D. 2007. *Partisan Politics and Public Debt: The Importance of the 'Whig Supremacy' for Britain's Financial Revolution*. New York University.

Swift, J. 1711. *The Conduct of the Allies and of the Late Ministry in Beginning and Carrying on the Present War*. London.

Walpole, R. 1712. *The Debts of the Nation Stated and Considered in Four Papers*. London.

Wells, J. and Wills, D. 2000. 'Revolution, Restoration and Debt Repudiation: The Jacobite Threat to England's Institutions and Economic Growth', *Journal of Economic History*, 60, 418–41.

Wennerlind, Carl 2011. *Casualties of Credit: The English Financial Revolution, 1620–1720*. Cambridge, MA: Harvard University Press.

Wright, R. E. 2007. 'US Government Bond Trading Database, 1776–1835', EH.net.

7 Financing and refinancing the War of the Spanish Succession, and then refinancing the South Sea Company

Ann M. Carlos, Erin K. Fletcher, Larry Neal, and Kirsten Wandschneider

Some European historians think of the War of the Spanish Succession (1701–1714) as the first true world war. Although the conflict was strictly European, fought over whether a Bourbon or Habsburg monarch would succeed to the Spanish throne after the death of the childless Charles II, it engaged European forces throughout the empires of Austria, Spain, France, the Netherlands, and Britain. The Great Northern War (1700–1721), which overlapped with the War of the Spanish Succession, was fought between the established empire of Sweden and the rising empire of Russia. Throughout Europe, therefore, the eighteenth century began with an extensive application of recently developed military technology: infantry, cavalry, and naval forces were fully armed with new, expensive artillery and other costly accoutrements. Thus, the battles waged in support of conflicting dynastic claims proved increasingly pricey for each belligerent (Parker 1988). Hamilton (1947) claimed that the mounting expenses of modern warfare encumbered each of the European powers with unprecedented amounts of debt.

As an uneasy peace settled over Europe after 1720, Britain's increasingly successful war finance demonstrated that only she had succeeded in devising a long-term solution to the problem of paying for the rising costs of modern warfare. How Britain managed to do so while also laying the basis for intermittent peacetime prosperity over the next century is the subject of this chapter. It argues that the key element was the existence of a large and diverse group willing and able to hold state debt in the form of easily traded securities, supported by London's efficient stock market. North and Weingast (1989) relied heavily on Dickson's magisterial work on the British Financial Revolution to bolster their argument about the importance of parliamentary power after 1688. This chapter also looks back to Dickson, elaborating on one of his key ideas, that 'If an efficient market in securities had not developed in London, where lenders could sell their claim to annual interest in return for a capital sum, the state would hardly have been able to float long-term loans without promising to repay them' (Dickson 1967, 245). Further, it explores in detail Britain's successful efforts, following 1688, to finance and refinance her war debts into tradable securities that were seen by investors as both appealing and liquid. In other words, it shows how successive British governments, with the assistance of corporate projectors and experienced market makers, worked to transform state debt into a credible investment choice for a broad segment of savers and investors – including a great many women.

Dickson's focus on Britain's increasing use of funded long-term debt has been augmented by later scholars' work covering other elements of the Financial Revolution. Jones (1988) showed how short-term financing of immediate war needs was developed over the course of William III's first war, the War of the League of Augsburg (1689–97), and then fully implemented during the War of the Spanish Succession. Brewer (1988) demonstrated how Britain's improved capacity for taxation provided the increased revenues necessary to service ever larger amounts of outstanding permanent debt. North and Weingast (1989) identified the key change as the rise of Parliament's power in relation to the king's. The instrument of this power became the Bank of England, which served as a bureaucratic 'delegated monitor' of the government's commitment to service the state's debt (Weingast 1997; Stasavage 2002), although Quinn (2004; Quinn 2005) and Sussman and Yafeh (2006) have questioned the Bank's ability to serve effectively in this role. The part that excise revenues would play later in assuring that Parliament could continue to service ever larger amounts of outstanding funded debt was just appearing at the time of the re-financing of existing government debt in 1720, as shown in Figure 7.1. Part of the revolutionary settlement had been to equalise the revenues deriving from the main interest groups represented in Parliament, but the extraordinary expenses of the War of the Spanish Succession created more pressure on the land tax. With the victory of the Tories in the election of 1710 (MacDonald, this volume), increasing reliance on the excise as the primary source of revenues emerged, laying the basis for reliable servicing of all future issues of British government debt.

All of this occurred in the context of a pre-existing secondary market for private debt and equity (Carlos, Key, and Dupree 1998; Carlos and Neal 2011). This chapter argues that the secondary market in tradable and transparently priced financial assets, which easily accommodated the new government securities, was the organisational innovation that generated 'credible commitment'. Although the stock market in London developed rapidly after 1688, the government's success in maintaining the marketability of the South Sea Company's securities after the

Figure 7.1. Main revenue sources of the British government, 1692–1750, £000. *Source:* Mitchell 1988, 575–6.

collapse of the South Sea Bubble in 1720 was the defining moment for this innovation (Neal 1990). In particular, debt refinancing through the Company in 1720 and the Company's reorganisation in 1723 were the key developments that allowed Britain to manage its debt successfully on through the wars of the eighteenth century, and into the nineteenth.

The War of the Spanish Succession

The death in 1700 of Charles II, the childless Habsburg king of Spain, was the proximate cause of the War of the Spanish Succession. His will specified that his successor was to be Philip, Duke of Anjou, the second grandson of Louis XIV, the Bourbon king of France, on condition that Philip waive any claim he or his descendants might have to the French throne. Philip's accession to the throne of Spain, however, with its control of Spain's possessions in America and northern Italy, and his filial relationship with the monarch of France, threatened both Britain and Austria. Britain was concerned about its Atlantic trade, whereas its new allies, the Dutch Republic and Portugal, were determined to maintain their hard-won independence from Spain. The Habsburgs in Vienna, ruling as Holy Roman Emperors, were concerned about their Italian borders in the aftermath of the siege of Vienna in 1683, and Archduke Charles of Austria, second son of the Habsburg Emperor, laid claim to the Spanish throne. Everyone was worried about the possibility that France and Spain could be united under the Bourbon dynasty.

Hostilities began in spring 1701 when Leopold I's invasion of northern Italy led to a series of land battles. The war was also waged at sea, where the British navy captured the key Mediterranean ports of Gibraltar and Port Mahon. Conflict spread to the Caribbean and North America, resulting in British conquest of Newfoundland and French Acadia (henceforth Nova Scotia). The Battle of Blenheim in 1704 was decisive in escalating the war, because victory by the Grand Alliance led the British and Austrians to persevere, whereas defeat persuaded the French to focus on the true prize, the crown of Spain. As a result, the war and its expenses continued to mount for another ten years, until the British and Dutch withdrew in 1713. The Austrian claimant, now Holy Roman Emperor Charles VI, abandoned his quest for Spain shortly afterwards. Under minor codicils of the Treaty of Utrecht, which transferred the Spanish Netherlands to Austria, France granted the *asiento* monopoly of the Spanish American slave trade to Britain, which in turn handed it to the newly formed South Sea Company.

Meanwhile the Great Northern War was waged sporadically, with occasional participation by Denmark, various German states (including Hanover, then governed by the future George I of Britain), and the Ottoman Empire. Consequently, all of Europe's states incurred enormous expenses in support of professional armies equipped with the latest and most expensive equipment, and forced to move large distances from their home bases, which entailed significant and very costly logistical support (Lynn 1993; Lynn 1997). When peace was finally achieved, the development of methods of financing and repaying the unprecedented debts incurred became a political and commercial priority across Europe.

Dealing with the debts created by the war

Intense experimentation with the management of each power's debt continued for a decade; by the end of 1723, each country had settled its war debts one way or another. Spain refinanced under Philip V, primarily by turning over control of silver imports from Spanish America to court favourites, but also by adding the revenues of the Kingdom of Aragon to those of Castile as crown privileges (Kamen 1969; Frey and Frey 1983; Kamen 2001). Austria, after refinancing long-term her wartime borrowing from England, turned to the mercantile riches of her newly acquired Austrian Netherlands, and even attempted to break into the East Indies trade through a dedicated company at Ostend. However, Austria failed to reform her tax base, which undermined her efforts in subsequent eighteenth-century wars (Dickson 1987). In the north, Sweden gave up its pretensions to being a great power centred on domination of the Baltic Sea, while Russia began its pursuit of great-power status under the aegis of Peter the Great. The Dutch Republic relied mainly on Holland, its richest maritime province, to increase its debt in the form of life annuities, which it serviced by increasing the excise duties on all consumption goods (Dormans 1991; Fritschy and Voort 1997; Gelderblom and Jonker 2009). France, bankrupt after the death of Louis XIV in 1715, turned to innovations that culminated in John Law's *système* in 1720 and a segmented default on its outstanding debt in 1723, ending with eventual stabilisation of the currency in 1726 (Murphy 1997).

By the end of the War of the League of Augsburg in 1697, Britain had established a workable war finance strategy. It depended first on issuing large amounts of short-term debt to mobilise resources quickly, and second on sustaining the market value of debt held by the public. The first component rested upon the payments mechanism operated by the Bank of England, within the existing framework of trade finance, and based upon the four-part foreign bill of exchange (Neal 1990). Key naval and land battles were fought overseas by British forces, so means of payment had to be found at home which were acceptable to provisioning merchants abroad. This was achieved through the issue of Exchequer bills to the Bank, which created credits drawn down by the government to purchase foreign bills of exchange from merchant bankers in London. These bills were drawn upon the bankers' correspondents in relevant foreign cities – Amsterdam most often, but also Hamburg, Lisbon, Naples, Barcelona, and Genoa. Merchant bankers in these cities accepted the bills from London, using their credits against London bankers to import consumer goods from England, Wales, Ireland, or Scotland, sometimes for re-export. The increased trade generated customs revenues used to retire the Exchequer bills held by the Bank. Adam Smith, in Book IV of *Wealth of Nations*, observed that England had managed to export soldiers in the form of pottery and cloth. However, these short-term debts mounted over the course of each war, causing the purchasing power of London bills to fall, as suppliers accepted them only at increasing discounts. This led to experimentation with different forms of funded long-term debt to be offered to the public. The goal was to exchange discounted short-term debt at face value for new long-term debt.

With the approval of Parliament, William's ministers tried several different forms of long-term debt in the 1690s. In 1693, single life annuities paying fourteen per cent were issued as an alternative to a complicated tontine scheme. A second series of annuities for one, two, and three lives

Table 7.1. *Government long-term borrowing, 1693–8*

Date	Sum raised	Interest	Form of loan
26 January 1693	£108,100	10% to 1700, then 7%	Tontine loan
26 January 1693	£773,394	14%	Single life annuities
8 February 1694	£118,506	14%	Single life annuities
23 March 1694	£1,000,000	14%	Lottery of £10 tickets
24 April 1694	£1,200,000	8%	Bank of England
24 April 1694	£300,000	10, 12, and 14%	Annuities for 3, 2, 1 life, respectively
16 April 1697	£1,400,000	6.3%	Lottery of £10 tickets (most unsold)
5 July 1698	£2,000,000	8%	New East India Company
Total	£6,900,000		

Source: Dickson 1967, 48–9.

paid interest at ten, twelve, and fourteen percent (see Macdonald, this volume). A 1697 offer of £10 lottery tickets at 6.3% was so unpopular that it raised only £17,630, and the Exchequer used the remaining tickets, with a face value of nearly £1,400,000, as cash until 1711. Debt-for-equity swaps were another innovation, and proved much more successful. In 1694 shares in the new Bank of England were exchanged for outstanding debt, with the government paying the Bank eight per cent on the converted debt it assumed (Dickson 1967, 48–9). The creation of the New East India Company in 1698 followed the same blueprint. Such use of the private equity market was more successful by far than the annuity conversions, as illustrated in Table 7.1, which shows how large sums of capital were mobilised in support of state debt at lower interest rates than were achievable with annuities.

Experimentation continued. A refinancing in 1705 involved the conversion of single life annuities into ninety-nine-year annuities, and in 1709 the capital stock of the Bank of England was doubled to £4,402,343 to allow for the debt-for-equity refinancing of outstanding annuities of this type (see Table 7.2) (Grellier 1805, 68). However, the greatest of the debt-for-equity swaps still lay ahead. Following the earlier successes of the Bank and the New East India Company, the projectors of the South Sea Company proposed, in 1710, to assume nearly £10 million of outstanding short- and long-term state debt at a reduced rate of 5.5 per cent. The following year, debt holders received the face value of depreciated debt instruments if they exchanged them for shares in the

Table 7.2. *Long-term government borrowing during the War of the Spanish Succession*

Date	Sum raised	Interest	Form of loan
24 February 1704	£1,382,976	6.6%	99-year annuities 1, 2, 3 life annuities
16 January 1705	£690,000	6.6%	99-year annuities
16 February 1706	£2,855,762	6.4%	99-year annuities
27 March 1707	£1,155,000	6.25%	99-year annuities
13 February 1708	£640,000	6.25%	99-year annuities
11 March 1708	£1,280,000	6.25%	99-year annuities
18 January 1710	£1,500,000	9%	Lottery of £10 tickets
13 March 1710	£900,000	9%	32-year annuities
6 March 1711	£1,928,570	6%	Lottery of £10 tickets
12 June 1711	£9,177,968	6%	South Sea Company
12 June 1711	£2,602,000	6%	Lottery of £10 tickets
22 May 1712	£2,341,740	6%	Lottery of £10 tickets
21 June 1712	£2,341,990	6%	Lottery of £10 tickets
Total	£28,796,006		

Source: Dickson 1967, 60–61, 63, 68.

capital stock of the new company. South Sea shares initially traded at the average depreciated level of the predecessor instruments, around seventy per cent of book value, and rose to above par after the War of the Spanish Succession, when the Company was awarded the *asiento* for the Spanish slave trade.

The War had caused an unprecedented increase in state debt, as shown in Figure 7.2 and Table 7.2. Total liabilities were £28,796,006, compared to the previous war's £6,900,000. Small issues of thirty-two-year lottery tickets had been made in 1713 and 1714 to complete the war financing, but as the peacetime economy revived, especially after the successful quelling of an abortive Jacobite rebellion in 1715, the Whig administration of George I began to seek ways to refinance accumulated debts. The Lords of the Treasury were most concerned about the ninety-nine-year annuities issued throughout the war, because they were irredeemable, with interest rates that had looked attractive to the government during the war, but were higher than seemed feasible during the peace. Their rates – 6.7% on the long annuities and 8.5% on the short – were the highest of all the remaining debts after earlier refinancing operations, and they could not be repurchased without the holders' consent.

Difficulty with Spanish authorities over the *asiento* prompted the South Sea Company to revisit its most successful endeavour – refinancing

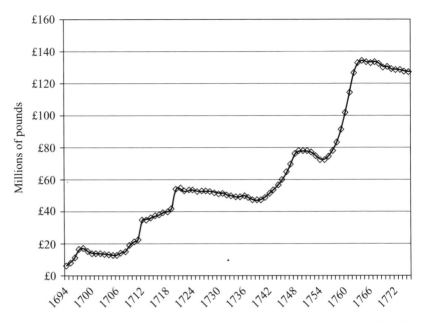

Figure 7.2. British national debt (funded), 1694–1775. *Source:* Mitchell 1988, 600–603.

illiquid state debt – in 1719, when it converted a series of illiquid annuities issued during the War of the League of Augsburg. The successes of earlier, small-scale refinancing efforts, combined with the evidence of the apparent success in that year of John Law's scheme for refinancing all of the French government's outstanding debt into capital stock of the Mississippi Company, lay the basis for the South Sea refinancing of 1720. The South Sea proposal was to convert all remaining forms of outstanding British debt, including some that remained from the Third Anglo-Dutch War (1672–4) and the War of the League of Augsburg. The project was largely complete by the end of the summer of 1720. The market price of South Sea Company shares rose substantially, but collapsed in early October, marking the end of the well-known South Sea Bubble. However, what happened next is of much greater importance.

In 1723, Walpole framed a solution for individuals who had converted their state debt into claims on shares in the expanded capital of the South Sea Company during 1720. Some £4 million of its capital stock was transferred to the Bank of England. Each claim against the remainder, some £38 million, was to be split equally between equity in the Company, yielding whatever dividends it might produce in the future, and perpetual annuities issued at five per cent for the first five years, and four per cent

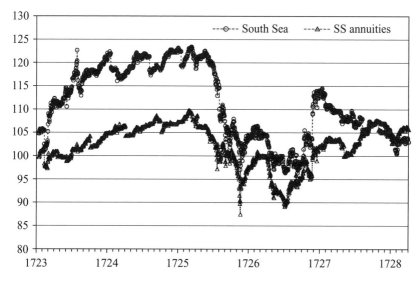

Figure 7.3. Prices of South Sea Company shares and annuities, 1723–8.

subsequently. (The rate was ultimately reduced to three per cent in January 1751, when the Company was wound up during the general consolidation of state debt carried out by Henry Pelham).

The restructuring was a defining financial innovation. It succeeded so well in reviving the market for state debt that, as future wars occurred, they were financed primarily by issuing comparable perpetual annuities as direct claims on the government, rather than issuing loans intermediated through company stock. Over time the initial interest rate fell to three per cent, and the accumulated mass of these instruments, issued nearly annually during the course of the War of the Austrian Succession (1740–48), led in mid-century to consolidation of all such annuities into Three Per Cent Consols. These became the dominant form of British national debt thereafter, overshadowing the continued holding of long-term national debt by companies. Britain financed its future wars with fresh issues of Consols.

An active market in the annuities developed immediately, and quickly surpassed the market for shares of the refinanced South Sea Company. The price of the annuities held remarkably steady during the following years (Figure 7.3). The successful reorganisation of the South Sea Company's affairs in 1723, which completed the refinancing of long-term government debt, meant that London stock market investors, as indirect government creditors, could put the turmoil of 1720 safely behind them. Successive Lords of the Treasury had successfully refinanced Britain's

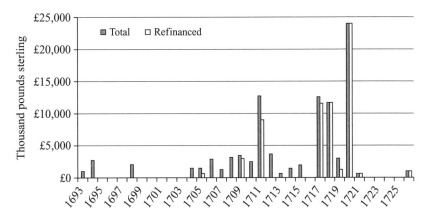

Figure 7.4. New issues of British funded debt, 1693–1726. *Source:* Quinn 2005. Data kindly supplied by author.

war debt on more favourable terms. The pattern of issuing funded, long-term debt, and then converting less liquid forms into investments that were more easily traded, is illustrated in Figure 7.4.

Figure 7.5 shows the ratio of British debt service to total revenue over the critical first decades of the Financial Revolution, and illustrates the early importance of debt-servicing cost when compared to increased revenue. The effects of the two wars bracketing the turn of the century show up clearly in the huge rises in the ratio. The War of the League of Augsburg raised the ratio from five per cent to over thirty per cent, whereas the War of the Spanish Succession took it from twenty per cent to sixty, before the refinancing efforts of Walpole (1717–19), Sunderland (1720), and Walpole (1723). Peaking at nearly sixty per cent of available revenue in 1718, the ratio was brought down sharply, in two stages, by 1731, to nearly thirty-five per cent. The first stage of these reductions was the restructuring under the South Sea Company; the second was the use of perpetual annuities paid directly by the government.

Figure 7.6 divides the components of the changes in the ratio into changes in debt service, which arose from refinancing operations or issues of new debt, and changes in revenue. The sharpest changes in both numerator and denominator occurred in the first quarter of the century. In short, refinancing operations were key to the Financial Revolution. The revenue increases that were achieved through taxation and were committed to debt service came afterwards.

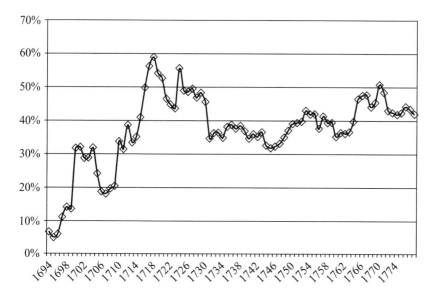

Figure 7.5. British debt service as percentage of revenues, 1694–1775.

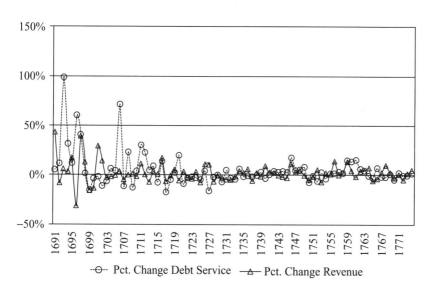

Figure 7.6. Components of changes in British debt-service ratios, 1694–1775.

Table 7.3. *Distribution of subscribers to initial funded debt issued in 1693–4*

	Tontine 1693				Bank of England, 1694			
Unit £	Nos.	%	£	%	Nos.	%	£	%
Under £500	1,107	88.1%	£180,000	60.5%	442	34.9%	£77,700	6.5%
£500–999	118	9.4%	£70,700	23.8%	435	34.3%	£227,150	18.9%
£1,000–4,999	32	2.5%	£46,700	15.7%	347	27.4%	£571,250	47.6%
£5,000–9,999	0	0	0	0	32	2.5%	£203,900	17.0%
Above £10,000	0	0	0	0	12	0.9%	£120,000	10.0%

Source: Dickson 1967, 255.

Investors in British state debt

Why was this refinancing so successful? Analysis of the holders of various forms of British debt issued during the War of the Spanish Succession shows that a liquid secondary market for this debt was re-established quickly after the collapse of the South Sea scheme. Encoding of individual holdings of various forms of long-term funded debt over the course of the South Sea Bubble provides an improved picture of the identity of debt holders. Dickson found no contemporary enumerations of holdings, and therefore made rough calculations of his own (Dickson 1967, ch. 11), reproduced in Table 7.3. This work reveals a clear distinction between holders of early tontines, which were issued in small denominations, and chartered companies' shares, which were purchased by syndicates of wealthy merchants and gentry: smallholders dominated the 1693 tontine.

Dickson's analysis of the ledgers preserved at the Bank of England considered relatively small samples of shareholders. He enumerated holders of the 1717 five per cent annuities in 1719, of South Sea shares in 1724, and of Bank of England and East India Company shares on 25 March 1724, when dividends were paid. Modern technology and funding from the National Science Foundation have facilitated a much broader analysis, which considered the holdings of each Bank of England shareholder in 1720 and 1725 (Carlos and Neal 2006), of each East India Company shareholder for 1719–21, of each South Sea Company shareholder in June 1723, and of each Royal African Company (RAC) holder of both its senior and engrafted issues of 1720 (Carlos, Fletcher, and Neal 2012). With the exception of the senior RAC issue, the sources of data are original ledgers. The result is the most complete list of shareholders yet assembled, unique in its breadth of coverage.

Table 7.4 compares Dickson's rough estimates with more precise calculations of the distribution of holdings both before and after refinancings

Table 7.4. *Distribution of numbers of holders of bank stock (1724), East India stock (1724), 5% annuities (1719), South Sea stock (1724), and South Sea annuities (1723)*

| | Bank (1724) | | Bank (1725) | | EIC (1719) | | EIC (1724) | | 5% A's (1719) | | SS (1724) | | SSA (1723) | |
	Nos.	%	Nos.	%	Nos.	%	Nos.	%	Nos.	%	Nos	%	Nos.	%
Under £500	1,116	24.0	1,309	26.6	305	18.9	479	25.3	1,073	62.9	466	55.2	14,932	69.2
£500–999	1,204	25.8	1,177	23.9	503	31.2	518	27.4	280	16.4	141	16.7	2,976	13.8
£1,000–4,999	1,941	41.6	2,038	41.4	665	41.3	765	40.4	315	18.5	184	21.8	3,100	14.4
£5,000–9,999	262	5.6	256	5.2	92	5.7	82	4.3	25	1.5	41	4.9	376	1.7
Over £10,000	139	3.0	141	2.9	47	2.9	48	2.6	11	0.7	12	1.4	193	0.9
Sum	4,662	100	4,921	100	1612	100	1892	100	1,704	100	844	100	21,577	100

Source: Dickson 1967, 275.

Table 7.5a. *Distribution of amounts held of bank stock (1724), East India stock (1724), 5% annuities (1719), and South Sea stock (1724)*

Distrib'n	Bank (1724) £	%	EIC (1724) £	%	5% Ann's. (1719) £	%	SS (1724) £	%
Under £500	£242,629	2.7	£92,480	2.9	£193,415	14.3	£94,528	8.8
£500–999	£684,323	7.6	£292,330	9.2	£182,842	13.6	£93,650	8.7
£1,000–4,999	£3,638,158	40.6	£1,427,708	44.7	£585,557	43.3	£387,392	36.2
£5,000–9,999	£1,692,021	18.9	£541,396	16.9	£155,617	11.5	£272,956	25.5
Over £10,000	£2,702,865	30.2	£840,166	26.3	£234,324	17.3	£222,696	20.8
Sum	£8,959,996	100	£3,194,080	100	£1,351,755	100	£1,071,222	100

Source: Dickson 1967, 275.

Table 7.5b. *Distribution of amounts held of bank stock (1725), East India stock (1719), and South Sea annuities (1723)*

Distrib'n	Bank (1725) £	%	EIC (1719) £	%	SSA (1723) £	%
Under £500	£282,317	3.2	£57,375	1.9	£2,293,404	13.7
£500–999	£680,482	7.6	£284,565	9.4	£1,992,112	11.9
£1,000–4,999	£3,787,003	42.3	£1,263,703	41.9	£6,215,900	37.0
£5,000–9,999	£1,631,705	18.2	£624,920	20.7	£2,470,549	14.7
Over £10,000	£2,572,328	28.7	£787,734	26.1	£3,820,385	22.8
Sum	£8,953,835	100	£3,018,296	100	£16,792,349	100

through the South Sea Company. It shows the dramatic expansion of the total numbers of individuals holding easily tradable forms of state debt. Successive pairs of columns compare Dickson's original estimates with the new data in each quantile of values available to them. Much to Dickson's credit, the general picture of distributions of stock in the Bank of England and the East India Company is much the same as he found it, both before and after 1720. However, the new data reveal an increase in small holdings of South Sea annuities from 1723. This is a clear effect of the absorption of the mass of earlier annuities held in small denominations into capital of the South Sea Company during the debt-for-equity swap carried out in 1720.

Tables 7.5a and 7.5b carry the comparison further by examining the total amounts of stock held by each quintile of holders, first as estimated by Dickson in Table 5a, and then using the new data in Table 7.5b. For the latter, the Gini coefficients of inequality are as follows: Bank shares, 0.64; East India shares, 0.62; South Sea annuities, 0.74. The increased inequality of holdings in the annuities is clearly due to the much greater number of small holdings in the South Sea Company after its capital expansion in 1720. To sum up, the tables and the figures show relatively similar distributions of holdings of Bank and East India stock in the years after the South Sea Bubble, compared to the estimates made by Dickson for the earlier years before the War of the Spanish Succession. In contrast, holdings of South Sea stock became much more unequal after the refinancing operations of 1720 and 1723.

The total number of Bank shareholders in 1725 was 4,921; East India Company shareholders numbered 1,610; and South Sea annuity holders 21,577 – a total of 28,108 shareholders. This does not include the remaining holders of the original government annuities that had not been converted into South Sea shares, which Dickson estimated numbered roughly 5,000, giving a rough total of 33,000 individuals directly or indirectly holding a piece of the British government's accumulated long-term debt after the collapse of the South Sea Bubble. (Dickson estimated 40,000.) Because very few investors – jobbers obviously excluded – held shares in more than one company, double count does not significantly inflate the total. (Of the 7,248 women investors found in the ledgers of the five companies by Carlos, Fletcher, and Neal (2012), only 731 ever held stock in more than one company, and only 130 in more than two, which was an upper bound given their methodology.)

Half of the shareholders in the Bank of England and East India Company were merchants and professionals, many of whom met or exceeded the £500 minimum required to vote in the companies' General Courts, assembled twice yearly to review the business operations of the companies. In contrast, South Sea Company shareholders after 1720 constituted a more diverse sample of the English population, and typically held much smaller stakes. For example, only 4,123 individuals were eligible to vote on the restructuring plan of 1723, meaning that 17,455 had stock but no vote. Of the 4,123 voters, only 243 were entitled to four votes, another 442 to three votes, and 639 to two votes. The remaining 2,799 were limited to one vote each (South Sea Company, 1723).

The standard interpretation of the skewed distribution of South Sea holdings is that the upper echelon of shareholders was very much an aristocratic interest, headed by George I as titular Governor of the Company. However, both the company's shares and annuities were more liquid than the securities they replaced. Not only could holders divest themselves more easily of these new securities if other investment or consumption needs arose, but also they could pledge them as collateral against loans of

Table 7.6. *Summary of financial statistics for major joint stock companies,*
1719–23

Company	Capital stock (£)	Transactions (#)	Book value of transactions (£)	Avg. book value of transactions (£)
Bank of England, 1719–23	5,559,995	12,580	10,342,091	822.11
East India Co., 1720–21	3,194,000	6,179	3,485,151	564.03
Royal African Company, Senior & Engrafted, 1720	2,091,000	5,437	4,910,650	903.19 (sr.) 979.02 (eng.)

varying amounts and durations for financing investment or consumption.
The number of trades in each of the major companies' shares shows that
these possibilities were realised by large numbers of shareholders.

Trading in long-term debt, 1719–21, and South Sea Annuities, 1723–8

Table 7.6 presents summary statistics for the securities of each company, including its capital stock, the number of transactions, their actual
book value, and the average book value of transactions. Each share had
a par value of £100, but all were trading above par at the beginning
of 1720, and rose substantially over the course of the Bubble, before
falling back to levels very close to those at the beginning of the year.
The authorised capital of each company determined the total number of
shares available for issue. The South Sea Company dominated the market
with over £30 million, followed by the Bank with £5.5 million, the East
India Company with £3.2 million, and the Royal African Company with
£2 million, three-quarters of which was engrafted during 1720. In all
four cases the value of the capital stock turned over at least once that
year, and in some cases more often, which illustrates the liquidity of the
market and the ample opportunities for those who wanted to purchase
shares. The average value came close to the £500 needed for a shareholder to vote at annual meetings. However, although the average value
of transactions was high, this reflects very large transactions by major
market makers during the height of the Bubble. Most individuals bought
only one share, or a fraction of a share.

Table 7.7 takes the analysis a step further by specifying the purchasing
activity in each company of an important emerging part of the investor
base – women. The final column specifies the number of women actually

Table 7.7. *Summary statistics: Women only*

Company	Purchases number	Purchases by women (number, % of total purchases)	Book value of purchases by women (% of total)	Avg. book value of transfers by women ($£$)	Number of women (% of total shareholders)
Bank of England, 1719–23	12,580	1,166 (9.3)	791,853 (7.7)	679.12	1,026 (17.3)
East India Company, 1720–21	6,179	968 (15.7)	279,351 (8.0)	288.59	495 (13.4)
Royal African Company, Senior & Engrafted, 1720	5,437	371 (6.8)	224,925 (4.6)	606.27	80 (8.4) 251 (9.3)
South Sea Annuities, 1723	21,577	6,282 (29.1)	3,016,844 (18.0)	480.24	5,396 (31.0)

trading (whether as buyers or sellers) in each company, and shows the percentage of women amongst total individual shareholders. Women's lower access to wealth is evident in the lower average book value of their transactions, but many women owned sufficient stock to garner a corporate vote. Considerable variation in their shareholding is evident when analysed by company. Women comprised only seventeen per cent of Bank shareholders, thirteen percent of EIC shareholders, and less than ten percent of RAC shareholders. The South Sea scheme, however, reveals a very high representation of women by 1723, at over thirty percent. The total number of unique women, 6,366, comprises over twenty-six percent of all investors. South Sea annuities were the precursors of the eventual Three Per Cent Consols created in 1751, which were considered to be especially attractive to women. This analysis shows that the feminisation of the Consol market began early in the eighteenth century. Despite various legal, cultural, and social impediments to their access to wealth in Early Modern England, women were a large presence in the securities market. Further, they came from all ranks of society.

Trading among the thousands of shareholders in the three major corporations holding long-term state debt required the services of professionals dedicated to finding counterparties quickly for investors wishing to buy or sell. Entries in the South Sea annuity ledgers permit identification of the three most active dealers in the instrument, and the results can be compared to those of earlier research identifying leading dealers in Bank of England shares during 1720 (Carlos and Neal 2006). Robert Westley,

Table 7.8. *Dealers' activities in South Sea annuities, 1723–8*

Henry Carington			
Buys 2,797	£525,233	Avg.	£187.72
Commissions	£5,252.33	Max.	£2,056.25
Brokerage	£656.54	Min.	£0.00
Sells 2,956	£523,525	Avg.	£177.05
Commissions	£5,235.25	Max.	£2,000
Brokerage	£641.41	Min.	£0.00
Christopher Whitmore			
Buys 2,546	£230,749	Avg.	£90.60
Commissions	£2,307.49	Max.	£1,000
Brokerage	£288.44	Min.	£0.00
Sells 2,775	£230,339	Avg.	£82.92
Commissions	£2,303.39	Max.	£1,000
Brokerage	£287.92	Min.	£0.00
Edward Elliott			
Buys 1,319	£116,201	Avg.	£88.10
Commissions	£1,162.01	Max.	£1,000
Brokerage	£145.25	Min.	£0.00
Sells 936	£114,946	Avg.	£122.94
Commissions	£1,149.46	Max.	£1,000
Brokerage	£143.68	Min.	£0.00

Source: BoE, AC27/6439, 6441, 6452.

the most active stock-jobber in Bank shares for small holders located in London, seemed an obvious candidate, but such a comparison shows that his main trading after 1720 continued to be in Bank shares. The three most active dealers in the new annuities were individuals who had done very little previous trading in Bank or East India shares: Henry Carington, Christopher Whitmore, and Edward Elliott. Their trading activity is summarised in Table 7.8.

By far the most active was Henry Carington. According to Dickson, he was a professional dealer in government securities in the 1730s and 1740s (Dickson 1967, 512). In the first five years that the new securities were traded, 1723–8, Carington was counterparty to 5,753 transactions with a total book value exceeding £1 million. If his average commission was one per cent of book, he would have earned more than £10,500 from these trades, possibly in addition to brokerage fees, which may have amounted to another £1,300. By 1727 he was also drawing annual returns of £150 from the five per cent dividends on his average holdings of £3,000. Perhaps, as a jobber in constant contact with the market, he imposed a bid–ask spread, and waived commissions to earn his income from the spread, or 'turn', as the jobbers called it.

Christopher Whitmore was nearly as active as Carington in terms of total transactions, but fell far short in terms of total value. His commission and brokerage fees, although still substantial, fell well below those of Carington. Dickson (1967, 498) noted that Whitmore 'of St. Andrews, Holborn, Broker' was an active jobber in the five per cent annuities of 1717. It is clear that Whitmore continued to be a professional jobber in the decade following the South Sea Bubble. His commissions alone would have made him one of the wealthier professionals in London at the time, and like Carington, he earned brokerage fees as well as dividends from the increased stock of annuities he had acquired by 1725.

Edward Elliott of Foster Lane, London, was also an active dealer. Elliott made 935 purchases and 1,319 sales of South Sea annuities over the period 1723–8. The average purchase was £122.91, with the largest only £1,000, and the smallest just two shillings and seven pence. The average sale was £88.19, the largest again only £1,000, and the smallest again less than a pound. This shows the low barriers to entry, even for those with only very small sums to invest. Eventually Elliott moved from being strictly a broker–dealer to holding a substantial amount of the annuities for his own account.

In summary, the 33,000 individual holders of the various forms of government debt issued by the British government up to 1725 were active, not passive. They appear to have had a functioning market in which to cash out or buy in, no matter how small the amount. A class of professional jobbers that had arisen previously – and been subjected to repeated calumnies in the press, poems, tracts, and parliamentary speeches – persevered in their activities on an even larger scale after the infamous episode of the South Sea Bubble. The service they rendered to the British public was appreciated in the most telling way possible, by the significant incomes they earned while providing instant counterparties to individual holders of state debt. By maintaining an open, transparently priced, secondary market for British national debt throughout the remaining century, the much-maligned stock-jobbers enabled the British government to issue new debt whenever the need arose. Consequently, Britain was able to finance its future wars efficiently, and also to benefit from a thriving capital market during peacetime.

Conclusion

This analysis presents a picture of remarkably widespread and long-term holdings of state debt in various forms. Consolidating swathes of state debt into easily transferable claims on chartered companies was the initial innovation that allowed this, achieved during the two wars that immediately followed the Glorious Revolution. The next step was refinancing earlier forms of debt into the capital stock of the South Sea Company. Even with the collapse of its share price in 1720 the conversion worked, because of a final innovation: The conversion of half of the Company's equity into perpetual annuities which channelled state debt-service payments to individuals, and which were supported by the easy transferability of these instruments on the London market, helped to maintain the liquidity of British state debt. By the end of 1723, the marketability of the debt reached an unprecedented level, one unparalleled until the conclusion of the Napoleonic Wars nearly a century later.

Analysing the turnover rate of the respective claims shows the importance of debt marketability to British success in war finance. This success, in turn, depended upon Walpole's response to the collapse of the share prices of the South Sea Company in 1720: continuing to use the existing secondary market to float an alternative, more attractive form of British state debt, this time directly to individuals who had previously bought either lottery tickets or parts of life annuities. Although the appeal of these new forms of state debt rested in large part upon the Parliament's commitment to the continued servicing of the interest on state debt, as has been well documented and argued by Brewer (1988), the main source of permanent revenue needed for Parliament to meet its commitment was the excise, which continued to grow relative to the other sources of revenue even in the first quarter of the eighteenth century. British debt became even more attractive well before the explosive rise in excise revenues that occurred after the middle of the eighteenth century because it could be re-sold readily in a secondary market at minimum cost and with little delay. Thus, the increased willingness of the investing public to hold British debt relaxed permanently the inter-temporal budget constraints faced by succeeding governments when confronted by the increased demands of war finance. Subsequent British tax-smoothing stands in sharp contrast to the repeated surges of direct taxes imposed on wealth holders in France, as the two countries waged repeated wars through 1815 (O'Brien and Hunt 1999). Thus, for Britain, experiments arising from the demands of financing the War of the Spanish Succession not only left a permanent economic legacy of that war, but also, in the long run, provided an enduring economic benefit.

Key to archive references

BoE: Bank of England archives

References

Brewer, John 1988. *The Sinews of Power: War, Money and the English State, 1688–1783*. Cambridge, MA: Harvard University Press.

Carlos, Ann; Fletcher, Erin; and Neal, Larry 2012. 'Share Portfolios in the Age of Financial Capitalism'. CEH Discussion Paper Series, 2012:6, Australian National University.

Carlos, Ann M.; Key, Jennifer; and Dupree, Jill L. 1998. 'Learning and the Creation of Stock-Market Institutions: Evidence from the Royal African and Hudson's Bay Companies, 1670–1700', *Journal of Economic History*, 58, 318–44.

Carlos, Ann and Neal, Larry 2006. 'The Micro-foundations of the Early London Capital Market: Bank of England Shareholders before and after the South Sea Bubble', *Economic History Review*, 59, 498–538.

Carlos, Ann, and Neal, Larry 2011. 'Amsterdam and London as Financial Centers in the Eighteenth Century', *Financial History Review*, 18, 21–46.

Dickson, P. G. M. 1967. *The Financial Revolution in England: A Study in the Development of Public Credit, 1688–1756*. London: Macmillan.

Dickson, P. G. M. 1987. *Finance and Government under Maria Theresia, 1740–1780*, 2 vols. New York: Oxford University Press.

Dormans, E. H. M. 1991. *Het Tekort – Staatschuld in de tijd der Republiek*. Amsterdam: NEHA.

Frey, Linda and Frey, Marsha 1983. *A Question of Empire: Leopold I and the War of the Spanish Succession, 1701–1705*. New York: Columbia University Press.

Fritschy, Wantje van der and Voort, Rene 1997. 'From Fragmentation to Unification: Public Finance, 1700–1914', in Marjolein t'Hart, Joost Jonker, and Jan Luiten van der Zanden (eds.), *A Financial History of the Netherlands*. Cambridge: Cambridge University Press.

Gelderblom, Oscar and Jonker, Joost 2009. 'With a View to Hold: The Emergence of Institutional Investors on the Amsterdam Securities Market during the Seventeenth and Eighteenth Centuries', in Jeremy Atack and Larry Neal (eds.), *The Origin and Development of Financial Markets and Institutions: From the Seventeenth Century to the Present*. Cambridge: Cambridge University Press.

Grellier, J. J. 1805. *The History of the National Debt from the Revolution in 1688 to the Beginning of 1800*. London (repr. New York: Burt Franklin, 1971).

Hamilton, Earl J. 1947. 'Origin and Growth of the National Debt in Western Europe', *American Economic Review*, 37, 118–30.

Jones, D. W. 1988. *War and Economy in the Age of William III and Marlborough*. Oxford: Basil Blackwell.

Kamen, Henry 1969. *The War of Succession in Spain, 1700–1715*. Bloomington: Indiana University Press.

Kamen, Henry 2001. *Philip V of Spain: The King Who Reigned Twice*. New Haven: Yale University Press.

Lynn, John A. 1993. *Feeding Mars: Logistics in Western Warfare from the Middle Ages to the Present*. Boulder, CO: Westview Press.

Lynn, John A. 1997. *Giant of the Grand Siècle: The French Army, 1610–1715*. Cambridge: Cambridge University Press.

Mitchell, Brian R. (ed.) 1988. *British Historical Statistics.* Cambridge: Cambridge University Press.

Murphy, Antoin E. 1997. *John Law: Economic Theorist and Policy-maker.* New York: Oxford University Press.

Neal, Larry 1990. *The Rise of Financial Capitalism: International Capital Markets in the Age of Reason.* New York: Cambridge University Press.

North, Douglass C. and Weingast, Barry 1989. 'Constitutions and Commitment: The Evolution of Institutions Governing Public Choice in Seventeenth-Century England', *Journal of Economic History*, 49, 155–86.

O'Brien, Patrick K. and Hunt, Philip A. 1999. 'England, 1485–1815', in Richard Bonney (ed.), *The Rise of the Fiscal State in Europe c. 1200–1815.* Oxford: Oxford University Press.

Parker, Geoffrey 1988. *The Military Revolution. Military Innovation and the Rise of the West, 1500–1800.* Cambridge: Cambridge University Press.

Quinn, Stephen 2004. 'Accounting for the Early British Funded Debt, 1693–1786'. Working paper, Texas Christian University.

Quinn, Stephen 2005. 'How Did the Early Bank of England Increase Government Credibility?' Presented at the 43rd Cliometrics Conference, Lake Tahoe, CA, June.

South Sea Company 1723. *A List of the Names of the Corporation of the Governor and Company of Merchants of Great Britain Trading to the South-Seas, and other Parts of America, and for Encouraging the Fishery, Who are Qualified to Vote at the ensuing Election for Governor, Sub-Governor, and Deputy-Governor, to be made on the Third, and of Directors on the fifth Day of February next, together with Part of the 7th By-Law concerning Elections.* London: December 25, 1723.

Stasavage, David 2002. 'Credible Commitments in Early Modern Europe: North and Weingast Revisited', *Journal of Law and Economics*, 18, 155–86.

Sussman, Nathan, and Yafeh, Yishay 2006. 'Institutional Reform, Financial Development and Sovereign Debt: Britain 1690–1790.' *Journal of Economic History*, 66(5), 906–35.

Weingast, Barry 1997. 'The Political Foundations of Limited Government: Parliament Sovereign Debt in 17th Century and 18th Century England', in John Drobak and John Nye (eds.), *The Frontiers of the New Institutional Economics.* San Diego: Academic Press.

8 Sovereign debts, political structure, and institutional commitments in Italy, 1350–1700

Luciano Pezzolo

The cities of northern and central Italy in the late Middle Ages have provided a great deal of material to scholars of finance. The early establishment of deficit financing through short- and long-term borrowing has attracted those seeking the origins of financial capitalism. A line of continuity – more or less ephemeral – has been drawn from Italian communes to eighteenth-century England, which is regarded as the birthplace of modern state debt (Kindleberger 1993; Macdonald 2003). This chapter does not deal as much with the degree of modernity of Italian financial systems, as with the means some governments exploited to raise resources to wage war. Renaissance and Baroque Italy offer an excellent field to verify the model linking institutions to financial efficiency. Republics, monarchies, and principalities presented different financial and economic structures and performances. A long-term approach permits one both to highlight major changes in financial development, and to control for relationships – if any – with political structures.

This chapter deals with the government debt of Genoa, Florence, the Papal States, and the Kingdom of Naples. The first part outlines the main features of deficit financing over time and shows how governments faced increasing cash requirements of financing their political and military engagements. During the later Middle Ages, Genoa and Florence resorted largely to both voluntary and compulsory loans, whereas the popes and the Neapolitan kings relied on short-term loans provided by merchant bankers, courtiers, and officials. From the early sixteenth century, however, the papal government and the Spanish rulers of Naples increasingly sold securities on the open market. The second part of the chapter examines differences and commonalities among the states. The third puts the Italian cases into comparative perspective.

The financial demands of warfare

The high degree of inter-state conflict that affected the Italian peninsula in the late Middle Ages led some governments to make financing tools more efficient. It is no coincidence that Tilly considered the Italian city-states to be the first protagonists of his model that links war, financial capital, and state building (Tilly 1992; Thompson and Rasler 1999; Tarrow 2004). The first financial innovators were Genoa and Venice, the great maritime republics engaged in the expansion and control of long distance trade (Pezzolo 2005), which mobilised substantial military resources – thousands of men and hundreds of ships – to monitor Mediterranean trade routes and to support merchants' interests.

The size of the armies that some Italian governments were able to raise was impressive. By the mid-thirteenth century, Florence was able to deploy 16,000 men, whereas in 1291 the Tuscan League amassed 20,000 infantry and 2,500 cavalry against Pisa. Beginning in the late thirteenth century, war claimed more and more financial resources (Settia 1993, 168–9; Grillo 2008, 116, 144). Communal armies, made up mostly of peasants and citizens, were gradually replaced by mercenaries who demanded huge amounts of money by way of wages and bribes (Bowsky 1970; Caferro 1998). The growing importance of heavy cavalry, supported on the battlefield by archers, had boosted the cost of war. Thus, only governments with a broad fiscal and financial base could support the growing burdens of warfare. The high rate of urbanisation and the extraordinary role of financial and commercial capital allowed Italian governments to resort to large mercenary armies. In the early fifteenth century both Venice and Milan counted as many as 20,000 soldiers under their standards. Furthermore, these governments tended both to reduce the size of the units under control of each condottiere and to keep them in permanent service (Mallett 1974; Green 1983).

Throughout the fifteenth century the political geography of the Italian peninsula was simplified, following the emergence of medium-sized political entities (the Kingdom of Naples, the Papal States, the republics of Florence, Venice, and Genoa, and the Duchy of Milan), along with a corollary of small states and lordships. Charles VIII's invasion in 1494 placed Italy in the context of the European dynastic conflict, which characterised the political history of the continent throughout the era. The political and material limits of the Italian city-states proved difficult to overcome, for they failed to expand in scale to become offensive powers during the late Renaissance. They were unable to exploit economies of scale in warfare, as other European great powers did. The southern kingdoms (Naples, Sicily, and Sardinia) and the state of Milan became dominions of the Habsburgs of Spain until the early eighteenth century, whereas Florence, Genoa, and Venice managed to maintain their independence. Table 8.1 shows the growth of indebtedness of the governments considered in this chapter.

.

Table 8.1. *Size of long-term government debts,*
1350–1700, tons of silver

	Genoa	Florence	Rome	Naples
1350	37	14		
1400	88	102		
1450	146			
1500	189	150		
1550	336			36
1600	363		343	261
1650	253	372	1,021	1,600
1700	221	300	1,108	

Genoa: A republic of bondholders

The Genoese government was among the first to resort to debt, and did so mainly to finance wars. At first, in the twelfth century, wealthy citizens were called upon to provide short-term loans to the government. Later, in the thirteenth century, a system of forced loans was created, as was the case in Venice and Florence. Citizens were compelled to lend a given amount of money according to their assessed wealth. They were entitled to receive interest payments as long as the government was repaying the principal. Unlike those in the other two cities, however, Genoa's state creditors enjoyed noteworthy control over the management of public finance. In 1323, eight *Protectores et defensores comperarum capitulo* (Protectors and defenders of debt shares) were established with a mandate to look after the interests of creditors. Whenever the government announced new loans – which were becoming increasingly voluntary – investors were promised a return at a set rate until the principal was paid back (Sieveking 1905–7, I: 107–8, 133; Gioffré 1966). Repayment of principal, however, rarely occurred, and so the amounts due to creditors from the state continued to accumulate, increasing the share of revenues earmarked for debt service.

In 1407, after much restructuring of the debt system, the House of St George was established, representing a consortium of creditors. The previous series of loans (with interest rates between eight and ten per cent) was merged and consolidated into one bundle, to be administered by St George, which also managed the revenues assigned to interest payments. Initially the interest rate was fixed at seven per cent, but returns were later linked to the yield of the taxes assigned to debt service. The return therefore depended on the general performance of indirect taxation. The new institution managed most of the city's fiscal income, whereas a small portion of the tax proceeds was used for the ordinary administration of the commune. Innovations by St George emerged in the following years. First, it began to offer banking services and approved transactions without using coins. Customers could open a deposit account, and could transfer money to other accountholders simply by providing a written note. Second, unlike previous attempts, the consolidation enjoyed notable success, and initiated a vibrant financial market based on both securities and interest claims. Finally, the importance of St George grew to such a point that it began to assume a governing nature, similar to that of a state (indeed, at one point the commune, unable to honour its obligations to St George, handed over control of some of its overseas territories in lieu of repayment).

Eight *Protectors* headed the House of St George. They were elected annually by the Great Council from among the principal bondholders (*Leggi* 1625). In the fifteenth century, as was customary, the *Protectors* were chosen, in equal measure, from among the ranks of the nobility and the *popolari*. In the following century, after political reforms, they represented in equal proportion the two factions of the Genoese ruling class, the 'old' and 'new' nobility (Heers 1961, 577; Bitossi 2006, 97–8). It is also important to note that the House exercised full jurisdiction over matters pertaining to state creditors. In 1568 the Great Council secured jurisdiction over the granting of loans both to private parties and to the state, which had until this time been held by the *Protectores*.

The House of St George is justly regarded as an efficient financial institution which defended the creditors of the state while demonstrating its flexibility in dealing with the difficulties challenging public finance. Financial information and money from taxation merged within the institution, and were in turn distributed to its *comperisti* (shareholders). The interest rate on the shares demonstrates that the Genoese investors preferred highly secure debt with relatively low returns to riskier investments (Fratianni 2006). Therefore St George perfectly represents the model which emphasises how strict control by creditors over state finances brings about stability. This connection is most evident in the Genoese case, as the administrators of St George belonged to the ruling class of the Republic. Despite the serious conflicts that afflicted the city, and the changes in its government, the bank maintained constant autonomy, and embodied a solid institution within the unstable Genoese environment.

This mechanism, however, fails to account thoroughly for the history of public debt from the establishment of the House of St George. Had it indeed managed to reassure its debt-holders fully, the price of the bonds would have been just as high as in the fifteenth century. Until the 1560s market prices fluctuated around fifty per cent of

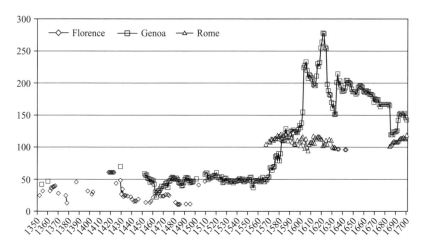

Figure 8.1. Market prices of some Italian government securities, 1350–1700.

par (Figure 8.1), and only after this time did they reach higher levels. This demonstrates that confidence in fifteenth-century bonds was not at all steady nor widespread, and that the degree of trust in St George was not much higher than that in other governments' securities, which were apparently less well protected. It is not easy to account for the difference in trends between the fifteenth and the mid-sixteenth century. In spite of the robustness of St George, it is likely that political and military vicissitudes strongly influenced the medieval Genoese market, as elsewhere. The high Genoese prices seem to be an exception in the panorama of Early Modern Italy.

The evident increase in prices from the 1560s could be due to a particularly fortunate moment in port activities, which during this period experienced intense growth (Di Tucci 1929–30; Grendi 1987, 358–64). Increased traffic and the consequent rise in dividends might have encouraged a strong demand for bonds, pushing up market prices. This, however, does not explain sustained high prices even during economic decline. Maybe politics offers some insight. A brief civil war broke out in 1576, which led to an adjustment in the constitution of the Republic to establish a substantial balance between the 'old' and 'new' nobility. The stabilisation of power relations in the political system probably reassured the market, which registered a boom in the value of securities. The rise of prices, however, started a few years before political reform. A further explanation might be the choice by St George in 1562 to relinquish its political jurisdiction over Corsica, which had been granted previously by the government in exchange for loans. It is likely that its abandoning such a considerable burden enhanced investors' confidence in the financial conditions of the bank, giving rise to a noticeable boost in market prices. In addition, it might be that the Genoese had incentives to invest elsewhere as the yields on municipal debt fell.

Florence: From a republican to a princely debt

The Florentine case is particularly interesting, as many scholars have recognised certain elements of modern financial capitalism in its system of deficit financing. The main features of Florentine finance since the late Middle Ages were the raising of loans from citizens, debt consolidation, and the emergence of a secondary financial market centred around government bonds.

Financial reforms between 1343 and 1347 mark the beginning of debt consolidation. Until that time, the Florentine government had used both voluntary and forced loans, promising repayment of principal over a relatively short term. Once the government had decided to launch a loan, the amount was set according to a tax register which should have reflected the fiscal capacity of citizens. However, the gradual accumulation of liabilities due to political and military commitments forced the commune to recognise its inability to meet its commitments to its creditors, and thus to decide upon consolidation (Barbadoro 1929, 534 ff, 629 ff). All the debts were gathered in the Monte Comune, interest rates were standardised at five per cent, and the revenues of selected *gabelles* (duties on trade and consumption) were earmarked to cover the interest. Above all, bondholders were allowed to negotiate their own credits. The advantage for government was evident, as earlier loans had borne interest at rates of between eight and twelve per cent, and peaked at fifteen per cent. The consolidation fostered the emergence of a vibrant secondary securities market which permitted shareholders to liquidate their credit quickly where needed, and speculators to act entirely legally. Immediately after the establishment of the Monte Comune, many Florentines started to sell their credits, most of which were bought by people who had liquidity (Brucker 1962, 19–21; Barducci 1979; Molho 1999; Ciappelli 2009, 113–18).

Military engagements, however, continued to place the Florentine financial system under considerable pressure. Over the next few years, the government had to launch new series of loans, which were far more attractive than those of the Monte Comune. The market price of the securities in 1352 was just twenty-five per cent of par, and in the 1360s fluctuated between thirty-two and forty, demonstrating, just a few years after the establishment of the Monte, the Florentines' lack of confidence in government debt (see Figure 8.1).

The difficult period of financial and political crisis ended in 1454 with the Peace of Lodi, which was signed by the major Italian states. The Florentine taxpayers' balance was unquestionably in deficit. Citizens of modest and considerable means alike had been facing serious financial difficulties. The second half of the century, characterised by relative peace, witnessed the government's efforts to contain the debt through the use of two instruments. First, all the creditors of the Monte Comune were urged – and sometimes forced – to pay taxes using credits from the arrears of interest claims (*paghe*) and securities. This practice had precedent in the early days of debt consolidation, but seems to have developed quite significantly after the Peace of Lodi. Second, the Monte dowry – an institution established in 1425 to provide dowries to Florentine citizens' daughters – collected as deposits a large amount of government securities, in lieu of cash. Interest payments were delayed until the dowries were disbursed (Molho 1971; Kirshner and Molho 1978; Molho 1994).

Together with the loans that were merged in the Monte, the Florentine government frequently used floating debt, which comprised short-term loans at high interest rates granted by a small group of wealthy citizens. Because of the length of time it took to collect taxes and forced loans, money had to be found quickly to meet the demands of the troops. Two financial institutions had the task of managing relations with moneylenders: the *Ufficiali del banco* (Officers of the bank) and the *Ufficiali del Monte* (Officers of the Monte). The former institution, established in the mid-fourteenth century as an extraordinary board, dealt with the short-term loans, whereas the latter obtained money under forced loans, which were destined to repay the principal of the accumulated short-term debts. However, the roles were not at all well defined, and often the *Ufficiali del Monte* would be in charge of the floating debt. The *Ufficiali* were required to lend in person and to look for potential investors within their circles of friends, clients, and acquaintances. These lenders usually came from the ranks of bankers, merchants, or traders, or those who were in some other way connected to business. The *Ufficiali* obtained money at a rate of around seven to eight per cent, which would be repaid with the proceeds of forced loans, and with a return of twelve to fourteen per cent. The *Ufficiali* could also raise funds on the exchange market, which was known to demand high interest rates. Between the end of 1430 and mid-August 1432, the *Ufficiali del banco* raised more than 560,000 florins from sixty-four Florentines, eleven of whom paid 437,000 florins, a little more than seventy-five per cent of the total amount (Molho 1971, 180). It seems that from 1480 the *Ufficiali del Monte* strengthened considerably its position within the Florentine financial system, playing a major role, and was strongly influenced by the clientage and ties to Lorenzo de Medici (Cambi 1786, 3; Marks 1960; Molho 1987; Tognetti 1999, 258–64; Ciappelli 2009, 189–203).

From 1530, with the stabilisation of the Medicis' power, Florence became a princely state. With just one variation, the deficit-financing system maintained its traditional feature of employing extraordinary taxes to repay loans from the *Ufficiali del Monte*. During the War over Siena (1552–9), Cosimo I (1537–74) borrowed huge sums on the international market. German and Genoese bankers were among the Duke's main financiers, whereas the role of Florentine investors was negligible (Teicher 1983; Parigino 1999, 56–74).

The elements of state debt intertwined with the debts of grand dukes, because according to the traditions of princely finance, personal and state resources are not clearly defined (Diaz 1976, 160). The creation in 1633 of a new Monte series at five per cent, for example, seems to have been justified by a loan made to Grand Duke Ferdinand II (1621–70) by the Genoese banker Alessandro Pallavicini, who in turn became its administrator. The interest should have been paid from the proceeds of a tax on salt, but actually the capital was used to purchase a fief for the Medici family (Parigino 2009, 508). It is evident, however, that the Grand Dukes of Tuscany used debt moderately and resorted to various forms of borrowing, primarily short-term loans provided by bankers, forced loans imposed on taxpayers, and the exploitation of the *Monte di Pietà* (pawn shop).

The *Monte di Pietà*, initially established to provide low-cost loans to the poorer classes, was authorised in 1533 to accept deposits at five per cent. In the 1560s it became a central Florentine financial institution (Pampaloni 1956; Menning 1993). Following the marked decline of the Monte dowries, for example, it raised money to fund new dowries. In 1616 the Monte issued a series of bonds for a total of two million scudi at five per cent (Cantini1800–1808, XV: 28–37). However, the Monte was also used as a tool to broaden and consolidate the Medici family's clientage system, thus endangering the financial condition of the institution. On the death of Grand Duke Cosimo II in 1621, his debt to the Monte was 600,000 scudi; under Ferdinand II it grew to nearly five million (D'Alaimo 1995, 367).

Rome: The pope's two debts

Like other medieval sovereigns, popes needed merchant bankers and specialised financiers to obtain loans when needed. A long tradition had secured close relations between the Holy See and trading companies, the majority of which were Tuscan and, on a smaller scale, Genoese. As the Pope did not have his own ad hoc apparatus, he exploited major commercial and financial trading networks to manage the cash flow – derived from spiritual revenues and taxes on the clergy, and the proceeds from benefices and rights – from the various regions of Christianity to the Curia. At the same time, corporate networks provided cash in time of need (Renouard 1941). A similar situation occurred in England between the thirteenth and fourteenth centuries, where agents of Italian companies held important positions in the royal treasury. However, unlike the English monarchy, the papacy did not employ a single firm, but had financial relationships with several merchant bankers simultaneously. By relying on a segmented credit supply, the popes were probably able to negotiate loans on relatively favourable terms.

Nevertheless, the increasing difficulties of papal finance caused by the Great Schism (1378–1417) brought about a progressive decline in spiritual revenues, which meant resorting to loans from merchant bankers. Thus, when money was needed, it was natural to turn to the merchants who regularly frequented the Curia. However, for both parties involved, the personal relationships which characterised the dealings between financiers and papal sovereigns brought about as many advantages as they did disadvantages. First, lending to the pope meant not only investing in lucrative financial operations with good prospects, but also, above all, entering a world that could offer enormous possibilities for weaving political and economic relationships. The papal court, more than courts in other countries, represented a social-capital-intensive environment, comprising cardinals and dignitaries from all over the continent. Moreover, the appointment as Depositary General, the highest position which could be held by a layman in the papal financial administration, opened up the way to further political and financial connections.

From the beginning of the fifteenth century, relations between bankers and the Curia were formalised through the establishment of the Depositary General, which sanctioned the role of merchant bankers and allowed regular resort to credit by the Apostolic Chamber (de Roover 1963, 194–224; Palermo 2000). From the late fifteenth century the papacy developed a system of long-term borrowing which eventually assumed the characteristics of a genuine public debt. Its early forms are linked to the traditional system of venality of offices: in 1463 Pope Pius II sold some offices in order to finance a crusade. The purchasers formed a college, and were to be paid through public fees (*sportule*) and taxes. This first set of offices implied an administrative function by the lender, and had no cost to the papal treasury, because payment of the yield was covered by office holders' customers. However, because these offices could not be expanded at will, new colleges were founded in 1471. They, too, assumed some administrative functions, but the return was paid directly from the papal treasury.

In 1507 a college was established which was composed of two new types of offices: those that were still active, and those that were completely free from any administrative responsibility. Finally, in 1513, the sale of this latter type of office began, and in 1520 the college of the Knights of St Peter was founded. It had characteristics similar to those of the third category of offices, but granted an honorary title to its members. It is important to underline that from the beginning of the sixteenth century some taxes were allocated to interest payments due to officeholders. Furthermore, through payment of a modest sum, it was possible to convey lifetime ownership of these offices, thus transforming so-called vacable offices into perpetual ones (Bauer 1928; Piola Caselli 1970–72; Reinhard 1984, 372–5; Frenz 1986, 193–233; Schimmelpfenning 1984). The full commercialisation of offices was legally ratified in 1514; in this way even small investors could buy shares in them. According to Bauer, this permitted a process of democratisation of the Papal State's debt (Bauer 1928, 488).

The most significant development with regards to papal public debt occurred, however, with the establishment in 1526 of the *Monte della Fede*, a new series of annuities to be sold on the open market (Monaco 1960). After some teething problems, from the mid-sixteenth century a long and successful series of loans was launched, which was to constitute the cornerstone of the popes' debt. The Monti maintained the supply of funding not only for the few wars of the Holy See, but most importantly for providing subsidies to Catholic powers, and for grandiose public works in Rome.

The Monti were divided into vacables (annuities with interest rates which would terminate on the death of the nominee) and non-vacables (whose reimbursement was at the discretion of the Apostolic Chamber). Each bond had a nominal value of one hundred scudi, but could be subdivided into smaller shares. The interest was paid every two months. The Roman Monti were rightly considered amongst the safest government bonds in Italy, with market prices which were generally positioned above par (see Figure 8.1), and thus provide proof of market confidence. This confidence in papal bonds was justified for many reasons. First, they were defined under specific rules and regulations. Second, the bondholders were assured that under no circumstances would they lose their property rights, and that the revenues tied to interest payments were guaranteed.

A very important issue that characterises the papal system concerns the creation of colleges, consortia of legally recognised bondholders.

The model is close to that of the Genoese House of St George (Piola Caselli 1970–72, 21; Colzi 1999, 36–43; Guidi Bruscoli 2000; Carboni 2009).When venal offices were first established, each series was run by a college which protected the interests of creditors. Usually a banker who had purchased the majority of securities directly from the Apostolic Chamber was the head (depository) of the college, while a Cardinal-protector carried out the intermediary role between the Chamber and the college. Towards the end of the sixteenth century terms were issued to regulate the role of bankers in relation to shareholders. In 1609, for example, this latter group had the right to collect interest from the bankers, even where the Apostolic Chamber had not yet paid the corresponding sum to the college (Piola Caselli 1991, 487). Not surprisingly, the participation of foreign investors was extensive (Piola Caselli 1988, 213; Colzi 1999, 153; Dandelet 2001).

Naples: The economic limits of financial innovation

The practice of borrowing money from merchants, mostly foreigners with business in Naples, became customary during Angevin rule (1266–1435). Bardi, Peruzzi, and Strozzi were among the companies most involved in trading and financial services in southern Italy in the late Middle Ages (Rivera Magos 2005). With the Aragonese conquest of Naples in 1442, the traditional Tuscan agents were joined by Catalan merchants. A 'royal mediator' was in charge of raising funds from the merchants of the capital, and personally assumed responsibility for loans.

With the success of the Catholic kings against the French, southern Italy entered the Habsburg dominions, and its financing methods were therefore incorporated into the broader context of Imperial finance. There were three available means by which the government of the Spanish viceroy in Naples obtained money quickly. One system tied the loan to the concession of rights to export wheat. For example, a merchant acquired an exemption from duty on the export of grain equal to the sum loaned plus interest. Ordinary loans also existed, which of course were the easiest means to raise money. Merchants, civic institutions, officers and court dignitaries, and Genoese financiers also provided money in times of urgency, sometimes in the form of donations, but this was not the most exploited type of funding. A crucial role was played by bills of exchange and the so-called *partiti*. The former were loans contracted on the international financial market, which had a pivotal role in the Bisenzone fairs (Pezzolo and Tattara 2008). The Genoese were the protagonists of this credit system, which linked the various Habsburg territories to the areas where money was needed most. The *partiti* were short-term loans stipulated directly by the Viceroy. From 1541 to the early 1580s the government borrowed more than eight million ducats in this way. Until the 1560s the Genoese underwrote ninety-four per cent of the total amount, after which their importance successively decreased, leading up to the financial crisis of Philip II in 1575. The Genoese capital, however, reasserted its primacy in Naples in the following decades (Calabria 1989; Calabria 1991; Calabria 2000).

The mechanism for the sale of long-term debt securities guaranteed by taxes took off during the sixteenth century. From the middle of the century fiscal income rose, thus providing the government with substantial resources to commit to the consolidated debt. Future tax proceeds, both direct and indirect, were used to pay interest on the sums borrowed. The creditor received interest in three annual instalments, and, as elsewhere, had the opportunity to sell his securities. The first decade of the seventeenth century saw a sharp rise in Imperial needs: besides the usual aids and subsidies for Milan and Flanders, Naples had to contribute to the Thirty Years War (Villari 1973, 119–75; Galasso 1984; De Rosa 1999). The overall economic climate had changed, however, and Neapolitan resources were no longer sufficient to meet growing demands from Madrid. Between 1600 and 1650 the debt increased sixfold, while the tax burden tripled. Even holders of government credits were hit with levies on interest payments (Foscari 2006, 262–92). Only Dutch taxpayers were able to cope with a similar tax pressure, thanks to their much better economic performance.

The great Neapolitan revolt of 1647–8 was clearly linked to taxation. The various aspects of the event are not examined here, but it is important to note that the middle of the seventeenth century saw a structural break in the financial history of the Kingdom of Naples, as in the rest of Europe at the conclusion of the Thirty Years War. First, in 1649, the government ceded most of its tax revenues, both direct and indirect, to creditors, keeping only a fixed income of 300,000 ducats, which was set aside for military coffers. Debt holders elected governors who were responsible for either farming out the collection of taxes, or collecting them directly. Furthermore, by granting requests that had emerged during the revolt, the government reduced the interest rate paid to those who had purchased securities in the market at very low prices (De Rosa 1958, 13–16; De Rosa 1999, 160–63; Zilli 1990, 47).

Comparisons

The papal debt underwent a structural change in the late middle and Early Modern ages. Until the early sixteenth century, links between lenders (usually merchant bankers) and popes were characterised by personal relationships, and therefore were subject to a high degree of uncertainty. In the early fourteenth century, Pope Clement V saw fit to donate Church goods to his family and associates, demonstrating that he made no distinction between public and private property (Piola Caselli 1987: 66–7). From the mid-sixteenth century the Apostolic Chamber had no difficulty in collecting loans at a relatively low cost. The success of the papal government was due, in the words of a Roman nobleman, to the 'greater faith and confidence that the merchants find here' (quoted in Casanova 1981, 104, author's translation).What factors made the Pope's debt so reliable? The decrees which established the Monti bore the names of twenty-four cardinals. They formed a secret consistory which ratified the document underwritten by the pope (Piola Caselli 1989, 3537).When new offices were sold in 1503, the *bulla* was underwritten by the pope and cardinals (Giustinian 1876, I: 453). Not only were state-specific tax revenues assigned to the repayment of the lenders, but also the loan was secured by a formal deed of a collective institution and made, in a sense, permanent. Second, the commitments of the Apostolic Chamber to the creditors were met with remarkable efficiency. The college system ensured easy debt administration, and regular payments were made. Over time, therefore, the papacy had been building a solid reputation as a debtor. This reputation is confirmed by comparing the interest rates on Roman securities with those on the private market (Figure 8.2).

To some extent a similar path can be seen in the case of Naples. The early sixteenth century saw a shift from the king's personal debt to the sale of securities on the open market. Although the concept of the domain state first arose in Naples rather than in Rome (Bulgarelli Lukacs 2004, 784–8), the mechanism of indebtedness in the late Middle Ages confirms the importance of the king as a figurehead. The financiers extended loans to the king or his representatives on both formal and informal guarantees with a promise of payment and the king's personal assurance. From the mid-sixteenth century the sustained increase in tax revenue allowed him to structure the debt on the sale of revenue, and to broaden the investor base. Furthermore, the use of public banks as intermediaries for the sale of securities (di Somma 1960, 4, 8, 13; De Rosa 1987) probably played a definitive role in removing uncertainty about the king's commitment.

The republics of Florence and Genoa, because of their constitutional organisation, did not undergo an evolution from princely to state debt. From the very beginning the funds raised from these communes evoked the citizen's sense of duty to contribute to the maintenance of the city in cases of need, and it was the same commune that undertook the tasks of repaying principal and paying interest. In some cases, faced with the

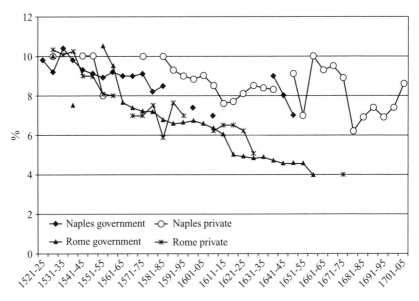

Figure 8.2. Interest rates compared at Rome and Naples, 1521–1705.

failure of the Florentine government against powerful creditors such as the pope, all the Florentines in Rome were involved in reprisals, and their goods were seized in the name of collective responsibility for the Florentine debt (Kirshner 1969, 352).

It is worth enquiring, therefore, whether the transition from a republic to a principality in 1530 had an impact on the system of borrowing in Florence. Most of the loans mobilised by Cosimo I for the war over Siena in the 1550s came from merchant bankers, according to the classic model of princely debt. It should be noted, however, that in Florence a long tradition of financial expedients had seen local figures called upon to advance money to the government. The only difference under the Medici seems to be from whence the Grand Duke drew money: from Genoese and German financiers. Further, in grand ducal Florence, short-term loans should have been repaid from future yields of forced loans. The institutional change which took place in Florence did not bring about a kind of devolution from public to personal borrowing. Subsequent events, however, demonstrate that, in general, grand dukes largely resorted to the open credit market, issuing bonds in times of need, at interest rates which were consistent with the more reliable government bonds issued in the peninsula. The Florentine case challenges the North and Weingast model that stresses the protection of property rights as a fundamental element for financial growth (North and Weingast 1989). The rise of the personal rule of the grand dukes, and the alleged reinforcement of the sovereign's discretion, did not undermine the credibility of the government as a borrower.

Until the late Middle Ages, institutional differences arising from political and constitutional constraints explain the different methods of debt-raising adopted by monarchies and republics. The institutional structure, however, cannot fully account for the apparent differences in the Early Modern period, at least in the cases examined in this chapter. From the middle of the sixteenth century, principalities and republics were similar in their approach to borrowing. It is likely that the increase in state budgets resulted in some convergence, although Naples is an obvious exception. There, *partiti* still seemed to play a fundamental role in financing the Spanish treasury, whereas the regular sales of securities appear to have been less important, and were used only to finance the *partiti*. The long and increasingly intolerable pressure on the finances and economy of the Kingdom of Naples provoked a serious economic crisis which resulted in major revolt. It is highly unlikely that investors were reassured by the state treasury, and only a few individuals, most belonging to the Neapolitan aristocracy, risked large amounts on loans. They were attracted by the extraordinary opportunity for profit: from 1630 to 1650 the government sold tax revenues for as little as ten per cent of their nominal value. The catastrophic devaluation of securities benefited those who were in an advantageous position with regards to political power. Some speculators were able to buy, 'for little or nothing', securities from creditors who could not hope to receive payment, and obtained the interest in arrears from the treasury, relying on acquaintances and clientele (Villari 1973, 148). Therefore, despite the apparent creation and development of a financial market centred on state bonds (Calabria 1991, 104–29), personal and asymmetric relations were established which favoured a narrow circle of people.

One of the most interesting aspects of the mechanisms of debt consent concerns the social composition of debt holders. Summarising, the social pyramid of government creditors was primarily driven by the wealthy class, be it nobility, patriciate, or wealthy bourgeois, with a substantial range of intermediaries able to invest discrete sums of money, and, finally, a wide layer of smaller investors. In the classic picture depicted by historians of Renaissance Florence, the ruling class implemented policies for the benefit of the richest holders of debt: the growing tax burden, arising from the increased indebtedness of the poorer classes of society through high consumption duties, channelled resources to the benefit of Monti shareholders (Becker 1965; Becker 1966; Molho 1971;

Armstrong 2003). However, this model does not hold in every situation. In the case of Venice, for example, the early stages of the development of government debt were actually funded by the proceeds of international trade, and thus indirectly by foreign consumers (Lane 1973; Pezzolo 2003).

On the other hand, governments had few alternatives. If it is true that resorting to debt meant avoiding direct taxation, then resources needed to be found through customs or consumption duties. In addition, direct taxation, at least until the sixteenth century, was regarded as a form of extraordinary taxation, subject to negotiation between local and governmental bodies, and therefore poorly suited to ensuring a regular flow of money to be paid to creditors. The economic environment represented a further limit on state finances. The relatively minor role of international trade in Naples and Rome limited the impact of customs proceeds on government income, unlike in Genoa. Thus, it was difficult for these governments to shift the burden of debt service onto foreign merchants.

This does not mean that there was no room at all for the power elite to manoeuvre. The widespread use of short-term debt in the Kingdom of Naples probably reflects the heavy influence of the aristocracy on the local Spanish government. Likewise in Genoa, on at least two occasions, it was proposed to reduce, if not cancel, the heavy public debt, but political groups involved in the income distributed by St George managed to prevent this reform (Savelli 1981; Savelli 1984). Genoa is the most obvious example of how the credibility of debt rested not on the republican institutions of a city-state run by merchants, but on the broad involvement of the interests of the ruling group in the management of public debt. Unlike Florence, however, the mechanisms of Genoa's indebtedness involved a wide stratum of citizens, and, most importantly, protected the creditors of the state. The most negative aspect of its debt was the privilege granted to the interests of St George over those of state finance.

Roman debt was no less reliable than Genoan. Despite an inherent weakness tied to the election of popes and the absence of a strong merchant class, the Apostolic Chamber was able to guarantee the continuity of the financial commitment of the head of the Church, and to ensure that Monti bonds were one of the soundest securities in Early Modern Europe. Prudent management and direct control by creditors underpinned this success, even though the institutional framework was not among the most favourable.

That said, all the elements that combined to make government debt either secure or unreliable ultimately depended on the states' military and political commitments, and their ability to tax their subjects effectively. Confidence in Roman securities was based on popes' cautious foreign policy, and on the gradual marginalisation of the Holy See from European conflicts. Naples, in contrast, had to participate heavily in Habsburg wars, and was forced to find money and soldiers urgently. In the context of almost continuous war, the weaknesses of the economic system and seriously unbalanced taxation prevented the development of a sound state debt.

Beyond the Alps

From the second half of the fourteenth century the Aragonese cities, to satisfy growing royal demand, began to sell long-term titles of credit, both redeemable (*censals*) and life annuities (*violarios*) (Furió 1999; Abella Samitier 2009). The principal characteristic of these instruments was that the debtor could decide when to return the capital, as long as the pension (interest) was paid on time. This financial practice helped to limit the suspicion of usury connected to the activity of money-lending. Relations between the king and the Aragonese cities contributed to important institutional and fiscal developments, such as the creation of an urban fiscal system that ensured the regular flow of income destined to repay the debt. It was not long, however, before local governments encountered difficulty in making regular interest payments to their creditors, and were thus forced to reduce the interest rate, to block payments, and to curry the king's favour to redesign their obligations to creditors.

In medieval Castile, apart from the case of Burgos near the Aragonese border, it seems that there was no stable financial system of loans (Ladero Quesada 1997, 52). It is likely that the consistent availability of collective goods, and above all, the sovereignty of the crown over fiscal resources impeded the development of a regular assumption of debt by municipal governments. During the fifteenth century the Castilian kings turned primarily to taxation and forced loans from cities (Olivera Serrano 1991). Starting at the end of the fifteenth century, the Catholic kings began to sell long-term loans (*juros*) which were irredeemable, and life annuities for one, two, or three lives, at a moderate rate of interest. These were backed by specific fiscal revenues indicated by the Cortes (Castillo Pintado 1963b). During the sixteenth century their level of indebtedness grew at an extraordinary rate, but the role of fluctuating debt, which was based on short-term loans (*asientos*) from banks, remained fundamental to the rapid disbursement of cash to various war fronts (Castillo Pintado 1963a). The *juros*, however, were used both for collecting money from diverse social strata, and for guaranteeing further *asientos*. In such cases it was financiers and important individuals who functioned as intermediaries between the government and the investors. Moreover, as was the case in France, both functionaries and courtiers were expected to buy titles to support the treasury (Castillo Pintado 1963b; Poncet 1993). Information on the secondary market for *juros* remains scarce, but there seem to have been transactions. One has the impression that, at least initially, the Castilian *juros* were analogous to the papal *monti* bonds which were assigned to financiers as a guarantee for short-term loans, or to be sold. As in the case of the French *rentes*, the Habsburg *juros* experienced a notable devaluation in periods of financial stress (Castillo Pintado 1963b, 63–4; Thompson 1994, 164; Sánchez Belén 1996, 87–99; Alonso García 2004, 113 ff; Álvarez Nogal 2009).

The case of the Dutch cities is similar, at least in the first phase, to that of Aragonese urban debt. Local governments made use of the available tools of the private credit market by selling *losrenten* (long-term loans with terms analogous to those of the *censals* and the *rentes*) and *lijfrenten* (life annuities). From the second half of the sixteenth century the *renten* spread throughout northern Flanders, and became the principal means of deficit financing (Tracy 1985; Zuiderduijn 2009). The move from public debt to collective public debt thus took place in the sixteenth century, with responsibility for the assumption of debt passing to the provincial states (Tracy 1985). Forced loans did not disappear, but the government counted increasingly on voluntary loans. Information about commercialisation of securities is scarce up to the end of the sixteenth century. In the next century, however, market prices of government credits were rather high, illustrating the impressive confidence that Dutch investors displayed towards the indebted government (Gelderblom and Jonker 2011).

In England the crown relied largely on loans from bankers, financiers, and courtiers, who provided money in return for presumed political or financial advantage. The dangerous liaisons between Tuscan and English merchant bankers between the thirteenth and fourteenth centuries are well known. If the negative aspects of the role of Florentine loans in the bankruptcy of large banking concerns have been re-evaluated (Kaeuper 1973; Hunt 1994), there is no doubt that well within the seventeenth century the Exchequer was unable to ensure the necessary conditions for a regular accumulation of long-term debt. In the late medieval period occasional creditors were assigned orders of payment to be presented directly to tax collectors, but these were merely IOUs that were never developed further. The crown, meanwhile, turned to the credit market of Antwerp, and to forced loans from guilds and prosperous subjects, without, however, developing a related financial market (Stone 1961; Outhwaite 1966; Outhwaite 1971). These were still 'archaic and cumbersome methods of financing deficits' (Outhwaite 1971, 263). During the Bishops' Wars of 1638–40 the government imposed tallies – as had been the practice since the Middle Ages – secured by royal income, with an interest of eight per cent, but the range of the lenders was restricted.

The image of government debt in mid-seventeenth-century England seems little different from that of the medieval period. It is true that the role of merchant bankers was notably refashioned, but government still relied on ad hoc, short-term practices. To address the deficit they turned to the sale of property and offices, as well as forced loans, whereas voluntary loans were negotiated with local governments and members of the political and financial elites. Starting from the mid-seventeenth century, however, a series of institutional and fiscal innovations led to a process of financial development that allowed the government to expand considerably the potential of lenders, and to guarantee their investments more securely (Nichols 1987; Braddick 1996; Coffman this volume). Nonetheless, as late as the 1680s, credit cost the government at least a couple of points more than the interest rate on the private market (Nichols 1971; Clay 1978, 35, 61–4, 89, 183, 186, 234).

The French crown, England's traditional rival, was not in better shape. During the conflicts of the late Middle Ages its ability to collect money depended, as in England, on merchant bankers (Kaeuper 1988, 69–75). In contrast to her rival, however, France could not count on the enormous resources derived from taxes on wool exports. France lacked both the advantageous concessions which existed between the major Italian mercantile houses, and the availability of ample credit. Despite the involvement of Italian lenders, the French market was always characterised by considerable uncertainty, which was magnified by the predatory behaviour of the king. He relied primarily on loans, which were more or less obligatory, from businessmen, officials, and citizens. The creation of the *rentes sur l'hôtel de la ville de Paris* in 1522 was thus in line with the monarch's past behaviour (Schnapper 1957; Morineau 1985). The *rentes* do not represent the 'beginning of French public credit' (Cawès 1895–6), because the sovereign asked Parisians to make loans with interest that was guaranteed by royal fiscal income, which would then be ceded to the municipality. Subsequently, these taxes were extended to other cities of the realm. The mechanism recalled the medieval Italian system, but with a few differences. As we have seen, the bulk of the loans in Italian cities was distributed on the basis of fiscal registers. It is not clear, in contrast, how the Parisian authorities chose lenders. Moreover, the main catalyst for the circulation of *rentes* seems to have been the desire of their holders to unload them (Hamon 1994, 191–2). During the seventeenth century the *rentes* that were sold on the open market spread throughout the country, but their reliability did not improve at all. The sums that were actually collected were less than predicted, and the sale price was often heavily discounted, so much so that in some cases the government transformed the *rentes* into forced loans once again (Ranum 1968, 56–8; Lloyd Moote 1971, 77–8; Dent 1973, 49–54; Bonney 1981, 141, 165–8; Béguin 2005).

The success of the *rentes* was pretty limited: on one hand, the crown could not count on certain and regular financial flows because of the grave uncertainties that burdened such loans; on the other, their low level of commercialisation had not led to the creation of a secondary market which, in turn, could have supported further financial development. Nonetheless, it is clear that the range of credit tools that the French king had at his disposal at the end of the seventeenth century was greater than that available in the medieval period. The participation of a wide swath of the population, even if this participation took place via loans issued by intermediaries at an interest rate that was inferior than the crown's, is perhaps the most striking element of the French scene at the death of Louis XIV (Potter and Rosenthal 1997; Potter 2003). The French government's policies functioned as a brake on the formation of a robust financial market. Worried about safeguarding royal loans, the government obstructed the negotiability of the *rentes sur la ville de Paris*, which markedly limited the growth of the credit market (Schnapper 1957, 215–20; Hoffman, Postel-Vinay, and Rosenthal 2000).

Certain common characteristics of urban financial systems emerge from this brief look at Western Europe. In Aragon, in the northeast, and some southern cities of France, in Germany and Switzerland, in Flanders, and in north central Italy, local governments turned, to different degrees, to long-term debt. In the fourteenth and fifteenth centuries the fundamental difference lay instead in the largely obligatory nature of Italian loans. Unlike the exceptional Genoa, which turned more and more to voluntary loans, Venice and Florence forced their citizens to hand over money that was unlikely to be given back, and which guaranteed ever-diminishing returns. Throughout the sixteenth century this coercion gave way increasingly to free choice, and the governments turned to the open market for capital. Forms of forced loans continued, but certainly were less dominant than in the past. Thus, in the Early Modern age, Italian debt assumed the characteristics of the Dutch system.

Although in the late Middle Ages the local governments of central Europe and Aragon sold life annuities, such loans were basically unknown in Italy. Venice began using them only from 1538, the Apostolic Chamber from 1550, and Florence from 1591 (Pezzolo 2003; Cantini 1800–1808, XIII: 255). Nonetheless, in Florence, the investments of the Monte delle Doti (dowries) were connected to the hope of young girls' survival, and thus could be considered a form of life annuity. It is not clear why the instances of annuities were so limited in Italian medieval debts. If it is true that the *rente* began as a financial tool in the ecclesiastical environment of the high Middle Ages, we can assume that it was not widely employed on the Italian peninsula.

Another marked difference between the debt of Italian cities and that of the rest of Europe leaps out: investors' geographical range. Usually in northern Europe a consistent proportion of creditors lived outside the city walls. This was both advantageous and disadvantageous. For governments in search of money it opened the possibility of a large market of investors to whom they could turn, because they could count on the willingness of even relatively distant investors. On the other hand, the administrative costs of managing foreign-held debt were higher. Above all, the government, when faced with insolvency, risked retaliation from creditor cities (Gilomen 2003, 144; Zuiderduijn 2009). Retaliation represented a powerful instrument for managing foreign debt. Nonetheless, recourse to this juridical tool could interrupt normal commercial relations, which in turn could worsen the general economic situation. The request to central authorities for a moratorium allowed debtors to avoid retaliation, and to gain time to satisfy their creditors. Moratoria, in turn, were the result of political negotiation between princes and cities, which weakened city power in relation to the central government. Furthermore, retaliations worked only when the defaulting government had no alternatives to its commercial ties to the creditor government (Tomz 2007). Thus, the wider the geographical distribution of titles of credit, the more effective was the threat of retaliation.

As far as Italy is concerned, there are very few cases of retaliation against an insolvent government, and only in Florence. Two powerful creditors, the Pope and the Marques of Ferrara, were able to pressure the Florentine authorities effectively to pay the monies due to them from the Monte (Kirshner 1969; Lang 2009, 349). The majority of Italian city governments' creditors lived within their city walls. It is thus clear that these were citizens called upon to lend to their communes. Secondary market transactions allowed foreigners to acquire available securities, but their presence does not appear to have been significant. However, in Genoa, where obligatory loans had declined, foreign presence was widespread, including merchants who likely held property to be used as a guarantee for their own business affairs (Heers 1961, 122). Many foreigners can also be found among the holders of papal and Neapolitan debt. As the centre of the Catholic Church and the seat of an international court, Rome attracted many potential investors who gathered information from relatives and friends residing in the Eternal City. In contrast, among the Neapolitan government were many Tuscans and Genoese. These long-term connections were reinforced during the sixteenth and seventeenth centuries. The Genoese, in particular, as important lenders to the Habsburgs, played a central role in the finances of the Neapolitan crown.

Why did other urban governments, such as those in England, Castile, southern Italy, and west central France, fail to create significant long-term debt? First, the quest for long-term financing arose from a growing need to finance the crown's wars. It seems that the level of financial autonomy of the Castilian and southern Italian cities was fairly limited until the fifteenth century. Most tax proceeds reached royal coffers without passing through them. This was the case for the export tax on English wool, as well as for the export of Sicilian wheat. Those sovereigns could thus make use of the tributary levy, counting on a widespread fiscal sovereignty over their land. Moreover, it is likely that the presence of parliamentary institutions, which offered a space for negotiation between the crown and various political classes, severely limited the need to turn to the financial mediation of the cities, the presence of the *Cortes* in Aragon notwithstanding.

In Aragon the creation of a system of regular taxation was the result of the growing debt of city governments, which were forced to find ordinary resources for paying interest to their creditors. In the Netherlands and England the process was different. The financial revolution identified by Tracy was supplanted by the fiscal revolution described by Fritschy as the necessary prerequisite for Dutch financial development in the late sixteenth century (Tracy 1985; Fritschy 2003). Similarly, changes to the English fiscal system which began in the middle of the seventeenth century were considered crucial for subsequent financial developments. In the case of the north central Italian cities, fiscal sovereignty was achieved by the twelfth century, with the assumption of Imperial fiscal prerogatives. The right of taxation thus went hand in hand with the ability to ask citizens for loans. Moreover, loans to the commune were considered the duty of a good citizen, alongside the duty to take up arms in defence of the city. In the southern cities, in contrast, the model was Castilian (Jago 1993; Drelichman and Voth 2008). The enduring presence of a monarchical power characterised the fiscal relationship between the crown and the cities. This limited the financial autonomy of the latter severely. As a result, city governments were not able to develop a robust system of financing their deficits with loans. Only heavy royal fiscal demand between the sixteenth and seventeenth centuries imposed a massive reliance on loans, which placed the financial health of many cities in jeopardy (Bulgarelli Lukacs 1993; Caracciolo 1994; Foscari 2006).

During the period under examination, governments significantly expanded their toolbox of financial strategies. The monarchies initially relied on the services of merchant bankers and courtiers to collect money in exchange for privileges, concessions, or patrimonial guarantees. Sometimes they turned to local bodies – cities or corporations – to impose forced loans. The picture became more complex at the end of the seventeenth century. The fiscal–financial system was by then populated by various categories of lenders. In the French case, alongside the merchant bankers who furnished short-term loans were officials who regularly made loans to the crown, and tax farmers who, like it or not, played an important role in advancing monies to government (Dent 1973; Bonney 1981; Dessert 1984; Bayard 1988; Hernández 2003). The range of local institutions involved in financing the monarchy expanded, which reinforced their contractual power in relation to the crown. In England, in contrast, the Glorious Revolution drastically changed the relationship between king and subjects, after the Stuarts' attempt to build a state that seemed to follow a Continental model failed in the struggle against Parliamentary armies. The reinforcement of a fiscal system, and the increase of taxation under Cromwell and during the Protectorate, were permitted by a consensus that was more widespread than before. As late as 1680 the government turned to financial intermediaries to collect money, though by the end of the century more innovative elements had emerged (see Carlos *et al.*, this volume).

Did innovations in the financial sector result in a reduction of the cost of deficit financing? Between the Black Death of the mid-fourteenth century and the death of the Sun King in the early eighteenth, everywhere the cost of money persistently fell (Clark 1988; Homer and Sylla 1991). Arguing against the North and Weingast thesis, Epstein noted how the interest paid by urban governments was less than that paid by the monarchies, and how the spread continued to diminish over the course of the modern age, until it disappeared altogether in the eighteenth century (Epstein 2007, 16–29). In effect, even in the age of Enlightenment, loans to monarchies were more burdensome than those made to republics (van Zanden 2009, 222–4). The institutional model emphasises institutional differences, whereas others focus on the increasing power of monarchies to collect taxes. It is once again worth stressing the role of war. Although they faced huge financial costs, in the long term the great powers succeeded in gaining advantage from conflicts 'by increasing returns to scale in military operations' (Stasavage 2007). The limits of the Italian territorial states lay in their small size, in terms of material resources and market dimensions, with respect to the great monarchies. The financial and military innovations of the later Middle Ages put the Italian city-states ahead in the European context, but in the Early Modern period the changes of scale were to favour the great polities.

References

Abella Samitier, Juan 2009. 'La deuda pública de los municipios aragoneses en los siglos XIV y XV', *Anuario de estudios medievales*, 39, 47–64.

Alonso García, David 2004. *Fisco, poder y monarquía en los albores de la modernidad: Castilla 1504–1525*. Unpublished Ph.D. thesis, Universidad Complutense de Madrid.

Álvarez Nogal, Carlos 2009. *Oferta y demanda de deuda pública en Castilla. Juros de alcabalas (1540–1740)*. Madrid: Banco de España.

Armstrong, Lawrin 2003. *Usury and public debt in early Renaissance Florence. Lorenzo Ridolfi on the* Monte Comune. Toronto: Pontifical Institute of Mediaeval Studies.

Barbadoro, Bernardino 1929. *Le finanze della repubblica fiorentina. Imposta diretta e debito pubblico fino all'istituzione del Monte*. Florence: Olschki.

Barducci, Roberto 1979. 'Politica e speculazione finanziaria a Firenze dopo la crisi del primo Trecento (1343–1358)', *Archivio storico italiano*, 137, 177–219.

Bauer, Clemens 1928. 'Die Epochen der Papstfinanz. Ein Versuch', *Historische Zeitschrift*, 138, 457–503.

Bayard, Françoise 1988. *Le monde des financiers au XVIIe siècle*. Paris: Flammarion.

Becker, Marvin 1965. 'Problemi della finanza pubblica fiorentina nella seconda metà del Trecento e dei primi del Quattrocento', *Archivio storico italiano*, 123, 433–66.

Becker, Marvin 1966. 'Economic Change and the Emerging Florentine Territorial State', *Studies in the Renaissance*, 13, 7–39.

Béguin, Katia 2005. 'La circulation des rentes constituées dans la France du XVIIe siècle', *Annales*, 60, 1231–32.

Bitossi, Carlo 2006. 'Il governo della Repubblica e della Casa di san Giorgio: I ceti dirigenti dopo la riforma costituzionale del 1576', in *La Casa di San Giorgio: Il potere del credito*. Genoa: Società di storia patria.

Bonney, Richard 1981. *The King's Debts. Finance and Politics in France 1589–1661*. Oxford: Oxford University Press.

Bowsky, William 1970. *The Finance of the Commune of Siena, 1287–1355*. Oxford: Oxford University Press.

Braddick, Michael J. 1996. *The Nerves of State. Taxation and the Financing of the English State, 1558–1714*. Manchester: Manchester University Press.

Brucker, Gene 1962. *Florentine Politics and Society, 1343–1378*. Princeton: Princeton University Press.

Bulgarelli Lukacs, Alessandra 1993. *L'imposta diretta nel regno di Napoli in età moderna*. Milan: Franco Angeli.

Bulgarelli Lukacs, Alessandra 2004. '"Domain state" e "tax state" nel Regno di Napoli (secoli XII–XIX)', *Società e storia*, 19, 781–812.

Caferro, William 1998. *Mercenary Companies and the Decline of Siena*. Baltimore: Johns Hopkins University Press.

Calabria, Antonio 1989. 'Finanzieri genovesi nel Regno di Napoli nel Cinquecento', *Rivista storica italiana*, 101, 578–613.

Calabria, Antonio 1991. *The Cost of Empire. The Finances of the Kingdom of Naples in the Time of Spanish Rule*. Cambridge: Cambridge University Press.

Calabria, Antonio 2000. 'What Happened to Tuscan Capital Investment in Sixteenth-Century Naples? An Unsolved Problem in the History of Early Capitalism', *Essays in Economic and Business History*, 18, 1–16.

Cambi, Giovanni 1786. *Istorie, in Delizie degli eruditi toscani*. Florence: Cambiagi, vol. XXIII.

Cantini, Lorenzo (ed.) 1800–1808. *Legislazione toscana*, 32 vols. Florence: Fantosini.

Caracciolo, Francesco 1994. *Sud, debiti e gabelle*. Messina: Caracciolo.

Carboni, Mauro 2009. 'Public Debt, Guarantees, and Local Elites in the Papal States (XVI–XVIII Centuries)', *Journal of European Economic History*, 38, 149–74.

Casanova, Cesarina 1981. *Comunità e governo in Romagna in età moderna*. Bologna: Clueb.

Castillo Pintado, Alvaro 1963a. 'Dette flottante et dette consolidée en Espagne, de 1557 à 1600', *Annales ESC*, 18, 745–59.

Castillo Pintado, Alvaro 1963b. 'Los juros de Castilla. Apogeo y fin de un instrumento de crédito', *Hispania*, 23, 43–70.

Cawès, Paul 1895–6. 'Les commencements du crédit public en France', *Revue d'économie politique*, 9, 97–123, 825–65; 10, 407–79.

Ciappelli, Giovanni 2009. *Fisco e società a Firenze nel Rinascimento*. Rome: Edizioni di storia e letteratura.

Clark, Gregory 1988. 'The Cost of Capital in Medieval Agricultural Technique', *Explorations in Economic History*, 25, 265–94.

Clay, Christopher 1978. *Public Finance and Private Wealth: The Career of Sir Stephen Fox, 1627–1716*. Oxford: Clarendon Press.

Colzi, Francesco 1999. *Il debito pubblico del Campidoglio. Finanza comunale e circolazione dei titoli a Roma fra Cinque e Seicento*. Naples: Esi.

D'Alaimo, Antonio 1995. *La finanza pubblica del Granducato di Toscana al tempo di Ferdinando II (1621–1670)*. Unpublished Ph.D. Thesis, Istituto Universitario Navale di Napoli.

Dandelet, Thomas J. 2001. *Spanish Rome, 1500–1700*. New Haven: Yale University Press.

de Roover, Raymond 1963. *The Rise and Decline of the Medici Bank, 1397–1494*. Cambridge, MA: Harvard University Press.

De Rosa, Luigi 1958. *Studi sugli arrendamenti del Regno di Napoli. Aspetti della distribuzione della ricchezza mobiliare nel Mezzogiorno continentale (1649–1806)*. Naples: L'arte tipografica.

De Rosa, Luigi 1987. *Il Mezzogiorno spagnolo tra crescita e decadenza*. Milan: Il saggiatore.

De Rosa, Luigi 1999. *Conflitti e squilibri nel Mezzogiorno tra Cinque e Ottocento*. Rome and Bari: Laterza.

Dent, Julian 1973. *Crisis in Finance. Crown, Financiers and Society in Seventeenth-Century France*. New York: David and Charles.

Dessert, Daniel 1984. *Argent, pouvoir et société au Grand Siècle*. Paris: Fayard.

di Somma, Carlo 1960. *Il Banco dello Spirito Santo dalle origini al 1664*. Naples: Università degli studi di Napoli.

Di Tucci, Raffaele 1929–1930. 'Le imposte del commercio genovese durante la gestione del Banco di San Giorgio', *Giornale storico e letterario della Liguria*, 5, 209–19; 6, 1–12, 147–69, 242–62, 340–60.

Diaz, Furio 1976. *Il Granducato di Toscana. I Medici*. Turin: Utet.

Drelichman, Mauricio and Voth, Hans-Joachim 2008. 'Institutions and the Resource Curse in Early Modern Spain', in Elhanan Helpman (ed.), *Institutions and Economic Performances*. Cambridge, MA: Harvard University Press.

Epstein, Stephan R. 2007. *Freedom and Growth. The Rise of States and Markets in Europe, 1300–1750*. London: Routledge.

Foscari, Giuseppe 2006. *Stato, politica fiscale e contribuenti nel Regno di Napoli (1610–1648)*. Soveria Mannelli: Rubbettino.

Fratianni, Michele 2006. 'Government Debt, Reputation and Creditors' protections: The Tale of San Giorgio', *Review of Finance*, 10, 487–506.

Frenz, Thomas 1986. *Die Kanzlei der Päpste der Hochrenaissance, 1471–1527*. Tübingen: Niemeyer.

Fritschy, Wantje van der 2003. 'A "Financial Revolution" Revisited: Public Finance in Holland during the Dutch Revolt, 1568–1648', *Economic History Review*, 56, 57–89.

Furió, Antonio 1999. 'Deuda pública e intereses privados. Finanzas y fiscalidad municipales en la Corona de Aragón', *Edad Media. Revista de historia*, 2, 35–79.

Galasso, Giuseppe 1984. 'Economia e finanze nel Mezzogiorno tra XVI e XVII secolo', in Aldo De Maddalena and Hermann Kellenbenz (eds.), *Finanze e ragion di Stato in Italia e in Germania nella prima Età moderna*. Bologna: Il mulino.

Gelderblom, Oscar and Jonker, Joost 2011. 'Public Finance and Economic Growth: The Case of Holland in Seventeenth Century', *Journal of Economic History*, 71, 1–39.

Gilomen, Hans-Jörg 2003.' La prise de décision en matière d'emprunts dans les villes suisses au XVe siècle', in M. Boone, K. Davids, and P. Janssens (eds.), *Urban Public Debts, Urban Governments and the Market for Annuities in Western Europe, 14th–18th Centuries*. Leuven: Brepols.

Gioffré, Domenico 1966. *Il debito pubblico genovese. Inventario delle compere anteriori a San Giorgio o non consolidate nel Banco (sec. XIV–XIX)*. Milan: Giuffré.

Giustinian, Antonio 1876. *Dispacci*. Edited by P. Villari, 3 vols. Florence: Le Monnier.

Green, Louis 1983. 'Changes in the Nature of War in Early Fourteenth Century Tuscany', *War and Society*, 1, 1–24.

Grendi, Edoardo 1987. *La repubblica aristocratica dei genovesi*. Bologna: Il mulino.

Grillo, Paolo 2008. *Cavalieri e popoli in armi. Le istituzioni militari nell'Italia medievale*. Rome: Laterza.

Guidi Bruscoli, Francesco 2000. *Benvenuto Olivieri. I mercatores fiorentini e la camera apostolica nella Roma di Paolo III Farnese (1534–1549)*. Florence: Olschki.

Hamon, Philip 1994. *L'argent du roi. Les finances sous François Ier*. Paris: Comité pour l'histoire économique et financière de la France.

Heers, Jacques 1961. *Gênes au XVe siècle. Aspectes économiques et sociaux*. Paris: Sevpen.

Hernández, Bernat 2003. *Fiscalismo y finanzas en la Cataluña moderna*. Barcelona: TEHI.

Hoffman, Philip, Postel-Vinay, Gilles, and Rosenthal, Jean-Laurent 2000. *Priceless Markets. The Political Economy of Credit in Paris 1660–1870*. Chicago: University of Chicago Press.

Homer, Sidney and Sylla, Richard 1991. *A History of the Interest Rates*, 3rd edn. New Brunswick: Rutgers University Press.

Hunt, Edwin S. 1994. *The Medieval Super-companies: A Study of the Peruzzi Company of Florence*. Cambridge: Cambridge University Press.

Jago, Charles 1993. 'Parliament, Subsidies and Constitutional Change in Castile, 1601–1621', *Parliaments, Estates and Representation*, 13, 123–37.

Kaeuper, Richard W. 1973. *Bankers to the Crown: The Riccardi of Lucca and Edward I*. Princeton: Princeton University Press.

Kaeuper, Richard W. 1988. *War, Justice, and Public Order. England and France in the Later Middle Ages*. Oxford: Oxford University Press.

Kindleberger, Charles P. 1993. *A Financial History of Western Europe*, 2nd edn. Oxford: Oxford University Press.

Kirshner, Julius 1969. 'Papa Eugenio IV e il Monte Comune. Documenti su investimento e speculazione nel debito pubblico di Firenze', *Archivio storico italiano*, 127, 339–82.

Kirshner, Julius and Molho, Anthony 1978. 'The Dowry Fund and the Marriage Market in Early Quattrocento Florence', *Journal of Modern History*, 50, 403–38.

Ladero Quesada, Miguel-Angel 1997. 'Las haciendas concejiles en la Corona de Castilla', in *Finanzas y fiscalidad municipal*. Avila: Fundación Sánchez-Albornoz.

Lane, Frederic 1973. 'Public Debt and Private Wealth, Particularly in 16th Century Venice', in Branislava Tenenti (ed.), *Mélanges en honneur de Fernand Braudel*, 2 vols. Toulouse: Privat, vol. I.

Lang, Heinrich 2009. *Cosimo de' Medici. Die Gesandten und die Condottieri. Diplomatie und Kriege der Republik Florenz im 15. Jahrhundert*. Paderborn: Schöning.

Leggi delle compere di S. Giorgio 1625. Genoa: Pavoni.

Lloyd Moote, A. 1971. *The Revolt of the Judges. The Parlement of Paris and the Fronde 1643–1652*. Princeton: Princeton University Press.

Macdonald, James 2003. *A Free Nation Deep in Debt. The Financial Roots of Democracy*. New York: Farrar.

Mallett, Michael 1974. *Mercenaries and Their Masters: Warfare in Renaissance Italy*. London: Bodley Head.

Marks, Louis F. 1960. 'The Financial Oligarchy in Florence under Lorenzo', in E. F. Jacob (ed.), *Italian Renaissance Studies*. London: Faber.

Menning, Carol Bresnahan 1993. *Charity and State in Late Renaissance Italy: The Monte di Pietà of Florence*. Ithaca and London: Cornell University Press.

Molho, Anthony 1971. *Florentine Public Finances in the Early Renaissance, 1400–1434*. Cambridge, MA: Harvard University Press.

Molho, Anthony 1987. 'L'amministrazione del debito pubblico a Firenze nel Quindicesimo secolo', in Donatella Rugiadini (ed.), *I ceti dirigenti nella Toscana del Quattrocento*. Florence: Papafava.

Molho, Anthony 1994. *Marriage Alliance in Late Medieval Florence*. Cambridge, MA: Harvard University Press.

Molho, Anthony 1999. 'Créanciers de Florence en 1347. Un aperçu statistique du quartier de Santo Spirito', in Charles-M. de La Roncière (ed.), *La Toscane et les Toscans autour de la Renaissance. Cadres de vie, société, croyances*. Aix-en-Provence: Publications de l'Université de Provence.

Monaco, Michelle 1960. 'Il primo debito pubblico pontificio: Il Monte della Fede' (1526), *Studi Romani*, 7, 553–69.

Morineau, Michel 1985. 'De la logique des finances de l'Etat', in J. Bouvier and J.-C. Perrot (eds.), *Etats, fiscalités, économies*. Paris: Publications de la Sorbonne.

Munro, John 2003. 'The Medieval Origins of the "Financial Revolution": Usury, Rentes, and Negotiability', *International History Review*, 25, 505–62.

Nichols, Glenn O. 1971. 'English Government Borrowing, 1660–1688', *Journal of British Studies*, 10, 83–104.

Nichols, Glenn O. 1987. 'Intermediaries and the Development of English Government Borrowing: The Case of Sir John James and Major Robert Huntington', *Business History*, 29, 26–46.

North, Douglass and Weingast, Barry 1989. 'Constitutions and Commitment: The Evolution of Institutions Governing Public Choice in Seventeenth-Century Britain', *Journal of Economic History*, 49, 803–32.

Olivera Serrano, César 1991.'Impréstitos de la Corona de Castilla bajo la dinastia Trastamara (1369–1474)', *Hispania*, 51, 317–27.

Outhwaite, R. B. 1966. 'The Trials of Foreign Borrowing: The English Crown and the Antwerp Money Market in the Mid-sixteenth Century', *Economic History Review*, 19, 289–305.

Outhwaite, R. B. 1971. 'Royal Borrowing in the Reign of Elizabeth I: The Aftermath of Antwerp', *English Historical Review*, 86, 251–63.

Palermo, Luciano 2000. 'La finanza pontificia e il banchiere 'depositario' nel primo Quattrocento', in Donatella Strangio (ed.). *Studi in onore di Ciro Manca*. Padua: Cedam.

Pampaloni, Guido 1956. 'Cenni storici sul Monte di Pietà di Firenze', in *Archivi storici delle aziende di credito*, 2 vols. Rome: Associazione bancaria italiana, vol. I.

Parigino, Giuseppe Vittorio 1999. *Il tesoro del principe. Funzione pubblica e privata del patrimonio della famiglia Medici nel Cinquecento*. Florence: Olschki.

Parigino, Giuseppe Vittorio 2009. 'Il patrimonio di Ferdinando II de' Medici. Una prima ricognizione', *Mediterranea*, 6, 479–516.

Pezzolo, Luciano 2003. 'The Venetian Government Debt 1350–1650', in M. Boone, K. Davids, and P. Janssens (eds.), *Urban Public Debts, Urban Governments and the Market for Annuities in Western Europe, 14th–18th Centuries*. Leuven: Brepols.

Pezzolo, Luciano 2005. 'Bonds and Government Debt in Italian City States, 1250–1650', in William Goetzman and Geert K. Rouwenhorst (eds.), *The Origins of Value. Financial Innovations That Created the Modern Capital Market*. Oxford and New York: Oxford University Press.

Pezzolo, Luciano and Tattara, Giuseppe 2008.'"Una fiera senza luogo". Was Bisenzone an International Capital Market in Sixteenth-Century Italy?' *Journal of Economic History*, 68, 1098–1122.

Piola Caselli, Fausto 1970–72. 'Aspetti del debito pubblico nello stato pontificio: gli uffici vacabili', *Annali della Facoltà di Scienze Politiche dell'Università degli Studi di Perugia*, 11, 1–74.

Piola Caselli, Fausto 1987. 'L'espansione delle fonti finanziarie della Chiesa nel XIV secolo', *Archivio della società romana di storia patria*, 110, 63–97.

Piola Caselli, Fausto 1988. 'La diffusione dei luoghi di monte della Camera Apostolica alla fine del XVI secolo. Capitali investiti e rendimenti', in *Credito e sviluppo economico in Italia dal medio evo all'età contemporanea*. Verona: Fiorini.

Piola Caselli, Fausto 1989. 'La disciplina amministrativa ed il trattamento fiscale dei luoghi di monte della Camera apostolica tra il XVI e il XVII secolo', in M. J. Peláez (ed.), *Historia economica y de las instituciones financieras en Europa. Trabajos en homenaje a Ferran Valls i Taberner*, 19 vols. Barcelona: Promociones y publicaciones universitarias, vol. XI.

Piola Caselli, Fausto 1991. 'Banchi privati e debito pubblico pontificio a Roma tra Cinquecento e Seicento', in *Banchi pubblici, Banchi privati e monti di Pietà nell'Europa preindustriale. Amministrazione, tecniche operative e ruoli economici*, 2 vols. Genoa: Società di storia patria, vol. I.

Poncet, Olivier 1993. 'Une utilisation nouvelle de le rente constituée au XVIe siècle: Les membres du conseil au secours des finances d'Henri III', *Bibliothèque de l'école de Chartes*, 151, 307–57.

Potter, Mark 2003. *Corps and Clienteles. Public Finance and Political Change in France, 1688–1715*. Aldershot: Ashgate.

Potter, Mark and Rosenthal, Jean-Laurent 1997. 'Politics and Public Finance in France: The Estates of Burgundy, 1660–1790', *Journal of Interdisciplinary History*, 27, 577–612.

Ranum, Orest 1968. *Paris in the Age of Absolutism*. New York: Wiley.

Reinhard, Wolfgang 1984. 'Finanzapontificia e Stato della Chiesa nel XVI e XVII secolo', in Aldo De Maddalena and Hermann Kellenbenz (eds.), *Finanze e ragion di Stato in Italia e in Germania nella prima Età moderna*. Bologna: Il mulino.

Renouard, Yves 1941. *Les relations des papes d'Avignon et des compagnies commerciales et bancaires de 1316 à 1378*. Paris: de Boccard.

Rivera Magos, Victor 2005. *Una colonia nel regno angioino di Napoli. La comunità toscana a Barletta tra 1266 e 1345*. Barletta: Rotary Club.

Sánchez Belén, Juan A. 1996. *La política fiscal en Castilla. durante el reinado de Carlo II*. Madrid: Siglo Ventiuno de España.

Savelli, Roberto 1981. *La repubblica oligarchica. Legislazione, istituzioni e ceti a Genova nel Cinquecento*. Milan: Giuffré.

Savelli, Roberto 1984. 'Tra Machiavelli e S. Giorgio. Cultura giuspolitica e dibattito istituzionale a Genova nel Cinque-Seicento', in Aldo De Maddalena and Hermann Kellenbenz (eds.), *Finanze e ragion di Stato in Italia e in Germania nella prima Età moderna*. Bologna: Il mulino.

Schimmelpfenning, Bernhard 1984. 'Der Ämterhandel an der römischen Kurie von Pius II. bis zum Sacco di Roma (1458–1527)', in Ilja Mieck (ed.), *Ämterhandel im Spätmittelalter und im 16. Jahrhundert*. Berlin: Colloquium Verlag.

Schnapper, Bernard 1957. *Les rentes au XVIe siècle*. Paris: Sevpen.

Settia, Aldo A. 1993. *Comuni in guerra. Armi ed eserciti nell'Italia delle città.* Bologna: CLUEB.

Sieveking, Heinrich 1905–7. *Studio sulle finanze genovesi e in particolare sulla House di S. Giorgio*, 2 vols. Genoa: Società di storia patria.

Stasavage, David 2007. 'Cities, Constitutions, and Sovereign Borrowing in Europe, 1274–1785', *International Organization*, 61, 489–525.

Stone, Lawrence 1961. *An Elizabethan, Sir Horace Pallavicino*. Oxford: Clarendon.

Tarrow, Sidney 2004. 'From Comparative Historical Analysis to "Local Theory": The Italian City-State Route to the Modern State', *Theory and Society*, 33, 443–71.

Teicher, Anna 1983. 'Politics and Finance in the Age of Cosimo I: the Public and Private Face of Credit', in *Firenze e la Toscana dei Medici nell'Europa del '500*, 3 vols. Florence: Olschki, vol. I.

Thompson, I. I. A. 1994. 'Castile: Polity, Fiscality, and Fiscal Crisis', in P. Hoffman and K. Norberg (eds.), *Fiscal Crises, Liberty, and Representative Government, 1450–1789*. Palo Alto, CA: Stanford University Press.

Thompson, William R. and Rasler, Karen 1999. 'War, the Military Revolution(S) Controversy, and Army Expansion. A Test of Two Explanations of Historical Influences on European State Making', *Comparative Political Studies*, 32, 3–31.

Tilly, Charles 1992. *Coercion, Capital and the European States: AD 990–1992.* Cambridge, MA: Blackwell.

Tognetti, Sergio 1999. *Il Banco Cambini. Affari e mercati di una compagnia mercantile-bancaria nella Firenze del XV secolo.* Florence: Olschki.

Tomz, Michael 2007. *Reputation and International Cooperation. Sovereign Debt across Three Centuries.* Princeton: Princeton University Press.

Tracy, James 1985. *A Financial Revolution in the Habsburg Netherlands: Renten and Renteniers in the County of Holland, 1515–1565.* Berkeley: University of California Press.

Tracy, James 2003. 'On the Dual Origins of Long-Term Debt in Medieval Europe', in M. Boone, K. Davids, and P. Janssens (eds.), *Urban Public Debts, Urban Governments and the Market for Annuities in Western Europe, 14th–18th Centuries.* Leuven: Brepols.

van Zanden, Jan Leuten 2009. *The Long Road to the Industrial Revolution.* Leiden: Brill.

Villari, Rosario 1973. *La rivolta antispagnola a Napoli. Le origini (1585–1647)*, 2nd edn. Rome and Bari: Laterza.

Zilli, Ilaria 1990. *Imposta diretta e debito pubblico nel Regno di Napoli: 1669–1737. La Terra di Lavoro.* Naples: Esi.

Zuiderduijn, Jaco 2009. *Medieval Capital Markets: Markets for Renten, State Formation and Private Investment in Holland (1300–1550).* Leiden and Boston: Brill.

9 Bounded leviathan: Fiscal constraints and financial development in the Early Modern Hispanic world

Alejandra Irigoin and Regina Grafe

One of the great merits of North and Weingast's insight into the importance of a ruler's 'credible commitment' to protecting property rights is that it both is parsimonious and lends itself beautifully to generalisation. These features explain its runaway success with economists, political scientists, and development advisors from the World Bank. In the last two decades the study of 'governance' has exhibited an unbroken tendency to return time and again to the basic New Institutional Economic (NIE) insight that, in the long run (economist-speak for 'historically'), what matters is that governments protect citizens' lives and property, and that citizens have ways to protect their livelihood from governments (North and Weingast 1989).

In contrast, much of the criticism of the ideas that emanated from 'Constitutions and Commitment' has been more narrowly based. Economic historians have put North and Weingast's data and interpretation of English fiscal and financial history to the test by exploring alternative explanations for the fall in English sovereign interest rates, by challenging the supposed link between public and private interest rates, by stressing the role of usury rates, and finally by wondering if sovereign interest rates reacted at all to institutional changes (Clark 1996; Epstein 2000; Temin and Voth 2005; Sussman and Yafeh 2006). This body of literature has – at least in the minds of many economic historians – seriously undermined the narrative of the Glorious Revolution as the origin of English fiscal, financial, and eventually economic growth. However, it has done little to lessen the faith of economists, political scientists, and development specialists that predatory states are the single largest obstacle to long-term growth.

The economics literature bases this conviction mostly on indirect evidence derived from large cross-country data sets, which suggest that what has been termed 'English legal origins' led to better judicial protection of investors' rights, or, put more simply, to a legal regime that protected them against private theft and public predation (La Porta, Lopez-de-Silanes, Shleifer, and Vishny 1998; La Porta, Lopez-de-Silanes, and

Shleifer 2008). English common law as used in Britain and her former colonies is contrasted with German, Scandinavian, or French civil law systems. Amongst the latter, the French tradition is usually singled out for particularly weak investor protection. Thus, North and Weingast seemed vindicated in principle with regard to the growth implications of institutions in post-Glorious Revolution Britain, even if the historical account of its fiscal and financial development was found to be less convincing. However, a number of recent papers bring the economics debate back more closely to that amongst economic historians. They acknowledge that growth in fact depends on 'state capacity' more generally. This encompasses not only the narrowly defined protection of investors but also the ability of the state to finance itself, that is, fiscal capacity. Besley and Persson (2009), for example, show that common-law countries might have been better at investor protection – that is, legal capacity – but they were less efficient in creating a fiscal state than most civil law countries, notably those of German and Scandinavian origin.

What this literature shows is that the protection of private property rights and that of public property rights to taxation are linked and most likely coevolutionary (Besley and Persson 2009; Besley and Persson 2010). However, the precise relation between the two is anything but clear. This chapter argues that at least part of the problem is that the original North and Weingast model contained a fundamental assumption that has been questioned too little. By arguing that the ability of rulers to commit credibly to protecting subjects' or citizens' property rights distinguished fast-growing European countries from laggards, the model laid the foundation of the belief that state predation was the most important political threat to economic growth in Early Modern Europe. This basic assumption in fact cannot be generalised, because the relationship between state fiscal capacity and legal capacity is not linear. This is especially true in the phase of European nation-state building. This chapter thus shifts attention away from the more narrowly defined historical accuracy (or otherwise) of the model within English fiscal and financial history. Instead, it focuses on the much more general claim that underpins the original North and Weingast model, and a whole literature in its wake.

The first section develops a very simple model of the relation between revenue and the coercive effort of the state that explains *why* the assumption of the predatory state should not be generalised carelessly. Instead, it posits that during the phase of European state building (at least to 1800), states faced one of two very different central challenges, depending on their *Verfasstheit* (the way states were constituted, rather than their constitution in the narrow Anglophone sense). On one hand, states' main challenge could be to keep in check the ruler's potential for pre-dation, just as North and Weingast argue. On the other hand, they were just as likely to face a coordination problem, instead of a predation issue. The second section provides empirical evidence to illustrate and fur-ther develop this argument, namely that in some Early Modern Euro-pean states, notably in Spain, predation was never a central issue, but coordination and integration were. The third section elaborates further the consequences of the coordination problem, zooming in on financial markets as an example of the potentially serious welfare problems that resulted from failing to solve the coordination problem. The final section concludes.

Model specifications

Through all ages rulers had to use some degree of coercion in order to collect taxes. The most benevolent ruler, who does not appropriate any of the revenue for his or her own purposes, and who miraculously decides to provide exactly the amount of public goods his or her subjects wish for, will be able to reduce the need for enforcement through bargaining and persuasion by, in Levi's words, increasing 'quasi-voluntary compliance'. But he or she will not be able to do away with the need for enforcement altogether (Levi 1988). A purely voluntarist political organisation, or a pure form of anarchy, will always founder in the face of overwhelming incentives for individuals to free ride on the contributions of others. Indeed, as Olson has shown, an entirely voluntary agreement to defray the costs of public goods is impossible to establish (Olson 2000). The threat of punishment is thus the selective (negative) incentive needed to establish collective organisation. Coercion is a *conditio sine qua non* for state capacity.

However, this chapter argues that the relationship between revenues collected and the state's coercive effort is not linear, but shaped like an inverted U. The basic notion underlying this relationship, depicted in Figure 9.1, is simple. Initially, increased coercive effort, say more tax col-lectors and a more complex administration, will increase the opportunity cost of tax evasion and avoidance for subjects. When an attempt to shirk taxes becomes likely to be discovered and prosecuted, the risk of not pay-ing up will become too great for many subjects. However, more coercive effort at some point runs into decreasing returns; that is, the marginal return in terms of net revenue of an additional tax collector (to stay within the example) will decrease once most of the territory is covered by a basic tax collecting structure. This relationship is represented in Figure 9.1 by the movement from the origin to point A, that is, by the ascending

Net revenue

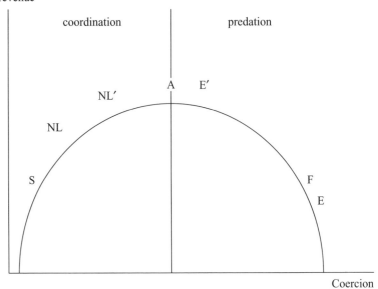

Figure 9.1. The relationship between revenue and states' coercive effort.

part of the inverted U. Arguably, this kind of slow movement towards improved state coercive capacity was what European state-building in the late medieval and Early Modern period was all about.

Beyond point A, however, investment in coercion in fact becomes counterproductive in terms of net revenue. The intuition here, too, is easy to see. Two effects are likely to appear. First, coercion is obviously costly, and because the marginal return to coercion in terms of additional revenue is decreasing, at some point the cost of the additional tax collector (to stay again with the simplistic example) exceeds the increase in revenue he or she will be able to collect. This is little more than a generalisation of Levi's model, in which a ruler's net revenue is reduced because the ruler is powerful, but has weak monitoring structures, and thus the ruler's agents pocket most of the revenue (Levi 1988). Even if the agents do not cheat the ruler, increased coercion will result in lower net revenue, because of decreasing returns to coercion. Second, once the coercive effort becomes overbearing, subjects are likely to engage in more sophisticated or coordinated ways of cheating the tax man, and simply reduce cooperation with the ruler. As resistance, open or more clandestine, increases, collection will actually fall, and collection costs rise further. At its most extreme, the legitimacy of the tax-raising ruler might be entirely lost, and revenue fall precipitously. Every Early Modern European ruler knew the cost of tax riots. They not only required a paid force to repress, but often wiped out the revenue of an entire town or region for a protracted period. This part of the relationship is depicted on the right-hand side of Figure 9.1.

It is important to note that in this – admittedly very simplistic – rendition of the relationship between net revenue and the coercive investment of the ruler, the authors have abstracted from tax rates and design. Although much thought has been given to them, the relationship described would hold even if tax rates remained fixed, and the only change was to the level of coercion applied to collect them. It is thus different from the Laffer curve of the same shape. The latter posits that as tax *rates* increase, so initially does net revenue. However, as the tax burden on the economy rises, people increasingly choose not to invest, work, and engage in taxed transactions, and thus net revenue falls because of the negative welfare effects of high tax rates. (Thus, the Laffer curve charts revenue on the *y*-axis and tax rates on the *x*-axis.) If one assumes that coercive effort, on one hand, and tax rates and the arbitrariness of impositions, on the other, are positively correlated, as would seem sensible, the effect described would be enhanced. However, the most important point for the debate that follows is that, *ceteris paribus*, the relationship between coercive effort employed to raise taxes and net revenue is non-linear, regardless of tax rates.

Let us (imperfectly) transplant the idea of 'credible commitment' into this simple figure. North and Weingast's argument was that England before the Glorious Revolution was somewhere around point E. The Stuarts employed high levels of coercion not just in the form of tax farmers but, more importantly, through forced loans, monopolies, and similar measures which carried very high enforcement costs and reduced compliance. Because the ruler's power to coerce, or in the preferred terminology of political economy, predate, was unconstrained, the ruler turned into the main threat to economic activity. Not surprisingly, net revenue was modest.

After the Glorious Revolution, in contrast, Parliament could impose enough control over the crown's tax-raising and spending that tax compliance improved, more favourable loans could be obtained, and they could be serviced more regularly and more cheaply. In short, net revenue increased while the level of coercion necessary to collect taxes decreased, as the legitimacy of the fiscal system increased. England had moved closer to point E' in Figure 9.1, that is, more revenue with less coercion.[1] In the credible-commitment view of European economic history, England had achieved a fiscally more sustainable and financially more beneficial position which fostered economic growth. More legal capacity apparently went hand in hand with more fiscal capacity.

In contrast, its unconstrained competitors, most importantly absolutist France, but by extension also Spain and the remaining European absolutists, struggled along for the next century and a half somewhere around point F in Figure 9.1, in a place where high coercive investment rendered mediocre fiscal returns. These were states that predated on subjects' property without being able to improve their own fiscal performance, and in the process hamstrung their own economies. The reason was that the states' coercive potential was not constrained by any constitutional guarantee, and both legal and fiscal capacities suffered.

A second look at Figure 9.1, however, reveals a serious issue. The story of the coercive power of the state that needed to be restrained by parliamentary representation makes sense as long as it is assumed that all Early Modern European states were placed somewhere to the right of point A in the graph. Here the combination of decreasing returns to coercion, increasing taxpayer resistance, and misappropriation of revenue by rulers' agents as states moved towards the right meant that less coercion (read predation) was associated with more revenue. Here a predatory ruler was indeed, in all likelihood, the main problem. The trouble is that much of the literature simply ignores the possibility that Early Modern states might have been located to the left of point A.

Economists, political scientists, and economic historians have assumed *ex ante* that all rulers are a threat to their subjects' or citizens' property because they need to maximise their disposable income (Brennan and Buchanan 1980; Brennan and Buchanan 1985). In Levi's words, all 'rulers are predatory in that they always try to . . . maximise their personal objectives, which, I argue, require them to maximise state revenue' (Levi 1988). Or, as North and Weingast argue (citing McNeill and Tullock), 'if rulers did not maintain a comparative advantage in coercion, they soon failed to be rulers'(North and Weingast 1989). The basis of this claim relies on Tilly's analysis of European state competition, which argues that the exogenous variable that compelled European states to compete for

---

[1] In the longer term English tax rates of course rose very fast. However, for the purpose of North and Weingast's original argument, this was in fact not necessary. They assumed that the positive effects of a more reliable and equitable tax system on growth would allow revenue to grow even if the rates had not increased. Thus, the dynamic part of their model came out of lower financing costs and higher rates of economic growth, not higher tax rates.

revenue was the technological and strategic innovations of the military revolution (Tilly 1975; Tilly 1990). With that basic assumption in mind, it would seem that there really is only the right-hand side of this chapter's little graph. The difference is simply that if a ruler is closer to E, he or she is an unconstrained predator, or to E', a constrained predator. Nothing else matters, and it would seem justified to generalise the notion that 'credible commitment' is the central political economy issue facing Early Modern European economies.

Alas, as scholars also note, rulers did and do not maximise revenue, but rule. Their ultimate constraint domestically was to stay in power, and arguably their main objective internationally was to extend their power (Lane 1958).[2] Revenue was a means to an end; coercion was but one means to collect revenue. However, Figure 9.1 suggests that whether more coercion was productive or counterproductive in terms of increasing revenue depended crucially on whether a ruler found himself or herself to the left or the right of the point of optimal levels of coercion at A. Revenue maximisation was not the only game in town, and Spanish fiscal and financial history can explain why.

Empirical evidence

Early modern Spain was nowhere near to point E (pre-Glorious Revolution England) or F (absolutist France, the spot NIE has reserved for European absolutists). Instead it was somewhere around point S. It combined low coercion effort with reasonable revenue collection. In other words, it was in territory that simply does not exist in much of the conventional NIE theory. The implications of this hypothesis are potentially far-reaching. If this assessment of the relation between coercion and revenues is correct in the case of Spain, the central assumption that underpins the generalisation of the model of 'constitutional commitment' is simply incorrect: not all rulers maximised revenue, and therefore the simple equation to test rule through the proxy of revenue has to be rethought.

This is a bold assertion, and it asks for at least three empirical tests to prove it. First, it should be possible to show that, in terms of its revenue raising, Spain was broadly comparable to France, but less successful than (post-Glorious Revolution) England. Second, it should be apparent that Spain was not afflicted by what North and Weingast identified as the

---

[2] Interestingly, Levi thought that this only applied to states that were run by a larger group of 'top management' (military and police), but not to monarchies. For a contrasting view, see La Manna and Stomp (1994).

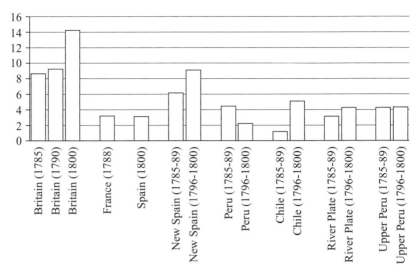

Figure 9.2. Net revenue per capita in European countries and Spanish territories in the Americas (1785–1800) (in Spanish American pesos). *Source:* For a complete list of sources see Grafe and Irigoin, 2012.

key characteristic of the unconstrained predatory ruler in Early Modern Europe: high sovereign interest rates. In the logic of the model a revenue-maximising ruler with absolute power would be expected to predate on subjects' property. The prime target was lenders' property, which could be expropriated by simply repudiating loans, by unilateral alterations of the terms of contract, or through currency manipulations. Thus, lenders naturally would require high *ex ante* interest rates. Third, coercion costs must be demonstrably low.

These three issues will be discussed in turn, using data from the authors' recent research on Spain and her territories in the Americas. The data presented are certainly subject to limitations in terms of geographical and temporal reach. However, it should be remembered that the goal here is not to prove that the Spanish case represents an alternative *universal* model. Instead, it is intended to disprove the claim of universality that has been attached to the model of 'Constitutions and Commitment'.

Revenue per capita

How successful was Spain at raising revenue relative to its direct European competitors? Figure 9.2 offers some data on the per capita revenue collection of Britain, France, and Spain for the late eighteenth century. The choice of period allows the inclusion of the Spanish territories in the Americas. Economists and historians have long worked on the assumption that the predatory nature of Spanish governance was more pronounced in the Spanish Indies than in the peninsula. Including newly available estimates for the Spanish Americas helps discussion of this notion. The data reflect the well-studied fact that the British state by the late eighteenth century was the most formidable fiscal apparatus in Europe (Brewer 1989; Braddick 1996; O'Brien 2010). Its fiscal capacity outdid that of pre-revolutionary France and peninsular Spain by a factor of two to three. This was the culmination of a history that had begun with the introduction of the fiscal reforms under Cromwell, and was pushed strongly by the excise reforms of the 1720s and 1730s, which successively increased the fiscal gap between Britain and her continental neighbours (Ashworth 2003).

The figure also confirms the claim that Spanish and French revenue-raising capacities were similar in per capita terms. Spanish fiscal capacity would be somewhat superior if the crown's American subjects were included in the equation. Yet these figures are not aggregated here, because they were separate fiscal units, and aggregations would suggest a unity that did not exist. Disaggregation also biases the results against the hypothesis. In any case, in the Americas revenue per capita was higher than in the peninsula, though closer to the peninsular Spanish or French range than to British figures. In other words, as the authors have argued elsewhere, the notion of massive extraction of revenue in the trans-Atlantic territories is not borne out by Spanish fiscal data (Grafe and Irigoin 2006; Irigoin and Grafe 2008; Grafe and Irigoin 2012). Per capita revenue in New Spain (today's Mexico) in particular was notably higher. Yet this was also by far the richest of Spain's territories. In sum, this suggests that with regard to revenue collection – the *y*-axis of Figure 9.1 – Spain should indeed be located closer to France than to England by the eighteenth century. On this most defenders of the NIE thesis would surely agree.

Interest rates

The more important question, however, is this: does this similarity in per capita revenue reflect more general similarities, as implied by the supposed dichotomy between parliamentary and absolutist regimes in Early Modern Europe? Was eighteenth-century Spain indeed in a situation comparable to that of France, that is, at a point where investors distrusted it, and the credit markets demanded much higher interest rates on French sovereign debt than on British sovereign debt? Within the NIE paradigm the answer should lie in the interest rates. Series of sovereign interest rates for Spain, especially in the eighteenth century, have been difficult to construct. In part this is the result of Spain's rather perplexing fiscal behaviour in this period. Throughout the sixteenth and much of the seventeenth century Spain had famously contracted sovereign debt through both loans and annuities. Large loans (*asientos*) had been provided by the German banking houses in the sixteenth century, and in the seventeenth they were syndicated by Genoese investors (Ehrenberg 1896; Drelichman and Voth 2011a; Drelichman and Voth 2011b). Annuities were issued in the form of *juros* throughout the sixteenth century, and until the 1670s. However, between the late seventeenth and the late eighteenth century, the Spanish central hacienda neither issued new *juros*, nor did it take up large loans nationally or internationally.

This led to two features of Spanish public finances that set them apart from those of Spain's European neighbours throughout much of the eighteenth century. On one hand, at a time when most European states struggled to service their debt, the share of Spanish expenditure spent on debt service was minimal. During the eighteenth century, Britain and France spent between one-third and one-half of their total expenditure on debt service, and the Netherlands spent between forty and seventy per cent. In peninsular Spain, debt service consumed on the average seven per cent over the century, and even in the financially very challenging 1780s, when new debt was issued in the form of the *vales reales*, it did not exceed twelve per cent. Between 1782 and 1794, the debt of the Spanish central treasury increased fivefold. But even on the eve of the French war in 1793, Spanish per capita debt was barely five per cent of British per capita debt (Grafe 2012). In the American territories these numbers were even lower. Debt service rose from about two per cent of total expenditure on the average in 1729–33 to seven per cent on the average in 1796–1800 (Grafe and Irigoin 2012).[3] On the other hand, the interest rate the Spanish central treasury would have had to pay for new debt is not known, because there was no regular issuance. The best proxy available is therefore the return that investors received on the old *juros*, on which interest continued to be paid, and which were traded in secondary markets. Anecdotal evidence on loans taken up in Europe and the Americas in the late eighteenth century adds to the picture.

Figure 9.3 displays the official rate of interest on *juros* established by the crown, which fell from ten per cent in the sixteenth century to

---

[3] Andrien (1981) reports that, at least in Lima, debt was higher in the seventeenth century. However, it is likely that debt was concentrated in the large treasury districts and rather lower on average.

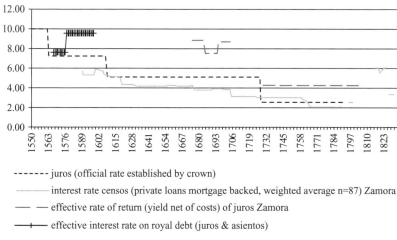

----- juros (official rate established by crown)

——— interest rate censos (private loans mortgage backed, weighted average n=87) Zamora

— — effective rate of return (yield net of costs) of juros Zamora

—+— effective interest rate on royal debt (juros & asientos)

Figure 9.3. Public and private interest rates in Spain (1550–1830)
Source: For a complete list of sources see Grafe, 2012.

2.5 per cent in the eighteenth. During much of the later sixteenth and especially the seventeenth century *juros* traded at substantial discounts on face value, and, thus, yields were considerably higher. The series of the effective rate on royal debt constructed by Drelichman and Voth and included in Figure 9.3 for the late sixteenth century reflects their estimate for the real cost of borrowing for the crown by combining annuities and large loans, which exceeded nine per cent. No comparable data are available for the first half of the seventeenth century.

For the later seventeenth and the eighteenth centuries, a small series has been constructed on the basis of the *juros* owned by the Cathedral Chapter of Zamora. It reflects the return the Chapter realised on their *juros*, and is perhaps the closest possible estimate of yields.[4] The difficult fiscal and therefore financial situation in the later seventeenth century is clearly visible. Returns were between 7.4 and 8.6 per cent. However, by

---

[4] *Juros* were redeemable and thus the crown was able to reduce the interest rate as long as investors were willing to hold the new annuities. Because in the case of *juros* the return (*réditos*) was generally held constant (an effective way of circumventing usury laws), technically a lowering of the interest rate was achieved through an increase (*crecimiento*) of the principal. In other words, rather than have the principal repaid, the investor agreed to top it up in order to guarantee the same future income stream. However, the real return on the *juro* was also altered because the crown began to levy taxes and surcharges on some of the older *juros* in the seventeenth century, effectively reducing returns. In short, the only way to get at the yields on *juros* is via the private account books of the annuity holders, which register the up-to-date principal and the real return they received after all deductions.

the mid- to later eighteenth century, these had dropped back to somewhere between 4.1 and 4.3 per cent on the average. When Spain returned to international markets in the very late 1700s, it paid 3.5 to 5 per cent in the Amsterdam market, comparable to what Britain paid at the time (Riley 1980; Marichal 2007). As late as 1805 Spain took up a loan in Paris at 5.5 per cent (Hamnett 1969). By then, of course, all of Europe was scrambling for funds to continue the first intercontinental war of the modern age.

In short, during the eighteenth century, the interest rate on Spanish sovereign debt was surprisingly close to British rates, and not at all facing the same problems that France confronted. During the eighteenth century Spain had retired some of the legacy debt issued under *juros*, and simply did not issue new debt. Yet it did not do so because it could not raise money in the face of high rates, but because it *chose* not to borrow. Thus, investors had to chase for old annuities in the secondary markets, and were willing to lend effectively at lower and lower rates. The crown did of course borrow short-term from suppliers and merchants and its own tax officials, yet here, too, modest rates were the rule.

Importantly, within the context of the North and Weingast argument, private interest rates in peninsular Spain were even lower than sovereign rates during this period. Private mortgage-backed loans, so-called *censos*, were agreed on between local debtors (in this case mostly farmers) and the Zamora Cathedral Chapter at just over five per cent in the early seventeenth century, and closer to two per cent in the later eighteenth (Figure 9.3). There are good reasons to doubt that private and public interest rates were ever as closely integrated as North and Weingast implied (Clark 1996). The only theoretical argument in favour would be that very high sovereign rates might have crowded out private investors, just as usury rates (which never mattered in Spain) might have caused crowding-out in Britain (Temin and Voth 2005). Yet a ruler who was increasing overall long-term borrowing only very modestly, such as the Spanish crown between the late seventeenth and the late eighteenth centuries, obviously did not crowd out private investors. Increases did occur, mostly because investors, for technical reasons, adjusted to the new lower rates by topping up the principal, rather than receiving a lower interest payment (see note four). Yet because they could choose repayment instead, this was also unlikely to crowd out private demand. Private interest rates rose again only in the first decade of the nineteenth century, but by then peninsular Spain was in the midst of a civil war caused by the Napoleonic invasion of 1808.

How different was the situation in Spanish America? Its fiscal system was run between the sixteenth and the eighteenth centuries through a network of almost 100 regional treasuries which enjoyed fairly great autonomy. Transfers between these treasuries were instrumental to the workings of the system. Elsewhere this has been described and analysed based on data for up to seventy-two treasuries (Grafe and Irigoin 2006; Irigoin and Grafe 2008). They financed the continued expansion of the Spanish state in the Americas, and with it the extension of the fiscal base territorially, and in terms of subject population. Yet there was no serious long-term debt in Spanish America. The crown initially offered *juros* in the Americas, but stopped doing so in 1639 at the behest of the Council of the Indies. Although the early sales were very successful, a renewed offer of *juros* in the late seventeenth century was not taken up by the public (Andrien 1981). Given what is known from the yields in peninsular Spain, this was of course a moment of great discounts on face value, and the reluctance of Spanish American investors is hardly surprising. This was, however, the last attempt to issue *juros* in the Americas. Theoretically, the crown's American subjects could still buy peninsular *juros*, but getting the coupon paid on a local tax in peninsular Spain was a costly enterprise for a Spanish American investor.

In the absence of a funded sovereign debt in the New World, public borrowing in the Spanish Americas revolved around the activities of the regional treasuries, which incidentally meant that the crown's American subjects could monitor both their investments and the local public borrowers much more easily. Throughout the sixteenth to eighteenth centuries local nonreligious and religious corporations gave loans and advances to their local treasuries. These could be part of civil or military purchasing, office holding or tax farming and revenue collection, or be part of the system of inter-treasury transfers. From at least the early seventeenth century there were also occasional large loans, which were usually syndicated through important local institutions such as the merchant guilds (*consulados*) or the mining guild (*tribunal de mineria*), which for a fee pooled resources, offering additional security to small investors and lower transaction costs to the local treasury (Grafe and Irigoin 2012).

Early American examples of syndicated loans reflect the generally very high interest rates in the early seventeenth century. Quiroz argues that the Lima *consulado* paid up to seventeen per cent in 1627 to the investors (Quiroz 1994). Yet it is hard to generalise from this information, and unlike the peninsular economy, Lima was in the midst of a boom at the time. In all likelihood, lucrative private business was crowding out public borrowing, not the other way around. Given the regional and local nature of public borrowing in the Americas, and the privatisation of large parts of the public finances, how much interest (explicit and implicit) the Spanish American treasuries paid for much of the period under consideration is simply unknown. In the late eighteenth century more large syndicated loans appeared. Where information exists, the interest rate was becoming more standardised. The syndicating institutions charged the local treasury around five to six per cent, while paying investors four to five, and keeping one per cent as their fee. For example, in 1793, the *consulado* of Buenos Aires syndicated a loan of over 100,000 pesos for six per cent. The crown guaranteed debt service by earmarking a number of local taxes for this purpose. The *consulado* raised the principal from local merchants, who participated with loans of different amounts, and with maturities between two and six years (Grieco 2005). Similar cases are documented for Mexico and Lima (Grafe and Irigoin 2012).

Even though there are substantial lacunae in the understanding of the financing of the Spanish state in Europe and the Americas, the available information suggests that for much of the period under consideration Spanish public finances were in better shape than once thought. Whereas thirty years ago historians simply referred to the repeated Spanish defaults of the sixteenth and seventeenth centuries, it is now quite clear that during the sixteenth century so-called defaults were essentially re-negotiations that turned loans into long-term bonds, and that reflected liquidity problems rather than insolvency (Rodríguez-Salgado 1988; Thompson 1994). More importantly, Drelichman and Voth (2011c) demonstrate that the defaults did not change lenders' expectations. In other words, they had been priced in all along. This explains why bankers and the public kept on investing in Spanish public debt. Rather than their being strong-armed by a predatory ruler, there were profits to be made.

The picture that emerges fits poorly with the model of a lack of 'credible commitment'. Spain was not expropriating the assets of its lenders, even in its hours of need. However, Spain's fiscal history in the eighteenth century presents an even bigger challenge to the idea of the predatory state. After the dire straits of the early to mid-seventeenth century, Spain did what Margaret Levi thought was impossible: it stopped trying to increase revenue (and borrowing), and it did so even though sovereign interest rates suggest that its subjects were keen to invest more in public debt. As Grafe (2012) has demonstrated, strong urban control over the Spanish fiscal system explained investors' faith to a large extent. Spanish rulers maximised rule. If that meant forgoing revenue, that was a price they were willing to pay (Irigoin and Grafe 2008).

Investing in coercion: Forced loans, currency manipulations, and monopolies

That Spain behaved differently from the underlying assumption of the necessarily predatory ruler becomes even clearer when we turn to a third 'test': the states' investment in coercion. This is a very complicated issue on a comparative basis, but a few short examples support the case that Spain spent relatively little on repression, and was thus able to raise an amount of per capita revenue that was quite similar to that in the French case (at least in the eighteenth century), but with a much lower investment in coercion. Indeed, it is that lack of coercion that explains the willingness of the crown's contractual partners to continue offering funds at low rates. Of course, the possibilities of rulers coercing their subjects into supporting them beyond the investors' will were manifold. Three often-cited examples follow: forced loans, depreciations, and the ubiquitous Early Modern monopolies.

The extent of confiscatory powers of the ruler is most obvious in outright expropriations of private property rights and repudiations of sovereign debts, which, as North and Weingast rightly pointed out, were not unusual in Early Modern Europe. The most common reference is to forced loans. Republican Florence relied on them in the fifteenth century, and so did the Netherlands into the seventeenth century (Martines 1988; Gelderblom and Jonker 2008; Pezzolo, this volume). In the Spanish context it is often claimed that the so-called *donativos* constituted forced loans, yet, notwithstanding their name, the level of coercion involved was at best modest. Grieco has shown beyond doubt that investors in *donativos* always expected a return (Grieco 2005; Grafe and Irigoin 2012). By the eighteenth century, for which more information is available, the *donativos* usually paid an interest rate that was attractive enough for investors to want to put their money into them. They were diligently serviced. Moreover, there is evidence that the king's subjects occasionally refused to pay into 'forced' loans when they were not convinced that they were a good investment, and the ruler did absolutely nothing about it (Grafe and Irigoin 2012). Not much predation there then.

That is not to say that Spanish rulers never performed expropriations. The possibly largest confiscations of wealth were the *temporalidades*. In 1767 Spain followed Portugal's example and expelled the Jesuits. The underlying and proximate causes for this expulsion were complex. The latter involved a large urban uprising in peninsular Spain in 1766, and conflicts with the Jesuits over their missions in territories that were contested between Portuguese Brazil and Spanish Río de la Plata. In other words, that the royal purse took over Jesuit property was the consequence, not the aim, of the expulsion. In the Americas, especially, the amounts involved were large. Real property was sold off, and debtors to the Jesuits had to either pay off their debt, or pay the local administrator of the *temporalidades* the same amount they had previously owed the Jesuits. Because the administration was local, well-to-do investors made large profits in the process by replacing the Order as financial intermediaries. Hence, this incidental confiscation created large windfalls for both the local treasuries and investors, but it fits poorly the bill of fiscally driven expropriation.

Indeed, towards the end of the eighteenth century it was a sign of the times that religious institutions found themselves under ideologically based pressure to give up some of their spectacular wealth. In the 1780s, for the first time in more than a century, the Spanish central treasury issued new public debt, the *vales reales*, Spain's first sovereign bond. They offered a four per cent coupon on twenty years' maturity, and their denominations were initially so large that they were obviously aimed at investors with deep pockets (Tedde de Lorca 1984). The treasury earmarked revenues to pay them off, and throughout the 1780s they performed well. After losing face value in the first two years, they traded at par or above between 1783 and 1794. Hamilton was famously puzzled by the trust that the public evidently had in the crown's commitment to service them (Hamilton 1944). After 1794, however, emissions increased exponentially, and discounts returned as Spain was dragged into war with revolutionary France, although the treasury created a sinking fund based on local taxes.

A depreciated bond turned into a confiscatory act of the crown only after 1798, when the crown began the *desamortización* (disentailment) of religious institutions, which received *vales* in return for the forced sale of real property. In 1803 the Spanish crown's financial situation took a dramatic turn for the worse. Desperate to avoid war with Napoleon's France, Spain agreed to pay an enormous monthly contribution directly into the French coffers. To restore the market for *vales*, Spain continued the confiscation process to the Americas and created a consolidation fund for the bonds. Here, too, the confiscation hit pious foundations which were forced by decree to contribute to the consolidation fund. Liens, loans, and mortgages that supported these pious works had to be redeemed, and the charities were forced to sell real property (Chowning 1989). Once again, however, the implementation of the decree was left to local *juntas* consisting of high local political and fiscal officials, the highest representatives of the Church in the region, and a delegate of the crown.

The commissions were charged with assessing the value of the loans, and, importantly, with negotiations with the debtor, who now owed the Consolidation Fund rather than the pious foundation. In the process, deals were cut, interest in arrears was cancelled, and principals were reduced. In Mexico, for example, the actual administration of the 'expropriation' consumed forty-four per cent of the total yield, which remained in the local economy (Hamnett 1969). In short, the crown's most blatant attempt at confiscation produced a negotiated outcome that shared the spoils by reducing the outstanding private debt which was to be converted into public borrowing. Thus, even under the existential threat from Napoleon, the confiscatory power of the Spanish ruler went only so far as local authority would collaborate. In the end, neither the histories of the *donativos*, the *temporalidades*, or the *vales reales* support the notion of confiscatory power being wielded by the Spanish crown.

Given European rulers' monopoly over currency emission, debasements were another well-established avenue for supposedly predatory rulers to change property rights unilaterally in their own favour. The Tudor kings of England had engaged in this practice in the 1500s; John Law's Scottish 'cure' for France's debt problem after the War of the Spanish Succession was the most notorious instance of the strategy. Traditionally economic history would follow Hamilton (1943) and add Spain's seventeenth-century experience to the list. However, this is a little disingenuous. Spain famously resorted to debasements of its small coin, the *vellon*, between the 1610s and 1686 (García de Paso 2000). However, with a very short-lived exception in 1642–3, Spain's large coin silver currency was not substantially debased over a period of almost three hundred years (Grafe 2012). The stabilisation of the copper coin in the 1680s was in part achieved through a minor debasement of peninsular silver coins (the *provinciales*), though American coins (the *nacionales*) remained untouched. *Provinciales* and *nacionales* were also subject to two very minor debasements in the eighteenth century, but these were directed at returning the *peso* to within a band that remedied problems with bullion flows. In other words, it was a technical monetary adjustment (Nogues-Marco 2010). In short, there were modest adjustments to the main metropolitan silver coinage, and the story becomes more complex when it includes territories beyond Castile.

By comparison with its European peers, the Spanish American peso was without a doubt the best store of value an investor could expect from any currency. No matter how uneasy North Americans grew over the credibility of the continental dollar as they saw the U.S. Congress print money, they never doubted the value of the coin to which the bearer of these first U.S. dollars was supposedly entitled in return, Spanish milled dollars, that is, Spanish American *pesos*. Economists comparing the trust investors had in different legal systems seem conveniently to forget that the Spanish American *peso* remained legal tender in the United States until 1856, and was the basis for the establishment of the U.S. dollar (Irigoin 2009). For most of the Early Modern period it was the only safe currency in Europe, Asia, and the Americas. 'Irresponsible' Spanish rulers could have expropriated holders of *pesos* residing in Madrid or

Lima, Philadelphia, or Canton. They chose not to, and merchants and investors everywhere evidently thought that the crown's commitment to the *peso* was credible.

Finally, a few words need to be said about rulers' ability to infringe on their subjects' property rights through the sale of monopolies, another of North and Weingast's key indicators for the predatory state. Again, somewhat careless economic historians are in part to blame for the confusing notion that monopolies were resorted to more intensely by Spain's Early Modern rulers than elsewhere in Europe. Two fields are often singled out: trade with the Americas and fiscal monopolies. In the case of the commercial monopolies this is ironic, because the Spanish Indies trade was in fact no monopoly, as opposed to the colonial trades of the republican-minded Netherlands and England. In contrast to the monopolies controlled by the English and Dutch East India companies, the *Carrera de Indias* and the Manila *Galleon* were structured according to an earlier form of mercantile organisation, one first built around wool exports to the southern Netherlands (Phillips and Phillips 1997), and more akin to a chartered company, essentially a licensing system. Those who wanted to participate had to be members of a guild (the *Casa de Contratación* or the *Ciudad y Comercio de Manila*). Barriers to entry thus existed, but the ability of the *Casa de Contratación* to exclude others from the trade was always limited by the incentives for members to serve as (paid) proxies for outsiders. Notwithstanding minor attempts in the eighteenth century to emulate proper English monopoly trading companies, economically speaking only a very reduced part of Spanish American trade was ever a monopoly.[5]

Fiscal monopolies were an altogether different story. The *estancos* formed an increasing share of Spanish revenue. If there was one area where one should expect the ruler's coercive and repressive hand to be clearly visible, tax monopolies would be the place. Amongst these in the eighteenth century, the tobacco monopoly was the crown jewel. Indeed, in the eighteenth century Spain derived about twice the share of its total revenue from the tobacco *estanco* that France collected from its own monopoly. As Kwass shows elsewhere in this volume, French enforcement of the tobacco monopoly was fierce.

Spain, too, tried its best to solve the problems that fragmented jurisdictions created in Castile, the Basque Provinces, the three Aragonese territories, and Navarre. The story of the actual introduction of the

---

[5] The exceptions were the *Guipuzcoana de Caracas* (created 1728) in the cocoa trade, the *Compañia de La Habana* (created 1740), which controlled part of the tobacco and sugar trade, and the *Compañia de Barcelona* (1755), which tried to monopolise Catalan trade. Their success was limited and they remained very controversial and contested. See Grafe (2012).

monopoly is complex and beyond the scope of this chapter. Suffice to say that it only ever became a real monopoly in Castile, but in order to achieve this the royal treasury had accept that (a) it would receive no revenue from the Basque Provinces, but had to subsidise the border enforcement of the Provinces; (b) it would have to become the subordinate tax farmer of the Navarrese parliament while again subsidising local administration; and (c) Aragonese consumers would overwhelmingly buy smuggled tobacco (Grafe 2012). Indeed, the prized tobacco monopoly might be one of the best examples of the choices Early Modern states had. France chose severe repression, and paid for it with a loss of legitimacy, high costs of coercion, and lower per capita net revenue (Kwass, this volume). Spanish rulers negotiated away constitutional and other conflicts, and though smuggling was illegal, prosecutions were in no way comparable to French levels. The outcome was an uneven application of the monopoly, but also lower costs of coercion and, most importantly, higher net revenue.

The discussion offered here is hardly exhaustive. However, the evidence strongly suggests that Spain was indeed combining an ability to collect per capita revenue that at least matched that of France with a regime of low coercive and predatory effort. This is consistent with the moderate interest rates presented above, a proven ability to borrow, and a treasury which on the whole paid its debts. It is also confirmed by a political regime that defended the Early Modern world's foremost currency and managed to organise its most important fiscal monopoly in such a way that it became a real revenue spinner at a relatively low coercive cost. To return to Figure 9.1, Spain was on the left of point A. This means that the generalised assumption that underpins the North and Weingast framework, and practically all of the relevant NIE literature – that all rulers are predators because they must maximise revenue – is simply incorrect. To put it another way, Spanish fiscal capacity might have been lower than that of Britain, but it was certainly equal to that of France. However, this was neither the consequence nor even the corollary of lower legal capacity resulting in higher levels of coercion. That represents an entry into political *terra incognita* in states such as Early Modern Spain, where predation was never the most important political economy issue. What then were the largest political economy challenges for growth in countries such as ancien régime Spain?

Coordination problems

Deep constitutional roots (again in the sense of the broader *Verfasstheit*) explain why, in states such as Spain, the ruler did not become a predator in the Early Modern period. These can be dealt with here only summarily, but are discussed in more detail in Grafe (2012) and Irigoin and Grafe (2008). In the Spains (tellingly, contemporaries used the plural), historic territories, and especially towns, retained most of the control over revenue and expenditure, meaning that local representation was powerful. The crown's role was that of a mediator of regional and local authorities, not that of a mandating central force. Spanish kings had never had divine rights over which the *cortes* could have tried to gain supremacy (as the English parliament did), or which could have been attacked by revolutionary citizens (as they did in France). The Spains lacked a repressive apparatus in the peninsula, and even more so in the Americas, where before the 1760s they did not even have a standing army to speak of, but relied almost entirely on local militias (Grafe and Irigoin 2012).

The state in the Hispanic world was never autonomous, nor, as North and Weingast would have called it, 'vertically integrated' (North and Weingast 1989). Power remained largely shared and negotiated between local, regional, and supra-regional administrative units, rather than hierarchically ordered. Decentralisation delivered governance that was perceived as legitimate: Spanish kings kept their heads on their shoulders, and Spanish American independence was triggered by the fact that the French removed (imprisoned) the Spanish king after their invasion of the European metropolis, and imposed French rule. It started as a movement in the name of the Spanish king, not as a rebellion against the crown. Frankly none of the major events, trends, and structures of Early Modern Spanish history fit the pervasive notion, which still appears in the pages of economics journals, of an unconstrained Spanish ruler hellbent on centralisation and revenue, and willing to ride roughshod over his subjects' and lenders' property rights.

This political regime thus generally did not threaten the economy with predation, and its costs were not primarily a distortion of incentives for investment. Instead, the lack of vertical integration manifested itself in poorly coordinated and integrated markets. Devolved state autonomy resulted in lower fiscal capacity in spite of high levels of legal capacity. Local control and representation was good for legitimacy and legal capacity, but hampered the widening and therefore deepening of markets. English historians such as Ashworth (2003) have recently begun to investigate how the application of a *national* excise not only flushed more revenue into Parliament's coffers, but also served to standardise productive processes in such areas as brewing. Weights and measures had to be unified for the excise man to do his duty, and the actual production technology involving alcohol degree and equipment became more standardised, too. Compare this to Spanish fiscality, which incidentally relied even more on indirect trade and consumption taxes than in England.[6] Each town and district created its own tax structure, even if, notionally, certain consumption taxes such as the *alcabala*, or trade taxes such as the *almojarifazgos*, should have been standardised. They were not, and their specific rates determined everything from the size of a wine barrel in town to the length of silk cloths. Not only did local representation fail to encourage the standardisation that could lower transaction costs, and thus support larger and deeper markets, but also it made any harmonisation of weights and measures, production processes, or product types virtually impossible (Grafe 2012).

What was true for goods markets also held for financial markets, even if the mechanism in this sector was slightly different. The example is interesting, because it addresses a puzzle that emerges directly from the discussion of Spanish public finances offered above. Spanish, and even more so Spanish American, economic historians have always struggled to explain the contradiction that is so obvious in the data presented. On one hand, interest rates in Spain and Spanish America seem to have been relatively low by international comparison, which would suggest that there was no shortage of capital, even though historians of colonial Spanish America have persistently claimed that 'money' was scarce. On the other hand, it is a well-known fact that financial institutions developed very late in the Spanish territories, and the entire banking sector, if it could be called that, was institutionally lagging behind all other western European countries. So what was the problem, if potential banking entrepreneurs had little predation to fear for from the ruler?

The common feature of credit markets in Spain and Spanish America was that they were largely localised. This is not surprising, given that they responded to the needs and demands of a private *and* a public sector that were in turn very local. Before the creation of the *vales* in the 1780s there was no 'national' or even imperial debt. Even if the *juros* were raised in the name of the ruler, they were secured against local tax income, which served to pay the interest. Their payment most likely involved a private notarial contract between the local tax farmer of a specific urban consumption tax and the equally local holder of the *juro*. That these annuities were backed by local revenue streams was precisely what made them so trustworthy in investors' eyes. In Spanish America most of the public debt was extended at a local or regional level to the

---

[6] Fiscal historians have long claimed that part of the English fiscal revolution was a strong reliance on indirect taxation rather than on direct taxes such as land taxes. Compared to France that is true. Compared to Spain (and the Netherlands), England was a latecomer to indirect taxation, and matched Spanish levels only in the eighteenth century.

regional treasury offices, as mentioned above. In short, demand was at most regional, and so was supply. This had benefits. Monitoring local borrowers, public and private, was easy, and enforcement costs were reduced. Information costs were low, and moral hazard issues limited in a market where everyone knew the reputation of other lenders and borrowers.

If there were no banks, who was lending? The sophisticated and well-developed culture of notarised contracts in the Hispanic worlds made it relatively easy to set up private debt obligations under the protection of the law, and to enforce them in court (Burns 2010). However, it appears that by far the largest sources of credit were religious institutions and charities, followed by merchant guilds (*consulados*), which began to syndicate large loans for the public purse, and a few other institutions such as indigenous trust funds and Madrid's *cinco gremios*, which had evolved from five traders' guilds, but moved into insurance and banking in due course (Capella Martínez and Matilla Tascon 1957). Monasteries, convents, religious confraternities, schools, cathedral chapters, and pious foundations all lent at interest, and in entirely commercial ways. With a strong interest in guaranteeing a regular income stream and the collateral and funds to offer a large loan volume, they were ideally placed to offer everything from small loans to peasants, to substantial amounts to merchants, officials, local treasuries, and noble estates. At the same time, they also took loans which offered individuals safe investment opportunities. The most commonly employed debt instrument was the *censo*, a collateralised loan, whereby there was little limitation as to what sort of asset could be used as collateral.

Hispanic financial markets are poorly studied, if only because it has simply not occurred to financial historians to examine the very extensive loan books of religious institutions. Further, most religious historians are uninterested in banking practices, although there are a few notable exceptions (Lavrín 1966; Greenow 1983; Chowning 1989; Quiroz 1993; von Wobeser 2010). This credit sector apparently provided efficient access to capital in rural and urban markets, at least from the sixteenth to the eighteenth century. As Figure 9.3 shows, in rural Extremadura (peninsular Spain), the average rate of interest fell to just over two per cent in the eighteenth century. In Spanish America, most of the evidence suggests a nominal interest rate of five per cent on *censos*, even in the eighteenth century. Too little is known, but given the well-known higher inflation rates in Spanish America, the real interest rate might have been closer to peninsular levels than it appears. In any case, it is clear that the volumes involved in these credit transactions were simply staggering.

Still, at present it is almost impossible to assess if credit rationing occurred. As much as monasteries and other religious institutions served as a functioning, reliable, and cheap local lender, they were multifunctional institutions. Their core business was religion, and their banking activities were a means to the end of financing their religious activities and maintaining their cadres. There was little room for learning and institutional innovation. Monks were not chosen for their financial aptitude, though arguably congregations that managed their businesses well were able to attract more donations and novices. Indeed, for a Peruvian merchant of the seventeenth century, the best way to guarantee that he would have regular access to credit was to send his daughter, accompanied by a nice dowry, to one of the richer convents in his town (Burns 1999; Gibbs 1989). Yet competition between religious institutions was always muted, and there were few economies of scale. Convents that grew very large tended simply to open sister convents nearby, limiting both spatial and vertical integration.

The local embeddedness of this credit sector allowed it to be close to the customer, and lowered monitoring costs. That the lender stood between the borrower and God probably further lowered the risk of shirking. Religious institutions had sufficient funds to ride out debt defaults caused by a bad harvest or a smaller commercial downturn, and to allow their customers to get over a bad moment. Yet, like all small local banks, they were susceptible to larger shocks to the local economy. Their lack of spatial integration could become a serious liability, and would potentially depress lending pro-cyclically if the local economy was hit by a serious crisis. Also, as multipurpose institutions, their ability to lend was subject to factors that did not respond in any way to the credit market. An expensive new chapel could well mean no agrarian credit in a rural monastery's district for a couple of years.

Worse, when religion, their core activity, came under attack in the later eighteenth century, the credit sector became collateral damage. The expulsion of the Jesuits seriously limited credit in the 1760s, but it is likely that other institutions took over their activities. However, disentailment in Spain and the consolidation of the *vales* in Spanish America effectively shut down large parts of the credit market. The ideological changes of the time, which demanded that the state take property away from the *mortmain*, ironically created severe interruptions in lending, mainly because the 'dead hand' had been very much alive and active in banking. Religious institutions had to call in existing loans and stop lending. Estimates for the investment of capital from ecclesiastical sources range from forty-four to fifty-nine million *pesos* in Mexico alone (Hamnett 1969). Even though, in the end, much of this was renegotiated, and the consolidation was called off before it affected smaller borrowers, the dislocation of credit markets was severe, and new lending much reduced.

The peculiar locally based credit market in the Hispanic world evidently served the economy reasonably well for much of the sixteenth to eighteenth century. Financial historians trained to search for something called a bank simply missed the fact that in the Hispanic world religious institutions accounted for much of the banking business. Nor was that unusual: Islamic *waqf* probably fulfilled a similar function. However, the latter were far more limited in terms of the design of financial contracts (Kuran 2010) than Spanish religious institutions, which faced no formal restrictions at all. In short, in the Hispanic world, capital was clearly available, and interest rates moderate, and so far there is little evidence that credit rationing was a major issue.

That is not to say that everywhere and at all times, would-be investors had easy access to loans. The local nature of the market meant that abundance in one town might well combine with scarcity in another. However, the insufficient institutional development of a specialised banking sector had little to do with a predatory state, and a lot to do with the persistently small scope and scale of credit markets, in which a rich convent might be better at offering credit than a specialised individual merchant banker.

As Grafe (2012) argues, capital was never a serious bottleneck in the Hispanic world. Instead, lower interest rates could be attributed to the fact that there was more capital available than was necessary to meet the needs of domestic production. Efficiency gains in financial markets were thus relatively unimportant in comparison, because capitalists found themselves chasing investment opportunities in search of returns. To put it another way, where nonspecialist bankers such as merchant guilds or monasteries mediated between lenders and borrowers for a commission of one per cent, the scope for the development of specialist banking was limited. There is no evidence that the few banking institutions that did develop, such as the *Cinco Gremios de Madrid*, were held back in any way by legal restrictions or a state that was interfering with business. They remained marginal to a market in which religious institutions were successful incumbents.

The reality was that there was little demand for more sophisticated banking services. Ironically, the development of specialised banking activities was seriously delayed by the combination of strong contractual law available absolutely everywhere in the Hispanic world through the apprenticed notary, and the fact that religious institutions' search for stable income streams created simple but well-functioning local credit markets. Strong legal capacity thus inhibited rather than fostered financial market development as long as an oversupply of capital kept interest rates low anyway. Maybe the creation of a unified 'national' debt instrument such as the *vales*, strongly backed by the state, might have created a demand for more specialised banks. But monasteries might still have been too good at what they were doing, and they had invested in *vales* even before they were forced to. Though specialist research is missing, it seems likely that what broke the financial back of the Hispanic economies was its would-be enlightened reformers, who failed to foresee the secondary effects of their attacks on religious institutions. When the ideological shift of the late eighteenth and early nineteenth centuries undermined their main trade, religion, the Christian moneylenders and their customers were in trouble.

Conclusion

The elegance and simplicity of North's and Weingast's model of 'credible commitment' has turned it into one of the theoretical pillars underpinning modern political economy, even though economic historians have steadily chipped away at their narrative of England's political, fiscal, financial, and growth trajectories. Rather than focusing on that story itself, this chapter has challenged the claim to universality which underpins it. It has offered a number of theoretical considerations to explain why the common assumption that rulers need to maximise revenue, and therefore will predate unless a constitution stops them from doing so, does not hold true. During the Early Modern period some states might have had the degree of vertical integration (hierarchy and centralisation) that afforded a ruler confiscatory powers. However, some states, maybe many, followed a different constitutional path.

The empirical discussion confirms that, in the terms of Figure 9.1, Spain was throughout the Early Modern period on the left half of the graph, where states combined reasonable revenue collection capacity with low degrees of investment in coercion. The Netherlands in the sixteenth century was in a similar position. However, as Dutch historians have pointed out, under the pressure of the Eighty Years War, power in the Netherlands became more hierarchically ordered, the fiscal system moved from being town-based to being mostly administered at the provincial level, and even some national taxes made an appearance (a move to NL') (Fritschy 2009). In other words, the Netherlands solved at least some of the fundamental coordination problems that rulers faced on the left-hand side of the graph.

Spain, in contrast, on the whole, did not solve these problems. The crude sketch of financial market development above starts to chart some of the consequences of this failure. Local control over fiscality and markets was good for representation and the legitimacy of governance. It was compatible with, and relied upon, very high levels of legal capacity, but by its very nature it limited fiscal capacity. It is not clear, however, that these fiscal limits were the most important problem. The main unintended consequence of this system was that it hamstrung the widening and deepening of financial and goods markets and affected growth negatively. In trying to explain economic development in the Hispanic world (and probably in quite a number of other Early Modern states and empires), the predatory ruler is a red herring. The problems were of an altogether different nature.

References

Andrien, K. 1981. 'The Sale of Juros and the Politics of Reform in the Viceroyalty of Peru, 1608–1695', *Journal of Latin American Studies*, 13, 1–19.

Ashworth, W. J. 2003. *Customs and Excise: Trade, Production, and Consumption in England, 1640–1845*. Oxford: Oxford University Press.

Besley, T. and Persson, T. 2009. 'The Origins of State Capacity: Property Rights, Taxation, and Politics', *American Economic Review*, 99, 1218–44.

Besley, T. and Persson, T. 2010. 'State Capacity, Conflict, and Development', *Econometrica*, 78, 1–34.

Braddick, M. J. 1996. *The Nerves of the State: Taxation and the Financing of the English State, 1558–1714*. Manchester: Manchester University Press.

Brennan, G. and Buchanan, J. M. 1980. *The Power to Tax: Analytical Foundations of a Fiscal Constitution*. Cambridge: Cambridge University Press.

Brennan, G. and Buchanan, J. M. 1985. *The Reason of Rules: Constitutional Political Economy*. Cambridge: Cambridge University Press.

Brewer, J. 1989. *The Sinews of Power: War, Money and the English State, 1688–1783*. London: Unwin Hyman.

Burns, K. 1999. *Colonial Habits: Convents and the Spiritual Economy of Cuzco, Peru*. Durham, NC: Duke University Press.

Burns, K. 2010. *Into the Archive: Writing and Power in Colonial Peru*. Durham, NC: Duke University Press.

Capella Martínez, M. and Matilla Tascon, A. 1957. *Los Cinco Gremios Mayores de Madrid. Estudio crítico-histórico*. Madrid: Cámara Oficial de Comercio e Industria.

Chowning, M. 1989. 'The Consolidación de Vales Reales in the Bishopric of Michoacan', *Hispanic American Historical Review*, 69, 451–78.

Clark, G. 1996. 'The Political Foundations of Modern Economic Growth: England, 1540–1800', *Journal of Interdisciplinary History*, 26, 563–88.

Drelichman, M. and Voth, H. J. 2011a. Funding Empire: Risk, Diversification and the Underwriting of Early Modern Sovereign Loans. Working Paper.

Drelichman, M. and Voth, H. J. 2011b. Risk Sharing with the Monarch: Contingent Debt and Excusable Defaults in the Age of Philip II, 1556–1598. Working Paper.

Drelichman, M. and Voth, H. J. 2011c. 'Serial Defaults, Serial Profits: Returns to Sovereign Lending in Habsburg Spain, 1566–1600', *Explorations in Economic History*, 48, 1–19.

Ehrenberg, R. 1896. *Das Zeitalter der Fugger: Geldkapital und Creditverkehr im 16. Jahrhundert*. Jena: G. Fischer.

Epstein, S. R. 2000. *Freedom and Growth: The Rise of States and Markets in Europe, 1300–1750*. London: Routledge.

Fritschy, W. 2009. 'The Efficiency of Taxation in Holland', in O. Gelderblom (ed.), *The Political Economy of the Dutch Republic*. Farnham: Ashgate.

García de Paso, J. I. 2000. 'La estabilización monetaria en Castilla bajo Carlos II', *Revista de Historia Económica*, 18, 49–77.

Gelderblom, O. and Jonker, J. 2008. Collective Spirit or Aggregate Wealth? Understanding the Structure and Growth of Holland's Public Debt, 1514–1713. Presented at the Rutgers Workshop in Money, History and Finance.

Gibbs, D. L. 1989. 'The Economic Activities of Nuns, Friars, and Their Conventos in Mid-colonial Cuzco', *The Americas*, 45, 343–62.

Grafe, R. 2012. *Distant Tyranny. Markets, Power and Backwardness in Spain 1650–1800*. Princeton: Princeton University Press.

Grafe, R. and Irigoin, A. 2006. 'The Spanish Empire and Its Legacy: Fiscal Re-distribution and Political Conflict in Colonial and Post-colonial Spanish America', *Journal of Global History*, 1, 241–67.

Grafe, R. and Irigoin, A. 2012. 'A Stakeholder Empire: The Political Economy of Spanish Imperial Rule in America', *Economic History Review*, 65, 609–52.

Greenow, L. L. 1983. *Credit and Socioeconomic Change in Colonial Mexico: Loans and Mortgages in Guadalajara, 1720–1820*, Boulder, CO: Westview Press.

Grieco, V. 2005. *Politics and Public Credit: The Limits of Absolutism in Late Colonial Buenos Aires*. Ph.D. Dissertation, Emory.

Hamilton, E. J. 1943. 'Monetary Disorder and Economic Decadence in Spain, 1651–1700', *Journal of Political Economy*, 51, 477–93.

Hamilton, E. J. 1944. 'War and Inflation in Spain', *Quarterly Journal of Economics*, 59, 36–77.

Hamnett, B. R. 1969. 'The Appropriation of Mexican Church Wealth by the Spanish Bourbon Government. The "consolidación de vales reales" 1805–1809', *Journal of Latin American Studies*, 1, 85–113.

Irigoin, A. 2009. 'The End of a Silver Era: The Consequences of the Breakdown of the Spanish Peso Standard in China and the United States, 1780s–1850s', *Journal of World History*, 20, 207–43.

Irigoin, A. and Grafe, R. 2008. 'Bargaining for Absolutism: A Spanish Path to Empire and Nation Building', *Hispanic American Historical Review*, 88, 173–210.

Kuran, T. 2010. *The Long Divergence: How Islamic Law Held Back the Middle East*. Princeton: Princeton University Press.

La Manna, M. and Stomp, G. 1994. 'Leviathan: Revenue Maximiser or Glory Seeker?' *Constitutional Political Economy*, 5, 159–72.

Lane, F. C. 1958. 'Economic Consequences of Organized Violence', *Journal of Economic History*, 18, 401–417.

La Porta, R.; Lopez-de-Silanes, F.; and Shleifer, A. 2008. 'The Economic Consequences of Legal Origin', *Journal of Economic Literature*, 46, 285–332.

La Porta, R.; Lopez-de-Silanes, F.; Shleifer, A.; and Vishny, R. W. 1998. 'Law and Finance', *Journal of Political Economy*, 106, 1113–55.

Lavrín, A. 1966. 'The Role of Nunneries in the Economy of New Spain in the Eighteenth Century', *Hispanic American Historical Review*, 46, 371–93.

Levi, M. 1988. *Of Rule and Revenue*. Berkeley: University of California Press.

Marichal, C. 2007. *Bankruptcy of Empire. Mexican Silver and the Wars between Spain, Britain and France, 1760–1810*. Cambridge: Cambridge University Press.

Martines, L. 1988. 'Political and Social Strains in "Quatrrocento" Florence', *Journal of Modern History*, 60, 300–311.

Nogues-Marco, P. 2010. *Bullionism, Specie-Point Mechanism and Bullion Flows in the Early 18th Century Europe*. Unpublished Ph.D. Dissertation, Sciences Po.

North, D. C. and Weingast, B. R. 1989. 'Constitutions and Commitment: The Evolution of Institutions Governing Public Choice in Seventeenth-Century England', *Journal of Economic History*, 49, 803–32.

O'Brien, P. 2010. 'The Nature and Historical Evolution of an Exceptional Fiscal State and Its Possible Significance for the Precocious Commercialization and Industrialization of the British Economy from Cromwell to Nelson', *Economic History Review*, 64, 408–46.

Olson, M. 2000. *Power and Prosperity: Outgrowing Communist and Capitalist Dictatorships*. New York: Basic Books.

Phillips, C. R. and Phillips, W. D., Jr. 1997. *Spain's Golden Fleece. Wool Production and the Wool Trade from the Middle Ages to the Nineteenth Century*. Baltimore: Johns Hopkins University Press.

Quriroz, A. W. 1993. *Deudas olvidadas: Instrumentos de crédito en la economía colonial peruana 1750–1820*. Lima: Pontificia Universidad Católica del Perú Fondo Editorial.

Quiroz, A. W. 1994. 'Reassessing the Role of Credit in Late Colonial Peru: Censos, Escrituras, and Imposiciones', *Hispanic American Historical Review*, 74, 193–230.

Riley, J. C. 1980. *International Government Finance and the Amsterdam Capital Market, 1740–1815*. Cambridge: Cambridge University Press.

Rodríguez-Salgado, M. J. 1988. *The Changing Face of Empire*. Cambridge: Cambridge University Press.

Sussman, N. and Yafeh, Y. 2006. 'Institutional Reform, Financial Development and Sovereign Debt: Britain 1690–1790', *Journal of Economic History*, 66, 906–35.

Tedde de Lorca, P. 1984. 'El Banco de San Carlos y la real hacienda (1794–1828)', in M. Artola and L. M. Bilbao (eds.), *Estudios de Hacienda: De Ensenada a Mon*. Madrid: Instituto de Estudios Fiscales.

Temin, P. and Voth, H.-J. 2005. 'Credit Rationing and Crowding Out during the Industrial Revolution: Evidence from Hoare's Bank, 1702–1862', *Explorations in Economic History*, 42, 325–48.

Thompson, I. A. A. 1994. 'Castile: Polity, Fiscality, and Fiscal Crisis', in P. T. Hoffman and K. Norberg (eds.), *Fiscal Crises, Liberty, and Representative Government, 1450–1789*. Stanford, CA: Stanford University Press.

Tilly, C. 1975. *The Formation of National States in Western Europe*. Princeton: Princeton University Press.

Tilly, C. 1990. *Coercion, Capital and European States, AD 990–1990*. Cambridge: Blackwell.

von Wobeser, G. 2010. *El crédito eclesiástico en la Nueva España. Siglo XVIII*. Mexico: Fondo de cultura económica.

10 Court capitalism, illicit markets, and political legitimacy in eighteenth-century France: The salt and tobacco monopolies

Michael Kwass

The financial revolution that catapulted Britain to great-power status in the eighteenth century never took root in old-regime France (Dickson 1967; North and Weingast 1989). France lacked the two institutions responsible for the spectacular rise in British public credit: a national parliament and a central bank. The only representative assembly in France that could conceivably have seized control over taxation and credibly serviced the public debt, the Estates General, lay dormant between 1614 and 1789, a casualty of Bourbon absolutism. The one great experiment with a French national bank, John Law's tentacular Banque Générale, went bust in 1720, casting a pall over French finances for decades to come.

Acutely aware of the limits of political representation and banking under the old regime, historians of Early Modern France have eschewed terms such as 'financial revolution' and 'financial capitalism', to speak instead of 'court capitalism'. Coined by George V. Taylor in 1964 to describe how credit markets evolved under conditions of absolutism, court capitalism initially referred to the private exploitation of 'government farms, state loans, joint-stock flotations and speculation' by high-ranking nobles and their clients. 'Without the royal court and the opportunities to which it held the key', Taylor asserted, 'Parisian finance and speculation on the scale on which it was practiced would have been inconceivable, and for that reason we may call it court capitalism' (Taylor 1964, 479). More recently, Bossenga has expanded the definition of court capitalism to highlight 'the capitalism in public functions' that lay at the heart of the Early Modern French state. She contends that institutions such as venal offices, tax farms, and government-chartered trading companies 'developed out of the chronically weak credit of the French monarchy' (Bossenga 2005, 3–464).

Just how effectively court capitalism functioned as a substitute for genuine financial revolution is a matter of some debate. Because a debt crisis brought down the old regime, most historians have described French finances in terms of severe institutional constraints (Marion 1919;

Bossenga 2011). Fiscal privileges limited tax revenues; revenue shortfalls led to debt repudiations; debt repudiations generated high default premiums on borrowing; high default premiums crippled the state. In the face of such strong financial headwinds, it is hardly surprising that the French monarchy could not keep pace with its powerful rival to the north, Great Britain. Yet, somehow, the French fiscal state endured – even thrived in certain respects. Cutting against the historiographical grain, some scholars have stressed how, in the absence of a national bank and an English-style parliament, the crown nonetheless found innovative ways to raise money. The monarchy learned to borrow through the intermediary of corporate bodies, which was cheaper than issuing annuities directly to the public (Bien 1987; Hoffman, Postel-Vinay, and Rosenthal, 2000; Legay 2000; Potter 2000; Swann 2003). Despite the proliferation of venal offices, it imposed partial reforms that improved the efficiency of direct and indirect taxation (Azimi 1987; Touzery 1994; Félix 1999; Kwass 2000; White 2004; Félix 2006). Although the eighteenth-century French state was clearly losing ground to Britain, especially when it came to the costs of servicing the public debt, it was hardly the sclerotic, decaying nation of historical caricature. As Félix has recently stressed, France remained the premier fiscal power in Europe, enjoying revenues that were more than a third higher than those of Great Britain (Legay, Félix, and White 2009, 189).[1]

Evaluating the efficacy of court capitalism is a worthy project, but this chapter strikes out in a new direction, and considers the impact of court capitalism on eighteenth-century public opinion. How did the flowering of court capitalism shape political ideas and attitudes in the decades before the French Revolution? How did commoners and elites react to the growth of public credit and taxation? It is the contention of this chapter that although court capitalism may have benefitted kings, financiers, and well-connected nobles, it alienated broad sections of French society, creating an environment hostile to its perpetuation. As much as any inherent structural weakness in the fiscal system itself, it was this wider hostility to French court capitalism that undermined the legitimacy of fiscal institutions, and helped to create the conditions for the French Revolution.

---

[1] Of course, relative to GDP, British taxation was much higher, reaching twenty per cent of national income, compared to ten to thirteen per cent in France (Bonney 2004, 202–3). Félix (1999, 34–6) revises upward the estimates for France given in Mathias and O'Brien (1976), but even after his correction is accounted for, Britain's eighteenth-century tax load was far heavier in per capita terms and as a proportion of GDP.

Fiscalising consumption

To illustrate the process by which royal financial institutions were discredited, this chapter concentrates on an aspect of European state formation that has yet to receive much attention: namely, the fiscalisation of consumption. In both eighteenth-century Britain and France, taxes that ultimately struck consumers became essential for servicing extraordinarily large public debts. Britain epitomised this trend. Over the eighteenth century, British customs duties (principally on imported tea, sugar, wine, foreign spirits, and tobacco) and excise taxes (principally on beer, malt, domestic spirits, and salt) pushed revenue receipts to new heights. By the reign of George III, indirect taxation had grown to eighty per cent of total tax revenues, providing the funding for Britain's debt, and launching the nation onto the global stage (O'Brien 1988; Brewer 1989; Ashworth 2003). This rise in indirect taxation was not merely a reflection of British commercial growth, as vigorous as that growth was. It was the result of a deliberate policy to generate higher revenues by creating new kinds of indirect taxes, and raising rates on those which already existed. Although it is true that such taxes fell on merchants and producers in the first instance, they were overwhelmingly passed on to ordinary consumers in the form of higher prices. Indeed, customs and especially excise taxes levied on price-inelastic commodities struck the labouring classes with such force that is not too much of exaggeration to say that the debt of the British Empire was carried on the backs of metropolitan middling and poor consumers, especially beer drinkers! The consumer society that historians have recently described as emerging in eighteenth-century England was increasingly exploited by the state as a valuable source of revenue.

In France, as well, consumption was increasingly fiscalised. The country's shift toward indirect taxes was not as dramatic as Britain's, but given France's comparatively large agricultural sector, the move toward trade and consumption taxes was impressive nonetheless.[2] Although Louis XIV created new direct taxes during the second half of his reign, the proportion of revenue derived from indirect taxes jumped from roughly a quarter of the budget in the first half of the seventeenth century to about half in the eighteenth (Durand 1971, 57; Bonney 1979; Riley 1986; Crouzet 1993, 62–5, 87–9; Hoffman 1994; White 1995; Félix 1999, chap. 2). By 1788, indirect-tax revenue amounted to no less than 270.5 million

---

[2] England's extreme reliance on indirect taxation seems to be a special case. Even in the Netherlands, a commercial nation where indirect taxes were high, the proportion of indirect taxes to direct taxes in the eighteenth century resembled that of France more than that of Britain (Fritschy 1990).

livres tournois (*lt*), or fifty-seven per cent of the budget, most of it coming from levies on salt, alcoholic beverages, tobacco, customs duties – which fell chiefly on poor and middling consumers – and a domain tax on private contracts (Morineau 1980). Direct taxes for the same year totalled 163 million *lt*, or 34.5% of the budget. It is clear that France increasingly found in consumption taxes a resource with which to wage war and fund war-related debt (Mathon de la Cour 1788, 93; Hocquet 1987). Thus, not only did France, like Britain, experience a surge of consumption in the eighteenth century (Pardailhé-Galabrun 1991; Fairchilds 1993; Roche 2000; Kwass 2006), but the French monarchy, like the English parliament, was learning to harness the power of that consumption. Although historians tend to emphasise the divergent trajectories traced by absolutist France and constitutionalist Britain, the paths of these two fiscal states actually converged in this one crucial respect.

Yet in France, where levels of taxation were, on the whole, lower than they were in Britain, the process by which consumption was fiscalised seems to have had a particularly corrosive effect on the body politic. To be sure, British consumers chafed at the rise in indirect taxes, especially during the excise crisis of 1733 and the wars with revolutionary and Napoleonic France (Ashworth 2003, 64–81, 357, 382). But resentment in Britain never boiled over to act as a catalyst to revolution. This apparent paradox raises the question: if the trend in both France and Britain was toward fiscalising nascent consumption, why did hostility to the state take on revolutionary proportions in France alone? Brewer provides one answer: the existence of Parliament lent an air of legitimacy and fairness to Britain's tax system (Brewer 1989, chap. 8). Another argument is that French sensitivity to the rise of consumption taxes stemmed not only from the absence of strong representative institutions, but also from the particular form such taxes took.

In the first place, French consumption taxes were not levied directly by the state. They were farmed. Whereas in England tax farming had been abandoned under Charles II, in France this system of revenue collection only grew stronger in the late seventeenth and the eighteenth centuries as a private consortium of financiers, the Farmers General, advanced ever-larger lump-sum payments in exchange for the right to collect indirect taxes. To modern eyes tax farming appears archaic, an inefficient and dangerous alienation of public power, but to cash-strapped French kings it offered substantial advantages. Not only did tax farming guarantee steady streams of revenue without the financial risks and bureaucratic hassles of direct administration, but also, more importantly, it provided the monarchy with an extraordinarily useful credit mechanism, as wealthy tax farmers advanced huge loans to the king on top of their cash payments. The lines of credit that monarchs tapped through tax farming were profoundly deep. In the mid-eighteenth century the Farmers General bankrolled Louis XV to the tune of sixty-eight million *lt* in long-term and sixty million *lt* in short-term debt (Mathews 1958; Bosher 1970, chap. 5; Johnson 2006).

In terms of public opinion, however, tax farming had serious liabilities, since it created the impression that indirect tax revenues were being diverted from their legitimate destination, the royal treasury, into the pockets of greedy financiers. With the royal finances cloaked in secrecy, writers speculated wildly about how much the Farmers General were skimming off the top. One 1755 tirade claimed that the Farmers annually siphoned off a third of the revenue they collected. This constant diversion of funds was so detrimental to the economy, the author lamented, that 'at the end of the day the *Traitants* [a pejorative term for financiers] will have all the money in the kingdom, and the king and the people will have none' (Goudar 1755). The widespread perception that financial 'blood-suckers' were preying on a defenceless population generated an enormous amount of resentment against the Farm.

Tax farming was only part of the problem, however. Equally if not more disturbing to French subjects was the fact that certain consumption taxes were not really taxes at all. In Britain indirect levies took the form of customs and excise taxes, which were collected at the border and at points of production, respectively, and then passed on more or less invisibly to consumers. In France, in contrast, two key indirect taxes, those on salt and tobacco, assumed the form of state monopolies, the revenues from which were collected from the consumer at the point of purchase. It would be difficult to conceive of a more conspicuous method of raising revenue. Rather than simply taxing salt and tobacco, the French monarchy monopolised their sale, and marketed them to consumers at prices far higher than those which an open market would have commanded. To be sure, monopolies were able to squeeze more revenue from consumer goods than customs or excise taxes. Continental tobacco monopolies established duties in excess of 1,000 per cent, whereas the British imposed a customs duty of one hundred per cent, much of which was rebated to merchants who re-exported their tobacco to the Continent (Price 1973, II: 840–41; Price 1998, 86, 97). As shall be shown, however, monopolies extracted such additional revenue at an exceedingly high political price.

The older of the two monopolies, that on salt, was particularly coercive. Salt was a good of absolute necessity in Early Modern France, and widely understood as such. The precious mineral sustained the human body, nourished farm animals, and preserved fish and meat. Yet since the fourteenth century French kings had ceaselessly exploited this necessity for fiscal purposes, monopolising the trade and establishing state retailers in certain areas. In the regions of the *grande gabelle* in northern France, where more than half the French population resided, the monarchy not only monopolised the sale of salt, setting its prices far above market value, but forced subjects to buy a fixed allotment of state salt (half a *minot*, roughly fifty pounds) every year. Northerners subject to the full weight of the *gabelle* were required by law to pay fifty-eight *lt* for a *minot* of salt, whereas their neighbours to the west, in Brittany, spent no more than three *lt* for the same quantity (Necker 1781, *carte des gabelles*). Little wonder the *gabelle* was the most loathed tax in French history. To price-sensitive Early Moderns, the salt tax seemed outrageously unfair.

A more recent institution, the tobacco monopoly, was structured quite differently. First, as its founding declaration of 27 September 1674 explained, the monopoly was to be based on voluntary consumption. Far from exploiting a good that was 'necessary for . . . the maintenance of life', it was now in the business of selling a non-essential commodity, a luxury, which consumers were free to buy in any amount they wished (AN AD XI 48 no. 15, declaration of 27 Sept., 1674). Because consumers would purchase tobacco of their own volition, as they did all luxury goods, they could hardly consider the monopoly oppressive. As Jean-Louis Moreau de Beaumont, a member of Louis XV's finance council, stressed, the tobacco levy 'is a purely voluntary tax for the people: if [tobacco] has in some way become a need, they are themselves the authors of this new necessity. Can the King find a less onerous resource to provide for the expenses of his State? . . . Should he not desire to see this part of his Domain make all the progress of which it may be susceptible?' (Moreau de Beaumont 1768, IV: 680). Present at the birth of the monopoly, this argument underpinned all major apologies for the taxation of tobacco (and other 'luxuries') down to the French Revolution (AN G-1 106, doss. 1; Forbonnais 1758, III: 225, 230; Gondolff 1914, 390).

Second, the tobacco monopoly went well beyond the regional confines of the salt franchise, drawing the French monarchy into a sprawling Atlantic economy that connected peoples from four continents and several empires. At first, adhering to the basic mercantilist principle that mother countries should, if possible, import raw goods from their own colonies rather than from those of rival nations, the crown procured tobacco from its Caribbean colony of Saint Domingue (modern Haiti), and then from Louisiana. But the Farm soon spurned the French colonies and turned to British merchants who could deliver cheaper, better-quality leaf from Chesapeake Bay (Price 1973). In opting to purchase

Chesapeake leaf from the British, the French crown deliberately put fiscal interest before mercantilist principle.[3] To the chagrin of French colonial planters, the Farmers General purchased millions of pounds of slave-produced Virginian tobacco, processed it in large French manufactories, and shipped the final product to forty-odd regional distribution centres throughout the kingdom. The centres supplied local warehouses, which in turn furnished some ten thousand tobacconists in cities, towns, and villages across France. It was through these local retail shops that the Farm marketed the weed to millions of French subjects. Consumers bought sticks of tobacco called carrots, which they took home, grated into powder, and snorted at their leisure.

Financially, the two monopolies were astoundingly successful. By the end of the old regime the salt monopoly yielded a whopping 58.5 million *lt* each year, with the tobacco monopoly adding another 30.5 million (Mathews 1958, 88, 118). Together the two levies comprised roughly a third of all indirect tax revenues, which themselves constituted more than half the budget. The windfall profits of the monopolies, along with the enormous loans advanced by the Farmers General, provided the monarchy with indispensable treasure. But the crown's exploitation of the monopolies, and its dependence on the credit provided by the financiers who managed them, came at a heavy political price. To the great majority of the French – ordinary subjects who did not have the wherewithal to purchase venal offices, invest in royal bonds, or buy shares in chartered companies – court capitalism came in the brute form of monopoly. It was against such monopoly that they directed their protests.

Opposition to fiscal monopolies

More than any other levies, the salt and tobacco monopolies provoked fierce resistance and controversy. More than the excise taxes on alcoholic beverages, and more than the *taille*, the main direct tax on the peasantry, the monopolies generated resentment and debate that directly challenged the French fiscal state. Opposition took three basic forms: passive resistance through illicit trade, active resistance through rebellion, and intellectual resistance through the publication of critical books and pamphlets. Taken together, these three forms of opposition did much to politicise French fiscality and to undermine the institutional foundations of the monarchy in the decades before the French Revolution.

---

[3] Not that the French crown always did so. The sugar trade in France was established as a colonial re-export system that closely paralleled what the British were doing with tobacco (Butel 1974).

At the most basic level, the monopolies had the unintended consequence of spawning a massive underground economy. Although customs and excise taxes generated black markets in France, as they did
in Britain, such markets paled in comparison to the vast web of illicit
trade stimulated by state monopolies. The yawning chasm between the
price of official goods and that of their clandestine substitutes presented
irresistible opportunities for illicit profit. Royal subjects of every stripe
entered the parallel economy in droves. Nobles, clerics, and magistrates
wheeled and dealed behind the scenes, while legions of indigent peasants shuttled contraband across customs borders, relayed it through the
countryside, and funnelled it into cities, where domestic servants stored
contraband in their masters' residences, and distributed it to dense networks of urban retailers, the capillaries of the distribution system. Paris
was positively crawling with petty tobacco dealers who, operating out
of cramped apartments, neighbourhood bars and cafés, and secluded
cemeteries, hawked half-ounces of snuff wrapped in paper cones. The
emergence of this underground economy is one of the great overlooked
effects of French court capitalism's proclivity toward monopoly.

The black markets for salt and tobacco overlapped, but were not identical. An ancient trade, salt smuggling remained a largely regional affair.
France was divided into five salt zones: the *grandes gabelles*, where the
tax was extremely heavy, and four other jurisdictions (the *petites gabelles*,
salines, *quart-bouillon*, and exempt lands), where it was moderate to non-
existent. To supplement their meagre agricultural incomes, peasants
hauled salt from low-priced to high-priced regions, earning as much
as twenty *lt* for transporting a single fifty-pound load (AN G-1 106 doss.
1). What took a fortnight to earn in the licit economy could be pock-
eted in a single day. Because the cost of access to the trade was low –
many smugglers simply carried sacks of salt on their backs rather than
using carts or horses – trafficking remained a relatively artisanal form
of commerce in which peasants, women, and children predominated. In
the *direction* of Laval, ground zero for the illicit salt trade from Brittany
to Maine and Anjou, almost sixty per cent of defendants hauled before
the local salt court were women. They plied their trade unarmed, worked
individually or in pairs (often with family members), and carried just over
twenty pounds of salt per trip (Durand 1974; Huvet-Martinet 1978).

The tobacco monopoly stimulated a whole new level of illicit activity. Easier to transport and, pound for pound, much more valuable than
salt, tobacco smuggling offered the prospect of extraordinarily high profits, attracting the attention of well-organised traders, as well as indigent
peasants. As a result, contraband tobacco flooded all quarters of the
French monopoly zone, from the coast of Languedoc in the south to the

littoral of Brittany and Normandy in the west. Supply ships hovered off the mainland as small craft ran the tobacco ashore, where locals picked it up and moved it inland for distribution. The most heavily trafficked routes into the territory of the French monopoly, however, lay to the north and east, where precious Virginian tobacco entered the Continent by way of Dunkirk and the Netherlands to pool just beyond the French fiscal border. From there it flowed in an arc that stretched across Alsace (a privileged French province not subject to the monopoly), down through the Swiss pays de Vaud, to Savoie. All along this trajectory the Virginian was mixed with cheap, home-grown European weed to create an inexpensive yet good-quality blend that was perfect for smuggling into the French interior. Traffickers purchased blends for as little as twelve *sols* a pound and sold them in the monopoly zone for as much as thirty-six *sols* in the provinces, and up to fifty *sols* in Paris, tripling their money, and helping to put tobacco within reach of poor consumers who could ill afford the sixty-two *sols* charged by the Farm (AN G-1 106, doss.1). Because demand for habit-forming, psychoactive products is, in principle, elastic for new users, it is likely that the lower cost of contraband leaf helped spread consumption among the lower orders (Fiorentini and Peltzman 1995; Schneider and Enste 2002; Findlay and O'Rourke 2007, 259). By the middle of the eighteenth century an estimated one third of the tobacco consumed in France was illicit (AN 129; AP 29; Price 1973, I: 407; Vigié and Vigié 1989, chap. 11).

The informal economy that flourished in the shadow of the salt and tobacco monopolies had important political implications. To begin with, it meant that countless French subjects – smugglers and consumers alike – were breaking the law on a regular basis, as they tested the crown's ability to police territory and control borders. This was a rather passive form of resistance; whatever political significance it held remained implicit. But the ubiquitous defiance of royal decree made a mockery of the Farm and its monopolistic claims.

Further, state efforts to crack down on illicit trade provoked more active kinds of resistance. During the final century of the old regime, the monarchy attempted to roll back the underground by expanding the corps of Farm police to 20,000 guards, the largest paramilitary force in Europe. It also overhauled the criminal justice system, hardening the penal code and creating extraordinary law courts funded by the Farm. Tens of thousands of smugglers – perhaps half of the more than 100,000 men who entered the galleys between 1685 and 1791 – were incarcerated for their participation in the underground economy. Indeed, the birth of the modern French prison owes much to the Farm's crackdown on smuggling (Zysberg 1975; Zysberg 1987; Johannic-Seta

2000; Kwass 2013), a point that Foucault, writing before the publication of major studies on the galleys, overlooked in his influential book on the genesis of the modern incarceration (Foucault 1979).

Rather than folding under the weight of such repression, however, many traffickers struck back, engaging Farm officials and guards in violent conflict. Lone smugglers resisted arrest, communities defended dealers in their midst, and armed gangs attacked customs posts at the border. Large bands were particularly prominent in the more professionalised tobacco trade. In the 1750s, for example, the celebrated gang leader Louis Mandrin headed a small army of over a hundred men who combated Farm guards as they whisked tobacco from Switzerland into towns and villages dotting southeastern France. Mounted and armed to the teeth, Mandrin's belligerent gang not only occupied provincial capitals in broad daylight, selling contraband tobacco in public marketplaces, but also busted the monopoly's supply lines by forcing Farm warehousers to buy his contraband leaf. Although Mandrin's exploits soon attracted the attention of Versailles, which dispatched several army regiments to stamp out the *chef*, such violence was endemic to France throughout the century. According to a path-breaking recent study, rebellion against Farm agents was the single most common form of revolt in France from 1660 and 1789 (Nicolas 2002, annexe 2). Far outpacing other (more closely studied) types of collective action, such as food riots, seigneurial disturbances, and labour conflicts, tax rebellions constituted no less than thirty-nine per cent of all documented cases of revolt. Within the category of fiscal rebellion, at least sixty-five per cent of cases involved contraband.

Such findings dramatically change our understanding of the history of popular revolt in *ancien régime* France. It has long been assumed that the shape of rebellion shifted from tax and conscription uprisings in the seventeenth century to food and seigneurial riots in the eighteenth century (Le Roy Ladurie 1974; Chartier 1991, 141–5). Yet, far from petering out after the reign of Louis XIV, fiscal rebellion remained the most prominent type of collective action down to the Revolution. To be sure, anti-fiscal sedition changed form. Contraband rebellions were much smaller in scale than the great peasant revolts of the *Grand Siècle*. But the newer rebellions were incessant and widespread, a part of daily political life in many border provinces. Although the eighteenth-century monarchy successfully relegated province-wide uprisings to the past, it never firmly established a double monopoly on taxation and violence, despite the oft-cited claim of Elias (Elias 1982, 91–225; Chartier 1991, 141–5). Behind the veneer of domestic peace and stability raged an ongoing guerrilla war between the elephantine Farm and legions of highly mobile traffickers.

If the fiscalisation of consumption, a project which lay at the core of French court capitalism, engendered widespread hostility to the Farm and its monopolies, it took the literature of the Enlightenment, an intellectual movement which subjected institutions to widening public scrutiny, to transform popular resentment into a powerful critique of the state (Habermas 1991). From the 1750s to the 1780s, two groups of thinkers – economists and legal reformers – launched a reform movement aimed at bringing down the General Farm and its monopolies. Although writers had long ridiculed state financiers as vulgar social climbers, after the middle of the eighteenth century, as the number of works on political economy skyrocketed, they reached beyond indictments of personal character to challenge the monarchy's entire fiscal-judicial complex. Just as the Farmers General were successfully integrating themselves in Parisian high society (Durand 1971, II), intellectuals laid siege to the whole apparatus of indirect taxation, focusing their attack on the repressive methods by which the Farm policed its monopolies.

The first salvo came from economists. Springboarding off Montesquieu's enormously influential *Spirit of the Laws*, which lambasted tax farming, high consumption taxes, and the creation of special smuggling courts (Montesquieu 1748, XI: chap. 18, XIII: chaps. 8, 19, 20), a small group of liberal economists surrounding *intendant* of commerce Vincent de Gournay jumped to the defence of smugglers. Although the group came to the issue of illicit trade through the controversy surrounding the importation of Indian calico (Meyssonnier 1989), one of its members, François Véron de Forbonnais, extended the discussion to the salt monopoly, which he slammed for forcing high prices on the poor and driving them into the underground economy. The so-called crime of smuggling was in fact no crime at all, but an artefact of a badly flawed fiscal regime. Impoverished smugglers might have broken political law, he conceded, but they 'in no way violated natural law', and should therefore be treated with leniency (Forbonnais 1758, III: 166).

The charge that smugglers were being punished cruelly for merely following their economic interests was further developed by a second wave of liberal economists, the Physiocrats. According to Physiocratic doctrine, indirect taxes violated a set of natural economic laws that, if properly followed, would produce the kind of large-scale, capitalist agriculture that France desperately needed for its regeneration. Because consumption taxes ended up gouging cultivators, so the theory went, such levies impeded capital investment in the land, and set France on a course for economic disaster (Larrère 2002). Only a single tax on landed income, combined with a free trade in grain, would bring prosperity to the kingdom. Thus, for the Physiocrats, the whole repressive apparatus of indirect taxation was damaging in the extreme. As the bombastic Marquis de Mirabeau (1760, 141–4) wrote of the Farm:

It seizes the opportunity to raise armies to guard the borders of regions prohibited from enjoying the gifts of nature, portending the coming of slavery on the whole territory. Prisons, galleys, gallows and sinister tribunals are established at the cruel whim of financiers to punish inhumanely the wretch who exercises his natural right. . . . Although the Farm feigns to draw blood from the capillaries, it bleeds the people at the throat.

Fellow Physiocrat Guillaume-François Le Trosne put it in colder analytical terms. Smugglers acted in accordance with 'the laws of the natural order', which recognised the liberty 'to buy and sell in a condition of full competition'. The imposition of fiscal monopolies had the perverse effect of turning legitimate merchants of salt and tobacco into criminals. 'Public opinion doggedly insists on absolving' the artificial crime of smuggling, but the crown 'persists in condemning' it (Le Trosne 1779, 78, 81). All this would change, he explained, as soon as indirect taxes were abolished. The levies 'will no longer require victims, the guilty parties will disappear, every subject will be submissive and faithful', and courts 'will prosecute only real crimes whose punishment will be applauded by all because it will be inflicted only to assure and avenge collective security' (Le Trosne 1770, 325–7). Widely diffused in books, journals, and agricultural societies, such logic directly challenged the fiscalisation of consumption and its judicial corollary, the criminalisation of smuggling.

In the 1760s and 1770s economists were joined by magistrates and legal reformers. As taxes mounted during the Seven Years War (1756–63), men of law stressed the abuses that the Farm committed as it went about policing monopolies and prosecuting alleged smugglers. Although magistrates across France participated in this rhetorical assault, it is worth noting that provincial magistrates, who possessed far fewer state bonds than their counterparts in Paris, were the most vociferous. Untroubled by the possibility that a sudden fall in indirect tax revenues might trigger a debt repudiation, they impugned the 'army' of guards and 'tribunals of blood' who did the Farm's dirty work (AD Isère B 2325, *remonstrances* of the *parlement de Grenoble*, 17 Aug. 1763; Kwass 2000, 182; Stasavage 2003, 132–8). In Paris, where bondholding magistrates were more docile, it fell to a firebrand barrister from the *cour des aides* to expose the 'monster' that was the Farm. In his 1763 *L'Anti-financier*, Jean Baptiste Darigrand, a former official in the Farm's wine tax division, used his inside knowledge of the company to launch a blistering attack. His book documented how the Farm's corrupt armed guards, the 'tyrants of the provinces', arbitrarily arrested and searched innocent men and women in the pursuit of personal gain. It also spoke movingly of convicts subjected to the summary justice of smuggling tribunals:

> The trial completed, they are weighed down with chains. I help them lift their arms from the depth of their prison cells toward the Throne. I join my cries with theirs: 'Oh my King! Oh well-loved King, deign to turn your eyes on these unfortunates. These are your Subjects, your children. They are guilty, I admit it. But when judging them, let it be remembered that they are only guilty of fraud.' We are not heard. Already the whips, the hot irons, the chains, the gallows are being prepared. (Darigrand 1763, 69)

The culmination of the legal critique of the Farm came in 1775 from the pen of Chrétien Guillaume Lamoignon de Malesherbes. Scion of a great *robe* family, Malesherbes was a pivotal figure in the Enlightenment. In the 1750s, while serving as director of the Royal Censorship Office, he protected the *Encyclopedia* and facilitated the publication of many liberal economic works. In 1766 he asked Morellet to translate Cesare Beccaria's *On Crimes and Punishments*, the text that galvanised the movement for French penal reform. As president of the *cour des aides* of Paris he had long voiced opposition to the abusive repression of smuggling. In 1770, however, a case came before his court that utterly radicalised him. A tradesman by the name of Guillaume Monnerat, suspected of smuggling tobacco, had been thrown into the *Bicêtre*, a notorious prison-hospital filled with the poor, sick, and criminal. There Monnerat was clasped in irons and confined to a dank, pitch-black, subterranean cell for two months before being transferred, for medical reasons, to an above-ground compartment for at least another year. Meanwhile, with the suspect incarcerated, Farm officials attempted to dig up enough evidence against him to initiate a trial, but to no avail. An apparent victim of mistaken identity, Monnerat was released into the streets of Paris after having been subjected to the misery of the *Bicêtre* and robbed of two years of his life. He immediately filed suit.

As president of the *cour des aides*, Malesherbes seized the suit as an opportunity to investigate the Farm's police procedures. What he found shocked him. Agents of the Farm were using special *lettres de cachet* (royal arrest warrants) to incarcerate whomever they suspected of dealing in contraband, whether or not there was sufficient evidence to do so. Appalled, Malesherbes awarded Monnerat 50,000 *lt* in damages, a remarkable blow against the Farmers General. But the tradesman never received his money. The Royal Council evoked the case, and cleared the Farmers General of any wrongdoing. Malesherbes responded by firing off remonstrances, but his campaign was cut short by a ministerial strike against the judiciary – the Maupeou coup – in which the *cours des aides* and the *parlements* were dissolved. Four years later, when the courts were recalled by the newly enthroned Louis XVI, Malesherbes resumed battle, now linking Farm abuse to a sophisticated theory of despotism.

Malesherbes' remonstrances of 1775 differentiated between royal absolutism, by which the king legitimately held unlimited authority, and outright 'despotism', a condition in which 'each of the executors of [the king's] orders also employs a power without limits' (Malesherbes 1775, 202) (Coffman, this volume). Malesherbes systematically applied this theory of despotism to every level of the Farm: Farmers General forced cash-starved monarchs to issue whatever penal legislation they wished; guards rode roughshod over defenceless provincial peasants; smuggling commissions handed down criminal sentences that were 'repugnant to humanity' (quoted in Grosclaude 1961, 350). For the president of the *cour des aides* of Paris, as for increasing numbers of magistrates, there was only one way to defeat the despotism that the Farm had implanted in the monarchy. The king would have to call the Estates General.

A renowned historian of the grain trade once noted that 'the history of the old regime is a history of a total failure of public relations' (Kaplan 1982, 66). What was true for food provision was doubly true of taxation, especially indirect taxation. By imposing monopolies on salt and tobacco, by subcontracting those monopolies to the General Farm, and by criminalising smuggling, the French crown not only stimulated the growth of a violent underground economy, but also drew public attention to the darkest practices of the eighteenth-century state. As the spectre of a despotic fiscal–judicial complex loomed, smugglers, economists, and men of law struck back, pounding the regime from above and below in an assault that would ultimately help bring down the absolute monarchy.

Revolution

In 1789, with bankruptcy looming, Louis XVI heeded the advice of his magistrates and convoked the Estates General, the momentous event that would usher in the French Revolution. Although historians have long observed that the financial crisis of the 1780s was a key short-term cause of the Revolution, they have overlooked how popular and elite hostility to consumption taxes converged to spark the Revolution and drive it forward. At the level of popular politics, the longstanding war against the Farm came to a head in 1789. In their *cahiers de doléances*, grievance lists compiled in anticipation of the meeting of the Estates General, the third estate drew a sharp distinction between direct taxes, which were salvageable and to be reformed, and indirect taxes, which were fundamentally illegitimate and to be abolished (Shapiro and Markoff 1998, chap. 20). Consumption taxes on monopolised goods were completely tainted, especially the *gabelle*, which was the object of more complaints than any other institution of the *ancien régime*. 'Are we not, with respect to salt and tobacco, the slaves of the most reviled men in public opinion?' asked the third estate of Vic, alluding to the detested agents of the Farm (quoted in Gondolff 1914, 341). Farm agents are 'leeches on the state', howled one Norman village. 'They are vermin who devour it; they are a plague that infects it. There are as many places where they are loathed as there are places where they exist' (quoted in Shapiro and Markoff 1998, 613 n. 48). The money such 'vermin' took from consumers, furthermore, lined the pockets of rich tax farmers. 'The Farmers General must be suppressed', declared the parishioners of Bicxeuil, 'for would it not be better that the immense sums which they gain, or rather which they extort, were sent to the royal treasury than to the hands of these avid *traitants*?' (quoted in Mathews 1958, 278).

The distinction made in the *cahiers* between direct and indirect taxes – those on property and those on consumer goods – was entirely consistent with earlier practices of popular revolt. In the decades before the Revolution, agents of the Farm were subject to repeated attacks, whereas direct-tax collectors were generally left in peace. The distinction was also consistent with the very first acts of the popular revolution, which began not with the storming of the Bastille, as is commonly thought, but with the destruction of the customs gates encircling the city of Paris. From 11 to 14 July, large crowds of men and women, many of whom were involved in the parallel economy, sacked the customs wall that had recently been erected by the Farm to clamp down on the flow of illicit tobacco into the capital (de Clercq 1938; Peysson 1982). For three days, the men and women of Paris demolished the elaborate neo-classical customs pavilions and expelled their inhabitants. Axes and hammers in hand, they ripped down the iron railings that closed off streets, burned down auxiliary stables and sheds, vandalised newly erected statues, and gutted the stone buildings of scales, documents, registers, receipts, beds, benches, tables, desks, chairs, and doors – anything that could be picked up and thrown out the window. The debris was then amassed into piles in the street and set ablaze. This was not the work of a handful of rogue rebels, but of huge crowds, some as large as the two or three thousand strong assemblage of men and women who sacked the post at the Fontainebleau road. As the city gates burned, consumers revelled in the dream of cheap tobacco, wine, and food, merchants delighted in the prospect of not having to share their profits with the Farm, and smugglers savoured the sweet taste of victory over an old and formidable enemy. The siege also sent the political message that, despite Louis XVI's apparent intention to shut down Paris and nip the Revolution in the bud, goods and citizens would continue to flow freely into and out of the capital. The will of the people as expressed by the National Assembly would not be denied.

After the Parisians sacked the customs gates, word of the rebellion spread to the provinces, where peasants followed suit, attacking customs barriers in their own towns and villages. In Picardy, crowds burned down customs posts, attacked the residences of company officials, freed traffickers from jail, and began openly trading in illicit salt and tobacco. As in Paris, smugglers played a vital role in such rebellions. As the *intendant* of nearby Soisson informed his superiors: 'smugglers profit from the fermentation that reigns in all minds; they enter towns, storm the toll gates, and, seconded by the people who find their advantage in it, publicly sell salt and tobacco. Farm agents and mounted police dare not confront these disorders, for fear that the populace that threatens them will knock them senseless' (quoted in Ramsay 1996, 177–9). Such unrest took on a distinctly revolutionary air when protesters shouted the rallying cry of 'the Third Estate', and tested the political allegiances of Farm guards. Popular uprisings against indirect taxation did not abate until a new fiscal regime was installed in 1791 (Marion 1916; Ragan 1992; Markoff 1996, 233–40, 275–6; Miller 2008).

Meanwhile, back in Paris, legislators turned to the project of defiscalising consumption, reversing a centuries-old trend by shifting the tax burden from indirect to direct taxes. In doing so, deputies were no doubt responding pragmatically to the pressure of popular insurrection. How could a revolutionary government purporting to uphold liberty and equality ignore the call to abolish abusive state monopolies and consumption taxes, especially the *gabelle*, the most detested tax of the old regime? The force of popular activism does not explain everything, however. Many deputies of the National Assembly were steeped in the ideas of the economists and legal reformers who had for decades been discrediting indirect taxes and the company that collected them. As Ernest Labrousse pointed out long ago (with a touch of exaggeration), the financial doctrine of the early revolution was 'but a compromise with the fiscal program of the Physiocracy' (Labrousse 1933, II: 631). So stained had indirect taxes become in the mind of the learned public that few moderate and left-wing legislators could imagine any significant place for them in the new regime.

Consequently, in 1791, the Constituent Assembly abolished tax farming and swept away the fiscal monopolies of the past. The odious *gabelle* was the first to go – no one dared to stand in the way of its abolition. The question of what to do with the tobacco monopoly was more complicated. Reluctant to dissolve an institution that yielded the state more than thirty million *lt* a year, right-wing deputies rehabilitated the argument that the tax was 'a voluntary contribution', a luxury tax that many consumers wilfully paid (AP, 20, 446). But deputies on the left and from the tobacco-producing province of Alsace countered that tobacco was now an 'object of prime necessity, a real need' and, as such, should be freed from the burden of excessive taxation (AP, 20, 412; Jones and Spang 1999). Upgrading the moral status of tobacco from a luxury to a necessity, legislators grouped the leaf with its formerly monopolised counterpart, salt, into a category of popular commodities that deserved protection from the fisc. On this the French people had already spoken, declared the Alsatian Jacobin C. L. V. de Broglie. 'If any doubts lingered about the people's profound aversion to this dreadful regime [of tobacco], recall what happened during that remarkable moment when the Revolution began. All the customs barriers that the general farm had erected against the circulation of tobacco in the kingdom were overthrown at once.' Only the 'enemies of the Revolution' would dare propose to re-establish the monopoly after the 'fiscal chains under the weight of which the people moaned' had finally been broken. Only when 'all the henchmen and the inventions of the fisc' are banished will 'France be able to believe in its liberty' (AP, 20, 412–14). On 20 March 1791 the Assembly voted to scrap the tobacco monopoly and nullify the contract between the king and the Farmers General. The company that had lodged itself at the heart of the French state, that for more than a century had provided the monarchy with huge cash payments and deep lines of credit, was destroyed.

Although the Assembly abolished nearly all of the old consumption taxes, it did not dispense with direct taxation. On the contrary, in 1791 it created new direct 'contributions' that were to be distributed equally among property owners, and administered by newly elected municipal governments. Based on the principles of equality and citizenship, this fiscal system was designed to slay the beast of court capitalism. If this was the goal of the abolition of indirect taxation, the newly reformed direct taxes, upon which the very right to vote was founded, were designed to forge a salubrious connection between the citizen and the revolutionary state (Kwass 2000, chap. 6; Delalande 2011). It is one of the most painful ironies of the Revolution, therefore, that the founding of the new tax system ultimately served to weaken successive revolutionary governments. Indirect taxes having been scrapped, the national treasury was now almost entirely dependent on direct taxation, the reform of which would take years to complete. As tax revenues plummeted, the state relied increasingly on *assignats*, paper money backed by proceeds from nationalised church land. Revolutionary governments might well have muddled through with such a minimal fiscal state had they been willing and able to maintain peace with other European states, but after the French marched back to war in 1792, deficits yawned, and the *assignats* began to ascend a hyperinflationary spiral – the first of its kind in the modern era – which completely destabilised the regime.

It was not until after the Terror, when the conservative governments of the Second Directory and the Empire came to power, that indirect taxes would be reinstated, and state revenues would reach and eventually surpass old-regime levels (White 1995, figure 1; Sutherland 2002). Napoleon raised taxes on alcoholic beverages, revived the regressive salt tax in 1806, and re-established the tobacco monopoly in 1810. The emperor undoubtedly put the government on a sounder financial footing, but in so doing violated the revolutionary principles of fiscal equality and local participatory government on which the new regime was meant to have been built. The most conspicuous forms of court capitalism had been expunged, but as revolution gave way to conservatism under the Empire, poor and middling consumers once again found themselves bearing the brunt of taxation. Conflicts over consumption taxes would reappear in the nineteenth century, until a political settlement was finally forged during the Third Republic (Delalande 2011).

Key to archive references

AD Isère: Archives départementales de l'Isère
AN: Archives Nationales
AP: Archives Parlementaires

References

Ashworth, William J. 2003. *Customs and Excise: Trade, Production, and Consumption in England, 1640–1845*. Oxford: Oxford University Press.

Azimi, Vida 1987. *Un modèle administratif de l'ancien régime: les commis de la Ferme générale et de la Régie générale des aides*. Paris: Éditions du Centre national de la recherche scientifique.

Bien, David D. 1987. 'Offices, Corps, and a System of State Credit: The Uses of Privilege under the Ancien Régime', in Keith Michael Baker (ed.), *The Political Culture of the Old Regime*. Oxford: Oxford University Press.

Bonney, Richard J. 1979. 'The Failure of the French Revenue Farms, 1600–1660', *Economic History Review*, 32, 11–32.

Bonney, Richard J. 2004. 'Towards the Comparative Fiscal History of Britain and France during the 'Long' Eighteenth Century', in Leandro Prados de la Escosura (ed.), *Exceptionalism and Industrialization: Britain and Its European Rivals, 1688–1815*. Cambridge: Cambridge University Press.

Bosher, John F. 1970. *French Finances 1770–1795: From Business to Bureaucracy.* Cambridge: Cambridge University Press.

Bossenga, Gail 2005. 'Markets, the Patrimonial State, and the Origins of the French Revolution', *1650–1850: Ideas, Aesthetics, and Inquiries in the Early Modern Era*, 11, 443–510.

Bossenga, Gail 2011. 'Financial Origins of the French Revolution', in Thomas E. Kaiser and Dale Van Kley (eds.), *From Deficit to Deluge: The Origins of the French Revolution.* Stanford, CA: Stanford University Press.

Brewer, John 1989. *The Sinews of Power: War, Money, and the English State, 1688–1783.* Cambridge, MA: Harvard University Press.

Butel, Paul 1974. *Les négociants bordelais, l'Europe et les îles au XVIIIe siècle.* Paris: Aubier.

Chartier, Roger 1991. *The Cultural Origins of the French Revolution.* Translated by Lydia G. Cochrane. Durham, NC: Duke University Press.

Crouzet, François 1993. *La grande inflation: La monnaie en France de Louis XVI à Napoléon.* Paris: Fayard.

Darigrand, Jean-Baptiste 1763. *L'Anti-financier, ou Relevé de quelqu'unes des malversations dont se rendent journellement coupables les Fermiers Généraux, & des vexations qu'ils commettent dans les Provinces.* Amsterdam.

de Clercq, V. 1938. 'L'incendie des barrières de Paris de 1789 et le procès des incendiaires', *Bulletin de la Société de l'histoire de Paris et de l'Isle de France*, 31–47.

Delalande, Nicolas 2011. *Les batailles de l'impôt: Consentement et résistances de 1789 à nos jours.* Paris: Seuil.

Dickson, P. G. M. 1967. *The Financial Revolution in England: A Study in the Development of Public Credit 1688–1756.* London: Macmillan.

Durand, Yves 1971. *Les fermiers généraux au XVIIIe siècle.* Paris: Presses Universitaires de France.

Durand, Yves 1974. 'La contrebande du sel au XVIIIe siècle aux frontières de Bretagne, du Maine et de l'Anjou', *Histoire Sociale*, 7, 227–269.

Elias, Norbert 1982. *Power and Civility: The Civilizing Process.* Translated by Edmund Jephcott. New York: Pantheon Books.

Fairchilds, Cissie 1993. 'The Production and Marketing of Populuxe Goods in Eighteenth-Century Paris', in John Brewer and Roy Porter (eds.), *Consumption and the World of Goods.* London: Routledge.

Félix, Joël 1999. *Finances et politique au siècle des Lumières: Le ministère L'Averdy, 1763–1768.* Paris: Histoire économique et financière de la France.

Félix, Joël 2006. 'The Financial Origins of the French Revolution', in Peter R. Campbell (ed.), *The Origins of the French Revolution.* New York: Palgrave.

Findlay, Ronald and O'Rourke, Kevin H. 2007. *Power and Plenty: Trade, War, and the World Economy in the Second Millennium.* Princeton: Princeton University Press.

Fiorentini, Gianluca and Peltzman, Sam 1995. eds., *The Economics of Organized Crime.* Cambridge: Cambridge University Press

Forbonnais, François Véron Duverger de 1758. *Recherches et considérations sur les finances de France, depuis 1595 jusqu'en 1721*, 6 vols. Liège.

Foucault, Michael 1977. *Discipline and Punish: The Birth of the Prison.* Translated by Alan Sheridan. New York: Vintage Books.

Fritschy, Wantje 1990. 'Taxation in Britain, France, and the Netherlands in the Eighteenth Century', *Economic and Social History in the Netherlands*, 2, 57–79.

Gondolff, E. 1914. *Le tabac sous l'ancienne monarchie: La ferme royale, 1629–1791*. Vesoul: Ancien Imprimerie Cival.

Goudar, Ange 1755. *Le Testament politique de Louis Mandrin*. Geneva.

Grosclaude, Pierre 1961. *Malesherbes, témoin et interprète de son temps*. Paris: Librairie Fischbacher.

Habermas, Jürgen 1989. *The Structural Transformation of the Public Sphere: An Inquiry into a Category of Bourgeois Society*. Translated by Thomas Burger with Frederick Lawrence. Cambridge, MA: MIT Press.

Hoffman, Phillip T. 1994. 'Early Modern France, 1450–1700', in Hoffman and Kathryn Norberg (eds.), *Fiscal Crises, Liberty, and Representative Government, 1450–1789*. Stanford, CA: Stanford University Press.

Hoffman, Phillip T.; Postel-Vinay, Gilles; and Rosenthal, Jean-Laurent 2000. *Priceless Markets: The Political Economy of Credit in Paris, 1660–1870*. Chicago: University of Chicago Press.

Hoquet, Jean-Claude 1987. 'Qui la gabelle du sel du Roi de France a-t-elle enrichi?' in Jean-Philippe Genet and Michel Le Mené (eds.), *Genèse de l'Etat moderne: Prélèvment et redistribution*. Paris: Editions du Centre national de la recherche scientifique.

Huvet-Martinet, Micheline 1978. 'Faux-saunage et faux-sauniers dans l'Ouest et du Centre à la fin de l'Ancien Régime (1764–1789), *Annales de Bretagne et des pays de l'ouest*, 85, 573–94.

Johannic-Seta, Frédérique 2000. *Le bagne de Brest, 1749–1800: naissance d'une institution carcérale au siècle des Lumières*. Rennes: Presses universitaires de Rennes.

Johnson, Noel D. 2006. 'Banking on the King: The Evolution of the Royal Revenue Farms in Old Regime France', *Journal of Economic History*, 66, 963–91.

Jones, Colin and Spang, Rebecca 1999. 'Sans-culottes, sans café, sans tabac: shifting realms of necessity and luxury in eighteenth-century France', in Maxine Berg and Helen Clifford (eds.), *Consumers and Luxury: Consumer Culture in Europe 1650–1850*. Manchester: Manchester University Press.

Kaplan, Steven L. 1982. 'The Famine Plot Persuasion in Eighteenth-Century France', *Transactions of the American Philosophical Society*, 72, 1–79.

Kwass, Michael 2000. *Privilege and the Politics of Taxation in Eighteenth-Century France: Liberté, Égalité, Fiscalité*. Cambridge: Cambridge University Press.

Kwass, Michael 2006. 'Big Hair: A Wig History of Consumption in Eighteenth-Century France', *American Historical Review*, 111, 631–59.

Kwass, Michael 2013. 'The First War on Drugs: Tobacco Trafficking, Criminality, and the Fiscal State in Eighteenth-Century France', in Renate Bridenthal (ed.), *The Hidden History of Crime, Corruption and States*. Oxford: Oxford University Press.

Labrousse, Ernest 1933. *Esquisse du mouvement des prix et des revenues en France au XVIIIe siècle*. Paris: Librairie Dalloz.

Larrère, Catherine 2002. 'Impôts directs, impôts indirects: Économie, politique, droit', *Archives de philosophie du droit*, 46, 117–30.

Legay, Marie-Laure 2000. 'Le crédit des provinces au secours de l'Etat', in Françoise Bayard (ed.), *Les finances en province sous l'Ancien Régime*. Paris: Comité pour l'histoire économique et financière de la France.

Legay, Marie-Laure; Félix, Joël; and White, Eugene 2009. 'Retour sur les Origines Financières de la Révolution Française', *Annales historiques de la Révolution française*, 356, 183–201.

Le Roy Ladurie, Emmanuel 1974. 'Révoltes et contestations rurales en France de 1675 à 1788', *Annales ESC*, 29, 6–22.

Le Trosne, Guillaume-François 1770. *Les effets de l'impôt indirect, prouvé par les deux exemples de la gabelle & du tabac*. Basel.

Le Trosne, Guillaume-François 1779. *De l'administration provinciale, et de la réforme de l'impôt*. Basel.

Malesherbes, Chrétien Guillaume Lamoignon de 1775. 'Remontrances relatives aux impôts, 6 mai 1775', in Elisabeth Badinter (ed.), *Les 'Remontrances' de Malesherbes, 1771–1775*. (Reprinted Paris: Flammarion, 1985.)

Marion, Marcel 1916. 'Le Recouvrement des impôts en 1790', *Revue Historique*, 121, 1–47.

Marion, Marcel 1919. *Histoire financière de la France depuis 1715*. Paris: Rousseau.

Markoff, John 1996. *The Abolition of Feudalism: Peasants, Lords, and Legislators in the French Revolution*. University Park: Pennsylvania State University Press.

Mathews, George T. 1958. *The Royal General Farms in Eighteenth-Century France*. New York: Columbia University Press.

Mathias, Peter and O'Brien, Patrick 1976. 'Taxation in Britain and France, 1715–1810', *Journal of European Economic History*, 5, 601–50.

Mathon de la Cour, Charles-Joseph (ed.) 1788. *Collection des comptes-rendus, pièces authentiques, états et tableaux, concernant les finances de France, depuis 1758 jusqu'en 1787*. Lausanne: chez Cuchet.

Meyssonnier, Simone 1989. *La balance et l'horloge: la genèse de la pensée libérale en France au XVIIIe siècle*. Paris: Passion.

Miller, Stephen J. 2008. *State and Society in Eighteenth-Century France: A Study of Political Power and Social Revolution in Languedoc*. Washington, DC: Catholic University of America Press.

Mirabeau, Victor de Riquetti 1760. *Théorie de l'impôt*. Paris.

Montesquieu, Charles-Louis de Secondat 1748. *De l'esprit des lois*. (Reprinted Paris: Flammarion, 1979.)

Moreau de Beaumont, Jean-Louis 1768. *Mémoires concernant les impositions et droits en Europe*, 4 vols. Paris: Imprimerie royale.

Morineau, Michel 1980. 'Budgets de l'état et gestion des finances royales en France au dix-huitième siècle', *Revue Historique*, 264, 289–336.

Necker, Jacques 1781. *Compte rendu au roi au mois de janvier 1781*. Paris: Imprimerie royale.

Nicolas, Jean 2002. *La Rébellion Française: Mouvements Populaires et Conscience Sociale 1661–1789*. Paris: Seuil.

North, Douglass C. and Weingast, Barry R. 1989. 'Constitutions and Commitment: The Evolution of Institutions Governing Public Choice in Seventeenth-Century England', *Journal of Economic History*, 49, 803–32.

O'Brien, Patrick K. 1988. 'The Political Economy of British Taxation, 1660–1815', *Economic History Review*, 41, 1–32.

Pardailhé-Galabrun, Annik 1991. *The Birth of Intimacy: Privacy and Domestic Life in Early Modern Paris*. Translated by Joyce Jocelyn Phelps. Philadelphia: University of Pennsylvania Press.

Peysson, Jean-Marc 1982. 'Le mur d'enceinte des fermiers-généraux et la fraude à la fin de l'ancien régime', *Bulletin de la Société de l'histoire de Paris et de l'Ile-de-France*, 109, 225–40.

Potter, Mark 2000. 'Good Offices: Intermediation by Corporate Bodies in Early Modern French Public Finance', *Journal of Economic History*, 60, 599–626.

Price, Jacob M. 1973. *France and the Chesapeake: A History of the French Tobacco Monopoly, 1674–1791, and of Its Relationship to the British and American Tobacco Trades*, 2 vols. Ann Arbor: University of Michigan.

Price, Jacob M. 1998. 'The Imperial Economy, 1700–1776', in P. J. Marshall and Alaine M. Low (eds.), *The Oxford History of the British Empire: The Eighteenth Century*. Oxford: Oxford University Press.

Ragan, Bryant T. 1992. 'Rural Political Activism and Fiscal Equality in the Revolutionary Somme', in Bryant T. Ragan and Elizabeth A. Williams (eds.), *Re-creating Authority in Revolutionary France*. New Brunswick: Rutgers University Press.

Ramsay, Clay 1992. *The Ideology of the Great Fear: The Soissonnais in 1789*. Baltimore: Johns Hopkins University Press.

Riley, James C. 1986. *The Seven Years War and the Old Regime in France*. Princeton: Princeton University Press.

Roche, Daniel 2000. *A History of Everyday Things: The Birth of Consumption in France, 1600–1800*. Translated by Brian Pearce. Cambridge: Cambridge University Press.

Schneider, Friedrich and Enste, Dominik H. 2000. *The Shadow Economy: An International Survey*. Cambridge: Cambridge University Press.

Shapiro, Gilbert and Markoff, John 1998. *Revolutionary Demands: A Content Analysis of the Cahiers de Doléances of 1789*. Stanford, CA: Stanford University Press.

Stasavage, David 2003. *Public Debt and the Birth of the Democratic State: France and Great Britain, 1688–1789*. Cambridge: Cambridge University Press.

Sutherland, Donald 2002. 'Peasants, Lords, and Leviathan: Winners and Losers from the Abolition of Feudalism, 1780–1820', *Journal of Economic History*, 62, 1–24.

Swann, Julian 2003. *Provincial Power and Absolute Monarchy: the Estates General of Burgundy, 1661–1790*. Cambridge: Cambridge University Press.

Taylor, George V. 1964. 'Types of Capitalism in Eighteenth-Century France', *English Historical Review*, 79, 478–97.

Touzery, Mireille 1994. *L'invention de l'impôt sur le revenu: la taille tarifée, 1715–1789*. Paris: Comité pour l'histoire économique et financière de la France.

Vigié, Marc and Vigié, Muriel 1989. *L'Herbe à Nicot: Amateurs de Tabac, Fermiers Généraux et Contrebandiers sous l'Ancien Régime*. Paris: Fayard.

White, Eugene N. 1995. 'The French Revolution and the Politics of Government Finance, 1770–1815', *Journal of Economic History*, 55, 227–55.

White, Eugene N. 2004. 'From Privatized to Government-Administered Tax Collection: Tax Farming in Eighteenth-Century France', *Economic History Review*, 57, 636–63.

Zysberg, André 1975. 'La Société des galériens au milieu du XVIIIe siècle', *Annales Histoire, Sciences Sociales*, 30, 43–65.

Zysberg, André 1987. *Les galériens: Vies et destins de 60,000 forçats sur les galères de France 1680–1748*. Paris: Seuil.

11 Institutions, deficits, and wars: The determinants of British government borrowing costs from the end of the seventeenth century to 1850

Nathan Sussman and Yishay Yafeh[1]

What determines differences in interest rates faced by borrowing developing countries? In light of the immense interest in the effects of institutions on economic development following North (1990) and North and Weingast (1989), this chapter uses historical data on sovereign debt drawn from various periods and countries from the 1690s to the 1990s to examine the extent to which changes in institutional quality have an immediate and direct impact on the cost of debt of borrowing nations, in comparison with the role played by wars and episodes of violent political turmoil. Its main conclusion is that, throughout historical periods, geographic zones, and data sets, wars and instability consistently affect borrowing costs, whereas institutional reforms typically do not elicit investor response in the short run, perhaps because a long period of time is needed to establish their credibility, or because the very nature of the reform process is gradual and cumulative.

The chapter begins by revisiting earlier work which focused on Britain following the Glorious Revolution (Sussman and Yafeh 2006) to extend the time series data on the cost of Britain's debt to 1850. During that period the cost of British government debt increased substantially. Although Barro (1987) attributes the higher borrowing rates to the effect of temporary military spending on crowding-out of private consumption, the results presented here demonstrate that the rising cost of debt reflects mainly a direct increase in the risk premium due to the uncertainty associated with the outcome of the war. The analysis includes a novel variable – the size of the British navy – that serves as a direct measure of the effect of

[1] We thank Roi Azoff and Tomer Yafeh for excellent research assistance. Some of the material presented in this paper draws on the book *Emerging Markets and Financial Globalization: Sovereign Bond Spreads in 1870–1913 and Today* (by Paolo Mauro and the present authors, Oxford University Press, 2006), as well as on two earlier articles by the present authors (Sussman and Yafeh 2000 and 2006). Financial support from Krueger Center at the Hebrew University (Yafeh) is gratefully acknowledged.

war-induced risk on government borrowing costs.[2] These findings confirm that risk associated with wars was the primary driver of variation in the cost of Britain's government debt, even when the country was already (relatively) rich, industrialised, and institutionally developed.

The rest of the chapter presents, in a unified framework, results from different data sets and time periods presented in previous work (Sussman and Yafeh 2000; Mauro, Sussman, and Yafeh 2002; Mauro, Sussman, and Yafeh 2006; Sussman and Yafeh 2007). The findings for Britain are echoed for Japan, which, following the dramatic victory over Russia in 1904–5, enjoyed nearly unrestricted access to foreign capital markets. Apparently Japan's surprising military victory over a European power reduced the uncertainty related to the sustainability of Japanese economic development and debt repayment capacity much more than nearly three decades of institutional and economic reforms. Finally, after moving on to a large sample of other developing countries of the period 1870–1913, the chapter concludes with evidence on the 1990s (Mauro, Sussman, and Yafeh 2006). For all of these countries and time periods, an examination of the determinants of spreads on government bonds indicates that institutional changes and reforms have never been a major driver of borrowing nations' cost of capital. Instead, the primary determinants of the cost of capital are peace and political stability. Although good institutions are likely to contribute to economic growth in the long run, historical support for the mechanism proposed by North and Weingast (1989) – that institutional reforms lower the cost of capital in the short run, and hence foster financial and economic development – is limited.

The present chapter is naturally related to previous studies which have cast some doubt on the importance of institutional changes in seventeenth- and eighteenth-century Britain in comparison with other changes.[3] The present study is also closely related to studies of the relationship between the cost of capital, institutional changes, and political events. For example, Epstein (2000) studies Europe between 1300 and 1750, and argues that differences in formal constitutional arrangements do not account for differences in interest rates. Summerhill (2005a; 2005b) studies Brazil in the nineteenth century and finds some impact of institutional changes on the government's ability to borrow (mostly domestically), although most of the 'structural breaks' he identifies seem to be closely related to revolts and instability. Finally, Saigheh (2009)

---

[2] O'Brien and Duran (2010) independently claim originality for the use of naval strength data in their work. However, the focus of their work is quite different from the focus here.

[3] See, for example, Brewer (1990), Ferguson (2001), O'Brien (2002), and Stasavage (2002, 2003, and 2007). All of these are reviewed in more detail in Sussman and Yafeh (2006).

examines the case of Argentina, and argues that the constitution of 1859 did lead to a 'break' in Argentina's cost of capital. The evidence in the literature on this issue is therefore mixed.

The remainder of the chapter is structured in chronological order. The next section, the main empirical section, presents the data and evidence for Britain between the end of the seventeenth and the middle of the nineteenth century. The third section reproduces the evidence for Meiji Japan. The fourth section discusses other emerging markets before World War I, and the fifth presents (very briefly) evidence from the 1990s. In presenting the findings for the various periods, this chapter focuses primarily on simple statistics and graphical presentations; the reader is referred to more rigorous econometric analyses presented elsewhere. The final section concludes.

Britain: From the Glorious Revolution to Waterloo

Figures 11.1a and 11.1b (reproduced from Sussman and Yafeh 2006) display estimates of the cost of British government debt starting soon after the institutional changes of the late seventeenth century highlighted by North and Weingast (1989). Figure 11.1a presents several estimates of the absolute cost of British debt (interest rates), and Figure 11.1b presents the interest rate differential ('spread' in modern parlance) between British government debt and debt issued by the Province of Holland.[4]

Both figures suggest that early in the eighteenth century, when Britain was involved in military conflicts, its cost of debt was high. Despite newly established institutions, the four decades following the Glorious Revolution can be characterised as a period of high and fluctuating cost of capital, rather than as an era of permanently low interest rates, suggesting that wars and military conflicts had a more direct effect on interest rates than the establishment of 'good' institutions. Subsequent major wars, such as the Seven Years War (1756–63) and the American War of Independence (1775–83), had noticeable effects on Britain's cost of debt nearly a century after the institutional changes of the Glorious Revolution.

To capture the effect of war intensity and the potential effect it had on the risk premium Britain had to pay on its debt, data on the number of enlisted men in the navy and land army were drawn from the British

---

[4] See Sussman and Yafeh (2006) for details on the construction of the various series used in these figures, as well as for comparisons of Britain's cost of debt with that of several continental European countries.

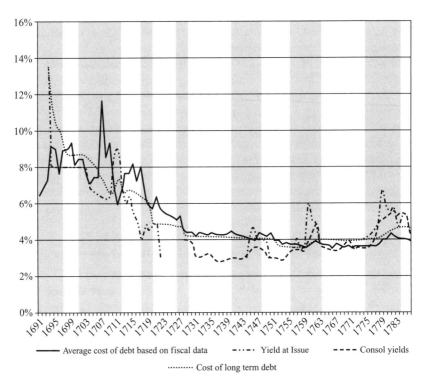

Average cost of debt based on fiscal data   ----- Yield at Issue   - - - Consol yields

·········· Cost of long term debt

Figure 11.1a. Estimates of the cost of debt, Britain 1692–1790. *Source:* Sussman and Yafeh (2006), Figure 1A, gives the definitions of the various measures of the cost of capital. War years (shaded) are 1688–97, War of League of Augsburg; 1701–12, War of the Spanish Succession; 1718–20, War of the Quadruple Alliance; 1727–9, War with Spain; 1740–48, War of the Austrian Succession; 1755–63, Seven Years War; 1775–83, War of American Independence. By permission of Oxford University Press.

Parliamentary Papers. Figure 11.1c shows that throughout the eighteenth century and until the end of the Napoleonic wars, the number of men in the British navy during peacetime was fairly low and stable at around 20,000 sailors. During war navy manpower increased dramatically, by a factor of three to seven, corresponding to the varying degrees of intensity of the different wars. Figure 11.1c suggests that the pattern by which wars were the primary driver of fluctuations in the cost of capital of Britain, the most economically and institutionally advanced country of the time, continued well into the nineteenth century. Consol yields – the interest rates on perpetual government bonds – increased during wartime

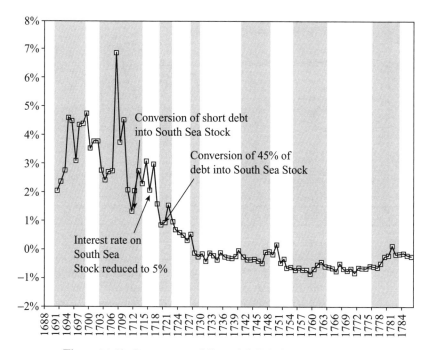

Figure 11.1b. Interest rate differential, Britain vs. Holland, 1692–1790. *Source:* Sussman and Yafeh (2006), Figure 1B. Interest rates are measured as the ratio of debt service to debt. By permission of Oxford University Press.

throughout the eighteenth century, hovering around six per cent during periods of turmoil. In the 1780s and in the first decade of the nineteenth century, levels were roughly similar to those of the 1720s.[5] Moreover, Figure 11.1c suggests also that the cost of British debt co-moved fairly closely with the number of enlisted men in the British navy, a proxy for the wars and the intensity of actual and impending military conflicts.[6]

The effect of wars on British long-term interest rates has been studied before. Barro (1987) claims that war finance accounts for most of their variation from 1700 to World War I. His interpretation is that wartime spending is largely unanticipated, and therefore crowds out investment

---

[5] The comparison of absolute interest rate levels should be treated with caution; the series for the early eighteenth century are based on a variety of indirect estimates described in Sussman and Yafeh (2006). Consol yields, which are used in Figure 11.1c, are only available starting in the middle of the eighteenth century.

[6] In the analysis we show that the number of seamen in the navy is more closely correlated with borrowing costs than the number of soldiers in the army.

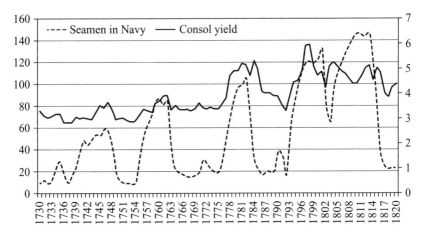

Figure 11.1c. British Consol yields and the size of the British navy.
Source and notes: On the right axis: three per cent British daily Consol yields for the period 1750–1809 drawn from data provided by Larry Neal in the European State Finance Database, www.le.ac.uk/hi/bon/ESFDB, and for the period 1809–1815, from the *London Times*. On the left axis: The number of enlisted men in the navy, in thousands, from the House of Commons Papers 1868–9 (366), pp. 1150, 1151, 1157, and 1158.

and consumption. Consequently, short-term real interest rates should rise at the end of a war, reflecting the higher return to the unexpected lower levels of capital. Long-term interest rates which, by assumption, incorporate the anticipated term structure should rise immediately at the beginning of a war. Barro's empirical analysis is consistent with this hypothesis. However, it cannot reject the traditional view that interest rates increase because of budget deficits that have to be financed by debt (a temporary effect), and also with an increased debt-to-GDP ratio (a longer-term effect). To disentangle the effects of deficits and temporary unanticipated spending, and to argue for his interpretation, Barro notes that

Over the sample of more than two hundred years, I found two examples of major budget deficits that were unrelated to wartime (or the business cycle). One episode featured compensation payments to slave-owners in 1835–36, and the other involved a political dispute over the income tax in 1909–10. Because of the 'exogeneity' of these deficits, it is interesting that interest rates showed no special movements at these times. (Barro 1987, p. 246)

In light of the evidence presented above, it may be possible to interpret Barro's findings in a different way. Wars had an additional effect on the British *risk premium* above and beyond the direct economic costs associated with temporary military spending. Although Barro claims that ordinary temporary deficits did not have an impact on long-term bond prices, those associated with wars did. This suggests that wars introduced a component of uncertainty regarding future ability to repay the loans, which could explain why investors reacted differently to deficits caused by wars, in contrast to deficits of similar magnitudes driven by other reasons.[7]

It is possible to design a more formal test of the hypothesis that wars had an independent effect on the cost of capital, beyond its fiscal implications in the period 1730 to 1850,[8] by using Mitchell (1988) both to reconstruct Barro's measure of military spending to GDP, and to obtain fiscal and export data, combined with data on Parliamentary approval of manpower to the navy and the land army.[9] Table 11.1a presents the results obtained from univariate regressions of the Consol yield on the likely explanatory variables: Barro's measure of military spending, the lagged debt-to-GDP ratio, the current budget-deficit-to-GDP ratio, and, in addition, two direct measures of the intensity of warfare – the size of the land army and the size of the navy.[10] It can readily be seen that the highest unconditional correlation between any of these variables and Consol yields is the correlation between yields and the number of navy seamen.

A multivariate analysis is needed to test directly for the added explanatory power of the number of seamen in the navy, conditional on the standard variables affecting the cost of sovereign borrowing. Table 11.1b, column one, examines the explanatory power of military spending versus the more standard government deficit to GDP: the deficit-to-GDP ratio has more explanatory power than measures of military spending.[11] When additional explanatory variables are included (column two), the military

---

[7] Note that Barro's (1987) analysis holds for a closed economy; Sussman and Yafeh (2006) show that Britain's capital markets were integrated with markets in Europe. Also, Barro (1987) acknowledges the possibility of a rising risk premium owing to the war, but ignores it in the rest of his paper.

[8] Annuities become available then for the first time. Consols were introduced in 1753.

[9] British Parliamentary papers 1868–9 (366) (366-I); estimates of land army personnel are for 1869–70.

[10] The number of enlisted men during this time period is not a constant fraction of the population and hence the analysis is based on the absolute number of soldiers or seamen.

[11] Barro's study (1987, 243) includes the First World War, and his regression results slightly favour the military spending hypothesis, but he concludes that 'the principal finding is an inability to disentangle the effects of spending from the effects of budget deficits'.

Table 11.1a. *The determinants of Consol yields, univariate analysis,*
1730–1850

	(1)	(2)	(3)	(4)	(5)
Military expenditure to GDP	0.0944*** (7.27)				
Debt to GDP $(t-1)$		0.00685*** (5.42)			
Deficit to GDP			0.126*** (8.99)		
Soldiers				0.00573*** (10.36)	
Seamen					0.0139*** (11.66)
Constant	3.160*** (30.62)	2.809*** (14.73)	3.494*** (56.64)	3.191*** (42.12)	3.081*** (40.37)
Observations	121	121	121	121	121
Adjusted R^2	0.302	0.191	0.399	0.470	0.529
AIC	229.1	246.9	210.9	195.9	181.4

Note: t statistics in parentheses. $^*p < 0.05$; $^{**}p < 0.01$; $^{***}p < 0.001$.
Sources: Annual British Consol yields and macroeconomic data are from Mitchell (1998). The number of enlisted men (in thousands) in the navy is from the House of Commons Papers 1868–9 (366), pp. 1150, 1151, 1157, and 1158. Military expenditures, debt, and GDP (extrapolated) are from Mitchell (1998) in millions of (constant) pounds.

spending ratio is insignificant. Therefore, in the remaining specifications (columns three through five), the government-deficit-to-GDP ratio is controlled for, and yet the number of seamen in the navy has an independent effect beyond that of the standard fiscal measures analysed in Sussman and Yafeh (2006). The marginal effect of increasing the number of seamen in the navy by 10,000 increases the cost of government borrowing by up to 0.16% (column two). Thus, in 1813, when naval forces reached a maximum of about 100,000 men above their average, the estimated coefficients suggest that the risk premium was up to 1.6% higher than normal, a very high figure given that Consol coupon yields at the time were three per cent.

These findings are related to recent work by O'Brien and Duran (2010), who emphasise the importance of British naval power in explaining the success of the Industrial Revolution. Although the results presented in this chapter imply that the British navy was perceived as crucial for the defence of the realm (and indirectly for economic growth), the increasing number of seamen in the navy had a crowding-out effect on investment through an increase in the cost of capital. The regression

Table 11.1b. *The determinants of Consol yields, multivariate analysis,*
1730–1850

	(1)	(2)	(3)	(4)	(5)
Gold	−0.0639***	−0.0181	−0.0168	−0.0186	−0.0242
	(−5.62)	(−1.38)	(−1.34)	(−1.50)	(−1.95)
Military expenditure to GDP	−0.00572	0.0130			
	(−0.21)	(0.90)			
Deficit to GDP	0.122***		0.0501**	0.0589***	0.0503**
	(3.75)		(3.50)	(3.77)	(3.17)
Debt to GDP ($t-1$)		0.00515***	0.00499***	0.00416***	0.00528***
		(3.88)	(3.90)	(3.82)	(4.64)
Exports to GDP		0.606	0.419	0.324	
		(1.94)	(1.37)	(1.09)	
Seamen (thousands)		0.0161***	0.0113**	0.00749***	0.00594***
		(4.82)	(3.24)	(4.77)	(3.47)
Soldiers (thousands)		−0.00313*	−0.00174		
		(−2.26)	(−1.23)		
Exports per seamen					−1.045*
					(−2.35)
Constant	3.709***	2.281***	2.443***	2.596***	2.913***
	(29.24)	(9.70)	(10.39)	(13.01)	(13.83)
Observations	121	121	121	121	121
Adjusted R^2	0.524	0.644	0.666	0.665	0.677
AIC	184.8	152.6	144.7	144.3	139.9

Note: t statistics in parentheses. *$p < 0.05$; **$p < 0.01$; ***$p < 0.001$.
Sources: Annual British Consol yields and macroeconomic data are from Mitchell (1998).
The number of enlisted men (in thousands) in the navy is from the House of Commons
Papers 1868–9 (366), pp. 1150, 1151, 1157, and 1158. Gold is a dummy variable for gold
standard periods. Military expenditures, debt, exports, and GDP (extrapolated) are from
Mitchell (1988) in millions of (constant) pounds.

specification in column five includes a variable which measures the 'efficiency' of naval forces in securing exports by taking the ratio of exports
to seamen in the navy. The results indicate that whenever the number of
seamen increases relative to the volume of exports, long-term borrowing
rates go up as well, potentially crowding out private investment.

Consol yields, as well as most other explanatory variables, contain
unit roots, and therefore it is impossible to reject the presence of serial
correlation. The unit root problem is addressed by finding a single co-
integrating equation using the Johansen procedure, and the issue of serial
correlation is addressed by estimating ARMA regressions (Table 11.1c).
Using both specifications with deficits (column one) and with Barro's

Table 11.1c. *The determinants of Consol yields, multivariate ARMA analysis, 1730–1850*

	(1)	(2)
Debt to GDP ($t - 1$)	0.00592***	0.00547***
	(2.91)	(2.69)
Deficit to GDP	0.0388*	
	(2.46)	
Seamen	0.00854***	0.0102***
	(5.02)	(5.82)
Exports to GDP	−0.687*	−0.598**
	(−2.46)	(−2.58)
Military expenditure to GDP		0.0145
		(1.18)
Constant	2.687***	2.626***
	(6.64)	(6.42)
ARMA		
L.ar	0.693***	0.666***
	(9.48)	(8.88)
L.ma	0.416***	0.513***
	(3.46)	(4.92)
Sigma		
Constant	0.251***	0.254***
	(16.03)	(15.76)
Observations	121	121
AIC	26.06	29.62

Note: t statistics in parentheses. *$p < 0.05$; **$p < 0.01$; ***$p < 0.001$.
Sources: Annual British Consol yields and macroeconomic data are from Mitchell (1998). The number of enlisted men in the navy (in thousands) is from House of Commons Papers 1868–9 (366), pp. 1150, 1151, 1157, and 1158. Military expenditures, debt, exports, and GDP (extrapolated) are from Mitchell (1998) in millions of (constant) pounds.

measure of military spending (column two), the statistical significance of the size of the navy, the proxy for war intensity, is confirmed.

Finally, it is also possible to test the hypothesis that the size of the navy mattered by using difference equations, thereby addressing potential concerns due to the unit root properties of the levels of the variables. The difference regressions presented in Table 11.1d show that the results still hold. For a given level of budget deficit, debt-to-GDP level, and military expenditure, an increase in the number of men serving in the navy increases the British government's cost of borrowing.

More direct measures of the effects of war on long-term yields can be obtained by focusing on the period of the Napoleonic wars. Using data on the actual dates of major battles, as well as on the dates in which battles were reported in the *London Times* (depending on the

Table 11.1d. *The determinants of Consol yields, difference equations, 1730–1850*

	(1)	(2)	(3)
Δ Military expenditure to GDP	−0.00230	0.0269	
	(−0.11)	(1.96)	
Δ Deficit to GDP	0.0577*		0.0507**
	(2.60)		(3.25)
Δ Debt to GDP		0.00542	0.00605
		(1.48)	(1.70)
Δ Exports to GDP		−0.749**	−0.869**
		(−2.74)	(−3.22)
Δ Seamen		0.00718***	0.00569**
		(3.47)	(2.77)
Constant	−0.00134	−0.00416	−0.00462
	(−0.05)	(−0.016)	(−0.19)
Observations	121	121	121
Adjusted R^2	0.101	0.179	0.223
AIC	46.57	37.53	30.93

Notes: t statistics in parentheses. *$p < 0.05$; **$p < 0.01$; ***$p < 0.001$.
Sources: Annual British Consol yields and macroeconomic data are from Mitchell (1998). The number of enlisted men in the navy is from the House of Commons Papers 1868–9 (366), pp. 1150, 1151, 1157, and 1158. Military expenditures, debt, exports, and GDP (extrapolated) are from Mitchell (1998) in millions of (constant) pounds.

location of the battles, these dates could be far apart), the regressions in Table 11.2 suggest that, on the average, a naval battle raised the yield much more than a land battle, presumably because the navy was regarded as the 'wooden wall' of Britain, whereas the army fought mainly overseas.

The regressions in columns two and three include both the size of the navy (log of the number of enlisted men, column two) and the size of the army (column three). In line with previous findings, the size of the navy seems to be a particularly important explanatory variable, because its size could be viewed as a proxy for the extent of foreign threats to Britain itself.[12] Dummy variables that take the value one on the dates of the Truce of Amiens (1801) and of war declarations(1803 with France, 1812 with the United States) have the expected signs (negative and positive, respectively). All of these results are consistent with the view that changes in the cost of capital associated with wars reflect more than their fiscal effects. The regression in column four allows for the possibility that it

---

[12] Interestingly, the (logs of the) numbers of enlisted men in the navy and in the army are not very highly correlated, with a correlation coefficient of about 0.28.

Table 11.2. *The determinants of Consol yields, 1790–1815*

	(1)	(2)	(3)	(4)
Naval battle	0.00400[*]	0.00221	0.00214	
	(2.31)	(1.66)	(1.62)	
Naval news reported	0.00472[**]	0.00302[*]	0.00294[*]	
	(2.73)	(2.28)	(2.22)	
Land battle	0.00272[*]	0.000861	0.000904	
	(2.27)	(0.94)	(0.98)	
Land battle reported	0.00281[*]	0.000605	0.000658	
	(2.09)	(0.59)	(0.64)	
War declaration	0.00468	0.00424	0.00440	
	(1.03)	(1.21)	(1.26)	
Truce	−0.00152	−0.00421	−0.00428	
	(−0.24)	(−0.85)	(−0.87)	
Day with coupon payment	−0.000666[*]	−0.000473[*]	−0.000487[*]	−0.000399
	(−2.34)	(−2.16)	(−2.23)	(−1.25)
Log (number of seamen)		0.00806[***]	0.00835[***]	0.00823[***]
		(70.46)	(57.53)	(52.40)
Log (number of soldiers)			−0.000366[***]	
			(−3.30)	
Naval battle ($t − 6$)				0.00790[***]
				(3.56)
Naval news reported ($t − 3$)				0.00471[**]
				(2.68)
War declaration ($t − 6$)				0.00479
				(1.36)
Truce ($t − 3$)				−0.00554
				(−1.12)
Constant	0.0470[***]	−0.0453[***]	−0.0446[***]	−0.0473[***]
	(585.88)	(−34.57)	(−33.53)	(−26.22)
Observations	7084	7083	7083	3901
Adj. R^2	0.003	0.414	0.415	0.416
AIC	−51359.7	−55115.4	−55124.3	−30317.5

Note: t statistics in parentheses. [*]$p < 0.05$; [**]$p < 0.01$; [***]$p < 0.001$.
Sources: Three per cent British Consol daily prices for the period 1750–1809 are from data provided by Larry Neal in European State Finance Database, www.le.ac.uk/hi/bon/ESFDB, and for the period 1809–15 from the *London Times*. The figures on enlisted men in the navy and in the army (in thousands) are from the House of Commons Papers 1868–9 (366), pp. 1150, 1151, 1157, and 1158. All other variables are dummy variables which take the value one on a day in which the event takes place or is reported in the *London Times*. Because of the large number of dummy variables, natural logs are taken of the number of enlisted men.

Table 11.3. *The most significant structural break points, British Consol yields, 1790–1815*

Date	Change in Consol yield (basis points)	Event
2 October 1801	−50	Truce of Amiens
8 July 1812	+50	US declares war on Britain
9 March 1803	+30	King informs Parliament of French war preparations
14 March 1803	+30	British ambassador leaves France (end of the Truce of Amiens)
8 April 1814	−30	Napoleon abdicates
23 July 1805	+15	Rumours of combined French squadrons not far from Britain
31 March 1815	+20	Reports of Napoleon in France, fear of another war

Sources: Three per cent British Consol daily prices for the period 1750–1809 are from data provided by Larry Neal in the European State Finance Database, www.le.ac.uk/hi/bon/ ESFDB, and for the period 1809–1815 from the *London Times*. Dates of major naval and land battles are from Cook and Stevenson (1980).

took some time before investors reacted to news reports. The results suggest that at most a week was needed to affect investor behaviour.

Table 11.3 presents a 'search for structural breaks' in the (daily) Consol yield series for the years 1790–1815 (see Sussman and Yafeh 2000 for a detailed description of this statistical procedure). Peace is associated with significant declines in Consol yields. Wars, or preparations for them, are associated with increases in yields. This is not surprising; the interesting finding here is that, more than a century after the fundamental institutional changes of the seventeenth century, British yields were still quite volatile and sensitive to political and war-related events, despite the institutional superiority of Britain over its rivals.

Moving to an international comparison, Table 11.4 suggests that the institutionally underdeveloped United States, soon after its independence, borrowed at rates which were comparable to those of Britain. Controlling for standard macroeconomic variables such as debt per capita and the government deficit (a proxy for the risk of default), Britain did not borrow at lower rates than the United States (the constant term in column three is not statistically different from zero). This finding echoes the comparisons made in Sussman and Yafeh (2006) between the cost of debt of institutionally developed Britain of the seventeenth century and its Continental European counterparts. Britain did not borrow more, or at a lower cost, than the Netherlands or other European powers.

Table 11.4. *Yields on United States bonds, 1792–1820*

	(1) Yield U.S.	(2) Yield U.S.	(3) Yield U.S. minus Consol yield
U.S. debt per capita	0.942	0.959	0.967
	(3.24)**	(5.71)**	(5.27)**
U.S. government deficit per capita	2.903	2.709	2.616
	(4.59)**	(4.85)**	(4.13)**
Consol yield		0.675	
		(6.18)**	
Constant	0.049	0.017	0.001
	(15.06)**	(3.52)**	−0.7
Observations	28	28	28
R^2	0.44	0.79	0.59

Note: t statistics in parentheses. $^*p < 0.05$; $^{**}p < 0.01$; $^{***}p < 0.001$.
Sources: Prices of U.S. six per cent Consols traded in New York are from the data set Early US Securities Prices, compiled by Richard Sylla, Jack Wilson, and Robert Wright, http://eh.net/databases/early-us-securities-prices. Annual data on outstanding debt (in dollars) are from Treasury Direct, www.treasurydirect.gov/govt/reports/pd/histdebt/histdebt_histo1.htm. Government deficit is from www.usgovernmentspending.com.

The basic statistics presented here (and more sophisticated econometric analyses presented in Sussman and Yafeh 2006) are consistent with the view that macroeconomic variables and wars were crucial for understanding fluctuations in Britain's cost of capital for a very long period after the fundamental institutional change comprising the Glorious Revolution. As noted before, this conclusion is consistent with the results of Barro (1987), who documents fluctuations in Consol yields during periods of war between the early eighteenth and early twentieth century, with Wright (1999), who calculates the volume of British debt in periods of war and in periods of peace, and with Brown, Burdekin, and Weidenmier (2006), who document substantial volatility in Consol yields during the eighteenth century, coinciding with military conflicts, in contrast with the stability of the 'Pax Britannica' of the nineteenth century. However, the emphasis in this chapter is not on the risk that government debt might crowd out private investment (as in Barro 1987), but rather on the special effect of military events and spending, especially with regard to the navy and naval battles, which appear to be a better proxy for risk than military spending in general.

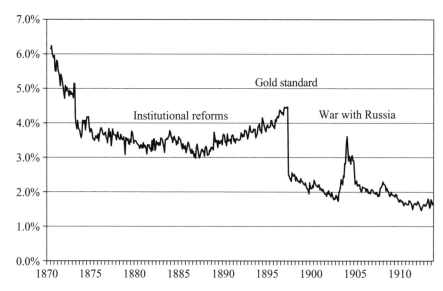

Figure 11.2. Japanese government bond yields vs. British Consols, 1870–1914. *Source:* Sussman and Yafeh 2000, Figure 1. By permission of Oxford University Press.

Meiji Japan

Figure 11.2, reproduced from Sussman and Yafeh (2000), describes the interest rate differential between Japanese government bonds and British Consol yields during the Meiji period. The figure suggests that the establishment of most state institutions in Japan (between the late 1870s and the 1890s) was not perceived as 'news' with an immediate effect on the risk associated with Japanese government debt in London. Almost none of the significant reforms of the Meiji period, such as the establishment of the Bank of Japan and the introduction of 'modern' monetary policy, the promulgation of the Meiji Constitution, or the introduction of parliamentary elections, produced any quantitatively significant market response in London. Nevertheless, the adoption of the gold standard in 1897 (an institutional change which can be viewed as a 'summary statistic' incorporating a number of preceding cumulative reforms) did lead to a dramatic decline in yields and an increase in volume of Japanese foreign debt.[13]

---

[13] The effect of the adoption of the gold standard by Japan has recently been re-examined. Sussman and Yafeh (2000) address the problem of using bond yields for 1897, because the adoption of the gold standard coincided with the maturity of the quoted bond. Mitchener, Shizume, and Weidenmier (2010) propose an alternative view.

In line with results for Britain, some international political events affected yields far more than did the introduction of new institutions. For example, with the onset of the 1904 war with Russia, yields on Japanese bonds in London increased significantly. However, Japan's victory in the war was followed by a small decline in yields, to a level below their pre-war level, and, more importantly, by a substantial increase in Japan's ability to raise capital abroad, described in considerable detail in Sussman and Yafeh (2007). Even during the war, when military spending was on the rise, commentary in the *London Times* (15 April 1904) attributed the rising prices (declining yields) of Japanese bonds (and the opposite trends of Russian bonds) to the surprising Russian naval defeat. In early May 1904, a new £10,000,000 Japanese loan was in such high demand that the *London Times* expressed regret that its scale was not large enough to satisfy all the investors who wanted to participate. The Japanese victory at Kin-chau elicited praise in the press: 'The recognition of the completeness of the Japanese victory at Kin-chau ... [led to] praise for Japanese skill, courage ... Even more than the Japanese valour, does the Japanese deliberation, thoroughness and scientific conduct of their military operations' deserve praise (30 May 1904, 5). Following a sequence of Japanese victories later in the year and commensurate headlines in the British press, the *London Times* commended Japanese bonds precisely because military victories 'show that Japan is as ready to work on the best modern methods in finance as in war' (27 August 1904, 11). Indeed, the news reports generate the impression of a direct link between the enthusiasm for Japanese bonds in London and developments on the front, ranging from relatively minor victories such as the sinking of a Russian battleship in early December 1904 to the fall of Port Arthur, around which Japanese bond prices rose by about fifteen per cent. Similarly, 'the progress of the Japanese army towards Mukden encouraged the bulls of Japanese bonds' (7 March 1905, 11), and the swift subsequent military successes raised bond prices even further, because markets were apparently concerned that any Russian military success might prolong the war.

Following the war with Russia, Japan became one of the largest borrowers on the London market, and was also able to issue debt in other foreign bond markets. Moreover, in the years after the victory, foreign debt was issued not only by the Japanese government itself, but also by quasi-governmental institutions such as Tokyo Harbourworks, Osaka Electric Tramway, the South Manchurian Rail Company, and the Imperial Industrial Bank of Japan, by municipalities, and even by some private Japanese companies, such as Kanegafuchi Spinning. Yet more evidence shows the impact of war on the perception of Japan in the London market: underwriting commissions on Japanese bonds, another measure of risk, declined by a third after the victory, and the Japanese government was no longer required to back its debt with securities such as customs income deposited in London (Suzuki 1994).

Further support for the claim that the military victory over Russia improved Japan's credit rating in subsequent years can be found explicitly in news articles. For example, starting in 1905, there was concern in Britain over the burden of Japan's war expenditures. *The Economist*, however, advised its readers not to worry because 'the sagacity with which the finances of Japan have been administered during a period of stress and anxiety is a good augury' (23 February 1905, 2072). A later *Economist* article, entitled 'Japan as a Borrower', explained the 'phenomenal success' of Japan's loan operations as 'due about equally to the enhanced reputation of Japan by reason of her military and naval exploits, and the skillful manner in which her loan flotations ha[d] been conducted' (20 July 1907, 1212). It seems that the reputation acquired during the successful war with Russia made it possible in later years for Japan to withstand investors' concerns (expressed in many news articles) regarding its increasing fiscal deficit. Apparently the London market for sovereign debt was much more interested in, and impressed by, the outcome of the war against Russia than by the institutional changes and reforms in the decades prior to the war.

Emerging markets 1870–1914

Mauro, Sussman, and Yafeh (2002, Mauro, Sussman, and Yafeh 2006) construct series of sovereign bond spreads (yields above those of British Consols) for a large sample of emerging markets in the period from 1870 to World War I. The authors (2006) combine the spread data with newspaper articles from the *London Times* and the Economist's *Investor's Monthly Manual*, and classify them into categories, including institutional reforms and wars and political instability.

Using this database, the authors list the events which corresponded to the largest (absolute) changes in the cost of capital of borrowing nations. Most of them are related to wars and other forms of instability, to stability, or to violence. Because of the large number of listed events, it is not reproduced here. Instead, Table 11.5 (reproduced from Mauro, Sussman, and Yafeh 2002) presents the events associated with 'structural breaks' in the spread series of eighteen emerging markets. Again, the vast majority are associated with rebellions, wars, and instability, rather

Table 11.5. *Events associated with structural breaks in the spreads of nineteenth-century emerging markets*

Country	Date	Sign	Event
Argentina	March 1876	Increase	Period of revolution and crisis
	June 1890	Increase	Baring crisis
	July 1891	Increase	Failure of national bank
	April 1879	Decrease	Success against rebellion
	April 1896	Decrease	Improvement in the fiscal position
Brazil	April 1898	Increase	Following the crushing of Canuda rebellion
	October 1890	Increase	Going off the gold standard, Baring crisis
	September 1895	Increase	Between revolt of military school and dissolution of congress
Canada	February 1912	Decrease	Pro-British Conservatives win important elections
Chile	November 1896	Decrease	Establishment of a financial inquiry commission?
	September 1891	Decrease	End of civil war
	March 1886	Decrease	New regime
	November 1879	Decrease	Doing well in a war with Bolivia and Peru
	July 1876	Decrease	New information provided to market about financial position
China	June 1885	Decrease	?
	May 1896	Decrease	End of war with Japan
	July 1900	Increase	Boxer rebellion
Egypt	May 1879	Decrease	July, Ismail pasha deposed
	September 1881	Increase	Armed uprising
	April 1885	Increase	War against Sudan
Greece	July 1893	Increase	Financial crisis
	April 1897	Decrease	End of war with Turkey
Hungary	May 1877	Decrease	Hungary to be neutral in Balkan conflict between Turkey and Russia
Japan	August 1897	Decrease	Going onto the gold standard
	March 1904	Increase	War with Russia
Mexico	March 1879	Decrease	?
	August 1886	Decrease	Ease of tensions with the US?
	July 1894	Decrease	?
Portugal	July 1902	Decrease	Renegotiation of debt
	March 1891	Increase	Going off the gold standard; bank moratorium
	September 1907	Increase	Franco dictatorship; end of monarchy
Queensland	January 1891	Increase	Banking crisis
	April 1893	Increase	Banking crisis
Russia	April 1877	Increase	War with Turkey
	February 1903	Increase	Tensions with Japan?
Sweden	June 1881	Decrease	?

Country	Date	Sign	Event
Turkey	July 1875	Increase	Trouble in Bosnia
	May 1878	Decrease	End of war with Russia, introduction of the gold standard
	September 1895	Increase	War against Greece
	October 1912	Increase	War in the Balkans
Uruguay	March 1892	Decrease	End of a financial crisis
	April 1877	Increase	Beginning of military rule
	February 1895	Increase	Instability leading to war
	January 1905	Decrease	End of civil war

Source: Mauro, Sussman, and Yafeh (2002, Table V). By permission of Oxford University Press. *Data Source: The Economist's Investor's Monthly Manual.* The breaks are listed in the order in which they are obtained; see Mauro, Sussman, and Yafeh (2002) for details. See also Bordo and White (1991).

than with institutional change. Table 11.6 presents regression results from one specification out of several examined in Mauro, Sussman, and Yafeh (2006). News on wars and instability is significantly correlated with spreads, unlike news about reforms. This result holds in a variety of regression specifications (including regressions with additional controls for macroeconomic effects), and is consistent with findings for Britain and for Japan described above.

Emerging markets in the 1990s

Table 11.7 presents regression specifications similar to those of Table 11.6 for a sample of emerging markets in the 1990s (also drawn from Mauro, Sussman, and Yafeh 2006). Although, in general, news reports have a weaker effect on bond spreads in the modern period (in part because of a much larger extent of co-movement in asset prices across countries in the 1990s in comparison with the pre-World War I period (Mauro, Sussman, and Yafeh 2002), wars and related instability are still associated with wider spreads in this period, too, whereas institutional changes are only weakly related to spreads in a manner that is not consistently statistically significant. This result, however, is not completely robust, and changes somewhat in alternative regression specifications.[14]

[14] Although the effect of war and instability on spreads remains unchanged in a variety of regression specifications, in some specifications which include additional macroeconomic control variables, there is some limited evidence for an effect of institutional changes on borrowing costs; see Mauro, Sussman, and Yafeh (2006), chap. 5, for further details.

Table 11.6. *Spreads and news, panel regressions, 1870–1913*

	News in logarithms						News in fractions					
	No fixed effects			With fixed effects			No fixed effects			With fixed effects		
Wars	0.114 [0.021]*	0.109 [0.020]**	0.095 [0.018]**	0.052 [0.017]**	0.044 [0.014]**	0.044 [0.014]**	0.640 [0.115]*	0.540 [0.106]*	0.509 [0.096]**	0.359 [0.084]**	0.232 [0.065]**	0.234 [0.065]**
Good/neutral economic	−0.165 [0.027]*	−0.098 [0.026]**	−0.049 [0.024]*	−0.147 [0.023]**	−0.033 [0.019]	−0.034 [0.020]	−0.302 [0.078]*	−0.108 [0.073]	−0.055 [0.067]	−0.314 [0.058]**	−0.088 [0.046]	−0.091 [0.047]
Bad economic	0.069 [0.032]*	0.066 [0.027]*	0.056 [0.023]	0.041 [0.023]	0.052 [0.018]**	0.051 [0.018]**	0.834 [0.241]*	0.910 [0.221]**	0.783 [0.200]**	0.163 [0.175]	0.260 [0.136]	0.254 [0.137]
Reform	0.010 [0.034]	−0.006 [0.031]	0.020 [0.028]	−0.008 [0.026]	−0.017 [0.021]	−0.018 [0.021]	0.160 [0.293]	0.003 [0.269]	0.248 [0.245]	0.241 [0.211]	0.123 [0.164]	0.119 [0.165]
Political	−0.119 [0.023]*	−0.126 [0.021]**	−0.162 [0.019]**	−0.014 [0.023]	0.014 [0.018]	0.014 [0.018]	−0.346 [0.160]	−0.273 [0.147]	−0.280 [0.133]	0.164 [0.124]	0.262	0.261
Foreign	0.071 [0.022]*	0.042 [0.021]*	0.019 [0.018]	0.007 [0.021]	−0.008 [0.017]	−0.007 [0.017]	0.360 [0.121]*	0.329 [0.111]**	0.249 [0.101]*	0.087 [0.108]	0.041 [0.084]	0.041 [0.085]
Default history			0.522 [0.041]**			0.027 [0.083]			0.488 [0.042]**			0.045 [0.082]
Portfolio spreads	0.453 [0.044]**	0.517 [0.040]**		0.561 [0.029]**	0.563 [0.030]**		0.498 [0.046]**	0.498 [0.046]**		0.545 [0.042]**	0.555 [0.028]**	0.559 [0.029]**

Source: Mauro *et al.* (2006), Table 5.2. By permission of Oxford University Press. The dependent variable is the yield differential (spread) relative to British Consol yields, and the sample consists of 627 country/year observations for eighteen contemporary emerging markets. Explanatory variables include news categories, which are calculated using all articles on each borrowing country in the *London Times* during the sample period. FE = Fixed Effects. Single asterisks indicate significance at the five per cent level; double asterisks indicate significance at the one per cent level. Standard errors are in brackets.

Table 11.7. Spreads and news, 1994–2002

	Annual data				Quarterly data			
	Logs		Fractions		Logs		Fractions	
	No FE	With FE	No FE	With FE	No FE	With FE	No FE	With FE
Wars/instability	0.166 (0.079)*	0.033 (0.086)	2.641 (0.699)*	1.683 (0.767)*	0.165 (0.056)*	0.041 (0.041)	1.155 (0.239)*	0.471 (0.177)*
Good/neutral economic	0.397 (0.108)*	0.262 (0.102)*	2.665 (0.503)**	1.316 (0.496)*	0.251 (0.047)**	0.121 (0.033)*	1.481 (0.206)**	0.542 (0.148)*
Bad economic	0.235 (0.089)*	0.089 (0.086)	3.381 (0.684)*	1.722 (0.732)*	0.218 (0.051)*	0.071 (0.035)*	1.527 (0.234)**	0.514 (0.166)*
Reform	-0.331 (0.109)*	-0.125 (0.105)	-1.282 (0.814)	-0.147 (0.681)	-0.217 (0.061)*	-0.103 (0.041)*	-0.013 (0.264)	-0.016 (0.174)
Political	-0.118 (0.087)	0.024 (0.082)	0.922 (0.539)	0.578 (0.476)	-0.031 (0.045)	0.098 (0.032)*	0.755 (0.200)*	0.463 (0.138)*
Foreign	-0.27 (0.087)*	-0.033 (0.103)			-0.317 (0.053)**	-0.103 (0.039)*		
Portfolio spreads	0.798 (0.241)*	0.849 (0.184)*	0.799 (0.240)*	0.876 (0.184)*	0.869 (0.104)**	0.885 (0.068)**	0.878 (0.111)**	0.918 (0.071)**
Constant	1.653 (0.229)**	1.376 (0.290)*	-1.221 (0.648)	-0.763 (0.554)	0.017 (0.222)	-0.054 (0.146)	-0.748 (0.274)*	-0.318 (0.182)
Number of observations	72	72	72	72	282	282	263	263

Source: Mauro *et al.* (2006), Table 5.5. By permission of Oxford University Press. The dependent variable is the yield differential (spread) relative to U.S. Treasury Bonds for a sample of eight emerging markets. News indicators are based on articles in the *Financial Times* on each borrowing country during the sample period and refer to the number of news or to the fraction of all news for the category indicated. 'F.E.' denotes regressions with country-fixed effects; single asterisks indicate significance at the five per cent level; double asterisks indicate significance at the one per cent level. Standard errors are in brackets.

Conclusions

This short chapter presents a comparative analysis of the determinants of the cost of sovereign bonds issued by borrowing governments over three centuries. The main finding is that wars and episodes of politically motivated violence have the most immediate and pronounced impact on the cost of borrowing. This effect seems to be driven by more than the standard fiscal concerns associated with military spending and is, this chapter argues, a reflection of the instability and risk associated with military conflicts. In contrast, institutional and political reforms (such as the introduction of a constitution) or efficiency-enhancing structural reforms seldom reduce the cost of capital quickly. Only in a few instances did reforms of the monetary framework, such as the introduction of the gold standard in nineteenth-century Japan or a currency board in Bulgaria in the 1990s, have a rapid and substantial impact on spreads.

Considering the evidence from all periods jointly, in the short run, peace and stability seem to matter more for countries' borrowing costs than does the establishment of investor-friendly institutions. Although there is little doubt that appropriate reforms can be beneficial in the long run, their benefits seem to accrue in a gradual manner. Novel institutions are rarely rewarded swiftly by financial markets. Thus, on the basis of the results presented both here and in previous research, a plausible conclusion would be that the aspects of institutional quality, broadly defined, that matter most for the cost of sovereign debt are related to the absence of violence, whether international wars or domestic turmoil and, more generally, to the quality of de facto rather than de jure institutions.

References

Barro, Robert 1987. 'Government Spending, Interest Rates, Prices, and Budget Deficits in the United Kingdom, 1701–1918', *Journal of Monetary Economics*, 20, 221–48.

Bordo, Michael and White, Eugene 1991. 'A Tale of Two Currencies: British and French Finance During the Napoleonic Wars', *Journal of Economic History*, 51, 303–16.

Brewer, John 1990. *The Sinews of Power: War, Money, and the English State, 1688–1783*. Cambridge, MA: Harvard University Press.

Brown, William; Burdekin, Richard; and Weidenmier, Marc 2006, 'Volatility in an Era of Reduced Uncertainty: Lessons from Pax Britannica', *Journal of Financial Economics*, 79, 693–707.

Cook, Chris and Stevenson, John 1980. *British Historical Facts (1760–1830)*. London: Macmillan Press.

Epstein, Stephan 2000. *Freedom and Growth: The Rise of States and Markets in Europe, 1300–1750*. London: Routledge.

Ferguson, Niall 2001. *The Cash Nexus: Money and Power in the Modern World, 1700–2000.* London: Penguin Press.

Mauro, Paolo; Sussman, Nathan; and Yafeh, Yishay 2002. 'Emerging Market Spreads: Then versus Now', *Quarterly Journal of Economics*, 117, 695–733.

Mauro, Paolo; Sussman, Nathan; and Yafeh, Yishay 2006. *Emerging Markets and Financial Globalization: Sovereign Bond Spreads in 1870–1913 and Today.* Oxford: Oxford University Press.

Mitchell, Brian R. (ed.) 1988. *British Historical Statistics.* Cambridge University Press.

Mitchell, Brian 1998. *International Historical Statistics.* New York: Stockton Press.

Mitchener, Kris James; Shizume, Masato; and Weidenmier, Marc D. 2010. 'Why Did Countries Adopt the Gold Standard? Lessons from Japan', *Journal of Economic History*, 70, 27–56.

North, Douglass 1990. *Institutions, Institutional Change, and Economic Performance.* Cambridge: Cambridge University Press.

North, Douglas and Weingast, Barry 1989. 'Constitutions and Commitment: The Evolution of Institutions Governing Public Choice in Seventeenth-Century Britain', *Journal of Economic History*, 49, 803–32.

O'Brien, Patrick 2002. 'Fiscal Exceptionalism: Great Britain and Its European Rivals – From Civil War to Triumph at Trafalgar and Waterloo', in Patrick O'Brien and Donald Winch (eds.), *The Political Economy of British Historical Experience, 1688–1914.* Oxford: Oxford University Press.

O'Brien, Patrick and Duran, Xavier 2010. 'Total Factor Productivity for the Royal Navy from Victory at Texal (1653) to Triumph at Trafalgar (1805)'. Working Paper 134/10, London School of Economics.

Saigheh, Sebastian M. 2009. 'Political Institutions and Sovereign Borrowing: Evidence from Nineteenth-Century Argentina'. CELS 2009 4th Annual Conference on Empirical Legal Studies Paper.

Stasavage, David 2002. 'Credible Commitment in Early Modern Europe: North and Weingast Revisited', *Journal of Law, Economics and Organization*, 18(1), 155–86.

Stasavage, David 2003. *Public Debt and the Birth of the Democratic State.* Cambridge: Cambridge University Press.

Stasavage, David 2007. 'Partisan Politics and Public Debt: The Importance of the Whig Supremacy for Britain's Financial Revolution', *European Review of Economic History*, 11, 123–53.

Summerhill, William 2005a. *Inglorious Revolution: Political Institutions, Sovereign Debt, and Financial Underdevelopment in Imperial Brazil.* New Haven: Yale University Press.

Summerhill, William 2005b. '*Political Economics of the Domestic Debt in Nineteenth Century Brazil*'. Unpublished manuscript, UCLA.

Sussman, Nathan and Yafeh, Yishay 2000. 'Institutions, Reforms, and Country Risk: Lessons from Japanese Government Debt in the Meiji Period', *Journal of Economic History*, 60, 442–67.

Sussman, Nathan and Yafeh, Yishay 2006. 'Institutional Reforms, Financial Development and Sovereign Debt: Britain 1690–1790', *Journal of Economic History*, 66, 906–35.

Sussman, Nathan and Yafeh, Yishay 2007. 'The Russo-Japanese War and the Perception of Japan by British Investors', in Rotem Kowner (ed.), *Rethinking the Russo-Japanese War, 1904–5: A Centennial Perspective*. Kent: Global Oriental Press, vol. I.

Suzuki, Toshio 1994. *Japanese Government Loans on the London Capital Market, 1870–1913*. London: Athlone Press.

Wright, J. F. 1999. 'British Government Borrowing in Wartime, 1750–1815', *Economic History Review*, 52, 355–61.

Index